KASHMIR IN THE CROSSFIRE

Kashmir
IN THE CROSSFIRE

VICTORIA SCHOFIELD

I.B.Tauris Publishers
LONDON · NEW YORK

Published in 1996 by
I.B.Tauris & Co Ltd
Victoria House
Bloomsbury Square
London WC1 4DZ

A full CIP record for this book is available from the British
Library

ISBN 1 86064 036 2

Set in Monotype Garamond by Philip Armstrong, Sheffield

Printed and bound in Great Britain by WBC Ltd, Bridgend,
Mid Glamorgan

Contents

Maps

Acknowledgements

'A country of such striking natural beauty must, surely, at some period of its history have produced a refined and noble people,' writes Sir Francis Younghusband in his *History of Kashmir*. So indeed, and during my own travels through Kashmir's history, I have been privileged to make contact with some of them. In the present day, I owe a tremendous debt of gratitude to the three main protagonists in the current struggle: the Indians, Pakistanis and the Kashmiris and, by this, I include all inhabitants of the once princely state. My thanks also go to the governments of India and Pakistan, whose representatives received me openly, as well as their respective High Commissions in London; in addition, I should like to thank the members of the Azad Government of Jammu and Kashmir for their assistance.

When I first went to the Indian High Commission in London to obtain my visa, I did so with some trepidation lest my long association with Pakistan might jeopardise my chances of entering the valley of Kashmir. But I was pleasantly surprised: 'You are well known to us as the friend of the Prime Minister of Pakistan,' the official said, 'but you are welcome also to travel to India.' On several occasions, I travelled between Delhi and Lahore and no effort was made to search my bags or look at any of my research material. I was also free to make my own contacts and itinerary in the valley of Kashmir. At times I felt I might be considered as yet another Western intruder, prying into local problems, only to return to the comfort of my home in London to write about them from a distant perspective. But I hope all those who read this book will realise that my intention has been to try and explain more clearly what proximity can, sometimes, cloud.

No book is written single-handedly. All those I interviewed, often at short notice, could not have been more willing to open their hearts and homes to me in order for me to understand their story. They too are contributors to this book. I am also grateful for permission to quote from numerous works listed in the bibliography; I have done so with special attention to those first-hand accounts which capture an event far better than it is sometimes possible to do with the wisdom of hindsight. In quoting the views and opinions of others, I have also wanted to give the reader the benefit of their analyses as well as my own.

My special thanks go to: Benazir Bhutto, a personal friend for over twenty years, who, despite the obvious sensitivity of the subject, neither discouraged nor attempted to influence me in my endeavour, and yet provided generous hospitality during my visits to Pakistan; Rashmi Shankar, who gave me a home in New Delhi and visited Ladakh with me; Rahul Bedi, a Delhi-based journalist who travelled to the valley of Kashmir with me in 1994 and 1995; Gulam Butt and family, on whose houseboat I stayed during my first and subsequent visits to the valley of Kashmir. I am very grateful to David Page who gave me invaluable advice, as well as Alastair Lamb, Leslie Wolf-Phillips, and Malcolm Yapp, who read my manuscript. I am also grateful to the staff of the British Library and the Oriental and India Office Collection for the many hours I have spent researching in these libraries, where, as always, there is a wealth of information. I am grateful for permission to quote from the books and manuscripts I have used from their collections. My thanks also to the London Library and their liberal lending policy, the United Nations Library as well as the Royal Geographical Society, whose collection of maps I have consulted.

Finally, I should like to thank my agent Murray Pollinger, who believed in my dream of writing a book on Kashmir long before it was commissioned, my publisher, Iradj Bagherzade, my editor, Anna Enayat, as well as Jonathan McDonnell, Maysoon Hamdiyyah and Phil Armstrong who was responsible for drawing the maps. Lastly, I am grateful to my family and friends, all of whom supported me emotionally and practically while the book was being researched and written. Unless otherwise stated all views and conclusions expressed in this book are my own.

Preface

That noble minded poet is alone worthy of praise whose word, like that of a judge keeps free from love or hatred in relating the facts of the past. Kalhana, *The Chronicle of the Kings of Kasmir* [1]

I first saw the valley of Kashmir in 1981. Like so many other visitors I stood by Dal lake in Srinagar admiring the lofty snow-capped Himalayas which seemed to determine the end of the world. The beauty and tranquillity of the valley was almost tangible, yet I came to realise that it belied an inner pain. It is not just in recent times that the Kashmiris have suffered because of a political struggle to control the mountains and the valley. For many centuries the inhabitants of this land have been fighting for a freedom which they themselves have seemed unable to define. At times courting outside interference, at other times rejecting it, they have reacted against domination by the Mughals, Afghans, Sikhs, Dogras. Today the rule of modern India is being challenged. So often in my travels in the valley when I asked: 'What are you fighting for?' 'Freedom', came the reply. 'We want our freedom and then we will think what to do with it.' It was an echo which resounded through the centuries.

In recounting the events which make up the valley of Kashmir's history from legendary times I have found it as important to write without 'love or hatred' as did Kalhana when he compiled his history of the ancient kings of Kashmir in the twelfth century. As with so many contentious political issues, the adage 'This is my truth now tell me your truth,' is applicable to Kashmir. The story related by the Pakistanis differs from that told by the Indians. The Kashmiris have a third viewpoint.

My objective in writing this book has been to let all sides speak their own truth. Where they have not been able to resolve their differences at the negotiating table I have attempted to sit with them independently, listen to their grievances and share their dreams. Most importantly, I have tried to let the voice of the Kashmiris predominate. Even then they do not speak with a united voice – Hindu Pandit differs from Muslim, yet both are Kashmiris from the valley. The Ladakhis, Gujars, Baltis, people from Jammu, Poonch, Mirpur, Gilgit, Hunza all have diverse cultural and linguistic traditions. Although my focus is on the valley where the present conflict arises, the other components of the state must not be forgotten. As parts of the former princely state of Jammu and Kashmir their future is directly affected by events in the valley. As in the past, objectives and priorities differ.

Amidst all the hardened attitudes I have been encouraged to find people who are prepared to concede their respective faults and mistakes. Even at government level there are those who admit a genuine desire to move forward rather than recriminate over the past. The challenge now is to have the courage to adopt a more enlightened approach to break the deadlock on all sides of the political divide. Until such time those who suffer most are the people caught in the 'crossfire' of conflicting political rhetoric. The tragedy is not that of the governments of Pakistan nor India, nor even that of the Kashmiri politicians, but of the people. They have been promised high sounding ideals, like special status, autonomy, self-determination. But it is fifty years since the independence of the sub-continent from British rule. What has that special status achieved for them? Where has the autonomy gone? What happened to the promise of self-determination?

In my own voyage of discovery I have also come, like the European travellers in the eighteenth and nineteenth centuries, to try and unravel the reasons why Kashmir has held such fascination for successive generations. During my research I read 'Lalla Rookh', written by the Irish poet, Thomas Moore. He tells the story of a princess, the youngest daughter of the Mughal emperor, Aurangzeb, who is betrothed to the king of imaginary Bucharia. The wedding is to take place in Kashmir and, with some trepidation, Lalla Rookh sets off on her long journey. On the way she is enchanted by a travelling minstrel who tells her four stories. She falls in love with the minstrel and begins to dread her marriage to the king, only to discover upon her wedding day that the minstrel was the king in disguise. Moore's poem was published in 1817 when the British had only just begun on their adventures in northern India. He never visited Kashmir, yet it had captured his imagination:

> Who has not heard of the Vale of Cashmere,
> With its roses the brightest that earth ever gave,
> Its temples and grottos, and fountains as clear
> As the love-lightened eyes that hang over the wave![2]

Why then is Kashmir so special? Is it just its natural beauty and fertile valley which others have wanted to possess or is it because the valley is the cross-roads of communication between China, Central Asia and the sub-continent that it has become so prized? Why were its indigenous kings unable to withstand foreign domination? Why today have so many of its youth been compelled to fight for the dream of independence which their forbears were not able to sustain?

And what makes Kashmir such an emotional issue for Pakistan and India? Why, when both countries have so many pressing problems of their own, does the fate of a few million people, compared with their own respective populations of 600 million in India and 130 million in Pakistan, mean so much to them? It is impossible to journey far into the issue without being told by Indians and Pakistanis alike that they have fought three wars since independence in 1947 and that Kashmir constitutes the single most important reason why their relations are so bad. It accounts for the inflated defence expenditure which both countries continue to undertake; and it has also meant that both India and Pakistan see nuclear capability as a necessary part of their defensive strategy.

On a world stage the dispute is more significant than at first might appear. As India and Pakistan continue to argue over Kashmir how much stronger can China grow at their expense? The creation of five new independent Central Asian republics undoubtedly serves as an inspiration for the Kashmiris wishing to achieve the same goal but is an independent Kashmir viable? The international community, facing the new world order in the aftermath of the collapse of the Soviet Union, is concentrating its diplomatic priorities on preventing regional disputes around the world from escalating into greater flash points. Strategically any territorial dispute or nationalist uprising carries the risk of a wider military conflict. The geographical position of the state of Jammu and Kashmir and the ethnic and religious characteristics of its people make this risk much greater. Is it therefore time for Britain, the United States, Russia and other concerned countries to take out their respective Kashmir files and focus on what is the oldest unresolved conflict on the agenda of the United Nations?

Notes

1 Translated by M. A. Stein, London, 1900, I, p. 7. A Brahmin Kashmiri praised as the Herodotus of Kashmir, Kalhana wrote his eight Tarangas (or chapters) in the mid-twelfth century. Sir Aurel Stein made the first English translation in 1900. After searching out the original manuscript, which had been divided between three owners, it took him over a decade to translate and annotate the work. R. S. Pandit, brother-in-law of Jawaharlal Nehru, also translated the Rajatarangini while imprisoned by the British during the Quit India movement in 1942.

2 Thomas Moore, *Lalla Rookh*, London, 1986, p. 256.

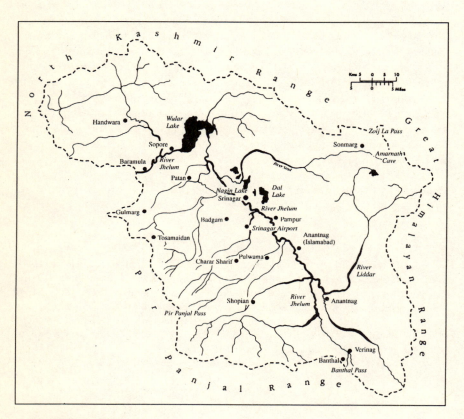

1. The Valley of Kashmir
(Source: Raghubir Singh, *Kashmir: Garden of the Himalayas*, London, 1983)

CHAPTER I

Introduction

Kashmir is a garden of eternal spring or an iron fort to a palace of kings

Emperor Jehangir, 17th century[1]

The beauty of Kashmir is legendary. The valley of Kashmir, an irregular oval of land, nestles picturesquely against the backdrop of the Himalayas: 'Bare, rugged and frowning rocks, a wilderness of crags and mountains, whose lofty summits tower to the sky in their cold and barren grandeur — a solitary and uninhabitable waste,' wrote William Wakefield, a medical officer who visited Kashmir in 1875. 'Yet in the midst of this scene of unutterable desolation, there lies spread out a wide expanse of verdant plain, a smiling valley, a veritable jewel in Nature's own setting of frightful precipices, everlasting snows, vast glaciers, which, while adding to its beauty by contrast, serve also as its protection.'[2] 'Each spot in Kashmir one is inclined to think the most beautiful of all,' observed Sir Francis Younghusband, who was Britain's resident in Srinagar at the beginning of the twentieth century, 'perhaps because each in some particular excels the rest.'[3]

Early Hindu legend describes how the valley of Kashmir was once a vast expanse of water called Sati Saras, or lake of Sati. In the lake lived Jalodbhava (meaning 'water born') whom the Lord Brahma had blessed with indestructibility under water. But as he grew up he became cruel and terrorised the Nagas or snake-worshippers who guarded the lake. When the father of one of the Nagas, the sage Rishi Kashyap, learnt about the oppression of his people by Jalodbhava, he appealed to the gods Brahma, Vishnu and Shiva. Since Jalodbhava was invincible while in water the Lord Vishnu called upon his brother, Balabhadra, to pierce the ring of closed mountains at Baramula thus draining the lake of Sati; Jalodbhava was beheaded with a discus. Kashyap then settled in the valley which is named after him: Kashyap-mar, 'the abode of Kashyap'. It also became known as Kasmira, Kasmir or Cashmere. Kashyap is credited with bringing the first Brahmins to the valley as penitents and philosophers who lived apart from the world. They came in summer to do penance; eventually they settled in the valley permanently, retaining their cultural identity.

The Nagas were the earliest known inhabitants; among other tribes were the Dars, Bhuttas and Damars. In 800 the Aryans from modern Uttar Pradesh populated the valley and predominated over the lesser tribes. Perhaps it is their struggle against the Aryans which inspired the legend about Jalodbhava. In time the monarchy became an established institution, and the king had almost divine status. The Brahmins came to form an important element in the society. As revered priests they exerted great influence over both religious and political life and were frequently given grants of land. They were also liable to pressurise the rulers to accede to their demands by undertaking fasts. Their liturgies were sung in Sanskrit, an Indo-Iranian classical language which became the official language of the court in Kashmir until the fifteenth century.[4] Since many Pandits, as they became known, were literate in Sanskrit, they were well placed to serve as royal advisers and ministers. Despite the frequent political upheavals in Kashmir's history the tradition of government service by the Pandit community persisted up to modern times.

On a world map the valley appears remote and landlocked, isolated by successive ranges of mountains high above the plains of the sub-continent. Its apparent impregnability is, however, illusory. Over twenty passes provide points of entry and the valley of Kashmir is both a cross-roads and a place of refuge. On account of its numerous tombs of saints and shrines, of which the holiest, Swami Amarnath, lies in the eastern mountains of the Kashmir valley, it also attracted outsiders as a place of pilgrimage. Three major routes open the valley to outside contact. The entrance from the west from Peshawar and Rawalpindi, favoured by the Afghans in the eighteenth century, leads to Baramula, where geologists give credence to the story of the valley's formation by stating that an earthquake most probably did shatter the ring of surrounding mountains. The second route, used by the Mughal emperors, became known as the 'Imperial route' and leads through the pass over the Pir Panjal, connecting Srinagar with the Punjab by way of Shopian and Bhimber. In the late nineteenth century the route over the Banihal pass via Jammu superseded both the Pir Panjal and Baramula routes.

Over time the valley of Kashmir's political borders have expanded and shrunk, the valley sometimes forming part of a great empire, at others comprising a kingdom in its own right. 'Under strong and magnificent kings, the Himalayan mountain ranges secured the valley from foreign intrusions,' says Dr Radha Krishan Parmu. 'Under weak kings – and there were a lot of them – owing to their complacency and laxity of control over the passes, Kashmir fell an easy prey to adventurers, missionaries and conquerors.' Yet even when the valley of Kashmir was part of an empire it has always retained a distinct identity. Kashmir assimilated foreign influences, 'like the sea receiving waters of different rivers from distant lands'.[5]

The princely state of Jammu and Kashmir, created in 1846, comprised several areas which themselves were also once independent principalities and regions: the valley of Kashmir, Jammu, Ladakh, Baltistan, Mirpur, Poonch, Muzaffarabad, Gilgit, Nagar, Hunza and other smaller kingdoms and hill states. In former times they too had their own 'river of kings' who guarded their independence as jealously as did the ancient kings of Kashmir. With

the formation of the state of Jammu and Kashmir into one political con-
glomeration peoples of different languages, cultures and religions learnt to
co-exist. Whereas Muslims predominate in the valley, there are also significant
numbers of Hindus and Sikhs who have traditionally lived in the Jammu
region and the valley; in addition a small number of Buddhists live in Ladakh.
The state covers some 84,000 square miles of land (it is about 10,000 square
miles smaller than the United Kingdom); the valley, 84 miles long, 20 to 25
miles wide, comprises only one-tenth of this land space. Today, however, the
state is effectively divided along a 'line of control' after a cease-fire imposed
by the United Nations in January 1949. Roughly two-thirds are held by India
and one-third by Pakistan; China also claims a section of Ladakh known as
the Aksai Chin. The total population on both sides of the line is estimated
at 12 million. Protagonists for an independent state of Jammu and Kashmir
point out that it is geographically larger than sixty-eight members of the
United Nations and more populous than ninety members.

A constant theme of Kashmir's history is not only its beauty but the
expectation, expressed so frequently, that almost because Kashmiris live in
such magnificent surroundings they should be able to lead peaceful lives;
another theme, equally apparent, is the political strife and oppression which
its people have experienced over many centuries; a third theme is the world-
wide attraction which this small valley has held for generations. As Sir Aurel
Stein observed: 'Small indeed the country may seem by the side of the great
plains that extend in the south, and confined the history of which it was the
scene. And yet, just as the natural attractions of the valley have won it fame
far beyond the frontiers of India, thus too the interest attaching to its history
far exceeds the narrow geographical limits.'

Topographically the state of Jammu and Kashmir rises at intermittent levels
towards the mountains and has often been compared to a house which is
situated on several storeys. Facing south, the ground floor is the Jammu region,
which is approached through level land bordering the Punjab; the first storey
is at 5,000 ft above sea level; the second storey is reached by climbing the Pir
Panjal, whose peaks rise to 16,000 ft. This includes the Kashmir valley. A
steeper flight of stairs, comprising the Pang Range with heights of 18,000 ft
leads to the top floor. Here Ladakh and Baltistan are situated. In the 'backyard'
is Gilgit which includes the mighty peaks of Nanga Parbat, the 'naked lady',
and Rakaposhi, the 'one who guards', rising to over 25,000 ft.

Kashmir's remoteness hides its strategic importance. The famed overland
trading route, the Silk Road, lies to the north. Linking Central Asia with
China by way of Tibet this route was well worn by successive caravans and
conquering armies some of whom included Kashmir in their grand designs.
The step down to the plains joins Kashmir with the sub-continent and so
the region also came to be prized by the empire builders of India who
wanted to secure their north-west and north-eastern frontiers by bringing
this 'iron fort' within their orbit.

PART ONE

River of Kings

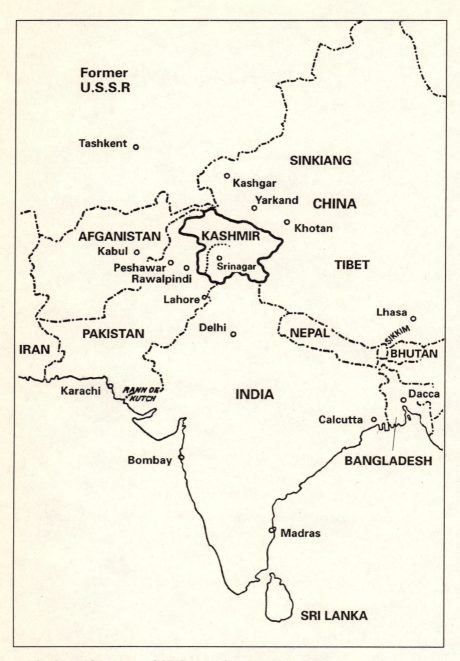

2. The State of Jammu and Kashmir and its Neighbours

CHAPTER 2

Ancient Kashmir

Now, gentle friend! drink freely, your ears serving as the mother of pearl glasses, of this River of Kings delightful with the flow of its sustained sentiment.

Kalhana[1]

Kashmir's first period of 'imperial' history begins in the third century BC with the rule of Asoka. Until then Kashmir was an independent valley ruled by men who were more likely to regard the sub-continent as a potential acquisition than themselves as vassals of a foreign magnate. Kalhana describes fifty-two kings belonging to the earliest dynasties but, 'on account of the loss of tradition', they have passed into oblivion.[2] Little is known about their early history because of the misdeeds of those kings, and, therefore, 'no creative poets existed who could have embodied them in glory.'[3]

Early rulers

As Hannibal fought the Romans in Europe, the Greeks who had remained in northern India after Alexander's campaign in 327 BC were pushed back to the west by Chandragupta of Magadh, who came from central India. Asoka was his younger brother and he succeeded in establishing the Mauryan empire. At its height the empire extended from Bengal to the Deccan, Afghanistan to the Punjab, and included Kashmir. Originally a devout Hindu, Asoka turned to Buddhism and sent Buddhist missionaries to Kashmir. When he died Kashmir once more regained its independence under Jaluka, who 'by the white stucco of his fame made spotless the universe.'[4] Initially Jaluka supported the Naga and Siva cults and persecuted Buddhists, but, like Asoka, he converted to Buddhism and built Buddhist stupas. He also set up eighteen departments to administer the state.

In the first century AD the valley was invaded by the Kushans from north-west China who had succeeded in conquering the whole of northern India. King Kanishka converted to Buddhism. He loved Kashmir and often held his court in the valley. 'During the powerful reign of these kings,' writes Kalhana, 'the land of Kasmir was, to a great extent, in the possession of the Bauddhas, who, by practising the law of religious mendicancy, had acquired great renown.'[5] Kanishka convened a Buddhist council and Kashmiri Buddhists spread their doctrine to central Asia and China. The Kushan kings were renowned for their love of art, architecture and learning and the period was marked by intellectual resurgence. Travellers and traders brought not only merchandise but also literary and artistic ideas. Kushan rule lasted until 178 AD after which Buddhism declined and Brahminism was revived. Buddhism had also moved away from its purist tenets and those who wanted to keep the freedoms established in the Buddhist era fused humanist preaching with the scriptures of Brahminism. This new religion, indigenous to Kashmir, came to be known as Shaivism.

Kashmir did not escape the invasion of the Huns who terrorised so much of Europe in the sixth century AD. Released from prison after his defeat by the kings of northern India, Mihiragula arrived in Kashmir as a refugee. He at first accepted hospitality from the King of Kashmir, but Mihiragula then turned upon the king and seized the kingdom for himself. There is a place on the Pir Panjal pass, called 'Hastivanj' - the destroyer of elephants, which later historians describe as exemplifying his cruelty. When Mihiragula was crossing the pass one of the elephants in his train slipped; so delighted was he by the shrieks of the elephant as it fell that he ordered a hundred more elephants to be thrown down so that he could enjoy the sound of their fear.

Kalhana describes Mihiragula as 'this terrible enemy of mankind who had no pity for children, no compassion for women, no respect for the aged'[6] 'Overwhelmed by the sense of his own innumerable misdeeds',[7] he committed suicide in 530 AD. Mihiragula had also persecuted the Buddhists and destroyed and plundered the monasteries. By the time the Chinese traveller, Hieun Tsiang, visited Kashmir a century later, he found that Brahministic Hinduism had superseded Buddhism: 'This kingdom is not much given to the faith, and the temples of the heretics are their sole thought.' He also acknowledged, however, that Kashmiris 'loved learning and were well instructed'.[8]

Conquering heroes

In the decades which followed Kashmir is remembered as enjoying a 'golden age'. The economic life of the people was simple. They worked the land and were expected to pay a proportion of what they cultivated to the state. 'The architecture of this period is magnificent and virile,' says the Kashmiri writer, Pandit Prem Nath Bazaz, who took special interest in researching the valley's early history. 'The kings of Kashmir excelled as conquerors.'[9] Kashmiris became famous throughout Asia as learned, cultured and humane and the intellectual contribution of writers, poets, musicians, scientists to the rest of India was comparable to that of ancient Greece to European civilisation. The Brahmins made a special study in astrology. Out of the sixteen best-known rhetoricians of ancient India fourteen came from Kashmir. One of the most famous poets, Bilhana, who lived in the eleventh century, found no outlet for his talents in Kashmir and wandered throughout India until he fell in love and married a princess in the Deccan.[10]

Lalitaditya is still regarded as the most celebrated king of the Karkota dynasty. He epitomised the type of conquering hero upon which Kashmiri pride in their ancient rulers is founded. A predecessor of the European emperor, Charlemagne, he ruled in the early eighth century. Writing over 300 years after his death Kalhana is lyrical about his exploits: 'The king, eager for conquests, passed his life chiefly on expeditions, moving round the earth like the sun.'[11] We hear of him conquering one kingdom after another 'round the whole of India', seizing the elephants of the King of Bengal, defeating small and big kings on the way to Turkestan, invading Tibet and sending embassies to Peking. Yet, as with so much of Kashmir's early history, fact is mixed with fiction and it is doubtful that his exploits were quite as extensive as Kalhana describes. Kashmir's links with the Tang dynasty in China also helped him to consolidate his position and when the Tangs declined so did Kashmir's policy of expansion. Lalitaditya, however, did successfully defend the frontiers of Kashmir from the Tibetans and Dards which was a considerable achievement.

Lalitaditya also made a significant contribution as an administrator. In addition to the eighteen departments established by Jaluka he created five new offices, including a high chamberlain, chief minister, master of horses, and keeper of the treasury. The fifth office was possibly a supreme executive administrator. He also showed surprising foresight in the need to curb the power of the landed elite, the 'damaras':

> Every care should be taken that there should not be left with the villagers more food supply than required for one year's consumption, nor more oxen than wanted for the tillage of their fields. Because if they should keep more wealth, they would become in a single year very formidable Damaras and strong enough to neglect the commands of the King.[12]

Lalitaditya's great failing, however, was that he drank and was prone to foolish acts when under the influence of alcohol. On one occasion he demanded that Srinagar be burned. Wisely his ministers did not obey his orders and instead burnt several haystacks while the king rejoiced. The next morning Lalitaditya was mortified by his request until his ministers informed him of their disobedience. Lalitaditya is also well remembered for what he constructed: 'There is no town, no village, no river, no sea, and no island where he did not consecrate a shrine,'[13] writes Kalhana. Indicative of his religious tolerance he built both Hindu temples and Buddhist stupas. The magnificent temple of Martand, whose ruins so impressed travellers in the nineteenth century, was built by Lalitaitaya. Captain Enriquez visited Martand in 1911:

> Those old grey walls are dumb like stricken men
> Striving to tell their tale, and die content;
> Whose speech has failed. Of what dim age, what men,
> What Gods, are they the silent monument?[14]

Younghusband calls Lalitaditya 'the most conspicuous figure in Kashmir's history who raised his country to a pitch of glory it had never reached before or attained since.'[15] He died most probably while on an expedition in northern Kashmir, perhaps against the Tibetans.

During the reign of Lalitaditya's grandson, Jayapida, for the first time the office of chief chamberlain was held by a woman, the queen. Jayapida also carried out administrative reforms, but towards the end of his reign he became avaricious and oppressed his subjects, especially the Brahmins, by demanding taxes. For three years he appropriated to himself the whole of the produce, including even the cultivator's share.[16] His death from serious injuries in an accident in 782 AD was followed by an increasingly familiar pattern of murder and misrule.

In 855 the throne was occupied by another king who merits note, Avantivarman, founder of the Utpala dynasty. In the context of events in Europe, while Charlemagne's successors were carving out their respective kingdoms, Avantivarman embarked on a process of internal consolidation, which earned him praise from Kalhana: 'When Avantivarman had obtained the sovereign power, after uprooting his enemies, he made, O wonder, the body of the virtuous feel thrilled on account of his great deeds.'[17]

During his reign terrible flooding of the Jhelum river caused great hardship to the local people. The story of how this was resolved is well known to Kashmiris to this day. An unknown man, named Suyya said that he could solve the problem but had no money to do so. Avantivarman heard about Suyya's boast and gave him the money he requested. Suyya then cast handfuls of coins into the water:

> There where the rocks, which had rolled down from the mountains lining both river banks had compressed the Vitasta (Jhelum) and made its waters turn backwards in whirls, the famine-stricken villages then searched for the money, dragged out the rocks from the river, and [thus] cleared [the bed of the] Vitasta. After he had in this manner artfully drained off that water for two or three days he had the Vitasta dammed up in one place by workmen.[18]

Wherever Suyya found that the river had been breached he constructed new channels. 'He made the different streams, with their waves, which are like the quivering tongues of snakes, move about according to his will, just as a conjurer does with the snakes.'[19] With better irrigation rice became cheaper and the people prospered. Suyya's irrigation feats are remembered with pride, and Sopore (Suyya-pur) on the banks of the Jhelum is named after him. When Walter Lawrence visited the valley in 1889 he remarked that things had not changed much since Suyya's time: 'The Valley is still in some places waterlogged, and the Kashmiris of the present day would work harder if paid by Suyya's system than they do on a daily wage.'[20] Avantivarman died peacefully in 883 listening to a recitation of the Bhagavadgita. This is perhaps the first mention of the Gita being used as a book of religious instruction.[21]

The reign of Avantivarman's son and successor, Samkaravarman, came to be known for its excessive taxation; more importantly for future generations of Kashmiris, he was the first king to systematise *begar* (forced labour for transport purposes), which 'is the harbinger of misery for the villages'[22] and which became a hated feature of Kashmiri rule until the late nineteenth century. Because of the terrain and lack of roads, the only way to transport goods and provisions was on the backs of people and inevitably the demand for labour fell on the villagers, who were obliged to leave their homes, perhaps never to return. At this time, says Kalhana, 'breathing is the only vital function which remains [free] for men.'[23] Samkaravarman revived the policy of making 'conquests in all directions'.[24] He did not achieve much, but his exploits demonstrate that the conquering tendency still came from Kashmir, and not as yet from the Punjab into Kashmir. By the end of the ninth century, however, the kingdom of Kashmir extended no further than the valley. Samkaravarman died while on a punitive expedition to Hazara, wounded by 'a swift flying arrow, and this pierced the neck of the unwary king.'[25]

Dark years

From the tenth century onwards the struggles for power intensified. 'It is a story of mediaeval times and often enough it is not a pleasant story,' writes Jawaharlal Nehru in his foreword to his brother-in-law's translation of Kalhana's *River of Kings*: 'There is too much of palace intrigue and murder and treason and civil war and tyranny ... We see the panoply of the middle ages, the feudal knights in glittering armour, quixotic chivalry and disgusting cruelty, loyalty unto death and senseless treachery; we read of royal amours and intrigues of fighting and military and adulterous queens.'[26] Nehru was no doubt referring to the Queens Sugandha and Didda who, for a while, dominated the politics of Kashmir. On the death of Samkaravarman, Queen Sugandha acted as regent for their young son. When both he and his brother died, she ruled uneasily for two years until 906. She took as her lover the keeper of the treasury, who, however, took advantage of his position to amass a fortune. Her main troubles came from two militarised factions, the Tantrins (praetorians) and Ekangas (gendarmes),[27] who both wanted to control the succession. Kapur describes how they 'practically sold and resold the crown to those who paid them the highest price.'[28] With chaos in Srinagar, Queen Sugandha departed to live near Baramula. In 914 the Ekangas encouraged her to march on Srinagar to seize power from the Tantrins. The attempt was unsuccessful and she was captured and executed.

The death of Yasaskara in 939 ended the Utpala dynasty founded by Avantivarman, nearly a century earlier. Yasaskara's son was deposed by his minister, Parvagupta. In 950 Parvagupta's son Ksemagupta succeeded him on the throne. 'Bad by nature,' writes Kalhana, 'he became still more terrifying through the society of wicked persons, just as a dark night becomes more terrible when obscured by a threatening cloud.'[29] He burnt Buddhist *viharas* and used the brass from the images of Buddha. When he died in 958, his wife Queen Didda, daughter of the Lord of Lohara, prepared herself to mount the funeral pyre. At the last minute, she changed her mind. For over forty years until her death in 1003, she dominated the succession as regent for her son, Abhimanyu, who died in 972, and for her grandsons. From 980 she reigned as queen in her own right.

Didda, a once beautiful woman, was now dissolute and unscrupulous. 'The officers who held charge of foreign affairs, the royal household, and other posts, visited the queen's bedchamber without scruples.'[30] Kalhana believed she made use of sorcery and murdered her grandsons Nandigupta and Tribhuvana. 'Then the cruel queen put without hesitation her last grandson, Bhimagupta, on the path of death which bore the name "throne".'[31] After the death of Phalguna, the prime minister, who appears to have had some restraining influence on her, Didda 'committed hundredfold excesses by open misconduct, infuriated just as a female elephant in rut which has torn off its face covering.'[32] As soon as Bhimagupta 'became a little more developed in intellect and recognised in his mind that the affairs of the kingdom and his grandmother's ways of living were not right, and in need of reform,'[33] he was imprisoned, tortured and killed. Queen Didda then assumed power in her own right. She developed a long relationship with Tunga, a herdsman from Poonch, who started his political career as a royal courier and was elevated to prime minister.

Towards the end of her days, surprisingly perhaps, after all her misdeeds, Didda was anxious to settle the succession peacefully on her brother's children. She made the selection by throwing apples for the numerous nephews to catch. Samgramaraja succeeded in obtaining the most and was remarkably unscathed by the scuffle. When she asked him how he had been so successful, he replied: 'I got the fruits by making those boys fight furiously with each other, while I kept apart, and thus I remained unhurt.'[34]

Samgramaraja became the founder of the Lohara dynasty; his and Didda's ancestors came from Lohrin near Poonch. Despite his show of promise when scrambling for the apples, he did not manage to assert much authority. Tunga remained as a rival to his power until Samgramaraja finally connived to have him murdered. During Samgramaraja's reign, the Sultan of Ghazni, Mahmud, son of Sabutakgin Ghazni, twice attempted to invade Kashmir. He crossed through the Tosamaidan pass on both occasions but was stopped on the southern slopes of the Pir Panjal mountains by the snows. Although the attempts were unsuccessful, it marked the return of invaders from the Punjab inwards to Kashmir.

During the next century, the succession passed from father to son, but there was no unanimity of spirit in continuing the dynasty. Samgramaraja's son, Ananta, succeeded him in 1028 cleverly thwarting an attempt by his mother, Queen Srilekha, to ascend the throne herself. As she was taking a ceremonial bath, in preparation for her coronation her opponents placed Ananta on the throne and had him crowned instead. Ananta passed his life under the influence of his wife Suryamati, who eventually made him abdicate in favour of their son, Kalsa, in 1063. But the feud between Kalsa and Ananta continued for nearly twenty years. Neither Ananta nor his wife accepted the secondary position they assumed under their son. On one occasion, Kalsa set fire to his parents' home in order to destroy their wealth. Kalhana records how Ananta chastised his wife as the person responsible for all his troubles: 'Pride, honour, valour, royal dignity, powers, intellect, riches, what is it, alas, that I have not lost by following my wife's will? People hold women to be a useless accessory for men, but in the end men are but an instrument of play for women. '[35] Ananta was finally driven to commit suicide and although his wife had berated him for being 'useless, past his time',[36] after his death she felt remorseful and 'leaped with a bright smile from the litter into the flaming fire of her husband's funeral pyre.'[37]

Ironically Kalsa is recorded as ruling rather more benevolently after the death of his father in 1081. 'He showed skill in keeping account of his wealth, like a merchant, was careful to spend it in the right way, and had ever an open hand,' writes Kalhana.[38] People were cheerful and happy. Kalsa waged a successful campaign to the west in Hazara, known as Urasa, and he succeeded in securing the position of his second son, Utkarsa, on the throne of Lohara. Initially, he also attempted to improve the poor relations which existed with his eldest son, Harsa. But the feud continued. Harsa even plotted to kill his father. Kalsa did not, however, follow the advice of his supporters to kill Harsa but avenged himself by raping his son's wives while Harsa remained in prison. He is also recorded as beginning to destroy the images of gods and confiscate the property of temples. Yet despite Harsa's attempts on his father's life, Kalsa wanted him to succeed to the throne. The ministers, however, who had worked against the prince and stood to lose by his succession, wanted to place Harsa's brother, Utkarsa of Lohara, on the throne.

In 1089 Kalsa died unable to secure the succession of Harsa. Instead Utkarsa ascended the throne, temporarily uniting the kingdoms of Lohara and Kashmir. But his rule lasted for only twenty-two days. He did not immediately put Harsa to death and so Harsa succeeded in inducing his captors to free him from prison. Utkarsa was, in turn, imprisoned and at the age of only twenty-four cut his throat with a pair of scissors. Harsa's rule alternated between 'wisdom and depravity', writes Kalhana. His father was a minister of King Harsa and so the poet's account is now that of a contemporary. The king was well versed in science, the arts and music. At the outset of his reign, Kashmir enjoyed unusual prosperity. Yet, as happened so often with the rulers of Kashmir, the dark side of his character emerged. According to Kalhana, 'the king, whose mind was perverted by the most sinful perfidies against his relatives, came then to be exploited by rogues as would be incredible even of simpletons.'[39] Misgovernment led to discontent and misery.

In an attempt to replenish his coffers, sacred shrines were plundered. 'In order to defile the statues of the gods, he had excrements and urine poured over their faces by naked mendicants whose noses, feet and hands had rotted away.'[40] It is tempting to explain the sudden attack on the shrines as due to the rise of Islam. The Sahi princes from the Punjab had taken refuge in Kashmir in the time of Ananta. But although they undoubtedly tried to influence the beliefs of those with whom they came into contact, it does not account for the despoliation of the Hindu temples and Harsa does not appear to have become a Muslim. The only explanation which Kalhana was able to give for Harsa's conduct was that he was raised in an 'immoral' atmosphere. 'The weakness of the king's moral character, which had become notorious everywhere, was such as was understandable in one begotten of King Kalsa.'[41] Whereas Kalsa raped his son's wives, Harsa in turn violated his father's wives and his own sisters. The moral degradation, which had begun under Queen Didda, reached its climax. 'In the form of Harsa, some demon had descended to the earth to destroy this land hallowed by gods.'[42] For the people it was a period of intense hardship. In 1099 a flood led to devastation of the crops, which in turn caused famine. Thousands died of disease and hunger. Harsa was killed in a palace uprising at the age of 43, together with his queens and the heir apparent.

By the time Jayashima ascended the throne in 1128 the country was in a piteous state. As was perhaps to be expected, since Kalhana was writing in the reign of Jayashima, the poet writes favourably of him: 'May the matured wisdom of this king which has been produced by the subjects merits and which has not been seen to such an extent in any other [ruler] last for years.'[43] In Jayashima's reign, the destruction of temples was reversed and there was a Buddhist revival. But a combination of misgovernment, floods, famine and epidemics took their toll on the people. Thousands died of starvation or were sold into slavery. Only a few amongst the upper classes who ruled the country were able to survive while the majority of the people lived in poverty. Assassination and power struggles continued.

Then, from the savage terrain of the Mongolian plateau, came the Mongols, a fiercesome race, famed for their horsemanship. In 1320 Zulqadar Khan, also known as Dulacha, swept through the Baramula pass with 17,000 horse and foot soldiers. The King of Kashmir, Sahadeva, fled and Dulacha spent eight months plundering Srinagar. The effect of his vandalism is noted by Pandit Jonaraja, who continues Kalhana's history: 'When the violence caused by the Demon Dulacha ceased, the son found not his father nor did brother meet brother. Kashmir became almost like a region before the creation, a vast field with men without food and full of grass.'[44] Dulacha, however, met his end on the Banihal pass. As he departed a storm trapped the whole army, leaving no survivors. In Sadaheva's absence Kashmir was also without a king.

Hindu rule was in decay. Part of the reason lay in the isolationist policy adopted by the later Hindu kings to counter emergent Islam in north India: 'To save their small kingdom from conquest by the new Muslim kings of north India, the rulers of Kashmir sealed the passes and behind the protecting walls of high mountains reduced the people of Kashmir to the plight of a beleaguered garrison,' writes Prithivi Nath Bamzai. But the resources of the kingdom, severed from contact with India, were not sufficient to sustain the population. Nor could a lavish court style be maintained and so the kings turned to despoiling the temples for additional treasure. It was a vicious circle: 'The masses being reduced to poverty, the state revenues dwindled, resulting in fresh taxation and more misery. The soldiers deserted the king's army and took service under the powerful barons.' Bamzai also admits that the 'incredible sensuality of the kings and queens' throws 'a lurid light on the manners and customs of the age and gives a rude shock to the fond illusion of benevolent despotism of our ancient rulers.'[45]

With hindsight, Pandit Prem Nath Bazaz is critical of the conduct of the Hindu kings: 'Again and again history afforded opportunity to the Hindu aspirants to kingship to start afresh but, on every such occasion they failed to grasp it and give a good account of themselves.' Thus 'politics had dehumanised the Kashmiris; Islam made them men again'.[46] But although the people may have been persecuted and oppressed, the Kashmiris retained their humanistic principles.[47]

Independent sultans

The story of the spread of Islam in Kashmir reads like a traveller's tale. A Buddhist prince, Rinchen, had left his home in Ladakh, after the murder of his father and taken refuge at King Sahadeva's court in Kashmir. At about the same time, a Muslim from Swat, Shah Mir, also came to Kashmir looking for work. After the Mongols, under Dulacha, had invaded Kashmir in the absence of Sahadeva, a new king had to be found. Supported by Shah Mir and some of the feudal lords, Rinchen killed his potential rival, the chief minister and married his daughter Rani Kota. After his accession to the throne, Rinchen wanted to convert to Shaivism, but was refused by the orthodox Brahmins. Searching for a new faith, he met a Muslim saint called Bulbul Shah and his teachings made a deep impact on Rinchen. Taking the name of Sadruddin, he became a Muslim. His conversion marks the beginning of Muslim rule in Kashmir. Rinchen is remembered as a just and wise ruler. Jonaraja calls him a 'lion among men'.[48] But his reign did not last long. He died in 1322, and for a short while Hindu rule was restored in Kashmir.

Rani Kota, Rinchen's widow, married Udyanadeva, the brother of the former king, Sahadeva, and invited him to become king. Shah Mir remained in the background gaining support amongst the feudal lords by assisting in the defence of Kashmir. When Kashmir was threatened once more by the Mongols, King Udyanadeva fled to Ladakh. Rani and Shah Mir remained to counter the attack. Although Udyanadeva returned to the throne he died soon afterwards in 1339. When Rani Kota attempted to become queen in her own right Shah Mir opposed her. After the murder of her chief minister she surrendered to Shah Mir, at first offering to marry him, then committing suicide. Shah Mir proclaimed himself sultan, and took the name Shamsuddin. The dynasty which he founded lasted for two hundred years. Shah Mir 'assuaged the troubles of Kashmir and changed its conditions,' writes Jonaraja.[49] He died in 1342 after a brief reign, aged eighty.

The first great king of the Muslim period was Shahab-ud Din who came to the throne in 1354. With peace restored after the devastation of the Mongols, Shahab-ud Din devoted his attention to foreign expeditions, conquering Baltistan, Ladakh, Kishtwar and Jammu. Shahab-ud Din also loved learning and patronised art and architecture. He was married to a Hindu, Laxmi, and had great regard for the religious feelings of all his subjects. In 1361 there was a devastating flood, but the atmosphere of general well being prevailed and on Shahab-ud Din's death in 1373 the succession passed peacefully to Qutb-ud Din.

During the reign of Qutb-ud Din, the pace of conversion to Islam increased. Muslims from west and central Asia, in search of refuge from the Mongols, arrived in Kashmir and the most influential was Mir Syed Ali. He came with hundreds of missionaries, or syeds as they came to be known, from Hamadan and other parts of Persia. 'Islam made its way into Kashmir,' writes Sir Aurel Stein, 'not by forcible conquest, but by gradual conversion.'[50] At the same time, Hinduism persisted. The administration, however, was still carried on by the Brahmins, who were recognised as the traditional official class, and Sanskrit remained the court language.

Qutb-ud Din was succeeded by his son, Sikunder in 1389. During his reign, Timur, successor of Genghis Khan and predecessor of Babur, threatened to invade Kashmir. He demanded a large tribute from Sikunder. In order to raise the money, Sikunder began to destroy the Hindu temples and called for the conversion of the people. Known as the Iconoclast, he sank all Hindu books in the lake, and forbade the use of the Hindu religious mark on the forehead. 'There was no city, no town, no village, no wood,' records Jonaraja 'where the temples of gods were unbroken.'[51] Extortionate taxes were levied. His persecution and torture of the Hindus is traditionally regarded as instigating the first migration of all but eleven Kashmiri Pandit families from Kashmir. The Kashmiri Muslims, however, did not condone his policy and against his orders, gave the Hindus refuge. Sikunder, writes Bazaz, was 'a ferocious bigot, a cruel fanatic and a religious zealot, who brought the noble traditions of the Kashmir culture and the fair name of Islam into disgrace.'[52]

Sikunder's younger son came to the throne in 1420. He took the name Sultan Zain-ul Abidin but was more popularly called Bud Shah (the great king). His rule was the antithesis of that of his father. 'It is puzzling that occasionally in history the sons and successors of tyrants are noble kings,' observes Prem Nath Bazaz.[53] During his long reign which lasted until 1470, the valley prospered. 'He embodied Plato's ideal of a philosopher-king,' writes N. K. Zutshi. 'A many splendoured genius ... zealous guardian of his kingdom's honour and the upholder of its territorial integrity'.[54] His chief concern was to protect the valley of Kashmir and he tried to strengthen the points of entry, such as the Tosamaidan and Pir Panjal routes. He tried to make friendly alliances, and although the Sultanate of Delhi under the Lodhis was already in decline, he maintained good relations with the ruler.

The court was full of poets and musicians. The historians Jonaraja and Srivara lived during Bud Shah's reign and he invited scholars and intellectuals to return. He was tolerant towards the Brahmins and rebuilt the temples, which his father had destroyed, and many Pandits, who had left, returned. He also introduced Persian as the new official language and offered government appointments to those who learnt the new language. His administrative reforms achieved 'what was beyond the power of the past sovereigns and what will be beyond the ability of future kings,' writes Jonaraja.[55] Bud Shah introduced the art of weaving and papier maché making, which have made Kashmiri handicrafts famous to this day. He also introduced the art of paper making, leading George Forster to comment three centuries later: 'The Kashmirians fabricated the best writing paper of the East.'[56] In his personal life he was 'free from all those vices which generally ruined the oriental rulers of early times. He was strictly moral in his conduct and never looked at the face of a strange woman.'[57] But although Bud Shah was a great king, his reign was not free from the usual power struggles. There was disruption from the Chaks, who came from Dardistan, and the Kakal Tash tribes. For the last eighteen years of his life, a war over the succession raged between his three sons.

During Bud Shah's reign a celebrated religious figure, Sheikh Nur-ud Din better known as Nund Rishi, was active. Inspired by the mystic Lal Ded or Lalla, he founded an indigenous order of Sufism known as the Rishi order which combined Buddhist renunciation with Hindu asceticism and traditional Sufism. The Rishis believed in the love of mankind and did not seek to make converts. They were therefore popular with both Muslims and Hindus.

When Bud Shah died in 1470 the dynasty of the Shah Mirs began to decline. 'Intrigues and plots became the order of the day and justice a thing of the past,' writes Bazaz.[58] A struggle for power persisted and the Magres and Chaks rose to prominence as king makers. Another important element to the cultural fabric of Kashmir was also introduced. In 1492 a Muslim preacher of the Shia faith, Shams-ud Din Iraqi, arrived in Kashmir. He rapidly gained converts of whom the most influential were the Chaks. As ardent Sunnis, the Magres therefore opposed them. Thus to Hindu-Muslim differences was added the potential for conflict between the Sunnis and Shias.

In the years to come, the fame of Kashmir attracted the Mughals but they failed in their early attempts to dominate the valley. Under the leadership of Kaji Chak, the Kashmiris temporarily united to resist Babur, the first Mughal emperor, who had defeated the Lodhis outside Delhi at the Battle of Panipat in 1526. In the reign of Babur's son, Humayun, Mirza Haider Dughlat, a cousin of Babur's mother, finally succeeded in conquering Kashmir in 1540. But as an orthodox Sunni, his persecution of the Shias led to his downfall and the Chaks regained power. In 1555, Ghazi Chak became king of Kashmir, which brought to an end the 200-year-old dynasty of the Shah Mirs. Under the new regime there was relative stability. Corrupt officials were punished and agriculture was promoted. The court was frequented by scholars, musicians and poets. Instead of contemplating further expansion, as had the Hindu kings and Muslim sultans in the past, the Chaks concentrated on consolidation. They reasserted control of Poonch, Ladakh, Kishtwar and some of the outer hill states.

The reign of the last two of the seven Chak kings, who ruled an independent Kashmir, led to the rise of warring social groups, which could not present a united front against a foreign enemy. Yusuf Shah was weak; his son, Yaqub Shah Chak, resorted to persecuting the Sunnis. In this triangle of religious conflict, the Hindus gave refuge to their Sunni compatriots. It was only a matter of time before the Mughal emperor, Akbar, who had succeeded to the throne of Delhi in 1558, sought to take advantage of the power struggle raging in the valley, leading to Kashmir's incorporation into the Mughal Empire.

So ended the valley of Kashmir's long history as a kingdom in its own right. When Kashmiris point to their political heritage, they remember the Hindu dynasties and the Muslim Sultanates. The depravity of Harsa and the unscrupulousness of Didda is almost forgotten compared with the magnificence of the exploits of Lalitaditya, Avantivarman and Zain-ul Abidin. Most importantly, although the lives of the people were undeniably harsh, none of the kings and queens were answerable to some alien power in Kabul, Lahore or Delhi; accordingly, their actions form part of a history which Kashmiris regard as undeniably their own.

Despite the ravages of so much cruelty and bloodshed during its early history, the valley of Kashmir, surrounded by its mountains, always retained its allure for future generations: 'On turning to catch a last view of the setting sun,' wrote William Wakefield 'we beheld in the distance the great Pir Panjal, with its spotless mantle of everlasting snow now appearing of a brilliant rose-colour, adding splendour and solemnity to a scene of such unspeakable beauty, that it was with a feeling of awe and reverence we gazed upon this glimpse of an almost earthly paradise.'[59] But, warned Dr Parmu: 'beautiful countries have often been the homes of tragedy. Happiness is rarely the lot of a beautiful land. So Kashmir, the desired land of men and monarchs, paid for her beauty. The desperadoes despoiled her, and emperors, like Akbar, embellished her.'[60]

CHAPTER 3

Monarchs and Demons 1586–1819

> God gave its control to the Afghan
> He gave Jehangir's garden to the demons
>
> (Persian poem)[1]

Mindful of the early attempts of the Mughals to dominate the valley, the Emperor Akbar considered Kashmir to be a rightful province of his inheritance. As the various factions vied for power in Srinagar, Akbar sent an invading force into the valley across the Pir Panjal. The King of Kashmir, Yusuf Shah Chak, prepared for war. But, as battle was about to be joined, he left the camp secretly at night and made an agreement with the Mughals; this action earned him the opprobrium of later Kashmiris, who condemned him for his subservience.

The conquest of the valley by the Mughals in 1586 is generally regarded as marking the beginning of Kashmir's modern history. For nearly two centuries, Kashmir was the northernmost point of an empire whose power base was situated in Delhi. 'Though the conservative instinct of the population was bound to maintain much of the old traditions and customs,' writes Aurel Stein, 'yet the close connection with a great empire and the free intercourse with other territories subject to it necessarily transformed, in many ways, the political and economic situation of the country.'[2]

Mughal emperors

When Yusuf Shah made his formal submission to Akbar's general, Raja Bhagwan Das, in February 1586, it was on the understanding that he would retain his throne. But he was taken prisoner and eventually exiled to Bihar where he died in 1592. Yusuf Shah's queen, Habba Khatoon, who was not allowed to be with her husband, gave vent to her anguish in songs which are remembered by generations of Kashmiris for their pathos:

> Say, friend, when will fate smile on me,
> And my love come to me again? Say when?[3]

As soon as the Mughals withdrew, however, Yusuf's son, Yaqub Chak, had himself crowned as King of Kashmir. His rule was unpopular and he reimposed the *jaziya* tax on the Brahmins. This tax, which was supposed to be a 'protection' tax levied on all non-Muslims because they were exempt from military service, was the most enduring grievance of the Hindus. Not only was it considered to be a symbol of their subordinate status, but, writes Henry Sender, it was perceived 'more often as a punitive device for those who declined to accept Islam.' Financial rather than ideological factors, however, were more likely to determine its actual collection.[4]

Yaqub Chak also antagonised the Sunni community by his execution of the religious leader, Qazi Musa. Therefore a delegation of Kashmiri nobles asked the Mughal Emperor to invade Kashmir once more. Before doing so Akbar agreed to certain conditions: the Kashmiris were not to be made slaves and servants, which was the customary practice meted out by the Mughals against subject peoples; they were to have complete freedom of worship; and they were not to be forced to do *begar*. Akbar consulted with astrologers who informed him that if some energy were exerted the conquest would be quickly made.[5] By September 1586 the Mughal force of 20,000 cavalry, infantry armed with muskets, and war elephants, reached Bhimber. Yaqub had assembled a large force to resist them. At first the Mughal army had difficulty crossing the passes, but the Kashmiris were unable to stop their advance and in October the Mughal army marched into Srinagar. Yaqub fled to Kishtwar. Akbar was proclaimed Emperor, the *khutba* was read and coins were minted.

Yaqub continued to fight against the Mughals and is remembered for his bravery in being the last independent ruler to resist foreign domination. But he too was finally obliged to submit to Akbar when the Emperor arrived in the valley in July 1589. His first journey to Kashmir was not without its difficulties. He was preceded by 3,000 stone cutters, mountain miners, splinterers of rocks and 2,000 diggers whose task it was to level the bumps on the roads. Yaqub died of poison in 1593. The Chaks, who remained a target of Mughal attack, disappeared into the countryside. They turned to breeding cattle and sheep and became known as Gulbans or Galwans (from Gwal, meaning breeder of cattle).

Although Akbar was illiterate his minister, Abul Fazl, kept a detailed record of his three imperial visits to Kashmir. 'Most of the trade of the country is carried on by water,' he observed 'but great burdens are also transported on men's shoulders'. He also noted how Kashmir's natural features had served to protect it in the past:

> On all the sides mountains, which raise their heads to heaven, act as sentinels. Though there are six or seven roads, yet in all of them there are places where if some old women rolled down stones, the bravest of the men could not pass. On this account former princes did not think of conquering it and prudence turned them away from such a wish.[6]

Once master of Kashmir, Akbar adopted a policy of conciliation and entered into marriage alliances with the Kashmiri nobles. His rule, both throughout India and in the valley, was known for its liberal-mindedness. He ended discrimination between Muslims and Hindus, and during his second visit in 1592, he joined in the celebrations of the Hindu festival, Diwali. His last visit was in 1597 when the valley was suffering a severe famine. The Portuguese Jesuit, Jerome Xavier, accompanied Akbar and has left a description of how the people bartered away their children for food.

Of all the rulers of Kashmir Akbar's son and successor, Jehangir, is perhaps best remembered for his love of the valley. He ascended the throne in 1605. During his reign Jehangir adorned Kashmir with over 700 gardens. Their names evoke the beauty of the place: Shalimar (abode of love) and Nishat (garden of gladness) are the two most famous. For several years in succession Jehangir and his wife, Nurmahal, remained in Kashmir during the summer. Their wanderings in the gardens were envisaged by the Irish poet, Thomas Moore, in Lalla Rookh:

> If woman can make the worst wilderness dear,
> Think, what a Heaven she must make of Cashmere!
> So felt the magnificent son of Ackbar,
> When from the power and pomp and the trophies of war
> He flew to that Valley, forgetting them all
> With the Light of the Haram, his young Nourmahal.[7]

On his deathbed Jehangir was asked if there was anything he wanted, to which he is reported as saying: 'Nothing but Kashmir.' He was succeeded in 1627 by his son, Shah Jehan. He too loved Kashmir and the valley became a popular place of refuge for the Mughal nobility away from the plains of India during the hot summers.

With Mughal rule a pattern of government which was to become only too familiar to the Kashmiri people was begun: a governor was sent to administer the province and demand taxes. Yet even though Kashmir was dominated by an outside power and once more comprised part of a great empire early Mughal rule is generally remembered as a period of relative stability and prosperity. Poets and scholars came to Kashmir. Land reforms were undertaken. Jehangir dismissed one governor because of his reported cruelty. When complaints were made of unfair taxes Shah Jehan had them annulled. Those who visited Kashmir in later years retained the belief that Mughal rule was, in some respects, also a golden age. 'The rule of the Moghals was fairly just and enlightened,' writes Younghusband 'and their laws and ordinances were excellent in spirit.'[8]

Aurangzeb, who came to the throne in 1658, was the last of the Mughal Emperors to make any impact on Kashmir's history. When he made his first and only visit in 1665 he was accompanied by the French doctor, François Bernier. The Emperor was attended, writes Bernier, by a force of 35,000 cavalry, 10,000 infantry, heavy artillery, light artillery and several thousand porters as well as a procession of women on elephants. 'So large a retinue has given rise to a suspicion that instead of visiting Kachemire, we are destined to lay siege to the important city of Kandahar.'[9] Aurangzeb was, however, visiting Kashmir to regain his strength after an illness.

Bernier's enthusiasm for Kashmir undoubtedly influenced future travellers:

> I am charmed with Kachemire. In truth, the kingdom surpasses in beauty all that my warm imagination had anticipated. It is probably unequalled by any country of the same extent, and should be, as in former ages, the seat of sovereign authority extending its dominion over all the circumjacent mountains ... It is not indeed without reason that the Moguls call Kachemire the terrestrial paradise of the Indies.[10]

Bernier wrote favourably of people who 'are celebrated for wit, and considered much more intelligent and ingenious than the Indians. In poetry and the sciences, they are not inferior to the Persians, and they are also very active and industrious.' By this time the shawl industry, begun by Bud Shah, was coming into its own and Bernier took note of the great number of shawls which the local people manufactured. He also noted the valley's general prosperity:

> The whole kingdom wears the appearance of a fertile and highly cultivated garden ... Meadows and vineyards, fields of rice, wheat, hemp, saffron, and many sorts of vegetables, among which are intermingled trenches filled with water, rivulets, canals and several small lakes, vary the enchanting scene. The whole ground is enamelled with our European flowers and plants, and covered with our apple, pear, plum, apricot and walnut trees, all bearing fruit in great abundance.[11]

There is no mention in Bernier's account of ruined towns and deserted villages which feature in the descriptions of later travellers.

While Aurangzeb was in Kashmir he was informed of an earlier promise made by the father of King Deldan of Ladakh to send tribute, which automatically implied vassal status. Deldan renewed the promises of tribute and promised that he would build a mosque and have the *khutba* (sermon) recited and coins struck in the name of the emperor. Although future Ladakhi kings might not take seriously their vassal status when Gulab Singh came to conquer Ladakh two centuries later this earlier relationship formed the basis of his claim.

Towards the end of Aurangzeb's reign an event occurred which had special significance for later generations of Kashmiris. In 1700 a strand of the beard of the Prophet Muhammad, the Mo-i Muqaddas, was brought by the servant of a wealthy Kashmiri merchant to Kashmir. It was originally displayed in the Khanqah Naqshband in Srinagar but the mosque could not accommodate the crowds who came to see it. It was therefore taken to another mosque on the banks of Upper Dal lake which was known first as Asar-i Sharif – shrine of the relic – and then Hazratbal – the lake of the Hazrat, or the Prophet. It has remained there ever since, with one brief interlude in 1963 when it mysteriously disappeared.

The memory of Aurangzeb's reign is tarnished by his persecution of the Hindus and Shias. Unlike Akbar, Aurangzeb was intolerant of other religions. Aurangzeb's governor, Iftikar Khan, tyrannised the Pandits. Yet Brahmins were still retained within the administration and opportunities existed for both Muslims and Hindus to prosper on merit and learning. 'The actual history of the Pandit community in Kashmir is neither a tale of paradise lost, nor of relentless oppression, ' writes Henry Sender.[12] The end of Aurangzeb's rule and the war of succession between his three sons after Aurangzeb's death in 1707 led to a steady decline of Mughal rule in Kashmir. But the occasional foreigner who passed by still seemed to be entranced. On his way to Tibet the missionary Ippolito Desideri reached Srinagar in 1714 and describes the town as:

> standing in a wide and most pleasant plain surrounded on all sides by high mountains and densely populated by both Muhammadans and pagans. A big river flows through the middle of the city, and nearby are large and beautiful lakes, whereon, with much pleasure and amusement, one can sail in small boats or in well-found larger vessels. A great many delightful gardens near or on the borders of these lakes form, as it were, a most ornamental garland round the city.[13]

Under Aurangzeb's successors the administration deteriorated and disorder spread. Rebellion, murder, lootings, arrests and assassinations were all common occurrences. During the rule of Muhammad Shah, who succeeded to the Mughal throne in 1719, the Brahmins also suffered at the hands of his governors. Inayatullah Khan, a Kashmiri who was appointed governor in 1717, set fire to the Hindu area of Srinagar and the Pandits were not allowed to wear their turbans. Major Hindu–Shia–Sunni conflicts erupted in 1720. A severe famine in 1723 meant rice became as precious as gold.

The exceptions to oppression are remembered favourably. Muhammad Shah sent Abdul Samad Khan as governor and he lifted the restrictions on the Pandits, who were once more permitted to wear their turbans and their caste mark on their forehead. In the early eighteenth century the number of Hindus leaving the valley increased. Although it was believed this was due to persecution, it is also possible that the Brahmins left because of the opportunities presented by contacts made while Kashmir was part of the Mughal empire.[14] In 1746 there was a devastating flood, followed by a famine, in which three-quarters of the people are believed to have perished. Nadir Shah's invasion of the seat of Mughal power at Delhi in 1738 had weakened their imperial hold on Kashmir still further. This in turn left Kashmir at the mercy of further predators.

Kabul reigns

Ahmed Shah Abdali, who took the name 'Durrani', meaning 'pearl of pearls', from the pearl earring he used to wear, was one of Afghanistan's most potent rulers. With the decline of Mughal power in India the governors of Kashmir became 'irresponsible and cruel, forcing the nobles to approach the rising Afghan power in the north-west and to seek its help for the liberation of the valley from the clutches of the Mughal tyrants,' writes Prem Nath Bazaz.[15] For centuries the Kashmiris and Afghans had been neighbours and friends and there seemed to be no reason why they should not continue as such under the overlordship of Durrani. The Afghan kingdom already reached the Indus Valley. The frontier towns of Peshawar and Attock, where the Kabul river joins with the Indus, were as much part of Afghanistan, as are Herat and Kandahar today.

The catalyst for the Afghan take-over came in 1751. A leading Kashmiri noble, Mir Muqim Kanth, was then the deputy governor and when he reduced the pay of the soldiers they rebelled under Abdul Qasim Khan. Subsequently, in yet another power struggle, Mir Muqim Kanth and Khwaja Zahir approached Abdali and asked him to annex Kashmir. In 1753 the Afghan general, Abdullah Khan Ishaq Aqasi, entered Kashmir with a force of 1,500 men. Abdul Qasim Khan opposed the invading force at Shopian and, in the ensuing battle, the Afghans triumphed. But, comments Bazaz: 'No sooner was the Valley annexed by Durrani to his Afghan kingdom than the Kashmiris found they were thrown from the frying pan into the fire.'[16]

Despite their shared religion, tribal, cultural and linguistic differences meant that the usual pattern of despotic rule began. Direct control was nominal and oppression took the form of extortion of money from the local people and brutality in the face of opposition. Both Kashmiri men and women lived in fear of their lives. Many were captured and sent as slaves to Afghanistan. Never before had the people in the valley experienced such barbarous administration. According to a Persian proverb at the time, during the rule of the Afghans cutting off a head was considered to be like plucking a flower to these 'stone-hearted' men.[17]

As in the days of the Mughals, Kashmir was ruled by governors. Their names are all but forgotten but not their cruelty, which was directed mainly towards the Hindus. 'A few Kashmiri Pandits were the instruments of the Afghans,' writes Sender 'and the majority were their victims ... Their wealth made them useful allies and obvious targets.'[18] The governors, however, disliked their subservience to the Afghan ruler and most of them attempted to rebel against Afghan authority in Kabul and to declare their independence. The first governor was Abdullah Khan Ishaq Aqasi, who had conquered Kashmir. He was a harsh ruler and extorted money from the province in order to amass a fortune for himself. He severely restricted the religious rituals of the Hindus. Temples were desecrated and idols broken.

A temporary lull in the oppression came with Governor Sukh Jiwan Mal. A Hindu, he had cleverly ousted Aqasi when he had been given temporary charge of the province while Aqasi was in Kabul. Sukh took as his adviser a Kashmiri Muslim, Abdul Hassan Bande, and together they attempted to improve conditions for the people. A contemporary chronicler, Ghulam Ali Azad Bilgrami, records how Abdul Hassan Bande 'bestowed favours on every visitor to the court, whether he was poor or not.'[19] The two men fell out, and Sukh then began to oppress the Muslims. In 1762, in alliance with the Dogra Rajput ruler, Raja Ranjit Dev of Jammu, the Afghans attacked Kashmir and captured Sukh. With characteristic cruelty he was taken to Lahore in chains where he was blinded and trampled to death by an elephant.[20]

A succession of governors brought no peace to the troubled valley, which was in a state of perpetual anarchy. When General Khurrum Khan was governor, the commander-in-chief of the Afghan forces in the valley ousted him and assumed power himself. He was Amir Mohammed Khan Jawan Sher Qazilbash. When the Afghan leader, Ahmed Shah Durrani, died in 1772 Jawan Sher set himself up as an independent ruler. As a Shia he revived the controversy between Shias and Sunnis. He is also remembered for his cruelty to Hindus. But there were some achievements. Writing a century later, Walter Lawrence believed that he was 'perhaps the best of the Pathan rulers'. He built the Amiran Kadal, a bridge at the entrance to Srinagar, and constructed the palace of the Shergarhi. 'But,' as Baron von Huegel was to observe, 'he showed petty spite in destroying the Mugal gardens on the Dal.' The entrance to the Shalimar gardens was completely disfigured by successive Pathan governors, 'who had erected an ugly flat roof over it, for the convenience of smoking their pipes.'[21]

Durrani successors

After Ahmed Shah Durrani's death never again did the Afghan kingdom reach the heights to which it had risen under his leadership. Constantly engaged in war, Durrani gave Afghanistan an empire which made it a power, both in Central Asia and on the sub-continent, with which to be reckoned. He was succeeded by his favourite son, Timur Shah. Initially Timur Shah attempted to assert the same authority over the empire as had his father. One of his first priorities was to recapture Kashmir. He sent Haji Karimdad Khan as governor with a punitive force against the self-proclaimed independent ruler, Jawan Sher. Reportedly the Afghan force was ill-equipped and could have been repelled, but there was no support from the Kashmiri Sunni Muslims who feared that, had Jawan Sher remained in power any longer, they would all be converted to the Shia faith. Jawan Sher was defeated and sent in chains to Kabul. Haji Karimdad conquered Skardu in the west and also defeated Raja Ranjit Dev, who, from neighbouring Jammu, had once more tried to annex the valley.

Karimdad was as cruel as his predecessors. This time it was the turn of the Shia Muslims, whom he suppressed mercilessly. The town of Amirabad, which Jawan Sher had built for the Shias, was destroyed. In order to extort money from the people, Muslims and Hindus alike, he levied a range of taxes; there was a tax on landlords and officials, another tax on merchants and bankers, a tax on grain from the farmers. And he levied an anna per rupee on the price of shawls from the weavers. At Karimdad's death he was succeeded by his son, Azad Khan. Known as the 'Nadir Shah of Kashmir' because of his bad temper, he unsuccessfully declared his independence from Timur Shah.

Persecution of Hindus was renewed. Turbans and shoes were forbidden as well as the caste mark on the forehead. The poll tax on the Hindus was revived and many Brahmins fled or converted to Islam. According to Walter Lawrence, Azad Khan made a practice of tying up the Pandits two by two in grass sacks and sinking them in Dal Lake.[22] But, warns Sender, the worst excesses of the Afghans have passed into legend: 'Lawrence conveys more what was remembered than what occurred.'[23]

During the time of the Afghans the Chaks or Gulbans reappeared, not in the guise of rulers but as robbers and dacoits. When the Sikhs came to govern Kashmir the Gulbans became notorious for kidnapping newly married brides and Godfrey Vigne talks of a place near Baramula as being 'particularly infested by the Gulbans.' Terrible punishments were meted out to them by the governors and they eventually were forced to become labourers and look after horses.

While Azad Khan was governor, George Forster visited Kashmir in 1783. A civil servant in the East India Company's Presidency of Madras, he travelled from Bengal to Kashmir and returned via Kabul and St Petersburg. Azad Khan appears to have been no less tolerant of foreigners. According to Baron von Huegel, who visited the valley over half a century later, 'to avoid persecution, which had nearly cost him his life, Forster was obliged to have recourse to disguises and concealments which, during his short stay there, under perpetual dread of discovery, prevented him from making any very important use of his time.'[24]

A later governor, Mir Hazar Khan, also aspired to independence. He attacked the Muslim Shias and Kashmiri Pandits by obliging them to pay special new taxes. He also drowned Hindus and Shias indiscriminately, says Lawrence, but instead of using grass he used leather sacks. He attempted to eliminate the Kashmiri Pandits from the revenue administration but failed. When Abdullah Khan Halokozai became governor in 1795 Nand Ram Tikku, a Kashmiri Pandit, succeeded in gaining considerable influence at the Afghan court to the extent that he was able to install his own protégé, Har Das, as Abdullah Khan's dewan (prime minister). When differences arose between the governor and his prime minister, Abdullah Khan was recalled to Kabul and imprisoned in the Bala Hissar fort. His imprisonment coincided with a struggle for power between rival claimants to the Afghan throne. After Timur's death in 1793 he was succeeded by one of his twenty-six sons, Zaman Shah. In 1800 Zaman was ousted by his half-brother, Mahmud Shah, who in turn was deposed in 1803 by a full brother of Zaman, Shah Shuja-ul Mulk. During the political upheaval Abdullah Khan managed to escape and returned to Kashmir, where he set himself up as an independent ruler. But a series of natural calamities followed. In 1804 there was a severe earthquake, in 1805 a devastating flood and, in 1806, the winter was so harsh that rivers and lakes remained frozen for many months.

The following year the Afghans returned to take control of the valley. Shah Shuja sent a punitive force under Sher Mohammed Khan against Abdullah Khan. The Afghans crossed the Jhelum river at Muzaffarabad and fought a battle at Sopore. Sher Mohammed continued his journey to Srinagar and laid siege to the Hari Parbat fort, built by Akbar and situated on an imposing hill overlooking the city. The siege lasted three months, until Abdullah Khan was killed. He is remembered as being a just and able administrator who gave some peace to the province. Sher Mohammed Khan's son, Ata Mohammed Khan, was then installed as governor, under control from Kabul. After the terrible famine he restored the agricultural and commercial structure. As a patron of art and learning he is credited with giving Kashmir a period of stable and effective rule.

A further struggle for power in Kabul, leading to the overthrow in 1809 of the Afghan king, Shuja-ul Mulk, by his half-brother, Mahmud Shah, provided the opportunity for Ata Mohammed Khan to declare his independence. He strengthened the defences of the valley by building forts at Sopore and Baramula. He revived trade and struck a coin in the name of Nund Rishi, the patron saint of the valley. But his declaration of independence was an open provocation to the Afghan king to send yet another expedition to Kashmir. Mahmud Shah made an alliance with the Sikh ruler, Ranjit Singh, Maharaja of the Punjab, and son of Mahan Singh, head of one of the twelve Sikh confederacies, known as 'misls'. Ranjit's rise to prominence had been at the expense of the declining Afghan empire. In 1799 he had acquired Lahore and the title of raja from Zaman Shah while he was king of Afghanistan. In 1801 he was confirmed as maharaja by a descendant of the great Sikh guru, Nanak. A year later Ranjit Singh had conquered Amritsar.

In order to gain control over Kashmir, the Afghan king's minister, Fateh Khan Barakzai, had promised Ranjit a substantial annuity. But the alliance between the Sikhs and Afghans fell apart and, in February 1813, the Afghans entered the valley first, defeating Ata Mohammed and installing another governor, Sardar Muhammad Azim Khan. Whereupon Fateh Khan stopped the promised payment to Ranjit Singh. According to J. D. Cunningham: 'he maintained that, as he alone had achieved the conquest, the Maharaja could not share in the spoils.'[25] But Ranjit Singh remained 'as anxious as ever to obtain possession of the valley.'[26]

The following year the Sikhs once more attacked Kashmir. In a pincer movement one force marched towards Shopian; another, under the personal command of Ranjit Singh, marched on Poonch. Initially successful, the campaign was impeded by bad weather; according to Godfrey Vigne 'a shower of rain rendered the Sikh muskets useless'.[27] The rains also brought cholera, which badly affected the Sikh forces. Ranjit Singh, who had personally taken up position in Poonch, retreated. But, says Walter Lawrence: 'Elated by this success [the governor] Muhammad Azim now gave himself up to the delights of torturing Brahmins.'[28] Doubting the loyalty of both Kashmiri Muslims and Hindus, who he believed had invited the Sikhs to enter Kashmir, Azim also discharged all Kashmiris from the army.

Afghans vanquished

After six years of famine, the Kashmiri exchequer was empty. Azim Khan, believed that one of his revenue collectors, Pandit Birbal Dhar, was guilty of embezzlement and he placed him under arrest until the accounts could be checked. When he was released on bail, Birbal Dhar fled from the valley. He left Srinagar in mid-winter, crossing the snow-capped mountains of the Pir Panjal range with his son Raja Kak. Historians of his mission are careful to point out that his flight was made possible by the help of two Muslim landowners, Malik Kamdar and Malik Namdar, as well as by Muslim peasants. It was not, therefore, a question of betrayal by a Kashmiri Hindu of his Muslim overlord, but a united movement by Kashmiris against an alien ruler.

Birbal Dhar made for Jammu, where he was received by one of Ranjit Singh's favoured vassals, Gulab Singh. He gave Dhar a letter of introduction to his brother, Dhyan, who was 'gatekeeper' of Maharaja Ranjit Singh's harem at Lahore. As an exponent of Muslim interests in the valley, Muhammad Saraf makes much of the fact that Pandit Birbal Dhar went to Lahore via Jammu, when a quicker route would have been by way of Poonch or Bhimber. It shows, says Saraf, that Birbal Dhar 'was under the impression that Gulab Singh was interested in the elimination of Muslim rule in the valley.'[29] Gulab Singh, however, had not yet been invested as Raja of Jammu and it was to be many years before whatever personal ambitions he might have nurtured in the valley came to fruition.

Birbal Dhar's message to Ranjit this time was one of support against the Afghans. Ranjit, however, was cautious of giving help and kept Pandit Birbal's son as a hostage until his mission was completed. When Azim Khan heard of Pandit Birbal's departure he sent for the women of his family. His wife committed suicide and his daughter converted to Islam and was sent to Kabul, where, according to Lawrence writing in the 1880s, 'she was living until quite recently.'[30]

Despite the troubled situation in Kashmir, Azim Khan returned to Kabul to give support to his brother, Wazir Fateh Mohammed Khan, leaving their younger brother, Jabbar Khan, in charge of affairs in Kashmir. His short tenure of power was characterised by a policy of senseless cruelty which made the Kashmiris even more determined to end Afghan rule. This time Ranjit Singh's invasion of Kashmir was accomplished with little resistance.

Godfrey Vigne describes how Ranjit Singh was helped by the 'treachery' of two chiefs whom Jabbar Khan had sent to Shopian to warn of the Sikh arrival. But they 'became traitors' and showed the way to the Sikhs, which enabled them to enter Kashmir. Ranjit Singh also secured the support of other local rulers on the way from Bhimber to Shopian to ensure a safe passage for his army.

An advance column left Lahore on 26 February 1819 under the command of Ranjit Singh's heir, Prince Kharak Singh. Ranjit left two months later and set up his base camp at Wazirabad. He took with him some of his ablest generals, including Gulab Singh. When he heard of the arrival of the Sikh army, Jabbar Khan marched from Srinagar to Hirpur, about five miles from Shopian. On 3 July 1819, the two forces engaged in battle. 'The choice of the Sikh cavalry marched on foot over the mountains along with the infantry soldiers, and they dragged with them a few light guns,' writes Cunningham.[31] Early on in his military career Ranjit Singh had learnt from the success of the East India Company's artillery and his Sikh guns predominated over the Afghans on their horses. When Jabbar Khan was wounded he retreated to Srinagar. The Afghans and Kashmiris panicked and Kashmir fell to the Sikhs.

Afghan rule in retrospect

Afghan domination lasted for little more than fifty years, but the period is generally remembered as one of the darkest of Kashmiri history. Despite common cultural links the repressive and extortionate nature of Afghan rule led to misery amongst the people. 'Owing to its remote situation, it became necessary for the Sovereign of Cabul to invest his representative in Cashmere with all the powers of a king, to be exercised without appeal or reference.'[32] When the Abdali dynasty was weakened, after the death of Ahmed Shah Durrani, the governors were even more tempted to rebel and the power struggles in Kabul provided them with the opportunity.

Lawrence, who came to the valley in the 1880s, believed that under the Afghans 'wealth had to be accumulated rapidly as no one knew how many days would elapse before he was recalled to Kabul, to make room for some needy favourite of the hour.' He believed that the defeat of the Afghans must have been a relief to the local people: 'I do not mean to say that the Sikh rule was benign or good, but it was at any rate better than that of the Pathans.'[33] Under the Afghans the shawl industry declined, probably due to their policy of taxation. In 1783 George Forster estimated that there were 16,000 shawl looms in use compared with 40,000 in the time of the Mughals, but by the beginning of the nineteenth century the demand for shawls in Europe meant that the number of looms rose to 24,000 by 1813.[34]

Although the Kashmiri Pandits undoubtedly suffered under the Afghans, Henry Sender points out that the 'collective memory of the community has preserved events of the Afghan period in somewhat distorted form, recalling

suffering as only directed to the Pandits of Kashmir.'[35] Despite the religious
oppression to which many of them were subjected, the Kashmiri Pandits
were useful to the Afghans because of their administrative experience. They
were not prevented from entering into government service and there were
some families whose names consistently appear in the administration – the
Dhars, Kauls, Tikkus and Saprus. Pandit Mahanand Dhar was prime minister
to the Afghan governor of Kashmir in the late 1750s. Sahaj Ram Sapru was
a revenue officer in Kashmir in the late eighteenth century. Nand Ram Tikku
and Lal Kaul both rose to become ministers at the court of the Afghan king
in Kabul.[36] But it is also true that by the end of Muslim rule in the valley
the lower castes of Hindus had either migrated or converted and those who
remained were the Kashmiri Pandits.

By requesting the assistance of the Sikhs and Ranjit Singh – a ruler who
had already mounted two expeditions against Kashmir and who had been in
nominal alliance with their oppressors, the Afghans – yet again the Kashmiris
had been responsible for asking for help from a foreign ruler. There seems
to have been no question of trying to re-assert their independence as in the
days of the Chaks. Submission to an external power was not only a matter
of expediency but also survival in a cruel world.

PART TWO

British Overlords

CHAPTER 4

Sikh Conquest 1819

It was the retribution of our sins that the Sikhs entered Kashmir. Attributed to Mullah Hamidullah[1]

After so much conquest, what can remain of originality to these inhabitants of the valley, after so many changes of rulers, each in turn eager to destroy the works of his predecessors?' Baron Charles von Huegel[2]

In the wake of the decline of the Afghan empire in northern India Ranjit Singh had shown himself both able and willing to fill the vacuum. Further expansion to the south was blocked by the British. On 25 April 1809 the British and Sikhs had concluded a treaty of 'Amity and Concord' by which the Sikhs acknowledged British supremacy in Sind and the British agreed that their territory would stop at the river Sutlej. 'Runjeet soon became sensible that it would be better policy to conciliate our friendship than to provoke our enmity.'[3] After subduing several chiefs in the Punjab, who had not acknowledged his supremacy, the 'Lion of the Punjab', as he became known, had turned his attention north towards Jammu and Kashmir.

'King log for King stork'

On 4 July 1819 a Sikh army estimated at 30,000 entered Srinagar. Contemporary accounts describe how the Sikhs 'routed the forces of Cashmeer' and 'the conquest of that province was effected without further resistance.'[4] In honour of the victory the Sikh capital of Lahore was illuminated for three days. Initially the Kashmiris, like Pandit Birbal Dhar, hoped that the defeat of the Afghans would improve conditions for the people. But, as Prem Nath Bazaz points out, the change of masters 'proved but a change of king log for king stork.' Sikh rule lasted for only twenty-eight years, but the Sikhs were 'no less cruel, rapacious, short-sighted intolerant and fanatical than the Afghans.'[5]

Their major concern was law and order and, as under the Mughals and Afghans, the Kashmiris were at the mercy of a foreign ruler. Unlike the Afghans, however, the Sikhs did not ride into the houses of the Kashmiris and make demands; traffic in women was more restricted. There was also one significant change. Whereas under the Afghans the majority of the population were ruled by their co-religionists, under the Sikhs the Kashmiri

Pandits had the opportunity to re-assert themselves. 'If the Afghans were less tyrannical towards the Muslim nobles, the Sikh governors treated the Hindu landlords less harshly,' writes Bazaz.[6] The poor sections of all communities, however, suffered equally.

As under the Afghans control of the province was effected by a series of governors, the first of whom was Dewan Moti Ram, the son of one of Ranjit's trusted military officers. Several measures which demonstrated the reassertion of Hindu belief were enacted. Cow slaughter was forbidden making it a crime punishable by death. Several butchers were publicly hanged to set an example. The *azan* – the Muslim call to prayer – was also prohibited.

Fearing discontent amongst the local population, Moti Ram closed the Jama Masjid to prevent crowds of disaffected Muslims from gathering there. Although the motive may have been political rather than religious, the closure of the mosque upset the local Muslim Kashmiris. It was rumoured that Moti Ram was also planning to destroy another mosque, the Khanqah-i Maulla, but Pandit Birbal Dhar, who was returned to his old post as a revenue collector, dissuaded him. The stone mosque at Srinagar built by Empress Noor Jehan was converted into a state grain store. The first mosque, built by Bulbul Shah, who in the fourteenth century had converted Rinchen, the Buddhist ruler, to Islam, was also closed.

But despite these actions Muhammad Saraf, a strong supporter of Muslim interests, considers that Moti Ram had the good of the people at heart. 'Realising that the peasantry was the backbone of the economy and on their contentment depended the government revenue, he tried to stop, as far as he could, their eviction from lands and its distribution among Hindus and Sikhs.' Saraf blames the troubles of the people on the revenue collectors who were liable to act independently from the governor, operating a dual system of administration. Moti Ram tried to encourage Birbal Dhar and his Pandit tax collectors 'to lessen their illegal exactions so that the Muslim peasantry could be persuaded to stop the abandonment of lands.'[7] On account of this, says Saraf, Birbal managed to get Moti Ram recalled and replaced by Hari Singh Nalva. Although a brave soldier Nalva was not a good administrator and initially remained under the influence of the Pandit officials. During this time some conversions of Muslims to Hinduism were reported. Nalva is, however, best remembered for introducing a new coin in his own name which remained legal tender until 1885.

Travellers' tales

Few Europeans had visited Kashmir. In 1823, however, William Moorcroft travelled throughout the country on his way to Bokhara. His objective was to locate a better breed of horse from amongst the Turkman steeds for the East India Company's military stud. Before becoming a veterinary surgeon he had trained as a doctor and while in Srinagar, where he remained for ten months, he treated the local people and observed their deprivation. 'Everywhere the people were in the most abject condition, exorbitantly taxed by the Sikh government and subjected to every kind of extortion and oppression by its officers. The consequences of this system are the gradual depopulation of the country.'[8] Moorcroft estimated that no more than one-sixteenth of the cultivable land surface was under cultivation; as a result starving people had fled in great numbers to India.

He also described how he had at one time no fewer than 6,800 patients on his list, 'a large proportion of whom were suffering from the most loathsome diseases, brought on by scant and unwholesome food, dark, damp and ill-ventilated lodgings, excessive dirtiness and gross immorality.'[9] Every trade was taxed: 'butchers, bakers, boatmen, vendors of fuel, public notaries, scavengers, prostitutes, all pay a sort of corporation tax', as well as the shawl makers. In a good year Kashmir was one of the richest revenue-yielding provinces of the Sikh kingdom. Moorcroft was astounded to hear from Governor Nalva that he had accumulated 25 lakhs of rupees for himself besides realising the provincial rental assessment for the maharaja.

During his stay Moorcroft travelled throughout the valley. Islamabad 'was as filthy a place as can well be imagined, and swarmed with beggars, some of whom were idle vagabonds, but the greater number were in real distress.'[10] Moorcroft left the valley by the Pir Panjal route, used by the successive Mughal emperors. About 500 Kashmiris were crossing at the same time, driven out by their abject circumstances. Their appearance, he noted, 'half naked and miserably emaciated, presented a ghastly picture of poverty and starvation. Yet, wretched as they were, the relentless Sikhs would have levied 'a "pies" a head to pass the post, had we not interfered.' During the journey the Sikhs seized some of the people accompanying Moorcroft across the pass to act 'as unpaid porters'; they were, he said, 'not only driven along by a cord tying them together by the arms, but their legs were bound with ropes at night to prevent their escape.' Surprisingly, in some places, conditions seemed to have deteriorated from the time of the Afghans. Shopian had at one time 200 houses and 100 shops, but 'upon hearing of the defeat of the Durannis by the Sikhs, the inhabitants fled, and many never returned, so that the place is not half inhabited.'[11]

Moorcroft's mission was never completed because he died of fever in 1825. But his journals, edited by H. H. Wilson, provide a valuable insight into the condition of the Kashmiris in the early years of Sikh rule. We can assume that conditions did not change much in the years to come and Godfrey Vigne who travelled throughout Kashmir in the late 1830s had a similar story to tell. The successive governors who ruled Kashmir did so primarily for their own benefit; as Moorcroft had observed, the Kashmiris were treated as 'little better than cattle'.[12]

In 1824 Moti Ram returned again as governor. Birbal Dhar was still working as a revenue collector but, comments Saraf, Moti Ram, 'tired of

Pandit intrigues and their large-scale corruption, ordered a thorough audit of the accounts which revealed that large sums recovered as revenues had neither been deposited in the treasury nor accounted for.'[13] Failing to account for the loss, all of Birbal Dhar's property was confiscated and he was put in prison, where he died. Saraf is unsympathetic: 'The end of traitors who foist foreign rule on their country for the furtherance of their personal or family interests is normally the same. It is no consolation that one foreign rule is sought to be replaced by another.'[14] Governor Chuni Lal who succeeded Moti Ram was remembered as an ineffective governor whose punishments were severe. When he was recalled in 1826, fearful of the consequences of his dismissal, he committed suicide by taking poison on his way to Lahore.

Of all the Sikhs governors, Dewan Kripa Ram enjoyed the best reputation. He loved luxury, especially boating, which gave him the name Kripa Shoin – after the sound of the boat paddle. He also spent time with dancing girls and prostitutes. While the governor was enjoying the pleasures of life, Sheikh Ghulam Mohi-ud Din from Jullundur was *de facto* ruler. Although Sheikh Ghulam attempted some reforms in revenue collection, according to Saraf he 'dutifully followed in the footprints of his predecessors and amassed a huge fortune through illegal means.'[15]

While Kripa Ram was governor a severe earthquake in June 1828 shook the valley. 'Perhaps a thousand were killed,' noted Vigne, '1,200 houses were shaken down ... the earth opened in several places throughout the city.'[16] This was followed by another cholera epidemic, the outcome of which seriously affected the economy. Kripa Ram's self-indulgence was disliked by the Lahore Durbar and in 1831 he was recalled and dismissed. It was also alleged that he was dismissed because the maharaja had been prejudiced against him by Gulab Singh, ruler of Jammu, for giving protection to the Raja of Bhimber, who had been dispossessed of his lands by the Jammu ruler.

Kripa Ram was replaced by Bhama Singh Ardli. During his governorship, a serious Shia–Sunni conflict erupted which caused further hardship to the people. He was believed to be a personal servant of Ranjit Singh and had only been made governor as a reward for some service because he had no other qualifications for the position and within a year he was recalled. In 1831 Victor Jacquemont, the French botanist, arrived in the valley. He kept in regular correspondence with Ranjit Singh and had taken the opportunity to visit Kashmir because he recognised it was still comparatively rare for a European to be allowed entry. The appearance of Srinagar, he said, was the 'most miserable in the world ... nowhere else in India are the masses as poor and denuded as they are in Kashmir. It is the only place where wages for labour are actually as low as we mistakenly believe them to be throughout India.'[17]

In 1832 Prince Sher Singh, one of the sons of Ranjit Singh, governed the valley. He chose to enter it from Muzaffarabad during winter by the difficult and treacherous Baramula route. Although in winter the route to Srinagar was virtually impassable, thousands of Kashmiris were forcibly driven out of their homes and compelled to break the ice all the way to Srinagar, a distance of 34 miles from Baramula. Sher Singh's two-year governorship was marred by another severe earthquake in 1833, which led to famine and a cholera epidemic. It was estimated that the population was reduced by three-quarters (from 80,000 to 20,000) because of death or migration. Ranjit Singh planned to visit the valley at this time. But the demand for grain to feed his anticipated retinue was so great that the consequences of the famine were exacerbated and the visit never took place.

Living conditions became so bad that people often tried to escape the valley. When Joseph Wolff visited Kashmir in 1832 he met some stragglers leaving the valley. In his memoirs, he describes how he prevailed upon Sher Singh not to prevent the poor people from leaving Kashmir. 'He promised to wink at it; and so it came to pass that hundreds of shawl weavers, with their wives and children' were able to leave Kashmir with Wolff on his return journey to India. Labour, however, was scarce and escape was normally impossible. Wolff also lamented the cruelty of the Sikhs against the Muslims. 'A whole Muhammadan family was burned alive for having killed a cow. It must, however, be confessed, that one cannot but see the retributive justice of God against the people for the cruelties which they had practised, when in power, against the Sikhs, and which are actually appalling to think.'[18]

In 1834 Ranjit Singh sent Colonel Mian Singh Kumedan, from Gujranwala as governor. Considered to be the best of all the Sikh governors, he attempted to bring the valley out of the economic chaos resulting from the 1833 famine. He made some attempt to revive trade and industry and bring order into the administration. He organised a land revenue system by ordering a new land settlement. He imported grain and fowls from the Punjab and distributed them among the people, recalled the shawl weavers who had fled to the Punjab after the famine to start their work afresh, and he fixed the rates to be paid as customs duties on certain articles. 'False weights were confiscated and unsocial elements were brought to book,' says Dewan Sharma.[19]

While Colonel Mian Singh was governor Godfrey Vigne was touring the valley. He noted the unease between Sikhs and Kashmiris:

> The lordly Sikh … is usually to be seen lounging about in the very plenitude of consequence … and, as is often the case, if he be the Commandant of the neighbouring guard house, and the officer in charge of the revenue, he will be always surrounded by a coterie of idle Kashmirians, and may be seen listening with the utmost complacency to lying representations and petitions for exemption, which it is quite out of his power to grant, from those who hate as cordially as they flatter him, and whom he as cordially despises in return.[20]

The Pandits, he said, 'justly complained of the oppression of the Sikhs, who are his brethren in religion; and the Musulman remarks with sorrow on the

present condition of his beautiful country, and compares it with what he has
read of the dominion of the Moguls or remembers the time of the Patan.'[21]

Despite the efforts made by Colonel Mian Singh, by the late 1830s the
valley and neighbouring areas were suffering under such terrible conditions
that any small improvement came too late. 'The oppression and rapacity of
the Sikhs had reduced the revenue to a paltry amount of a few thousand
rupees per annum,' writes Vigne.[22] The Kashmiris even ridiculed their own
poverty: 'Kishtwar is the causeway of distress, where people are hungry by
day and cold by night; whoever comes there, when he goes away is as meagre
as the flagstaff of a fakir.'[23] 'Not a day passed,' says Vigne, ' whilst I was on
the path to Kashmir, and even when travelling in the valley, that I did not
see the bleached remains of some unfortunate wretch who had fallen a
victim either to sickness or starvation.'[24] Baron Charles von Huegel, an officer
in the Prussian army, was also in the valley while Mian Singh was governor
and met him personally. 'To judge by his countenance, one would pronounce
him good-natured and kind; but, in many respects, he is not the governor
required in the present critical state in Kashmir.' Von Huegel witnessed the
feudal nature of the relationship of the local rulers with their overlords. 'On
the ground ... sat many Muhammadan Rajas, from the Baramula and
Muzaffarabad mountains, tributaries of Ranjit Singh. One of every family is
detained as a hostage in Kashmir and from time to time they are obliged to
bring large gifts to the governor, otherwise their tribute is raised.'[25]

The effect of Sikh rule, according to Prem Nath Bazaz, dealt a severe
blow to the pride of the local people. 'The people of the valley gradually
forgot their glorious martial traditions and became timid and cowardly.'[26] But
in some senses the 'modern age' also began to creep in. European visitors
provided detailed studies of the area. Captain Wade's map, presented to
Ranjit Singh, was the first up-to-date map of Kashmir. Cameras, watches,
barometers, binoculars, telescopes, clocks were all introduced into Kashmir
at this time. The beginning of a modern postal system was also set up.
Whereas under the Afghans trade was in the hands of the Pathans and the
Durranis, the Sikhs encouraged the Kashmiris and Punjabis to enter into
commercial contracts for business.

Ranjit Singh never visited the valley of Kashmir; but there is a well-
known story of how he once wrote to Colonel Mian Singh: 'Would that I
could only once in my life enjoy the delight of wandering through the gardens
of Kashmir, fragrant with almond-blossoms, and sitting on the fresh green
turf!' To please the maharaja, the governor ordered a special Kashmiri carpet
to be woven with a green background, dotted with little pink spots and
interspersed with tiny little pearls like dots. When he received it, Ranjit was
delighted and rolled himself on it as though he were rolling in the Kashmiri
grass.[27] A shawl was also prepared for Ranjit depicting a map of the Kashmir
valley; but by the time it was completed thirty-seven years later, the Lion of
the Punjab was dead.

Power to the Dogras

On the sidelines of Kashmir, in the neighbouring plains of Jammu, the Dogras were keenly interested in events in the valley. Gulab Singh, the ruler of Jammu, a feudatory of Ranjit Singh, was a man whom Lord Ellenborough, the governor-general, came to recognise 'was extending his power with unscrupulous disregard to the rights of others and the supremacy of the state he pretends to serve.'[28] Born in October 1792 with his two younger brothers, Dhyan and Suchet, Raja Gulab Singh had succeeded in making himself indispensable at the court of Ranjit Singh. For over twenty years the triumvirate of brothers dominated events in the Sikh kingdom. As vassals of Ranjit Singh, they succeeded in amassing land and wealth both in the plains and hill states to the north of the Punjab. By the time of Ranjit's death, they had acquired such power that the struggle for the succession in Lahore was bound to affect their own future. For Gulab Singh, the demise of the Sikh empire enabled him to obtain the most prized of his territorial acquisitions: the valley of Kashmir.

The Dogra Rajputs had settled around the lakes of Mansar and Siroinsar in the tract of land rising from the plains of the Punjab to the mountains to the north. They took their name from the word 'Dogirath' which in Sanskrit means 'two lakes'. Former vassals of the Mughals, the Rajputs had been left free to pursue their own political ambitions by the decline of the empire after the death of Aurangzeb. Gulab's great-grandfather was Surat Dev, younger brother of Ranjit Dev, the great Dogra leader who gave his kingdom, centred on Jammu, over thirty years of stable government. In 1770 Ranjit Dev was obliged to pay tribute to the Sikhs after they had taken power in central Punjab following the decline of the Afghan empire. But Gulab's immediate predecessors lost control of Jammu, and it was ruled by another branch of the Dogra family. Gulab was brought up by his grandfather in neighbouring estates.

In 1808, when Gulab was only sixteen, Ranjit Singh was preparing an expedition to re-assert Sikh authority over Jammu. 'Without even obtaining permission from his grandfather, Gulab Singh borrowed a charger from the stables and appeared on the battlefield,' writes his biographer K. M. Pannikar.[29] The Dogras were defeated and Jammu became part of the Sikh kingdom. Gulab had originally intended to enlist in the army of the Afghan king, Shah Shuja-ul Mulk, who was assembling an army in Peshawar to reassert his claim to the Afghan throne. But Gulab's attendants refused to go to Afghanistan and he therefore joined the army of Ranjit Singh at Sialkot in 1809. Sent for training to Lahore, he soon came to the attention of Ranjit Singh.

Gulab took part in Ranjit Singh's unsuccessful expedition to annex Kashmir in 1813. When Pandit Birbal Dhar went to Lahore to ask for Ranjit Singh's help against the Afghans he was received by Gulab Singh in Jammu. Gulab

Singh also assisted in the successful 1819 expedition, when Ranjit Singh finally captured Kashmir. When there was an open revolt against the Sikhs around Jammu, led by Mian Dedo, who claimed to be a direct descendant from Ranjit Dev, Gulab Singh asked to be entrusted with the duty of putting down the insurrection. As a reward, following the mediaeval practice of farming out provinces for revenue, he was granted Jammu in 1820. In 1822 the principality was conferred on him, together with the hereditary title of raja, in a ceremony on the banks of the river Chenab. The formal investiture demonstrated Ranjit's growing trust in Gulab Singh and his brothers:

> On this auspicious occasion, with extreme joy and with heartfelt love, I grant to Raja Gulab Singh in recognition of his conscientious and loyal service, the government of the Chakla of Jammu, which from time immemorial has been in the possession of his family. He and his brothers Dhyan Singh and Suchet Singh appeared in my Court at a very early age and loyally and devotedly served me and the State.

Gulab was just thirty years old; at the same time his youngest brother Suchet was invested as Raja of Ramnagar. In return, the brothers promised to render services wherever or whenever called upon. K. M. Panikkar describes how, when Dhyan asked why there was no kingdom for him, Ranjit replied that he was going to make Dhyan 'Raja of Rajas'.[30]

In 1828 Dhyan was promoted to Wazir. He was also granted the jagir of Poonch and other hill territories. His son, Hira, was given the jagir of Jasrota. Over the next ten years the three brothers increased the number of jagirs they held to eighty-five in the hill country bordering the valley of Kashmir. Their rise to prominence at Lahore did not endear them to the Sikh nobles. As contemporaries noted, they were 'more feared than liked and looked upon with great jealousy by the other sirdars.'[31] Unlike other chiefs of the Lahore court who held jagirs and yet spent most of their time at Lahore, Gulab Singh remained in Jammu unless called to Lahore: 'He took great personal interest in the management of his property and the government of his dominions,' writes Panikkar, 'which, by their hilly nature and by the independent character of their people, called for personal attention.'[32]

As a vassal of the maharaja, Gulab Singh was also obliged to perform certain duties, undertake expeditions and present himself at Lahore for ceremonial occasions. Most important of all, he had to contribute his share of revenue. In 1836 Gulab Singh transmitted 14 lakhs and 125 camels to Lahore. Unable to read or write, the rajah of Jammu combined barbaric cruelty with a strangely urbane personality. Victor Jacquemont who met him in the 1830s gave a favourable impression of his physique: a 'man of middle height, and extreme beauty, a superb head, with long, curly black hair, an aquiline nose of extreme delicacy, great oval black eyes and a small mouth with perfectly cut lips. His proportions combine grace with adroitness and strength.'[33] When Godfrey Vigne had an audience with Gulab Singh, he was asked whether the king of England paid tribute to the king of France 'and some other questions equally absurd by way of ascertaining whether I was disposed to deceive him.'[34]

Vigne also witnessed Gulab Singh's fearful cruelty. In 1837 Shams-ud Din, the governor of Poonch, one of the jagirs awarded to Dhyan Singh, led a rebellion against excessive taxation. He and his supporters were severely punished. Some of the prisoners captured by Gulab Singh were flayed alive. Gulab Singh:

> then ordered one or two of the skins to be stuffed with straw; the hands were stiffened, and tied in an attitude of supplication; the corpse was then placed erect; and the head, which had been severed from the body, was reversed as it rested on the neck. The figure was planted by the way-side, that passers by might see it.[35]

The Jammu ruler then called his son 'to take a lesson in the art of governing.' Shams-ud Din, his wife and children were all killed. To this day the Poonch governor's exploits against the Dogras are recalled in song:

> 'Praise be to your mother, O, Shams Khan
> A son like you no other mother will ever bear.'[36]

Vigne also noticed a surprising side to Gulab Singh's otherwise autocratic behaviour:

> Gulab Singh has made himself feared by his cruelty and tyrannical exactions, but effects to be tolerant and liberal in his religious opinions. Jammu is, accordingly, the only place in the Panjab where the Mullahs may call the Mussulmans to prayers. Runjit had forbidden them to do so; but Gulab Singh, his powerful vassal, allowed them to ascend the minars of Jamu, in the exercise of their vocation. A pious Brahmin, or Sikh, having complained that the Mullah's cry disturbed his devotions, Gulab Singh told him that he would order him to desist, if the applicant would take the trouble to collect his flock for him.[37]

Dogra expansion

In his first decade as Raja of Jammu, Gulab Singh had already extended his territory to include some of the surrounding hill states like Kishtwar, which he subdued in 1821. In the 1830s he expanded his lands in the name of the Sikh kingdom still further to include first Ladakh and later Baltistan. Ever since its nominal suzerainty to the Mughals, under Aurangzeb, Ladakh had continued to send tribute to the Afghans and Sikhs. The Sikh annexation of Kashmir, however, made the Ladakhis apprehensive that the Sikhs would turn their attention to the east. When Moorcroft had visited Ladakh he was encouraged by the local ruler to entertain the idea of securing Ladakh as a British sphere of influence against Russia. The East India Company, perhaps fearing that any moves in that direction would jeopardise the Anglo–Sikh treaty of 1809, or because of lack of interest in the area, disassociated themselves from Moorcroft's initiative.

In the summer of 1834 Gulab sent an army of 10,000 men to Ladakh under his famous general, Zorawar Singh. The following year Ladakh became a vassal kingdom of Jammu. But although the victory had been carried out in the name of Lahore the Sikhs were uneasy about Gulab Singh's personal ambitions. In order to assuage their fears Gulab sent Zorawar Singh to see Ranjit in person, whereupon the general boasted that he would carry the standards of the Sikhs to Tibet and China. Whatever doubts Ranjit Singh may have had about Gulab Singh's activities he did nothing to curtail them.

Dogra interest in the valley of Kashmir was a natural extension of this process of consolidation. Gulab's predecessor, Ranjit Dev, had attempted to invade Kashmir when it was ruled by the Afghans. It is therefore not surprising that Gulab Singh kept a watchful eye on the valley to the north, as much out of loyalty to Ranjit as for his own ambitions. Well before Ranjit Singh's death Godfrey Vigne was convinced that Gulab Singh's 'chief object was to further his designs upon Kashmir which he and his brother have been constantly endeavouring to obtain possession of, by every other means in their power.' Ranjit Singh had retained little of Kashmir's revenue for himself 'excepting the shawl duty and Gulab Singh had, I believe, his revenue officers in the city, at Shupeyon (Shopian) and Islamabad.'[38] Officers of Gulab Singh were already collecting revenue from a tax on salt and other commodities which went from the plains to Kashmir. For a while, when Sher Singh was governor, in order to gain the confidence of Gulab's brother, Dhyan, at Lahore, Sher Singh had permitted Gulab Singh to administer an area around Banihal. To the east, the Zanskar region of Ladakh was also transferred to Gulab Singh; but the people of Banihal objected and both these areas were returned to the Sikh administration.

When Ranjit Singh died, Gulab Singh had been his protégé for thirty years; aged forty-seven, he was well-placed to control events not only in the heart of the Sikh empire in Lahore but also in Kashmir. 'Judging from the manner of the Jammu Rajas rise,' writes B. S. Singh 'it may be safely assumed that in the wake of Ranjit Singh's death, they not only intended to maintain their position of strength, but to extend it.'[39] The events in Lahore are significant because, as Gulab Singh's power increased, so did his ability to look after his territorial ambitions. The probable plan was for Gulab Singh to acquire the whole of Jammu, Kashmir and the lands to the north east and for his brother Dhyan to be the power behind the throne at Lahore.

By the time of Ranjit Singh's death Kashmir was impoverished. Godfrey Vigne believed there was a political reason for this: 'Runjit assuredly well knew that the greater the prosperity of Kashmir, the stronger would be the inducement to invasion by the East India Company. "Après moi le déluge" has been his motto; and most assuredly its ruin has been accelerated by his political jealousy, which suggested to him, at any cost, the merciless removal of its

wealth and the reckless havoc which he has made in its resources.'[40] The
struggle for the succession at Lahore also intensified the neglect of Kashmir.

From Ranjit Singh's twenty-two wives and numerous concubines his
legitimate successor was Kharak Singh. He was, however, not of the calibre
of his father and died after a year in power. When Kharak Singh's nineteen-
year-old son, Nao Nihal Singh, together with the eldest son of Gulab Singh,
was accidentally killed by a falling archway at his father's funeral the succession
settled on Ranjit's 'reputed' son, Sher Singh, former governor of Kashmir.
Sher Singh's claim to the Sikh throne was challenged by Kharak Singh's
widow, Rani Chand Kaur, who threatened to adopt Dhyan's son, Hira Singh,
as her heir. The Dogra brothers evolved a strategy whereby Dhyan and
Suchet would back Sher Singh, and Gulab Singh and Hira would support
Rani Chand Kaur's claim. The Rani and her assistants were lodged in the
Lahore fort. Sher Singh laid siege to it with 17,000 Sikh troops. This action
took Gulab Singh by surprise. He had feigned loyalty to Chand Kaur, but he
had not expected a clash between himself and Sher Singh, much less a fight
between his Dogra troops and the Sikh army. Sher Singh was, however,
unable to storm the fort and after a series of negotiations peace was made.
Sher Singh became maharaja and Rani Chand Kaur received a lucrative jagir,
which, because of Gulab Singh's support, she entrusted to him. He protested
his loyalty to Sher Singh and said that he had only been protecting the
daughter-in-law of the great maharaja.

When Gulab Singh evacuated the fort he succeeded in carrying away a
great deal of Sikh treasure: 'sixteen carts were filled with rupees and other
silver coins', wrote a contemporary, Latif Muhammad, 'while five hundred
horseman were each entrusted with a bag of gold mohurs [seals] and his
orderlies were also entrusted with jewellery and other valuable articles.'[41] The
carts were covered with ammunition in order to 'hoodwink' the Sikh soldiers.
Although Sher Singh reproached Gulab Singh for having taken the treasure
his response was that whatever he had taken had been agreed by the Rani
and was to cover expenses incurred in the fort. When, however, only a few
years later, Gulab Singh came to purchase Kashmir, his appropriation of the
Sikh treasure was remembered. 'Gulab Singh,' observed another contemporary
writer, Lepel Griffin, 'laughing in his sleeve at the success of his and his
brothers' plans, marched off to Jamoo amidst the curses of the Sikh army,
carrying with him a great part of the treasure, principally jewels, which
Maharaja Runjit Singh had stored in the fort, and which plunder, five years
later, helped to purchase Cashmere.'[42] In the wake of his victory over the
Rani, Sher Singh was obliged to grant the Dogras additional favours which
included grants of land and the right to maintain their own troops, a privilege
they had already enjoyed, but which was tantamount to sanctioning a Dogra
state within that of the Sikhs.

In the chaos of the succession the Dogras had also been given a free
hand to further their territorial acquisitions bordering Jammu, obtaining 'the

casket which enclosed the jewel of Kashmir'.[43] At the end of 1840 Zorawar
Singh led a contingent of Dogras and Ladakhis to conquer Baltistan.
Although the Baltis had destroyed the only bridge by which the army could
cross the river Indus, the Dogras were eventually able to cross a part of the
river which was frozen. They surprised the Baltis and overwhelmed them. A
puppet ruler and a garrison of Dogras was installed at Skardu, annual tribute
was assessed and Zorawar retired to Leh.

Gulab Singh's next venture was to revive an ancient Ladakhi claim on
Tibet. At first his combined force of soldiers from Jammu, Ladakh and
Baltistan met with little resistance. The British, who had not paid much
attention to Gulab Singh's incursions into Ladakh and Baltistan, reacted
strongly to the Jammu ruler's new venture, which they believed would interfere
with their trading links from Tibet into the British-dominated areas of
Baskahr and Almora. With pressure both from the British and Sher Singh,
Gulab was eventually obliged to request Zorawar to withdraw. Before he
could do so, the Tibetans engaged the Dogras in battle. Zorawar was killed
and most of the army also perished. 'The Jammu commander's death determined the outcome of the battle. The weather had chilled the bodies of the
Dogra soldiers; their leader's loss now froze their spirits,' writes B.S. Singh.[44]

Sher Singh and the Dogras also had a new force with which they had to
contend: the rising power of the Sikh army – the Khalsa – which, after
Ranjit Singh's death, had become unrestrained and riotous during the anarchy
and chaos. They no longer respected the authority of the government and
each battalion elected an executive body of its own, known as a *panch*.
Lawlessness spread to the battalion in Kashmir and in Spring 1841 they
mutinied and murdered Governor Mian Singh. Once more, Gulab Singh was
able to take advantage of the situation to extend his influence into Kashmir
and he requested Sher Singh's permission to crush the rebellion.

Sher Singh was reluctant to lose control of the operation to Gulab Singh
and therefore agreed to send a force, which would be under the joint control
of his son, Partab Singh and Gulab Singh. With 5,000 men, Gulab Singh
quelled the mutiny and installed a Muslim governor, Sheikh Ghulam Mohi-
ud Din, who had risen to prominence under Governor Kripa Ram in the
early 1830s. In 1843 Sheikh Ghulam re-opened the gates of the Jama Masjid
and also ordered repairs to the Shiva temple. Attempts, however, to restore
order and reverse corruption came too late. He was apparently hated by the
Kashmiris, who had even petitioned for his removal. When Sheikh Ghulam
died in 1845, he was replaced by his son Imam, who was not well disposed
to the Dogras.

Prelude to Amritsar

Until the death of Ranjit Singh, the East India Company had maintained
cordial relations with the Sikhs; they in turn did not wish to upset the

British. After his death, the relationship soon fell apart. When Ranjit's son, Kharak Singh, and grandson, Nao Nihal, both died in 1840, British annexation of the Punjab was seriously considered, especially in the light of Britain's troubled policy in Afghanistan where they were trying unsucessfully to re-instate Shah Shuja-ul Mulk on the Afghan throne. In January 1841, H. B. Bayley, the chairman of the Board of Directors of the East India Company wrote to John Hobhouse, the president of the company's Board of Control:

> I believe we should have no difficulty in withdrawing from Afghanistan if we occupied the line of the Indus – but even if the holding of a force in Afghanistan should be necessary, we should find in the resources of the Punjaub, resources necessary for their maintenance; we could reinforce them without difficulty; and with Cashmere on our flanks, the whole line of the Indus in our possession, we might defy all attacks whether from European or Asiatic enemies.[45]

This aggressive stance was not adopted and the British decided to wait and see what happened within the Sikh empire. They did, however, observe that the Dogra brothers no longer had the same unity of spirit with the Sikhs and that there might be some advantage for the British in an eventual split between the Dogras and the Sikhs. In the Spring of 1841, George Clerk, the British Agent at Lahore, wrote to the political secretary of the governor-general: 'The recognition of the separate autonomy of the Jummoo rajas would doubtless afford great facility to the British government of establishing a due control over their aggrandisements.'[46] Clerk's suggestion was ignored by higher officials in the East India Company, who were annoyed by Gulab Singh's ongoing expedition to conquer Tibet. When, in June 1841, Sher Singh considered replacing the Italian born general, Paolo de Avitabile, with Gulab Singh as governor of Peshawar, the British prevailed upon him not so do so. Over the next five years the attitude of the British towards Gulab Singh changed so completely that he became the only man in the Sikh leadership with whom the members of the East India Company felt they could deal.

In 1842, after a humiliating retreat from Afghanistan the British decided to send a new force under General Pollock. Anticipating that the progress of the army might be hindered by hostile tribes in the north-west, they requested Sher Singh to send an escort for the British army along the Khyber Pass. Sher Singh obliged and sent Gulab Singh to Attock at the head of a force of 20,000 men. By this time the official British attitude was softening towards Gulab Singh and, in return for his assistance, Major Henry Lawrence, who rose to become a staunch supporter of Gulab Singh, even offered to help him to obtain Peshawar and Jalalabad. Gulab Singh, however, appeared to be in no hurry to move onwards to please the British. Herbert Edwardes, Lawrence's biographer, paints a vivid picture of his procrastination:

> As easily can those whose lot it has been to parley with that Ulysses of the hills, call up before them the sweet deference of attention, the guileless benevolence,

the childlike simplicity, and the masterly prolixity of fiction, parenthesis and anecdote, with which Raja Goolab Sing stroked his silver beard while listening to the question and then charmingly consumed the hours avoiding a reply.[47]

Eventually, with the intercession of both Sher Singh and Dhyan Singh from Lahore, Gulab Singh moved with his troops to escort Pollock and the British army through the Khyber in April 1842. Governor-General Ellenborough once more offered to grant Jalalabad to Gulab Singh on the understanding that he would withdraw from Ladakh. Ellenborough believed it would suit British objectives to have a hostile buffer between their territory and Afghanistan. But, not surprisingly, Gulab rejected the offer, which was less advantageous to him than it would have been to the British.

Gulab Singh's growing friendship with the British was treated with suspicion by the Sikhs. When Lord Ellenborough proposed decorating Gulab Singh for his services, Sher Singh refused. Yet there was little the Sikh leadership, beset by its own internal feuds and rivalry, could do to prevent the burgeoning relationship between their feudatory and the British. The message which Henry Lawrence sent to Gulab Singh through George Clerk in April 1842 could not have been more effusive.

'The fruit of the long-sown seed of friendship between us which was concealed for a long time has now come to light ... you who are the flower of the garden of this world ... we remember your troubles and difficulties in rendering help to our army: we shall never forget that.'[48]

Meanwhile, the power struggle continued in Lahore. Doubting Rani Chand Kaur's loyalty, Sher Singh had her murdered in 1842, whereupon Gulab Singh added to his lands the jagir, which the Rani had entrusted to his safe-keeping. Soon afterwards, both Dhyan and Gulab Singh connived to have Sher Singh, and his son, Partab, murdered in April 1843. Dhyan, however, fell victim to the same plot and was also murdered. In a wave of sympathy, Hira Singh, Dhyan's son, was made wazir. This was much against the wishes of their youngest brother, Suchet Singh, who had wanted the post for himself. Another of Ranjit Singh's wives, Rani Jindan, became regent and her young son, Dulip Singh, reputed to be yet another son of Ranjit Singh, was instated as maharaja.

Gulab Singh lost no time in turning the situation to his advantage by attempting a reconciliation between the opposing factions. In gratitude for his support, Hira enhanced Gulab's position still further: the affairs of Kashmir province were 'to be managed by Raja Golab Singh alone and no orders could be given about them in Lahore.' Although Gulab Singh did not actually acquire possession of Kashmir at that time, Hira's announcement was 'at least a partial renunciation of Lahore's unquestionable supremacy over Kashmir and an acknowledgement that the northern province now lay in Jammu's sphere of influence,' writes B. S. Singh.[49] Yet again the status quo did not last long. The anti-Dogra faction of Sikhs murdered Suchet Singh in 1843. With the connivance of Rani Jindan, Hira Singh was also murdered in 1844. Both Lal

Singh, the Rani's lover, and Jowahir Singh, her brother, competed to become wazir, but neither had the confidence of the Khalsa. Gulab Singh retired to Jammu. At this juncture, relations with the British, which had been strained since the death of Ranjit Singh, reached breaking-point.

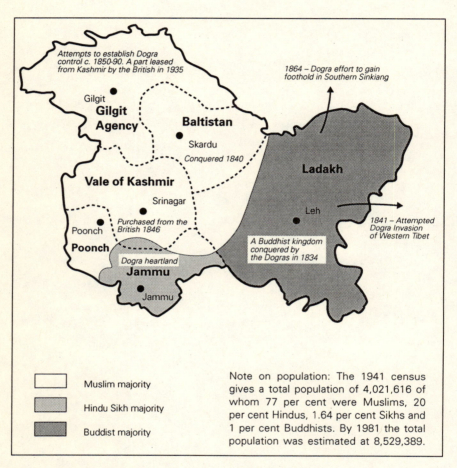

Attempts to establish Dogra
control c. 1850-90. A part leased
from Kashmir by the British in 1935

1864 – Dogra effort to gain
foothold in Southern Sinkiang

Gilgit •

**Gilgit
Agency**

Baltistan

Skardu •

Conquered 1840

Ladakh

Vale of Kashmir

Srinagar •

Leh •

Poonch •

*Purchased from the
British 1846*

1841 – Attempted
Dogra Invasion
of Western Tibet

Poonch

A Buddhist kingdom
conquered by
the Dogras in 1834

Dogra heartland

Jammu

Jammu •

☐ Muslim majority

▨ Hindu Sikh majority

▓ Buddist majority

Note on population: The 1941 census
gives a total population of 4,021,616 of
whom 77 per cent were Muslims, 20
per cent Hindus, 1.64 per cent Sikhs and
1 per cent Buddhists. By 1981 the total
population was estimated at 8,529,389.

3. The Creation of the State of Jammu and Kashmir with Communal Groupings
(Source: Alastair Lamb, *Crisis in Kashmir*, London 1966)

CHAPTER 5

Kashmir For Sale 1846

Each hill, each garden, field, Each farmer too they sold.
A nation for a price, That makes my blood ice-cold. Muhammad Iqbal[1]

As relations deteriorated between the British and the Sikhs prior to the outbreak of war in 1845, Gulab Singh played an important role, which ultimately helped to further his own territorial ambitions, enabling him to become a maharaja in his own right. But his role before and during the first Anglo–Sikh war, has aroused considerable controversy. He was in direct contact with the British yet he assumed the role of wazir in the Sikh state. Was he therefore a traitor to the Sikhs to whom he owed allegiance or did he play some useful role in mediating between the Sikhs and the British, which helped to defuse a yet more bloody conflict? In addition, why at the end of the war, when the British obtained Kashmir from the Sikhs, did they then agree to sell to it Gulab Singh? Amongst commentators at the time, the treaty of Amritsar was regarded as 'a piece of state expediency, a temporising with a great difficulty.'[2] The transaction was to have repercussions which have persisted to this day.

The treasure of the mountain

In April 1844, Lord Ellenborough, the governor-general, was informed by George Clerk's successor as political agent in Lahore, Colonel Richmond, that Gulab Singh would probably align himself with the British in a future conflict with the Sikhs. In return he would want to be recognised as the independent sovereign of Peshawar and Kashmir as well as the hill states between the Indus and the Sutlej. Ellenborough, however, was opposed to making any promise of independence to Gulab Singh. His successor as governor-general, Sir Henry Hardinge, a veteran of the Peninsular War, arrived in India in July 1844. He at once took note of the special status, which Gulab Singh held at the Lahore Court.

Hardinge was, however, also unsure of how to deal with the Dogra ruler, whose position seemed less secure now than it had been throughout his thirty year relationship with the Sikh leadership. Rani Jindan's dislike of Gulab Singh was exacerbated by the disastrous state of the Sikh finances. With barely enough money in the treasury to manage the government, the

49

Sikhs hoped to improve their position by sending an army against Gulab Singh in Jammu in order to oblige him to surrender control of the hill territories on which, in recent years, he had paid no revenue and to seize his treasury, which was rumoured to contain crores of rupees. In February 1845 a substantial army of about 35,000 men set off for Jammu.

Gulab was able to extricate himself from their initial death threats by offering bribes and convincing the soldiers of his loyalty to the Sikhs. 'He and his family were, as they ever had been, the creatures and slaves of the Khalsa, and nothing should induce him to raise his hand against them,' wrote Major Smyth in his contemporary history.[3] Mesmerised by his oratory, the soldiers were divided over whether to kill him or make him wazir in place of Jowahir Singh, Rani Jindan's brother, who had finally succeeded in assuming the premiership. Before making any decision, they took Gulab to Lahore, where he was kept under protective custody, until a settlement was negotiated. Gulab agreed to return the lands of his brother, Suchet, and nephew, Hira, which he had appropriated on their death. He also agreed to pay the State 68 lakhs. He finally returned to Jammu after an absence of four months without a firm obligation that he would honour his commitments.

The murder of the last main descendant of Ranjit Singh, Peshora Singh, in September 1845 was yet another catalyst in the intrigue and rivalry which was tearing the Sikh kingdom apart. Jowahir Singh was held responsible for the murder and was himself killed by the Khalsa, with the result that Lal Singh took over as wazir. Meanwhile, Gulab Singh was secretly offering his services to the British, promising to help them occupy the Punjab if only he would be confirmed in his possessions. At this stage, however, Hardinge did not wish to increase the territory of the East India Company to include the Punjab and Gulab Singh's overtures of friendship went unheeded. Although the British did not respond to Gulab Singh's initiatives, they did not forget them; nor did they disclose his potentially treacherous intentions to the Sikhs. As the Sikh state crumbled, ruled as Hardinge said by 'a drunken prostitute, her counsellors, her paramours',[4] his attitude towards Gulab Singh changed.

The Sikh Darbar was also mistrustful of the by now uncontrollable actions of the soldiers who had little confidence either in Rani Jindan or Lal Singh. They had reluctantly acknowledged Tej Singh as their commander-in-chief. Lal Singh's strategy was to encourage the militancy, which, he hoped, would work to the Darbar's advantage: if the Sikhs crossed the Sutlej and engaged the British in battle and were defeated, their power would be curbed. If they were victorious then their power would be increased, and consequently the reputation of the Sikh Darbar. 'Their desire was to be upheld as the ministers of a dependent kingdom by grateful conquerors,' writes J. D. Cunningham, who was in the Punjab at this time. They therefore 'assured the local British authorities of their secret and efficient good will.'[5] Gulab Singh remained in Jammu strengthening his army. Yet again his overtures to the British met with a negative response.

On 11 December 1845, in what became known as the First Anglo–Sikh war, the Sikh army, unaware that its leaders were in communication with the British, moved across the river Sutlej.[6] The governor-general, Hardinge, who had arrived personally in the Punjab in November 1845, joined the battlefield as second-in-command of the British army under Sir Hugh Gough, the commander-in-chief. Two encounters – at Mudki on 18 December and Firuzshar on 21/22 December – left the Sikhs defeated although not conclusively. As *The Times* (London) noted: 'The Sikh army has been repulsed but not destroyed, and although we have won a great battle, we have only begun the war.'[7] Had the British wished to annex the Punjab at this juncture, their less than decisive victory put an end to this dream.

For Gulab Singh the outcome was favourable. As a vassal of the Sikhs, a total Sikh collapse at the hands of the British would have meant that he could lose all his possessions and his repeated overtures to the British must be seen in this context. In January 1846, during the stalemate which followed, he once again contacted the British offering help. This time his message was delivered by Bansidhar Ghose, who claimed to have been Gulab Singh's physician for seven years. The recipient was Lieutenant Edward Lake, assistant agent to the governor-general at Ludhiana. According to Lake's report dated 15 January to his superior, Captain Mills, he was handed two pieces of paper, one was the signature of Gulab Singh, the other his message in Persian. In return for his assistance Gulab Singh requested to be confirmed in the jagirs which were held by him and his family members. He also wanted to be left in possession of his territory with a tribute of four annas in every rupee which he derived from it. In the absence of precise instructions Lake had responded to Gulab Singh:

> He who wishes to climb the summit of a lofty mountain must start at day break. Should he delay, night may close o'er him, 'ere he has gained the desire of his heart. The Treasure which is buried in the depths of the mountain will become the prize of that man who is the first to reach the summit.

When he reported his action to Mills, Lieutenant Lake explained why he had responded in what he believed were ambiguous terms: 'I feel that while I may be promoting the interests of the British government, I have in no way compromised them.' But Mills was told by Frederick Currie, secretary to the government of India, to reprimand Lake for his response to Gulab Singh, which 'is susceptible to a very distinct meaning, far different from the vague answer which it was his intention to convey.' Lake was, however, directed to refer the emissary to Currie or Major Henry Lawrence 'by either of whom a fitting answer to his communications will be given.'[8]

On 25 January 1845, after slow progress, Gulab Singh reached Lahore with a force of 12,000 men. His arrival increased the expectations of the Sikh army, but his motives were out of self interest. 'He had come to the conclusion that only by assuming control of the Lahore government,' writes

B. S. Singh, 'could he pursue the policies which would persuade the British
to be more receptive to him and his aspirations.' Unaware that Gulab Singh
was offering his services to the British, the Sikhs were still prevailing upon
him, as their most powerful feudatory, to assist them and accept the position
of wazir in place of Lal Singh at the court of Lahore. They also expected
to him to come to the river Sutlej and declared, 'when he did, they would
fight again.'[9] A desultory action at Aliwal on 28 January further increased
their desire to be led by the Jammu Raja.

Through their intelligence reports the British kept a careful watch on
Gulab Singh's relations with the Khalsa. In ridicule of Rani Jindan he told
the Sikh soldiers that he had:

> Neither necklaces nor bracelets that he should order them to fight – that when
> they crossed the River and caused the war – he (the Rajah) was ignorant by what
> stretch of wisdom they have gained such boldness, considering that the English
> Company were sovereign down to the furthest boundary of Sindh – where now
> was that boldness gone?

Whereupon the panches answered that they had seen the English defeated
by the Afghans. They also complained that the East India Company had the
power of 'showering down cannon shot like drops of rain – if the English
armies would leave off the use of their cannon and come out and fight with
the sword and musket, it would then be seen who were the best men.' The
British were also well aware of the pressure Gulab Singh was under from the
Khalsa to assume the wazarat. Despite such overtures, the intelligence report
signed by Henry Lawrence continued: 'The Rajah answered them in a wise
manner and made no certain promises.'[10]

Rani Jindan regarded Gulab Singh's presence in Lahore with dismay since
she believed that he was plotting to oust her young son, Dulip, from the
throne. She had already instigated several plots to murder Gulab, but she was
also being threatened by the panches who were demanding that Gulab Singh
should be made wazir otherwise they would murder her, Dulip and her
officials. At the end of January she hastily convened the Darbar and appointed
Gulab Singh as wazir. Gulab lost no time in making a scathing attack on Lal
Singh, accusing him of embezzlement, which further enraged the panches
against Rani Jindan's lover.

On the eve of his appointment as wazir Gulab Singh immediately contacted the British. Hardinge confided to his wife: 'I have a communication
from Raja Golab Singh which may lead to overtures for an arrangement; he
is to be made minister and says he is ready to do what we like to order. I
am obliged to be very cold and haughty; but propose to allow him to come
to propose terms and make a beginning.'[11] Three days later, after Gulab
Singh became wazir, Hardinge drew up a blueprint of possible territorial
arrangements once the war was over, which included an independent kingdom
under Gulab Singh.

In the days to come, Gulab Singh continued to play upon the Sikhs' extraordinary belief in his ability to lead them to victory; at first he encouraged them, by outlining a plan for guerrilla war against the British, but then he failed to put it into action. He also demoralised the troops by interrupting their food supplies. Colonel Gardner, who later commanded the Dogra army, notes: 'Gulab Singh cajoled the whole of the leading panches of the Sikh army, affecting to see every visitor from the battle at any moment, whether he was bathing or eating, as if his whole heart was with the Sikhs'.[12] But, despite his protestations of support, he never led his own troops into battle and procrastinated on the sidelines. 'He came from Jummoo as ready to throw himself into the scale of the Lahore state as to our own. He was ready and willing to espouse the strongest cause.'[13]

On 10 February 1846, the Sikhs fought the British at the battle of Sobraon, a small village on the banks of the Sutlej. 'While the brave Khalsa soldiery were busy making ready for one more stand on the Sutlej,' writes Lionel Trotter, 'Gulab Singh busied himself in plotting with the British government.'[14] Without any support from the ruler of Jammu, Sikh defeat at the hands of the British was inevitable. Neither Lal Singh nor Tej Singh made any significant contribution towards the battle. Tej Singh had once more assured the British that he too did not wish to fight and would be willing to come to terms, but the troops would not obey him. 'The battle was over by 11 in the morning,' reported Sir Hugh Gough. 'I caused our engineers to burn and so sink a part of the bridge of the Khalsa army across which they had boastfully come once more to defy us, and so threaten India with ruin and devastation.'[15] The Sikh losses numbered between 8,000 and 12,000 men, killed or wounded, and for days afterwards the ground was littered with their bodies.[16]

When representatives from both sides met at Kasur, where the two armies had halted, about thirty miles from Lahore, the British treated Gulab Singh as a welcome ambassador. Hardinge recognised 'the wisdom, prudence and good feeling evinced by him in having kept himself separate from these unjustifiable hostilities of the Sikhs.'[17] But the Sikhs bitterly resented Gulab Singh's duplicity. Rani Jindan dismissed him at once as wazir, reinstating Lal Singh in his place. She also made a bold suggestion to the British, which would instantly reduce Gulab Singh's power. Instead of the war indemnity for which the Sikhs were to be liable, she offered to hand over to the British the lands of Jammu and Kashmir. Gulab Singh was still only a feudatory of the Sikh empire and this plan was designed to pay off the Sikh war debt as well as stripping Gulab Singh of all the lands he had so painstakingly acquired in the name of the Sikh kingdom.

The vendor of human flesh

Uppermost in Sir Henry Hardinge's mind after the first Anglo–Sikh war was the need to curb the military power of the Sikhs and reward Gulab Singh

for his assistance. Immediately after the war, Hardinge outlined his intentions
to Queen Victoria:

> It was 'desirable to weaken the Sikh state, which has proved itself too strong,
> and to show all Asia that although the British government has not deemed it
> expedient to annex this immense country of the Punjab, making the Indus the
> British boundary, it has punished the treachery and violence of the Sikh nation.'

In order to achieve this objective he suggested adding 'Cashmere to the
possessions of Golab Singh and thus make it independent of the Sikhs of
the plains.'[18] He later confirmed how, after Gulab Singh had been made
wazir, he was in direct contact with the British: 'Raja Golab Singh, on being
installed as Minister [of the Sikh Darbar] put himself in communication
with us, proffering every assistance in his power for the furtherance of any
ends in regard to the State of Lahore which we might have in view.'[19] It was
therefore far more expedient for the British to allow Gulab Singh to become
an independent maharaja of Jammu and Kashmir, lands in whose management he had been directly involved for twenty-five years, rather than attempt
to take over the area themselves. Hardinge's plan was doubly attractive because
Gulab Singh was willing to pay for it.

As the chief architect of the Treaty of Amritsar and the decision to sell
Kashmir to Gulab Singh, Henry Hardinge came under strong criticism for
his role. Sir Charles Napier, who subsequently took over from Gough as
commander-in-chief, wanted to continue the war against the Sikhs and annex
the Punjab. He was scathing about the decision: 'What a king to install!
Rising from the lowest foulest sediment of debauchery to float on the highest
surge of blood, he lifted his besmeared front, and England adorned it with
a crown!'[20] Herbert Edwardes, who had recently arrived in the Punjab as
ADC to Gough, had no illusions about Gulab Singh's methods in achieving
his objective: 'He has the cunning of the vulture. He sat apart in the clear
atmosphere of passionless distance, and with sleepless eye beheld the lion
and the tiger contending for the deer, And when the combatants were dead,
he spread his wings, sailed calmly down, and feasted where they fought.'[21]

Muhammad Saraf calls Hardinge 'the man responsible for the unprecedented sale of such a vast number of people with at least a three thousand
years old history and one who stands universally condemned as a vendor of
human flesh.'[22] Hardinge's motives were also ambiguous. On the one hand
the sale was necessary because the Sikh treasury was empty; on the other, it
was important to reward Gulab Singh for his loyalty to the British and what
might therefore be termed treachery to his former overlords, the Sikhs.

British policy, however, was directed by expediency. Hardinge was not
beyond admitting that Gulab Singh was 'the greatest rascal in Asia'. But
Gulab Singh's neutrality had tipped the balance of war in favour of the
British, and, as he explained to his wife in a letter dated 2 March 1846, it was
necessary

... to improve his condition because he did not participate in the war against us and his territories touching ours, we can protect them without inconvenience and give him a slice of the Sikh Territory which balances his strength in some degree against theirs; and as he is geographically our ally, I must forget he is a rascal and treat him better than he deserves.[23]

As he subsequently outlined to the Secret Committee on 14 March, two days before signing the Treaty of Amritsar, in his opinion, it was simply not possible for Britain to keep Kashmir:

It is not my intention to take possession of the whole of this country. Its occupation by us would be, on many accounts, disadvantageous. It would bring us into collision with many powerful chiefs, for whose coercion a large military establishment at a great distance from our provinces and military resources would be necessary. It would more than double the extent of our present frontier in countries assailable at every point and most difficult to defend without any corresponding advantages for such large additions of territory.[24]

Writing his father's biography in the late nineteenth century, Viscount Hardinge acknowledged the unpopularity of Gulab Singh as a future ruler of Kashmir but defended his father's actions on purely practical grounds. There was a deficit in the Indian treasury, the hot season was setting in; four military actions had 'palpably weakened the strength of our European regiments.' Gulab Singh's character was not without reproach. 'But where was there a native chief or minister to be found without similar blots on his escutcheon?'[25]

A slave bought by gold

The terms of the settlement embodied in the Treaty of Peace, ratified at Lahore on 9 March 1846, between the young Sikh Maharaja Dulip Singh and the British, required the Sikhs to cede:

... to the Honourable Company in perpetual sovereignty, as equivalent for one crore of rupees, all forts, territories, rights and interests in the hill countries which are situated between the rivers Beas and Indus, including the provinces of Kashmir and Hazara. (Article IV).

In recognition of the 'services rendered' by Raja Gulab Singh to the Lahore state, or as Lionel Trotter says 'in plainer English, as a reward for his secret desertion of a failing cause,'[26] the Sikhs were also obliged:

to recognise the independent sovereignty of Raja Golab Sing in such territories and districts in the hills as may be made over to the said Raja Golab Sing by separate agreement between himself and the British government ... and the British government in consideration of the good conduct of Raja Golab Sing also agrees to recognise his independence in such territories and to admit him to the privilege of a separate Treaty with the British government. (Article XII)

The treaty gave further protection to Gulab Singh, stating that:

> In the event of any dispute or difference arising between the Lahore State and Raja Golab Sing, the same shall be referred to the arbitration of the British government and by its decision the Maharaja [Dulip Singh] engages to abide. (Article XIII)[27]

A week later, on 16 March, the British signed the Treaty of Amritsar with Gulab Singh. Article I stated that:

> The British Government transfers and makes over for ever in independent possession to Maharaja Gulab Singh and the heirs male of his body all the hilly or mountainous country with its dependencies situated to the eastward of the River Indus and the westward of the River Ravi, including Chamba and excluding Lahul, being part of the territories ceded to the British Government by the Lahore State according to the provision of the Article IV of the Treaty of Lahore, dated 9 March 1846.'

Gulab Singh was to pay the exact sum in lieu of which the British had taken possession of Kashmir one week earlier: one crore of rupees towards the indemnity. Twenty-five lakhs were later waived in consideration of the British being allowed to retain the area of Kulu and Mandi across the river Beas. Article IX stated that the British government would 'give its aid' to the maharaja in protecting his territories from external enemies. Article X stipulated that the maharaja would 'acknowledge the supremacy of the British Government.' In token of such supremacy, he was to present annually one horse, twelve perfect shawl goats and three pairs of Kashmiri shawls. In addition, by the terms of Article IV, the limits of his territories 'shall not be at any time changed without the concurrence of the British government.'[28]

Rani Jindan's plan to deprive Gulab Singh of the lands he held in fief from the Sikhs had backfired. She wrote angry letters to Hardinge warning that if Kashmir were given to Gulab Singh, she would appeal directly to Queen Victoria. Her protests, however, were in vain. As contemporary sources note, her 'spiteful suggestion was apparently at the same time acceded to and prostrated.'[29] Gulab Singh was able to sever his allegiance from the Sikhs and, for the first time after nearly forty years, attain the status as a maharaja in his own right. It was an extraordinary feat for a man who, at the age of sixteen, had left his grandfather's home to seek his fortune in the Sikh kingdom. Instead of being a feudatory of the Sikhs, he was now a suitable counterpoise against them. Moreover, Hardinge also believed that both Sikhs and Dogra Rajputs would have a common interest in resisting the rise of any Muslim power, which was a concern to the British after their experiences in Afghanistan.[30]

Yet again after the signature of the treaty, Hardinge, who had been given a peerage for the role he had played in the Sikh war, pointed to the impracticalities of the British retention of Kashmir when British dominion still ended at the river Sutlej: 'The distance between Kashmir and the Sutlej is 300 miles of very difficult mountainous country, quite impracticable for six months. To keep a British force 300 miles from any possibility of support would have been an undertaking that merited a straitwaistcoat and not a peerage.'[31]

It was not until three years later, after the Sikhs had once more attacked British forces, that the British annexed the Punjab, bringing the boundary of their dominions closer to the valley of Kashmir. Prior to that it was not considered logical for the British to annex Kashmir. Thus the cession of Kashmir to the British was only ever an interim measure on the understanding that, upon suitable terms, it would go to Gulab Singh. The new maharaja was delighted to be acknowledged in his retention of Kashmir. As Vigne had noted during his travels, he had been working towards this objective even during the lifetime of Ranjit Singh. In a note of gushing thanks, which as M. J. Akbar points out, had unfortunate overtones, Gulab Singh described himself as *zar kharid* (a slave bought by gold). 'The phrase would haunt Kashmiri sentiment for many generations after Gulab Singh was dead and gone.'[32]

Hardinge also defended Gulab Singh against a charge of treason towards the Lahore state and referred to their earlier contacts before the war began. 'He had done good service to us, which we had recognised before he was a Sikh Commissioner. After the war commenced, were we to abandon our policy and to treat the only man who had not lifted up his arm against us with indifference?'[33] Gulab Singh's biographer, K. M. Panikkar argues against the transaction being a sale, on the grounds that Kashmir had been promised to Gulab Singh before the Treaty of Lahore. 'The view that Kashmir was sold for a paltry sum by a Government whose main interest was to fill its coffers is a travesty of facts and a misreading of history.'[34] But neither Panikkar nor any other apologist for Gulab Singh could deny that money was exchanged in return for land and people and that, 150 years later, the transaction still causes deep resentment. 'Each one of us was purchased by the Dogra ruler for 3 rupees,' said Mian Abdul Qayum, president of Srinagar's Bar Association in 1994.[35]

The British, who needed to replenish their coffers after the war, had no scruples about accepting the money as soon as it was made available. 'I have called upon Maharaja Gulab Singh to lose no time in sending the balance of his first instalment;' Henry Lawrence wrote to Hardinge, at the end of March 1846. 'and have told his Vakil [lawyer] to say that the payment of the whole seventy-five lakhs at once will be very acceptable. As soon as the remittance reaches and has been counted at Jullundhur, it should be pushed on to Delhi with the least possible delay.'[36] On 12 May 1846, Hardinge reported that the maharaja had paid the first instalment of 50 lakhs. By the end of July 1848 he had paid most of the balance. The remainder, totalling less than 4 lakhs, was paid by March 1850.[37]

King of the hills

The legal title to Kashmir may have been transferred to Gulab Singh, but not the land. Initially, the maharaja appeared to be in no hurry to take physical possession of his new acquisition. When finally in August he chose to do so, he did not anticipate any opposition, and sent a small force commanded by Lakhpat Rai, who had been in his service since the conquest of the hill state of Kishtwar in 1821. Lakhpat installed himself in the Hari Parbat fort overlooking Srinagar; but to his surprise, Sheikh Imam, the governor, refused to relinquish his authority. In the armed clash which followed, Lakhpat Rai was killed. After this Gulab Singh decided to go to Kashmir in person at the head of a Dogra force. He was accompanied by two British officials, Captain Broome and Lieutenant John Nicholson, who had been assigned to the maharaja to train the Jammu army.

Yet again the Dogras were attacked. Broome and Nicholson fled and Gulab Singh retreated to Jammu. Encouraged by his success, Sheikh Imam managed to attract some of the other hill tribes to join him. Finally, Hardinge ordered British troops to assist. Eight regiments of native infantry and twelve field guns were dispatched under Henry Lawrence, now a colonel, and Lieutenant William Hodson. The Sikhs were also obliged to send a contingent of 1700 'of those very Sikhs who had fought against us,' writes Hardinge's son.[38] This time Sheikh Imam, who had only a force of 8–9,000 men, surrendered personally to Lawrence, stating that Lal Singh had instructed him not to hand over the province to Gulab Singh. In November 1846 Gulab Singh entered Kashmir. Lawrence stayed for a brief period and noted that during this time he had not heard 'a whisper against the Maharaja or his government.'[39]

Sir Charles Napier remained one of the new maharaja's fiercest critics. He described the operation to install Gulab Singh in Kashmir as 'cramming down the throats of the Cashmerian people a hated and hateful villain'.[40] Gulab Singh, however, retained the support of the governor-general, Henry Hardinge and Henry Lawrence, who were the two most influential men in India at the time. His proven ability to survive also made him a useful ally: 'Had it been otherwise,' wrote Dr Arthur Neve who came to Kashmir in 1882, 'had the Rajah been a petty chief of the outer hills, such as his brother ... it is highly unlikely that the government of India, would have forced the Sikh governor of Kashmir, Sheikh Imam-ud Din, who held the country for the Sikh Raj, to make over the country to him.'[41] By this time, however, the British were bound to assist Gulab Singh because they had already received over half the money in payment.

By the terms of the Treaty of Amritsar, Gulab Singh had gained possession of the land to the west of the Indus including Hazara. But when he encountered armed resistance to the extension of his rule, he suggested exchanging Hazara for some Sikh territory around Jammu. Each transaction was evaluated with due regard to what might be given in exchange. On 3

March 1847 Henry Lawrence wrote to James Abbot, the political officer at Hazara, who was demarcating the western boundary of the new state:

> Gulab Singh can only have lands opposite Jummoo or elsewhere, in such quantities beyond his rights as he can give up equivalents for in other places. He (Gulab Singh) has lately written to me that you are taking from him villages allowed to be his at Kangra; I suppose it is for an equivalent. I have replied that Govt. orders have been issued and that you are on the spot to carry them out in the spirit of the Treaty.'[42]

The British were also anxious not to favour Gulab Singh unduly. In another letter to Abbott, Lawrence wrote: 'The Maharaja is king of the hills and of their dependencies and of no more or no less. I am anxious and have been that he should have a road below and a strip of territory in front of Jummoo, but it is too much to expect that we are to plunder Lahore for his satisfaction.'[43] Hazara eventually reverted to the Sikhs and subsequently to the British; in return Gulab Singh obtained the districts of Suchetgarh, parts of the district of Gurdaspur and a section of the territory of Kangra. The Jhelum river became the western boundary of the state of Kashmir between Jhelum and Muzaffarabad. Abbott completed the boundary demarcation by December 1847. Lahul and Spiti bordered the state of Jammu and Kashmir to the south. The border of northern Ladakh along the Kunlun mountains proved more complicated and was never fully defined.

The sale in retrospect

'Poor Kashmir!' wrote Lieutenant Colonel Torrens in 1861. 'When, after so many vicissitudes of slavery to a foreign yoke, the hand of a powerful, just, and merciful Government acquired the territory by force of arms in a fair fight, and it seemed that at last its condition was about to be ameliorated, its old ill-luck stuck by it still!' As with many Englishmen of his time Torrens, who spent his three month leave in Kashmir, adopted the attitude that the people would have been better off under a 'just' British rule, rather than that of a 'native Prince'. Equally he recognised that it would have been beneficial to British interests to have retained such an important buffer on the northern frontier of the British empire: 'No Englishman can leave Kashmir without a sigh of regret that a province so full of promise should ever have been allowed to slip through our fingers.'[44] His views were echoed in the next century by Sir Francis Younghusband, who had to deal with the practical effects of the Dogra rule over the state of Jammu and Kashmir at a time when the British were nervously watching for a potential Russian advance towards the northern frontier of the sub-continent. 'Surprise has often been expressed that when this lovely land had actually been ceded us, after a hard and strenuous campaign, we should have parted with it, for the paltry sum of three-quarters of a million sterling.'[45]

In his contemporary history, J. D. Cunningham, who had served under both Napier and Hardinge, chose to recall that the reason why the Sikhs were unable to pay their war indemnity was because Gulab Singh had not only made himself rich at their expense, but also because he had not paid the fine, which had been imposed on him in 1845.

> The transaction seems scarcely worthy of the British name and greatness, and the objections become stronger when it is considered that Gulab Singh had agreed to pay sixty-eight lakhs of rupees as a fine to his paramount before the war broke out, and that the custom of the East as well as the West requires the feudatory to aid his lord in foreign war and domestic strife. Gulab Singh ought thus to have paid the deficient million of money as a Lahore subject, instead of being put in possession of Lahore provinces as an independent prince.

Cunningham also noted how Tej Singh had offered another twenty five lakhs for 'a princely crown and another dismembered province'. But he was reprimanded for 'his presumptuous misinterpretation of English principles of action; the arrangement with Gulab Singh was the only one of the kind which took place.'[46] The two surviving sons of Dhyan Singh, Jawahir Singh and Moti Singh who were in possession of Poonch, requested the British to give them a share of the state and wealth on the grounds that Gulab Singh owed his rise to their father. Although the British refused, they were confirmed as rajas in their own right under the jurisdiction of the Kashmir Darbar.

British commentators also expressed concern for the well-being of the Kashmiris under a man famed for his cruelty. 'Towards the people of Cashmeer we have committed a wanton outrage, a gross injustice, and an act of tyrannical oppression,' wrote Robert Thorp in 1870 'which violates every human and honourable sentiment which is opposed to the whole spirit of modern civilisation, and is in direct opposition to every tenet of religion we profess.'[47] Lieutenant Thorp, whose mother was a Kashmiri Muslim from Kishtwar had travelled extensively in the villages reporting on the poor condition of the people. He pointed to several considerations which gave the sale 'a peculiarly odious aspect, and render it a dark stain upon the history of British rule in India.' No provision was made for the 'just and humane' government of the people. 'For purposes entirely selfish, we deliberately sold millions of human beings into the absolute power of one of the meanest, most avaricious, cruel and unprincipled of men that ever sat upon a throne.' He went on to compare the situation in Afghanistan where the British had finally declared in favour of Dost Mohammed, after their disastrous attempt to install Shah Shuja as King of Afghanistan in 1839, because they realised they could not force an unpopular ruler 'upon a reluctant people'. In the case of Kashmir, the British had not only forced a ruler on the people 'but a crowd of rapacious and unprincipled ministers, courtiers, hangers-on of every grade who followed in the fortunes of Gulab Singh.'[48] Furthermore, there was no consultation with the people of Kashmir. Younghusband warned that 'needless to add, a weighty responsibility lies also upon the British government that it should guide their destinies aright.'[49]

Britain was, however, becoming a paramount power in the sub-continent and all relationships were based on what was perceived to be in the best interests of the new imperialists. Some commentators, like Teng, Kaul and Bhatt, believe that the transfer of the territories to Gulab Singh was only a temporary phase in Britain's grand design to subjugate the Dogras after the Sikhs had been vanquished.[50] As early as 1843, Lord Ellenborough had written to the Duke of Wellington: 'I look to the protection of our Government being ultimately extended to the Sikhs of the plains and the Rajputs of the

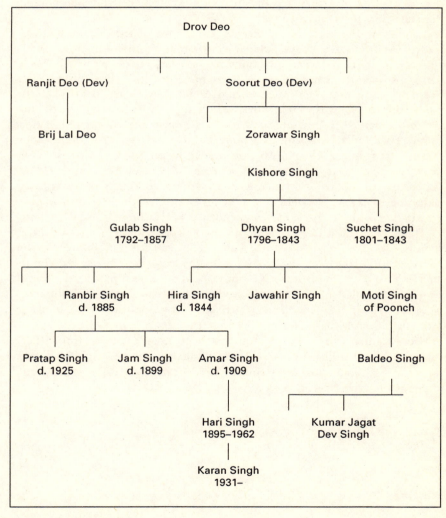

The Dogra Dynasty

hills and the Mussulmans of Mooltan ... I do not look to this state of things as likely to occur next year, but as being ultimately inevitable.'[51]

The Treaty of Amritsar made sure to bind the maharaja to a subordinate position. Disputes were to be submitted to British arbitration and the territories of the state were not to be altered without their agreement. The Dogras were not to employ any British, American or European subjects without the permission of the British government. But, although at the end of the nineteenth century Britain came close to controlling the internal affairs of what came to be known as the princely state of Jammu and Kashmir, they never took the final step of subjugating the Dogras and incorporating the state into the British Empire.

Prem Nath Bazaz remonstrated that, at the time of the sale, no Kashmiri leader was consulted. 'It was altogether a sordid, shameful affair devoid of all sense of fairness, justice and equity ... the treaty consisting of ten articles makes no mention whatsoever of the rights, interests or the future of the people'.[52] A hundred years later, Sheikh Abdullah made an issue out of the sale during the Quit Kashmir movement in 1946. 'We challenge the political and moral status of this sale deed, this instrument of subjugation, handed by the East India Company to a bunch of Dogras,' he wrote in an angry telegram sent to the Cabinet Mission headed by Sir Stafford Cripps. 'A sale deed does not have the status of a treaty.' Abdullah even entreated the people to contribute one rupee each towards a collection of seventy-five lakh rupees 'so that we could return the investment of the present Maharaja's grandfather and buy back the independence of Kashmir.'[53]

The sale of the valley of Kashmir and its incorporation into a princely state is also considered to have had an adverse effect on its future development. In 1925, the *Muslim Outlook* newspaper commented that but for the 'ineffable folly' of the British: 'Kashmir would have been part of the Punjab and the Education Minister would have been able to apply to Kashmir the vigorous regenerative measures which are being applied to the Punjab.'[54] More significantly, had Kashmir been annexed by Britain and become part of British India when the sub-continent became independent from British rule in 1947, according to the principle of the partition it could have been divided along communal lines and the predominantly Muslim valley would undoubtedly have been allocated to Pakistan.

CHAPTER 6

Dogras in Perpetuity

And now he is a king, and has a wide field wherein to reap. Every living man is to him a blade of golden corn, which he will never leave till he has gathered, and threshed and winnowed and garnered. Herbert Edwardes, 1846[1]

By the terms of the Treaty of Amritsar, Gulab Singh had succeeded in severing his feudatory allegiance to the Sikhs to become an independent ruler of lands including not only his native Jammu but the Himalayan kingdom of Kashmir. He also retained his sovereignty in Baltistan and Ladakh. Both his brothers, Dhyan and Suchet, had died pursuing their territorial ambitions. Gulab Singh alone had survived and, at the age of 54, he was at the pinnacle of his power.

Although the valley of Kashmir had been added to the Dogra possessions, unlike earlier rulers who settled there permanently, the Kashmiris always felt that the Dogras considered Jammu as their home and the valley as a conquered territory. 'They established a sort of Dogra imperialism in the State in which the Dogras were elevated to the position of the masters and all non-Dogra communities and classes were given the humble places of inferiors,' wrote Prem Nath Bazaz in the 1950s. The feeling of discrimination under the Dogras, which both the Muslims and Hindus experienced, was to manifest itself in the next century in a series of protests against the maharaja's descendants. But, says Bazaz, the Dogras were themselves vassals of British 'super-imperialists'; and this had some advantages for the people of the valley. 'By coming under the British suzerainty, the valley began to have the impact of Western ideas and modern civilisation which finally awakened the people to demand their birth-right of independence and freedom.'[2]

A fairly wise landlord

As one of the leaders of the movement against the Dogras in the 1930s, Prem Nath Bazaz has little good to say about the founder of the Dogra dynasty: 'The methods he applied were of a savage nature and he was very rapacious and greedy.' Contemporaries were also critical of his conduct. 'Gulab Singh went beyond his predecessors in the gentle acts of undue taxation and extortion,' wrote Lieutenant Colonel Torrens after his visit in 1861: 'They had taxed heavily it is true, but he sucked the very life blood of the people. They had laid violent hands on a large proportion of the fruits of the earth, the profits of the loom and the work of men's hands, but he skinned the very flints to fill his coffers.'[3]

There was a tax on grave-diggers, gambling houses and tobacco. *Begar* - forced labour for transport purposes - remained in force. The marriage tax was increased although eventually the British prevailed upon Gulab Singh to dispense with this. Corruption was still prevalent and the government retained its monopoly of grain. Gulab Singh showed no signs of introducing economic reform and retained the Sikh system of taxation, whereby the government took between two-thirds to three-quarters of the gross produce of the land. Any attempt at opposition was firmly crushed.

One of the earliest concerns of the British was to pressurise Gulab Singh to dispense with suttee, female infanticide and the killing of illegitimate children. A week after the maharaja's entry into Kashmir in November 1846, Lawrence discussed the issue with him: 'The Maharaja expressed his entire willingness to put down both infanticide and suttee; the first crime he agreed to make penal by proclamation; but he remarked he was not yet strong enough to insist upon the abolition of suttee, though he would do all in his power to prevent the rite by giving maintenance to widows.'[4] Although Gulab Singh was not in a position to carry out many of his promises, he did open orphanages.[5] He continued to allow universal freedom of worship and, although he did not approve of Hindu-Muslim marriages, he did not prevent them.

Domestically, there was not a great deal the British could do to improve the lot of the Kashmiris. Despite their position as 'super-imperialists' and the constraints placed on Gulab Singh by the Treaty of Amritsar, they had no mandate to interfere in his conduct of the state. The British were, however, aware of sensitive issues arising from the rule of a Hindu over a majority Muslim population. Punishments for cow-killing had been meted out since the Sikhs took over; and the British realised that it was an issue which could not immediately be resolved. 'Let Gulab Singh take his own measures about cow-killing except as to death or maiming,' instructed Lawrence,' but don't interfere one way or the other actively. Government expects the prejudices to wear out; though this I doubt; but though we must not authorize or sanction it, we need not do more than is necessary.'[6] Favoured though Gulab Singh might have been, Lawrence was also concerned that the new maharaja's interests should not be paramount and that the interests of the Sikhs at Lahore had also to be considered: 'We may fairly do our best to meet the Jummoo views as long as it is not to the injury of Lahore, or at variance with the spirit of the Treaty ... While we must try to be patient and to hear and be all that is to be heard or seen, we must act decisively for the common good, first of the people and then of the sovereigns.'[7]

In June 1847 Henry Lawrence, who had been appointed resident at Lahore, dispatched a mission under Lieutenant Reynell Taylor to recommend reforms.

Taylor's attempts to hear the people's grievances were thwarted not only by the maharaja's officials but also by the people's fear. Even if the Kashmiris did speak out, Taylor had little to offer them. He told one delegation who had come to meet him: 'The Maharaja was king of the country and likely to remain so; that we could do nothing but recommend and intercede, etc.; but that I believed our advice would meet with attention'.[8] In order to keep informed of the maharaja's activities, from 1846 onwards the British kept a spy at the court of Gulab Singh, Saif-ud Din, whose father Mirza Afzal Beg, had also spied for the British. Although, when Gulab Singh came to know about him, his lands were confiscated and he was forbidden to attend the Darbar, the maharaja did not dare remove Saif-ud Din completely for fear of upsetting the British. Saif-ud Din's reports, both critical and laudatory of the maharaja, indicated that he was becoming very superstitious and frequently resorted to astrologers to determine the actions of the British towards his state.[9] The British also made sure that his feudatory status suited their convenience; the tribute required of him was frequently varied to suit British interests. In 1853 he was requested to submit money instead of the customary shawls prescribed by the Treaty of Amritsar. Subsequently, when the shawls were once more requested, the governor-general, asked for the finest to be sent, since they were 'to be laid each year at the feet of the Queen of England.'[10]

'One of his chief faults was an unscrupulousness as to the means of attaining his own objects,' writes Frederic Drew, who spent ten years in the service of Gulab's son, Ranbir. 'He did not draw back from the exercise of cruelty in the pursuit of them, but he was not wantonly cruel.'[11] Walter Lawrence, who came to Kashmir as settlement commissioner in 1889, judged Gulab Singh more favourably than most. He regarded as exaggerated the reports which state that the purchase money paid for Kashmir was recouped from the local people in a few years. 'This is not correct. Maharaja Gulab Singh took care that the revenue reached the treasury, and he also took care that there should be no unnecessary expenditure.' Walter Lawrence's assessment of Gulab Singh was that he was 'an able, just and active ruler, and a fairly wise landlord ... a man of great vigour, foresight and determination.'[12] But despite Gulab Singh's gradual abandonment of some of his worst traits, which were so evident in his early career, and comparative stability throughout the state, most British officials remained critical of his conduct. In 1848 Lord Hardinge left India. In his farewell letter to the maharaja he had warned that the British government could not be 'the blind instrument of a ruler's injustice towards his people.'[13]

The end of the Sikh empire

The status to which the British had elevated Gulab Singh did not prevent him from coming under suspicion when the Sikhs once again confronted the

British in 1848 in the second Anglo–Sikh war. 'Gulab Singh,' writes B. S. Singh, 'deliberately chose to pursue a policy of friendly neutrality toward the British at the start of the conflict. He was indeed a self-seeking man and considered non-entanglement to be politically and financially the most expedient course open to him.'[14] Yet when the British demanded his support, as they were entitled to do under the terms of the Treaty of Amritsar, he gave it. On 7 February 1849, Lord Dalhousie, who had replaced Hardinge as governor-general, wrote to the Secret Committee:

> I have considered it necessary to address Golab Singh in strong language of advice and warning, intimating to him what part the British government expect him to adopt, conformably with the obligation imposed upon him by treaty, and pointing out to him the consequences of even a lukewarm conduct, at a time like the present, when the British look, and have the right to demand his cordial and strenuous co-operation.[15]

From Gulab Singh's point of view Sikh victory could possibly have revived the controversy over his acquisition of Kashmir and he was undoubtedly relieved that the British were the victors at the battle of Gujrat on 21 February. Sikh defeat at the hands of the British led to the total dismemberment of the Sikh empire and the annexation of the Punjab on 29 March. No sooner had the Punjab been annexed by the British than rumours began to spread about the impending annexation of Kashmir. The Earl of Dalhousie already had a reputation for being less inclined than his predecessors to leave territory in the hands of friendly Indian princes. Gulab Singh still retained a supporter in George Clerk who had written to the commander-in-chief of the Indian army, Sir Charles Napier, in March 1849:

> My belief is that he is a man eminently qualified, by character and surrounding territorial possessions, for the position of Ruler there, that all his interests lie on the side of friendship with us ... if Rajah Goolab Sing of Cashmere ever goes against us, it will be owing only to his having been handled stupidly by our government, or by our officers on the Frontier and in the Punjaub.[16]

Napier was not convinced and rumours persisted that Gulab Singh was reinforcing his army and Sikh soldiers were flocking to Kashmir. It was also reported that Dalhousie was about to mount an attack on Kashmir in order to make Gulab Singh return some heavy artillery. Dalhousie dismissed the reports: 'All is going on quietly here. You will see, I daresay, gossiping letters copied into "The Times" as to the prospect of war with Golab Sing, and my having demanded his guns. It is all stuff.'[17] Napier, however, remained in the forefront of those favouring annexation which led to a bitter controversy between the commander-in-chief and the governor-general. 'The C in C was strangely impressed with a notion of Golab Sing's vast power, and his intention to use it,' Dalhousie confided to his friend Sir George Couper on 17 November. Napier's concerns were 'troublesome, because of course he writes it home; and equally of course, a Government will believe anybody rather than its own officer, and therefore will be alarmed by him rather than be guided and comforted by me.'[18]

Napier was also concerned about a possible third war with the Sikhs in which Gulab Singh could be tempted to side with them.

> Golab Sing will probably be faithful to us, he knows our power; yet he has also seen our weakness in the two wars of the Punjab ... his country is perhaps the strongest in the world for defence; he can ensconce himself in snow for half the year; he has forts of various strength, quantities of small arms, and in the depths of his jungles and snows can conceal his preparations. To quell such an enemy will not be easy.[19]

Although Dalhousie did not share Napier's concerns, he did concede that it was expedient to maintain 'the army on a footing of full preparation against all possible risks in a country whose warlike population have been but recently subdued.'[20]

Calling Gulab Singh a 'modern Tiberius for horrible cruelty and villainy,' Napier proceeded to recommend that the British should fortify a military post at Sialkot to the south of Jammu: 'while it holds the Maharaja's capital in check, it is on the road to Cashmere for aggressive operations on our part.' Napier also recognised Gulab Singh's ability to attract others to his side. 'He has a rich treasury, quantities of cannon, small arms in abundance, and no prince in India ever wants men if he abounds in money.'[21]

In August 1850 a rumour that Henry Lawrence had been imprisoned by Gulab Singh while touring Kashmir on holiday made Sir Charles Napier demand an immediate invasion. Although the rumour was unfounded Gulab Singh, nervous that the purpose of Lawrence's visit might be to inspect the internal situation in Kashmir, kept himself well informed of his influential visitor's movements and made sure than no discontented Kashmiri gained an audience with Lawrence.

Soon afterwards, Dalhousie arranged a meeting with Gulab Singh to put their relations on a firmer footing. At first the maharaja was reluctant to see the governor-general and consulted an astrologer to determine whether it would be auspicious to do so. The meeting eventually took place at Wazirabad, north of Lahore, in December 1850. 'Our visits were mutually satisfactory and infernally civil,' Dalhousie later wrote to Couper:

> The presents on both sides really rich, and the protestations of friendship – undying fidelity on his part, benevolent and uncoveting protection on ours – were most edifying. He pressed me again and again to visit him in Cashmere, and to stay all summer. "It is yours; why should you leave it? Cashmere is your house, the boats are on the lake – they are yours, the horses are on the land – they are yours – why leave it?" This is, of course, orientalism; but a visit he really desires, and I am well inclined to pay it.[22]

The maharaja's gun salute was raised from 17 to 19 and during the meeting Dalhousie reported how Gulab Singh had grabbed his clothes: 'Thus I grasp the skirts of the British government and I will never let go my hold.'[23] Dalhousie, however, was not won over by Gulab Singh. 'In 1846 we unwittingly handed over [Kashmir] to a chief who had proved himself a veritable tyrant and who already appears the founder of a race of tyrants.'[24]

After ten years as maharaja, Gulab Singh's health began to fail. He had had diabetes since 1851 and was also suffering from dropsy. In order to smooth the succession and prevent rival claims from his nephews to the throne, he asked the governor-general to install his third son, Ranbir Singh, as maharaja on 8 February 1856. Although Gulab Singh had formally abdicated, he became governor of the province and retained full sovereignty until his death on 7 August 1857.

The 1857 mutiny

The general uprising of sepoys, the local troops used in the army of the East India Company, started in Meerut near Delhi on 10 May 1857. It soon spread to other towns and hundreds of Europeans were massacred. The simple cause for the mutiny was regarded to be the introduction of the Enfield rifle, which was valued for its greater accuracy. It was still a muzzle loader and required the soldiers to bite off the end of a greased powder cartridge. When news spread that the lubricant was made from pig and beef fat, it offended both Muslim and Hindu sentiment. It also aroused fears that the British were intending to convert the entire population to Christianity. The titular head of the former Mughal empire, Bahadur Shah II, supported the mutineers. The rebellion, which lasted for over a year, not only undermined British confidence in their rule in India, but it also called for loyal allies.

The state of Jammu and Kashmir, under the joint leadership of the ailing Gulab Singh and his son, Ranbir, responded favourably to British appeals for help. They sent a large amount of money to the Punjab for the troops whose pay was in arrears. The mutineers were also forbidden to seek asylum in Kashmir which, after British annexation of the Punjab, now bordered British India. When 200 rebels reached Jammu they were arrested and handed over to the British. Shelter in the valley was also provided to English women and children seeking refuge from the plains. Most importantly, the Dogras agreed to send a Kashmiri force to assist the British in the siege of Delhi but continuing doubts about their loyalty to the British kept the soldiers inactive for several months. Only after Gulab Singh's death in August 1857 was the force – comprising 2000 infantry, 200 cavalry and six guns – under the command of Lieutenant Richard Lawrence, the youngest of the Lawrence brothers, allowed to depart. It saw only limited action, but the psychological significance of the decision to commit Kashmiri troops on the side of the British outweighed their possible contribution in the fighting.[25] As Herbert Edwardes recognised, had the Dogras chosen to revolt and to call upon the

Sikhs, Gulab Singh's 'late comrades in the Punjab, to rise against us, no doubt they would have risen at his command.'[26]

Ranbir Singh

By amending the terms of the Treaty of Amritsar in 1860 His Highness Maharaja Sir Ranbir Singh, Indar Mahindar, Sipar-i-Saltanat, General, Asakir-i-Inglishia, Mushir-i-Khas-i-Qaisara-i-Hind, Grand Commander of the Star of India, Grand Commander of the Indian Empire was rewarded for his loyalty and assistance during the Indian mutiny by being allowed to adopt an heir from a collateral branch of the family. This was confirmed by George Canning in 1862 that 'on failure of natural heirs, the adoption of an heir into your Highness' House, according to its usage and traditions will be willingly recognised … so long as your House is loyal to the Crown.'[27] This would secure the succession of the Dogras in perpetuity in the event he or his successors did not have a direct heir. Queen Victoria had conferred on Maharaja Ranbir Singh the title of the Most Exalted Order of the Star of India at the same time and his gun-salute was raised from 19 to 21. Rather more popular – and less formidable than his father, Ranbir, was not able to improve conditions for the people. The country remained in the hands of officials, who were neither motivated nor intellectually equipped to undertake any reforms.

The reign of Ranbir Singh, observed Torrens after his visit in 1861, 'is marked by an evident wish to govern wisely; but he is still surrounded by advisers of the old regime who use their influence "not wisely, but too well".' He also scorned the atmosphere of superstition under which the maharaja lived. The edict forbidding the people to catch fish because a Hindu fakir had announced that Gulab Singh, reincarnated as a bee, had been swallowed by a fish 'is an instance of the height of folly to which a weak mind, awed by superstition and swayed by priestcraft, can attain.' As an orthodox Hindu, the maharaja aimed at building as many temples in Jammu as there were in Varanasi on the river Ganges. He also promoted religious literature, education, and festivals. Torrens pointed to the neglect of Muslim buildings 'while on every side Hindoo temples are being erected.'[28] The Dogri language was promoted in the army and Dogras gradually took over as officers.

Frederic Drew's ten years in Ranbir Singh's service meant that the 'ways and doings' of the maharaja's Darbar became almost as familiar to him 'as the customs of my own country.' During the winter months, which were spent in Jammu, Drew describes how the maharaja listened to petitions twice a day in a public Darbar. 'Perhaps an employee will ask leave to return to his home, or to take his mother's ashes to the Ganges; next, maybe, a criminal is brought to receive final sentence; then a poor woman with face veiled, will come to complain of some grievance or other, or a dispute about a broken contract of marriage will have to be decided.'[29] Drew spent several summers exploring the geology of the mountains for which purpose he was originally engaged. Later he managed the maharaja's Forest Department and in the last year of his service he was made Governor of Ladakh.

Colonel Ralph Young visited Kashmir in 1867. As he travelled along the road to Srinagar he found 'that it had all been once under cultivation but it is now desolate. Certainly the country is not now flourishing.' Cholera took lives daily and Young remarked on the maharaja's idea to print invitations to the Hindu god, Sri Krishna, for protection against cholera, which he sold to the local people. During his travels he met Frederic Drew, from whom he formed the impression that all ranks were 'discontented with the Jummoo rule and that they would rebel but for the belief that the English would interfere to put down the rebellion.'[30]

William Wakefield who visited Kashmir in the summer of 1875 commented that the maharaja 'desires to act fairly and honestly to his people in this part of his dominions, aliens as they are for the most part both in race and creed. If the same could be justly said of many of his advisers, the future of Kashmir would, perhaps, look brighter.'[31] Walter Lawrence called him 'a model Hindu prince, devoted to his religion and to Sanskrit learning, but kind and tolerant to the Mussulmans, to whom he allowed free exercise of their religion.' Writing soon after Ranbir's death, Lawrence observed, somewhat charitably perhaps, that he 'would have done much towards the development of the valley if he had possessed the stern determination of his father, and could have kept his servants in hand.' Lawrence also believed that throughout its history Kashmir's location had placed its inhabitants 'at the mercy of short-lived governors, ignorant of their language and customs, who worked their will on the Kashmiris regardless of the policy of the courts of Delhi, Kabul and Lahore, and looked upon Kashmir in the same light as that in which the Roman proconsuls regarded Africa.'[32]

As with many visitors who came to Kashmir, Torrens also believed that the Kashmiris with whom he came into contact during the reign of Ranbir Singh were 'a much abused race' who had been oppressed for so many years that their past grandeur was all but forgotten. 'Our boatmen were possessed of vague notions of a happy time, long, long ago, when the men were all brave, hardy and warlike, the women all virtuous.'[33] Robert Thorp, who openly expressed his outrage at the sale of Kashmir to the Dogras in 1846, believed that the British had some responsibility to 'the people whom it sold into the slavery of Gulab Singh.' He described a people 'whose characteristics (both intellectual and moral) give evidence of former greatness, trampled upon by a race in every way inferior to themselves and steadily deteriorating under the influence of an oppressive despotism, which bars the way to all improvement, whether social, intellectual or religious.' Death or migration was the only escape from this form of servitude. The shawl makers worked for a pittance. 'Of almost everything produced by the soil, the government takes a large proportion and the numerous officials who are employed in collecting it are paid by an award of so much grain from the share of the landlords.' Thorp also described how the sale of young girls 'to established houses of ill-fame, is both protected and encouraged by the government.' Pointing out that Ranbir Singh rarely visited the valley: 'he sits apart in his luxurious palace at Jamoo, contented to receive such reports of the state of his country as his officials may choose to furnish him with.' Although Thorp believed that the maharaja was ignorant of a large part of the repression of his government, 'such ignorance is equivalent to guilt'.[34] Thorp's comments were circulated to British officials in Calcutta and Lahore. Described by Muhammed Saraf as Kashmiri's 'first foreign martyr' he was mysteriously murdered in 1868.[35]

Ranbir Singh's twenty-eight year reign was marked by a combination of indifference to local government and a series of natural disasters. The famine of 1877 was so severe that for generations it was recalled with dread. The crops in the valley were destroyed by torrential rain. Thousands died – perhaps one third of the population – and dead bodies lay unburied by the roadside. For several months those who wished to flee to the Punjab, where food was more plentiful, were refused permission to leave the state. When finally they were allowed to depart, hundreds of shawl-makers were amongst those who left, never to return, inflicting irreparable damage on the already declining shawl industry.[36] Although the maharaja ordered supplies of grain to be imported from British India, much of it was siphoned off by corrupt officials before it reached those in need. Aloof in his court in Jammu, it is doubtful that the maharaja ever truly appreciated the suffering of his people, which was exacerbated by misgovernment and incompetence.

Dr Arthur Neve, who arrived in Kashmir in 1882, discovered that there was a general feeling that the famine could have been avoided: 'In those days all taxes were levied in kind and the wage assessment was not made until the crops were ripening. It was commonly believed by all the Mohammedan cultivators that in 1877 the delay was deliberate.' According to reports which Neve heard, the assessment had not been made in time for the crops to be harvested 'to punish the Mohammedans who had the previous year sent a deputation to complain to His Highness of the exactions of one or two of his officials.'[37] Neve, who had arrived in Kashmir five years after the famine still saw 'emaciated bodies and scanty garments' recalling its ill effects.

In 1884 the lives of the Kashmiris were convulsed by a tremendous earthquake. Neve was in bed: 'For half a minute I lay expecting the noise and shaking to subside, but it seemed to increase, and to the loud creaking of the roof timbers and the swinging of doors, windows and pictures were added the crashing of bricks and plaster falling on the staircase.' Sopore and Baramula were almost wiped out. The cheaply built huts and double storey barracks with heavy mud roofs fell 'flat like a pack of cards'. 'It was a heart rending spectacle. In many instances, tho life was not extinct, the crushed skull or chest forbade any hope of recovery; but some had escaped with merely a dislocation and a fracture.' For the wounded of Sopore and Baramula, Neve set up a temporary hospital. A fortnight after the earthquake he found men and women still with fractures and dislocations unset. 'The few survivors had been so stunned by the calamity that they thought little of minor injuries.'[38] Neve noted that surprisingly few houses fell in Srinagar:

> To a European traveller the city of Srinagar looks tumble-down and dilapidated to a degree; very many of the houses are out of perpendicular, and others semi-ruinous ... But the general construction is suitable for earthquake country; wood is freely used, and well jointed; clay is employed instead of mortar, and gives a somewhat elastic bonding to the bricks.

In 1884 Lord Kimberley, secretary of state for India, wrote to the Government of India: 'As to the urgent need for reforms in the administration of the State of Jammu and Kashmir, there is, unfortunately, no room for doubt.' He went on to say that, given the circumstances under which the Dogras came to rule over Kashmir, 'the intervention of the British government on behalf of the Mohammedan population has already been too long delayed.'[39] However, concerned as they were by the internal situation in the state, there was a more important reason why the Government of India chose to intervene more assertively in Kashmiri affairs. The state of Jammu and Kashmir effectively constituted the northern frontier of Imperial India. 'Whether we believe that Russia has designs upon India or not, we are bound to secure ourselves in India,' wrote Major William Sedgwick in 1886'. 'For if we do not do so, assuredly the mere proximity of such an aggressive power as Russia, will unsettle the minds of the people and will cause a deep feeling of unrest.'[40]

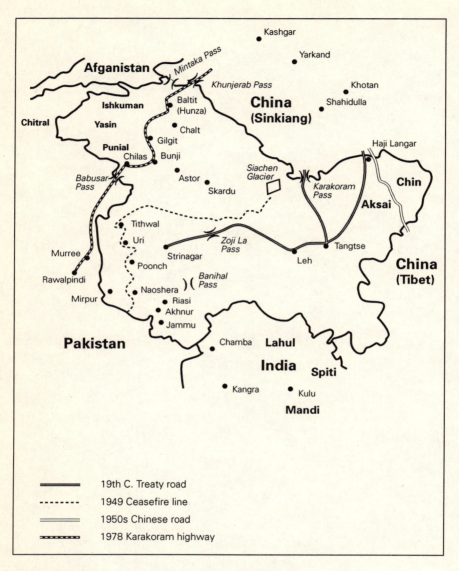

Afganistan

Kashgar

Yarkand

Mintaka Pass

Khunjerab Pass

Khotan

Shahidulla

Ishkuman

Baltit
(Hunza)

China
(Sinkiang)

Chitral

Yasin

Chalt

Punial

Gilgit

Chilas

Bunji

Haji Langar

Babusar
Pass

Astor

Skardu

Siachen
Glacier

Karakoram
Pass

Chin

Aksai

Tithwal

Uri

Zoji La
Pass

Murree

Strinagar

Leh

Tangtse

China
(Tibet)

Rawalpindi

Poonch

Naoshera

Banihal
Pass

Mirpur

Riasi

Akhnur

Jammu

Pakistan

Chamba

Lahul

India

Spiti

Kangra

Kulu

Mandi

————————	19th C. Treaty road
- - - - - - - -	1949 Ceasefire line
═══════════	1950s Chinese road
▪▪▪▪▪▪▪▪▪▪	1978 Karakoram highway

4. The State of Jammu and Kashmir: Routes to China
(Source: Alastair Lamb, *Kashmir: A Disputed Legacy*, Herts, 1991)

CHAPTER 7

An English Fortress

Expensive as the Gilgit game may have been, it was worth the candle. Colonel
Algernon Durand[1]

In Kashmir we have ready at hand, a great fortified camp, which can be made
absolutely impregnable. Major William Sedgwick[2]

British imperial policy towards the state of Jammu and Kashmir in the late
nineteenth century was guided primarily by fear of a Russian advance towards
India through the Pamir mountains as well as by events in the expanse of
land, north of the Hindu Kush and Himalayas, known as Turkestan, the
eastern part of which was under the nominal rule of China. In addition, the
British were continually troubled by the independent policy adopted by the
Amir of Afghanistan whose lands also extended as far as the north-western
frontier of the sub-continent. On account of its strategic location, the state
of Jammu and Kashmir appeared to be an ideal buffer against potential
incursions from Russia, Afghanistan and China into the sub-continent.
Provided the British could maintain a workable alliance with the maharaja
they would not be obliged to incur the expense of fortifying the northern
frontier themselves.

Such a policy, however, implied a degree of control over the maharaja
which the British did not have. The Treaty of Amritsar made no provision
for a British representative at Gulab Singh's court. Although technically a
feudatory of the British, there was no clause preventing the Maharaja of
Jammu and Kashmir from conducting his own independent diplomatic
relations. In the late nineteenth century the British attempted to assert
sufficient control to enable them to use the state of Jammu and Kashmir for
their own imperial objectives. By 1880 their first attempt had ended, in the
words of the outgoing viceroy, Lord Lytton, in 'complete failure'.[3]

A broken instrument

During the mid-1860s, when John Lawrence was viceroy, the British government did not attempt to interfere with the maharaja's conduct of policy.
Lawrence did not give as much credence to the dangers of the Russian
advance as some of his colleagues and was not inclined to jeopardise the
advantage of having the state of Jammu and Kashmir as a buffer between

India and Central Asia. When, in 1867, Charles Aitchinson, the commissioner at Lahore, urged Lawrence to establish direct control over the diplomatic relations of Ranbir Singh, he replied that it would be 'distasteful to the Maharaja and any attempt to enforce it, would be found nugatory.'[4] Lawrence believed the British were bound by their gratitude to Gulab and Ranbir Singh for their support during the Mutiny, during which his brother Henry had died.

The maharaja was, therefore, given a free hand in conducting his external relations. With a keen interest in trade, he sent his agents to the khanates of Turkestan in Central Asia. He also established a Russian language school at Srinagar, which was the first of its kind in India. In 1870 a mission from Ranbir Singh arrived in Tashkent, led by Baba Karama Prakash, who emphasised the maharaja's desire to establish relations with Russia and said the maharaja was 'almost a free ruler' and paid only 'symbolic' tribute to the British. The Russians did not, however, take up his offer.[5]

Since the Treaty of Amritsar was vague regarding the western boundary of the state, the maharaja was interested in bringing the neighbouring border states under his control. Chilas, on the route to Gilgit, already paid tribute to Kashmir. In 1852 the Dogras had been obliged to give up the strategically-placed area of Gilgit over which they had gained nominal control and which bordered the independent kingdoms of Hunza and Nagar. In 1860 Ranbir Singh therefore sent a force to recapture Gilgit which was 'annexed' to the state of Jammu and Kashmir. By the end of the decade Hunza and Nagar, traditional rivals, both paid tribute to the maharaja in return for which they received an annual subsidy. The Mir of Hunza, however, was not happy with this state of affairs and considered that his allegiance lay with his traditional overlord, the Manchu ruler in China.

Lord Mayo, who became viceroy in 1869, was much more concerned about the Russian threat and directed his policy towards Kashmir with Britain's imperial considerations firmly in mind. 'How this treaty [of Amritsar] can be carried out without exercising direct control over the diplomatic transactions of the Kashmir state, I cannot understand.'[6] In the light of evidence of the maharaja's activities in Yasin and Badakhshan, Mayo determined to put a check on his ability to conduct his external affairs without reference to the British government. Since 1852 an officer on special duty had been allowed in the state for six months, ostensibly to monitor the activities of the visiting Europeans. In 1871 the Government of India insisted that the officer on special duty should be the viceroy's nominee rather than an official representative of the Punjab government. Mayo's main concern was that the maharaja should not create disturbances in the neighbouring areas, which could upset peaceful relations with the tribes and which the Russians might then use as a pretext for advancing towards India. Mayo's successor, Lord Northbrook, did not have the same qualms about permitting the maharaja to extend Kashmiri influence if, at the same time, it served

British interests; in 1874, the period for which the officer on special duty in Srinagar could stay in Srinagar was extended from six to eight months and with each new viceroy, his powers increased. Northbrook's thinking was accepted by Lord Lytton who took over as viceroy in 1876.

The Dardi principalities, which included Hunza, Nagar, Chilas, Punial, Yasin and Gilgit were still considered vulnerable if Russia crossed the Baroghil and Iskhkoman passes to the north-west. 'It would be suicidal,' Lytton wrote to the Secretary of State for India, Lord Salisbury in 1876, 'in our present uncertain and menaced position to leave to the mercy of chance, in the hands of any weak chief surrounded by powerful and aggressive neighbours that strip of territory containing the Baroghil and Ishkoman passes.'[7] At the same time, the extension of Dogra power into Dardistan was viewed with concern by the Mehtar of Chitral, who, as ruler of an independent kingdom, regarded the maharaja as an unwelcome competitor, particularly in Yasin.

The British, however, were prepared to let the Maharaja of Kashmir occupy the territory of Yasin and secure the two passes with their help in return for a permanent British resident in Srinagar and an agent in Gilgit, which would give access to Hunza and eastern Turkestan. But the maharaja was most alarmed at the proposal to station a British officer in Gilgit who would report directly to the British government on border developments, and the discussions – which took place in November 1876 at Madhopur, south of Jammu in British India – nearly broke down. Only when Lord Lytton assured Ranbir Singh that the British would not interfere in the domestic management of the state, did he agree. Colonel John Biddulph was sent as the first British OSD in Gilgit in 1877 with instructions 'to collect and furnish reliable intelligence of the progress of events beyond the Kashmir frontier ... to cultivate friendly relations with the tribes beyond the border in view to bringing them gradually under the control and influence of Kashmir.'[8]

Lytton had also been exploring the possibility of redefining British relations with Afghanistan before sanctioning an extension of Kashmiri influence to the west. He believed that the obvious estrangement of Sher Ali, the Amir of Afghanistan, from the British was due to their own neglect of him. Describing the amir as an earthen pipkin between two iron pots – Russia and Britain – Lytton proffered friendship and in 1877 the British and Afghans met in Peshawar. Had their negotiations been successful, the viceroy was even considering letting Afghanistan absorb Chitral under strict conditions, which would have diminished Britain's perceived need to rely on the Maharaja of Kashmir to safeguard the northern frontier. But, as relations deteriorated with Sher Ali, leading to war in 1878, British reliance on the maharaja became more significant. Ranbir Singh, however, was also playing his own game. Biddulph was not welcomed in Gilgit and the maharaja never fully co-operated with him. The Mehtar of Chitral, who was obliged to accept Kashmiri suzerainty in 1878, was also an unwilling partner in the relationship. He was far more disposed to treat with his fellow Muslims in Afghanistan, rather than Hindus and 'Kafirs' on his eastern borders. Hunza remained outside the British sphere of influence.

By 1880 the British were forced to admit that their Kashmiri policy had failed. Lord Lytton described the maharaja as 'a broken instrument which we can neither mend nor employ again with any safety.'[9] F. Henvey, the officer on special duty in Srinagar, made a serious indictment of Kashmir's administration, which partially explained the failure of British policy:

> A state which is rotten to the core within can scarcely show a bold front without. A state whose soldiers are always in arrears, and therefore discontented, forms a sorry bulwark to the Indian empire. A state which cannot keep its people alive would meet with difficulty in equipping and supplying a force for distant warfare in a barren country.[10]

In 1881 the Gilgit Agency was withdrawn. It had not proved to be a particularly valuable listening post and the maharaja was left to guard the northern frontier on his own. Blame for the failure of the agency was also laid on Biddulph. 'In a few weeks he found himself surrounded by a network of local intrigues. He was apparently quite unable to cope with such tactics and he seems to have been grievously wrong in his judgement of the character and capacity of the chiefs and others with whom he came in contact.'[11] According to Indian assessments: 'He by passed the Kashmiri authorities, established direct contact with the tribal chieftains, played one against the other and deliberately created disaffection among the tribal leaders against the Dogras. The active political interest the Dogras took in the region and the indiscriminate intervention in the internal affairs of the tribal chieftainships by the British officer, turned the tribals against both.'[12] The premise of Lytton's policy was also that Kashmir was completely loyal to the British government in preference to both Russia and Afghanistan. The maharaja, however, was found to have had dealings with both.

The Russian perspective on events in Northern India had clearly led them to take advantage of every opportunity which presented itself. Tsar Nicholas perceived that it would be to his advantage to squeeze Imperial Britain in an area where it hurt in order to force the British to loosen their grip elsewhere. In 1865 the Russians had annexed Tashkent; the following year they took Khojand; two years later Samarkand and Bokhara came under Russian control. But in addition to Russia's expansion south into the khanates of Central Asia, the tsar's emissaries were keeping a watchful eye on events in China.

The route through Ladakh

The significance of Kashmir as the guardian of India's northern frontier lay not only in its western border areas of Gilgit and Hunza, but also in the east because of Ladakh, which Gulab Singh had acquired in 1840. From Srinagar access to Leh led onwards to Khotan, Yarkand, and Kashgar in Turkestan. After the creation of the state of Jammu and Kashmir, one of the Boundary Commission's tasks was to define the borders of the new state, which was the first time its officials became officially aware of the Ladakh route to China. By the 1860s, as the Russian empire moved ever closer to the north-western frontier, the British became concerned that their interests might extend still further to Chinese Turkestan, which would deprive Britain of the opportunity of expanding their own commercial links into the region. The Manchu dynasty was in decline and Chinese rule over its Muslim subjects in Central Asia was greatly weakened after the Chinese Muslims in Gansu had rebelled in 1861.

With the rise of a potentially independent state in Kashgaria, centred on Kashgar, in the western corner of Chinese Turkestan, under Yaqub Beg (who had seized power from another warlord from Kokand in 1868) the British became even more concerned that the Russians would use this opportunity either to annex the whole area or make a puppet out of Yaqub Beg for their own objectives. 'That the Russians were extremely interested in what was happening in the former Chinese dominion and that they were trying to establish a special diplomatic relationship with Yaqub Beg was soon apparent to the British,' writes Alastair Lamb.[13] In 1870 Colonel Douglas Forsythe was sent to Yarkand to assess the strategic importance of the region for the defence of India against a possible Russian invasion. Much British thinking was also based on conjecture, which gave rise to unrealistic expectations of the wealth of Central Asia. Mayo was encouraged by 'optimistic reports received from a tea planter who had recently visited Turkestan and urged the establishment of an India–Yarkand trade route.'[14]

Ranbir Singh was not oblivious to the fluid situation on his northern frontier and attempted to take advantage of it to expand his trading links with Eastern Turkestan. To this end he established a small garrison in 1864 at Shahidulla, which lies on the road from Leh to Kashgar, across the Karakoram Pass. He also established relations with the Amir of Khotan, the ruler of a small area centred on the town of Khotan who had assumed power for himself in the absence of Chinese authority. In these uncertain times he too was looking for allies. Ranbir Singh also permitted William Johnson, a former member of the British survey team, to map out the state's north-eastern boundary, which he placed several hundred miles to the north of the 18,000 foot Karakoram Pass, to within about fifty miles of Khotan. Although the British were annoyed by Johnson's activities, in an area which might conflict with Chinese interests, his map, writes Alastair Lamb 'found its way into the official corpus of Indian cartography to influence British maps for years to come (and to lay one of the foundations for the post-1947 Indian claim to the Aksai Chin).'[15]

Ranbir Singh's independent initiatives were, however, watched with concern by the British, who were still making up their minds as to the extent to which they would permit him to conduct an independent foreign policy. Since they were also anxious to benefit from possible trade, in 1863 they had negotiated a commercial treaty with the maharaja. But concern that his agents were imposing heavy taxes on the transit trade led to the demand for a commercial agent to be stationed at Leh. In 1867 Dr Henry Cayley was appointed to this position. An additional treaty in 1870 enabled the British to pass along a route, known as the Treaty road, in the region of Shahidulla, but which avoided the Karakoram pass. The route went from Tangtse towards the Aksai Chin plain to Haji Langar. Its maintenance, and the supervision of its traffic, was supervised by two joint commissioners, one appointed by the maharaja and the other by the Government of India. In 1874, after a series of missions, the British signed a commercial treaty with Yaqub Beg. During this time the Treaty road was used extensively. After a decade, the Chinese were able to reassert control over the whole of Chinese Turkestan, which they then renamed Sinkiang, meaning 'the New Dominion'. The Treaty road fell into disuse, and the name was applied to the old Karakoram route, which was supervised by the joint commissioners. The idea of a more northerly route, however, was revived in the 1950s when the Chinese saw the benefits of constructing an all-weather road across the Aksai Chin for wheeled vehicles, which would link Sinkiang with Tibet.

Although in the decades to come Central Asia became the arena for intense rivalry, Ladakh remained outside the field of immediate conflict for the rest of the century. Subsequent British attempts to define the border in the Aksai Chin were not reciprocated by the Chinese.[16] Thus the border and the area still under dispute between India and China was left ill-defined at the Kunlun range of mountains. 'This legacy of the British Government of India,' writes Madhavi Yasin, 'is taking its toll in the present times, when a powerful China is progressively nibbling at the outlying regions of Jammu and Kashmir state.'[17]

Pratap Singh: reform and deposition

Throughout the 1880s the British put into practice a plan of direct action in the affairs of the state of Jammu and Kashmir or a policy, as M. J. Akbar puts it, of 'wriggle and crawl, of excuse, pretence and deceit'.[18] In 1882 Ranbir Singh had considered nominating his youngest son, Amar Singh, as his successor as he was 'wiser' than his brothers Pratap or Ram. But the British did not agree. Although the maharaja repeated his request in 1884, the British chose to let Pratap Singh accede to the throne when Ranbir died in September 1885; they stipulated, however, that a resident political officer would be appointed, in place of the officer on special duty, who would act as his adviser in the reform of the administration.

The new maharaja, 'was a story book Indian prince,' writes Patrick French 'vacillating and oppressive, bedecked in silk pyjamas, pearls and a diamond-encrusted turban.'[19] He was also addicted to opium. The Government of India refused Pratap Singh's request to have more time to put his state in order. On the same day Pratap Singh was installed as maharaja, Colonel Oliver St John was appointed as the resident. At the Darbar in 1885, the maharaja announced a series of reforms, which included the abolition of state monopolies, reorganisation of the financial administration of the state, rationalisation of taxes, construction of roads and the removal of restrictions on emigration. But the reforms envisaged were, as later Indian commentators observed, beyond the ability of the maharaja whose officials 'were incapable, corrupt and devoid of any administrative acumen. The maharaja was surrounded by an inner coterie of personal advisors among whom were sycophants, quacks, fortune tellers.'[20]

The view expressed by St John after four months as resident, that the maharaja was unfit to rule, persisted throughout his long reign. In January 1886, St John was replaced by T. C. Plowden, who formed an equally unfavourable opinion of the maharaja. In 1886 the Government of India obliged Pratap Singh to appoint a new Council which included his younger brothers Amar and Ram Singh. In 1887 a Land Settlement was instituted in order to redress the inequities of the land tenure system which had existed since the time of the Afghans and Sikhs. Walter Lawrence was appointed settlement commissioner. His report, which was modelled on the lines of the Punjab gazetteers, gives a valuable insight not only into the distribution of land but into the lives and history of the people. Lawrence worked for six seasons in Kashmir. 'I found the people sullen, desperate and suspicious. They had been taught for many years that they were serfs without any rights but with many disabilities.' So dejected were they that Lawrence believed they had become *zulm parast* – worshippers of tyranny. 'They were forced by soldiers to plough and sow, and the same soldiers attended at harvest time. They were dragged away from their houses to carry loads to Gilgit and every official had a right to their labour and property.' He described their position as worse than that of the Third Estate in France before the French Revolution.[21]

Lawrence believed that 'the system of administration had degraded the people and taken the heart out of them.' He blamed the officials but not the maharaja.[22] The peasants, one and all, attributed their miseries to the deputies through whom the maharajas ruled, and they have always recognised that their rulers were sympathetic and anxious to secure their prosperity. But the officials of Kashmir would never allow their master to know the real condition of the people or to find out that the revenue of the country was diminishing.[23]

Lawrence's recommendations for the reform of land tenure were the most significant domestic achievement of the British during the reign of Pratap Singh. Theoretically the cultivator was able to retain 70 per cent of the yield of his land, whereas before he had been left with only the minimal amount for survival. As a friend of Walter Lawrence, E. F. Knight, a journalist who came to Kashmir in 1891, saw the determination of the British reformers: 'I was in no sleepy oriental state that had been allowed to go on in the same way from time immemorial and would continue doing so. Kashmir is in a transitional state and reforms of the most radical description are taking place.'[24] Educational institutions were also set up, the first census was taken and an attempt was made to check the corruption of the judiciary. But in practice the reforms benefited the peasants less than they should have done. The *jagirdars*, those to whom the maharaja had granted revenue rights over large amounts of land, were able to diminish substantially the earnings of the cultivator, who often found himself in debt to moneylenders. During his one year stay Knight noted the hatred of the 'Hindoo official class, whose privileges to rob and oppress the people are now being curtailed.'[25] Lawrence was not optimistic about the effects of reform: 'It is well to remember that a people so broken and degraded as the Kashmiris do not in a few years harden into a resolute and self-respecting community.'[26]

At the end of 1888 the Residency disclosed that it had discovered over thirty letters of a treasonable nature from the maharaja to the tsar. Although the maharaja denied having written them and it was subsequently proved they were forgeries, the episode was sufficient to undermine the last vestiges of confidence the British had in him. On 27 February 1889 Parry Nisbet, who had replaced Plowden as resident, wrote to Sir Mortimer Durand, foreign secretary of the Government of India: 'The maharaja is timid and a very superstitious man at the entire mercy of a set of unscrupulous scoundrels, who take advantage of his fears and imbecility to plunder the state to any extent, and there appears to me, weighty reasons for advising the practical setting aside of the maharaja's authority.' The suggestion was for the maharaja to relinquish all the powers of government for five years. In his edict confirming his 'voluntary' resignation, the maharaja stated: 'In the interests of the "State" and for better administration of the country, and with a view to remodel it, as near as possible on the English system, I hereby authorise a Council, the members of which for a period of five years will conduct all the public affairs of the State.'[27]

On 1 April 1889 the maharaja was divested of all but nominal powers. The Council comprised his two brothers, two ministers and an English member 'specifically selected by the Government of India.' Amar Singh became prime minister, then president of the Council and executive head of the administration; the real power lay with the British resident. William Digby, journalist, author and founder of the Indian Political Agency in 1887, appealed to the House of Commons for the restoration of Pratap Singh, stating that all that had happened was the transference of the government of Kashmir from one autocrat to another (i.e. the British resident). 'His will is law, he is King, and has surrounded himself with his own friends and protégés, and turned out many an old and faithful servant to the State.'[28] But his protests were dismissed as paid propaganda.[29] Indian contemporary belief was that the maharaja had been deposed because of British designs on Gilgit, and that the allegation of maladministration was merely an excuse to take over control of the state.[30]

Formation of the Gilgit Agency

In 1888 Colonel Algernon Durand went to Gilgit to work out a defensive strategy which would utilise the recently formed Kashmir Imperial Service Troops. The viceroy, Lord Dufferin, had decided to make all the rulers of the princely states share in the defence of the empire by contributing both men and money. When Durand returned from Gilgit, he reported to his brother, Sir Mortimer Durand, that he had heard that a Russian officer, Captain Grombchevsky, had been in Hunza. This news added to British fears that the Russians could pass through the Pamirs into the sub-continent and that India therefore was within range of their forces.

The following year, in July 1889, Durand was sent back to Gilgit to re-establish the Gilgit Agency. Despite the earlier failure to maintain a British presence in Gilgit, Durand was optimistic about the prospects of success. 'Our first year in Gilgit passed in peace and hard work, tempered by "excursions and alarms" born of the wild and ever-varying plots and intrigues indulged in by my native friends on all sides.'[31] He also understood British compulsions in taking over a poor valley 'separated from India by snow passes, situated at the far side of the Indus at the very extreme of Kashmir territory. Why, it has been asked should it be worth our while to interfere there whatever happened? The answer is, of course, Russia.'[32] Durand succeeded in drawing up an agreement with the rulers of Hunza and Nagar to keep the road to Kashgar open, in return for which both chiefs were granted a subsidy from the Government of India. Durand's position in Gilgit also highlighted the anomalies of British policy towards Kashmir:

> I was the representative of the British government on the frontier, and the external relations with the neighbouring states were under my control. But the rule within the Gilgit border was in the hands of the Kashmir governor, while the command of the forces rested with the Kashmiri General, with the provision that no important move of troops should be undertaken without my sanction.[33]

One of his first priorities focused on improving lines of communication between Gilgit and Srinagar. The somewhat unnatural geographical link between Srinagar and Gilgit, over the 13,775 ft Burzil pass, was finally improved by the construction of a military road. For the first time the Kashmiris could sleep more easily in their beds. As noted by Dr Arthur Neve, in earlier times, because of the demand for labour for transportation purposes 'the mere name of Gilgit struck terror into the Kashmiri. For him it had the most alarming meaning; it spoke of forced labour, frost bite on the lofty passes, and valleys of death, where the camps were haunted by cholera and starvation.'[34] With the construction of a military road, it was no longer necessary to call upon their services for transportation and *begar* was finally abolished in 1893, (although in practise, it continued in effect until 1947, especially in remote areas). As Durand noted, with a better road mules were more economical: 'Over bad roads, coolies can only carry a load of from sixty to eighty pounds in addition to the five days food for themselves. After the first few days they begin to consume what they carry, and bad roads make short marches. Mules carry four and five times as much as men, and only eat twice as much.'[35]

No sooner had the British established themselves at Gilgit, however, than their position was once more threatened by the activities of the rulers of Hunza and Nagar, who made a temporary alliance. In 1890 another Russian delegation was received in Hunza by the ruler, Safdar Ali. The following year, Uzr Khan, the heir to the ruler of Nagar, closed the Kashgar road and expelled the Kashmiri troops stationed there. Francis Younghusband, who had been surveying the passes between the Pamirs and the Karakorams, was also asked to leave. Since Younghusband was trying to negotiate an agreement between the Afghans and Chinese over their frontier, to thwart potential Russian designs, the British government regarded Younghusband's expulsion as a setback to their policy.

In one of the most famous actions of British imperial history, at the end of November, the British forces took up their position at Chalt, strategically located north of Gilgit, on the Hunza river, where the great Rakaposhi mountain dominates the landscape. Documents full of oriental imagery were exchanged. Demanding the evacuation of Chalt, Safdar Ali's court scribe described it as being 'more precious to us than are the strings of our wives' pyjamas.' Safdar Ali also expressed his readiness to cut off Durand's head and 'then report you to the Indian government.'[36] Throughout the night of 30 November war drums were beaten calling the tribesmen to fight. The Hunza–Nagar forces occupied the Maiun and Nilt gorges upriver and fortified their position on the clifftops at Nilt on the edge of a great chasm.

On 1 December the British forces – comprising Gurkhas, Kashmir State Forces, Punjab Infantry, Pathans employed on building roads and Punial irregulars with swords and shields – crossed the river Hunza at Chalt using a bridge hastily constructed by the sapper Fenton Aymler. E. F. Knight, who was reporting for *The Times*, and had come with his golf clubs, was placed in charge of a platoon of Pathans. The main gate of the fortress at Nilt was barricaded and in order to force entry Aymler, in full view of the enemy, placed explosives and attempted to light the fuse. His first attempt failed and, although he was wounded in the leg, he returned to light it a second time when, as Knight recorded, 'he received another wound, his hand being terribly crushed by a stone that was thrown from the battlements.'[37] The 'terrific explosion' created a breach into the fort and fierce hand-to-hand fighting followed. Durand was severely wounded by a bullet which 'when extracted, was found to be a garnet enclosed in lead.' The cliffsides, observed Knight, 'are studded with hard garnets which are of convenient size and shape ... so the tribesmen, by employing them thus in their projectiles, economise on the lead, with which they are not too well provided.'[38]

Despite taking the fort at Nilt, the Kanjutis, comprising the Hunza–Nagar forces, still had the advantage of height. 'From the glaciers to the river bed, we were faced by these impregnable cliffs, lined with marksmen, and easily defended by what is so far more terrifying to men than any rifle fire, the avalanche of rocks, only requiring the displacing of a single stone to start it from above.'[39] Knight estimated that 4,000 men held the line from the Rakaposhi glacier to the Maiun nullah. For over two weeks, the opposing forces faced each other. 'So far all was well' Durand wrote, 'the question was, how to break through their guard'.[40] The fort at Maiun was regarded as too difficult to approach. Finally, Nagdu, a sepoy of the Kashmir Bodyguard, planned a route up the opposite cliff along the nullah from the fort at Nilt. An advance party led by Lieutenant Manners-Smith with fifty Dogras and fifty Gurkhas ascended the 1,200 ft cliff and succeeded in storming the breastworks, whereupon the Kanjutis fled from the surrounding forts including Maiun.

Dr Hugh Luard was in Gilgit during the siege of Nilt and subsequent operations tending the sick and wounded:

> Seventeen very busy days. I was the only effective white officer within sixty miles, though myself intermittently ill with diarrhoea; for the wounded I was sole doctor, nurse, quarter-master, caterer and comforter; for the officers ahead, forwarder of all kinds of supplies; for the outposts and convoys I had to supply medical subordinates, transport, supplies and supervision: and for the Nilt force I had to concert with the clerks and native governors, pushing on supplies, ammunition, old guns, etc. and cope with an outbreak of pleuro-pneumonia in our cattle.[41]

Durand, who heard news of the victory from his sick bed, summed up the result of the war 'in the words of a well known Russian statesman, who said, when he heard of the occupation of Hunza: "Ils nous ont fermé la porte au nez." [they have slammed the door in our faces][42] Safdar Ali was deposed, Uzr Khan was exiled and his father continued to rule. Lieutenant Manners-Smith won the Victoria Cross; as did Lieutenant Aymler and Lieutenant Boisragon for their part in the storming of Nilt.

In peace time, the Gilgit garrison was manned by about 2,000 Jammu and Kashmir state troops, paid for mostly by the Jammu and Kashmir State Treasury, and for the rest of the century, the British maintained their presence. It was not until 1913 that local troops were found to man the garrison with the foundation of the Corps of Gilgit Scouts. Over 600 men, recruited locally and trained by British officers, formed the Scouts. It was not expected that the Gilgit Scouts would be able to resist a major encounter, their main use was to guard the passes and offer resistance in the event of an attack before reinforcements could be sent.

Foreigners in the vale

The reason for obliging the maharaja of Kashmir to accept an officer on special duty in Srinagar had been in order to monitor the activities and possible misconduct of Europeans in Kashmir. Ever since François Bernier, one of the first Europeans to enter Kashmir, had reported on its beauty, Europeans had been attracted to this mountainous region.

One of Srinagar's great attractions was picnics on Dal lake in boats, known as doongas. Narain Das, a Kashmiri Pandit, started a small shop to supply the Europeans with essential items. When his shop was destroyed by fire, he removed his stores to a doonga, fitting planks to replace the matting walls and roof. When a British officer offered to buy it, Narain Das started building houseboats.[43] The idea was improved upon by many others including Martin Kennard who in 1918 built the famous two storey 'Victory.' A whole community of Kashmiris known as the Hanjis, forming a separate social class, came to depend on the houseboats for their livelihood. 'We were known as Hanjis because whenever we were asked to do something we would say "*Han ji*", meaning " yes – very well, sir",' says Iqbal Chapra, a leading member of today's Hanji community.

As the popularity of Kashmir grew, so did the number of houseboats. 'The British, who came to Kashmir to escape the scorching heat, taught us how to furnish a houseboat, how to make it a decorative one with beds, chairs, tables,' says Chapra.[44] A century later, there were estimated to be 1,500 houseboats on Dal lake. Since the British were not allowed to own property in Kashmir, it was also a favoured way of having some form of accommodation. The houseboats also gave Kashmir the reputation as a place for rest and pleasure for foreign guests, around which the social and economic life of a great number of the people revolved. Makers of shawls, embroidery, carpets, papier maché boxes all benefited from the presence of officers, with their wives and children, who arrived in the valley every summer to escape the heat of the plains. Tongue in cheek, Lieutenant-Colonel Henry Torrens explained the reason why the palace of the maharaja in Srinagar was empty because he preferred 'the dignified retirement of Jummoo to a residence in his capital':

> It must be such a horrid bore for such a potentate to have his dominions annually invaded by a crowd of shooting-coated subalterns, who, as he passes them in his gilded barge, vouchsafe to acknowledge his presence by a condescending nod or a patronising wave of the hand, not withstanding that these Goths and vandals put indirectly so many Company's rupees into His Highness's pocket.[45]

The activities of all foreigners were subject to a set of 'Visitors Rules'. In 1916, an updated version to those of 1888, was issued under the authority of the Government of India by the resident, incorporating 167 rules and appendices to be observed regarding shooting rights, boating, camping and general rules.

In 1898 David Lorimer, who was briefly posted to the Kashmiri Residency, took his '3 months of Privilege leave' on a shooting expedition in Kashmir and Ladakh. Although he marvelled at the scenery, he did not develop any special love for the people. He called the Kashmiri language 'a hopeless gabble with an occasional Persian phrase thrown in.' The Kashmiri, he found to be:

> perhaps the most aggravating being in existence. He will continue to make the same mistakes in the face of all remonstrance and correction daily for three months, without any loss of self respect. And if called a fool, as he frequently is, he puts it down to a sad want of discrimination on the part of the hasty and discontented Sahib.

Yet he was prepared to concede that many of the Kashmiri coolies were 'wonderfully tough walkers and climbers and, without the stimulus of sport, will uncomplainingly undergo a wonderful amount of hardships.'[46] His appreciation of Ladakhis was different: 'although the very opposite of a rollicking people, they seem to have a strong vein of cheerfulness in their temperament and strike one as a contented and happy tho' poor community.'[47]

When Sir Francis Younghusband was resident in Kashmir in the early 1900s, British rule in India was witnessing a lavish era at the beginning of the reign of Edward VII. 'Every June, Lady Younghusband gave a "Moonlight at Home" in her exquisite garden amidst the climbing roses, gladioli, lilies, apricots and scarlet salvias.' According to the *Civil and Military Gazette* her party in June 1907 was the 'success of the season'. 'Political officers up from Rajputana rented villas above the Bund and strode the golf links,' writes Younghusband's biographer, Patrick French. 'Fresh chaperoned girls wandered through the Mughal Gardens with feverish young subalterns.'[48] Younghusband, however, did not particularly enjoy the 'social whirl'. He was more interested in the political implications of his presence and the need to maintain good relations with the maharaja.

The influx of light-hearted holidaymakers was in total contrast to the harshness of the lives of the local people, most of whom lived in abject poverty. Only a small minority, centred around the Dogra rulers, enjoyed unparalleled affluence. In 1911 Captain Enriquez of the 21st Punjabis travelled throughout the Kashmiri state in order to make a study of Hinduism and Animism. But it was impossible for him not to notice the misery of the poor people. The agricultural classes, he said, had reached about its lowest level. 'I have never seen elsewhere such vacant, empty, expressionless faces, or such distorted, shapeless limbs, as amongst a herd of these human cattle, driven together into Srinagar to carry some great man's baggage up to Gulmarg.'[49]

Europeans also made their presence felt as doctors and teachers. Under the direction of the Church Missionary Society, as in other parts of the empire, the British founded mission schools and hospitals. In the Spring of 1864 the Reverend Robert Clark started regular work in Kashmir. When Dr Elmslie arrived the following year he encountered considerable hostility from the local authorities to his work. The opposition reached a surprising climax during the 1867 cholera epidemic.[50] In time, however, the Kashmiris began to realise the benefits of European medicine, especially when the first dispensary was opened and chloroform, as an anaesthetic, was introduced.

Canon Tyndale Biscoe, who arrived in Srinagar in 1890, took over as headmaster of the Mission School founded by the Reverend Doxey in 1882. He remained in Kashmir for fifty years and made himself famous by sending the boys onto the streets to put out fires, which occurred regularly. He also insisted that the boys learn to swim, which had been considered improper, so that they could help save lives during frequent flooding. What the boys, who were mainly the sons of the influential Rajputs, needed, Biscoe believed, was 'not brain training but heart changing'.[51]

Dr Arthur Neve, who had arrived in Kashmir in 1882, realised that there was no point expecting converts just because of the medical help he gave to the Kashmiris:

> It is a great mistake for the missionary to suppose that he really promotes the spread of truth by allowing the mission to be regarded as a milch-cow. In times of special distress, missionaries should be foremost in the endeavour to organise and distribute effective relief, but should be equally on their guard against expending money in such a way as to bribe pseudo-inquirers, thus attracting an undesirable adherent.[52]

In 1889 and 1892 there were further severe outbreaks of cholera which 'decimated the city of Srinagar, and spread most disastrously to the villages, in which over 6,000 deaths occurred.' Efforts at anti-cholera inoculation proved successful although Neve still believed that improved sanitation and a trustworthy water supply were essential. 'But the habits of the people are as yet unchanged and the Augean stable is yet but little cleared.' He also attributed many ailments to the intemperate climate. Liver complaints and malarial fever were common as well as lung complaints in winter because of deficient clothing.[53]

Elizabeth Mary Newman came to Kashmir in 1888 and she became famous as the Florence Nightingale of Kashmir. Tyndale Biscoe described how women such as Elizabeth Newman were generally regarded as 'low caste' Europeans, because they did work, like midwifery, which only the lowest class of Kashmiri women would do. There was no hospital for women and the house which Newman used as a makeshift hospital was severely damaged in the flood of 1893, which washed away most of the bridges in Srinagar and many of the houses. According to Tyndale Biscoe, Newman was criticised by certain missionaries for not giving enough importance to evangelism, to which she responded: 'I know I am not what I ought to be, but I cannot preach to these poor people when they come to the hospital in pain. Would you like to be preached to when you are in pain? I try to make them comfortable, and later on, when they are ready and able to listen, I talk to them.'[54] In Leh, for a long time, the only European residents were the Roman Catholic and Moravian missionaries. 'I do not think they entertain any hope of proselytising for a long time to come,' writes E. F. Knight 'but these missionaries have tended the people in their sickness, have fed the poor and have, in short, by the example of their own devoted lives ... given an excellent demonstration of what the religion of a true Christian is.'[55]

Maharaja reinstated

Ever since his deposition, Pratap Singh held his brother, Amar Singh, responsible for all his problems. On 14 May 1889 he wrote to the viceroy, Lord Lansdowne: 'Since the very day I succeeded to the throne, he caused to set afloat all sorts of rumours against me, about my incapacity, insanity, etc.' He begged to be reinstated and if that was not possible, for the viceroy to shoot him 'through the heart with your Excellency's hands, and thus at once relieve an unfortunate prince from unbearable misery, contempt and disgrace for ever.' The viceroy declined both to shoot the maharaja and to reinstate him.[56] Nor did he attempt to curtail the activities of Amar Singh, in whose abilities as an administrator, the British evidently had more confidence.

Other Indian princes, however, were not happy with the unprecedented British interference in Kashmir. The Indian press had also taken up the cause of Pratap Singh and had requested Charles Bradlaugh, a well-known exponent of free speech, to attend the recently formed Indian National Congress in 1889 in order to focus attention on the deposition of Pratap Singh. Although Bradlaugh was criticised for pleading the cause of a Hindu 'despot', rather than focusing on the plight of the poor Muslims, the maharaja was gradually rehabilitated. Successive residents and viceroys did not, however, have any faith in his capabilities. When in 1891 the Council was reconstituted and the maharaja was offered the presidency, Amar remained as prime minister. In 1899 he also took over as commander-in-chief of the Kashmir State Forces after the death of Ram Singh. In 1905 the Council was finally abolished by the viceroy, Lord Curzon, and nominal power was restored to the maharaja. The Government of India, however, retained control over the finances of the state, the armed forces, tax, appointments to administrative services and foreign relations. The maharaja was also obliged to follow the advice of the British resident whenever it was offered to him.

On account of the enmity between Amar and the maharaja, in 1907 Pratap Singh decided to adopt a 'spiritual heir', the second son of the Raja of Poonch, descendant of Dhyan Singh, referred to by the British as 'the

Poonch boy'. His intention was evidently to prevent his brother from inheriting the throne and he argued forcefully that the 1860 amendment to the Treaty of Amritsar permitted him to do so:

> Raja Amar Singh can only aspire to be an heir in case I leave no natural issue or adopted son. As, however, I mean to exercise my right of adoption before I die without a direct issue, and Raja Amar Singh can on no account whatever be adopted as a son, his succession to the gaddi [throne] should be taken as entirely out of the question.[57]

The British argued equally forcefully that he was only permitted to adopt an heir if a natural heir did not exist. They were therefore prepared to recognise his 'spiritual heir' but made it quite clear that the succession would pass in the first instance to his brother and then to Amar's son, Hari Singh.

The maharaja was evidently displeased at this outcome and continued to protest about Amar's presence in his administration to the extent that he even suggested appointing a British officer in place of Amar as prime minister. In 1908 he wrote to Sir Francis Younghusband, the resident: 'If, notwithstanding his character and selfish ambitions and bad attitude towards me, he is considered indispensable for the State, then the Government may declare him straightaway the ruler of the State in place of me and order me to clear out.'[58] Younghusband told the maharaja to leave his prime minister alone 'as the Emperor leaves the Prime Minister of England free to perform all minor duties of a Chief Minister' and for the maharaja 'to perform the larger and the more important functions of a Ruler himself.'[59] Only when Amar Singh died in 1909 did the long feud between the brothers finally end.

In order to improve the administration of the Kashmir government, the Government of India had prescribed the appointment of 'respectable' officials amongst the principal measures of reform. But the lack of educated or trained Kashmiris to fulfil these positions meant that Bengalis and Punjabis from British India were introduced into the administration. The court language was changed from Persian to Urdu to attract more qualified people, but this upset the local Kashmiris. 'Thus at the beginning of the present century,' writes Prem Nath Bazaz ' a new problem confronted the people; that of facing the outsider who had occupied every position of vantage in the administration of the country.'[60] While the poor people were burdened with taxes, the middle classes felt resentful. In 1903 the 'Dogra Sabha' was formed in Jammu. Conservative by nature, its objective was political reform and improved social conditions under the existing regime of the maharaja.

The Pandit community, which had links in India, especially in Lahore and Lucknow, since the days of emigration during the time of the Mughals and Afghans, were also influenced by the reform movements which were developing in the late nineteenth and early twentieth century in British India. After the efforts of Annie Besant, who later founded the Home Rule for India League, in 1905 a college was set up in Srinagar which came to be known as the Sri Pratap College. Another college was started in Jammu. But education inevitably meant exposure to new ideas, which from a British point of view was not always welcome. At the end 1906 Prime Minister Pandit Daya Kishen Kaul went to take part in the Indian National Congress meeting. Soon afterwards, Younghusband received an intelligence report: 'While the Maharaja of Kashmir is deporting sedition mongers from his state, his own Dewan, Pandit Kishen is supporting the extremists and has helped them with money.'[61] Younghusband's response was placatory: 'For my own part, I have purposely spoken very strongly to Daya Kishen upon agitators in general and left him to put the cap on his head if it happens to fit.'[62]

The employment of Punjabis in Kashmir also brought allegations of sedition, especially during serious agitation against the British in the Punjab in 1907. Amar Nath, the Prime Minister of Jammu, came under scrutiny, but Younghusband was equally calm: 'I think we may take it for granted that every Hindu from the Punjab sympathises with [the agitation]. I doubt if there is a single Punjabi Hindu up here in Kashmir who does not.'[63] Colonel Ramsey, the resident in 1910, was pleased to note that he did not find the maharaja had any anti-European feelings. He also took a more sympathetic view of Pratap Singh, pointing out that, although at certain times of day he was affected by opium, he was in fact quite shrewd and when matters were put to him by word of mouth, he understood them far better than when they were written down.[64]

While the Kashmiri Pandits began to benefit from better education, the Muslims, although numerically superior, remained excluded. As Canon Tyndale Biscoe had noted when he came to Srinagar in 1890 as headmaster of the Church Missionary School: 'the Mohammedan did not send their sons to school as all Government service was closed to them.'[65] Muslims, said Sheikh Abdullah, who rose to prominence in the politics of Kashmir in the 1930s, were not interested in education 'because of their abject poverty and the indifferent and discouraging attitude of the rulers.'[66] The All India Muslim Kashmiri Conference, formed in 1896 and supported by many Muslim Kashmiris who had settled mainly in the Punjab, was, however, beginning to support the Kashmiris in the state, both morally and financially, by offering scholarships for them to study in British India. In 1905 the Mirwaiz of Kashmir, the religious leader of the Muslims of the Kashmir valley, founded an association called the Anjuman-i Nusrat-ul Islam which aimed at improving the conditions of the Muslims, especially in education. In 1916 the Government of India sent its educational commissioner, Mr Sharp, to examine the educational system. Although his recommendations were for an increase in the number of schools throughout the state, the goals set by him were never achieved and his report was never publicised. Fifteen years later when Sir Bertrand Glancy, political secretary to the Government of India, presided over an official enquiry commission, he was obliged to admit that no·one was aware of Mr Sharp's report.[67]

In the opinion of the Government of India, the main obstacle to effecting change remained the maharaja: 'The idiosyncrasies of His Highness the Maharaja are too well known to need description. With a considerable measure of personal shrewdness and intelligence he is incapable of taking a consistent view of things and his activities are chiefly confined to interference and obstruction in departmental work.' The Government of India policy therefore was to rely on what efficient ministers could be recommended to the maharaja, while focusing attention on 'a most promising young man', Amar Singh's son, Hari Singh. But, given the long-standing hostility between Amar and Pratap, there was 'no love lost' between them and Pratap was jealous of his nephew, which was 'not unnatural altogether having regard to the Maharaja's personality, seeing that His Highness is quite aware that, on his demise, the full powers which have been withheld from himself, will, if all goes well, be conceded at once to Hari Singh.'[68] Hari Singh, however, was not as energetic as the British hoped. He did not show himself 'desirous of having any considerable amount of work which would keep him busy for more than three and a half to four hours in the day.'[69]

The orbit of empire

Initially, political awareness in the state of Jammu and Kashmir was not linked to the movement for 'responsible' government which was making itself increasingly evident to the British in the opening decades of the twentieth century, spearheaded by the activities of the Indian National Congress Party, founded in 1885, and the Muslim League, which was established in 1906. The 1909 reforms, sponsored by the Earl of Morley as secretary of state and Lord Minto, the viceroy, were designed to give the people of British India wider opportunities of expressing their views on how they should be governed, but this did not apply to the princely states.

During the First World War, the Indians from both British India and the princely states had demonstrated their loyalty to the British crown by their willing support of the war effort. 'They have shown that our quarrel is their quarrel ... they were a profound surprise and disappointment to the enemy; and a cause of delight and pride to those who knew beforehand the Princes' devotion to the Crown.'[70] Throughout the war, Pratap Singh placed all the forces of the state of Jammu and Kashmir at the disposal of the British. Contingents of Kashmiris fought in East Africa, Egypt, Mesopotamia and France. They also took part in operations which led to the defeat of the Turks in Palestine.

In 1917 there was considerable discussion about Hari Singh leaving the state in order to get away from the atmosphere of intrigue at court, with the suggestion that as commander-in-chief of the Kashmir Army, he might do active service in the war in Mesopotamia or France. This idea was welcomed by the military adviser to the state of Jammu and Kashmir, provided he did not consider his trip abroad as a holiday: 'If he went to the front on someone's staff, it would be all right and not give rise to comment but if he went on pleasure bent travelling about the world, it would give rise to talk and would be very unpopular in the Kashmir army and not be setting a good example.'[71] Eventually, due to the reluctance of his family, the idea of a trip abroad, either to the Front or to observe Britain at war, was postponed.

While the Indian people fought on behalf of the British Empire overseas, within British India Indian political leaders were exerting pressure to increase the pace of change. In response, on 20 August 1917, the secretary of state for India announced in the House of Commons that the policy of the government was for: 'increasing association of Indians in every branch of the administration and the gradual development of self-governing institutions with a view to the progressive realisation of responsible government in India as an integral part of the British Empire.'[72]

The implementation of this declaration was subsequently embodied in the Montagu–Chelmsford reforms, effected by an Act in 1919. In their report the secretary of state and the viceroy recognised that the rulers of the princely states would undoubtedly want a share in any control, 'if control of matters common to India as a whole is shared with some popular element in the government ... .' They also pointed to a stronger reason why the present stir in British India could not be a matter of indifference to the princes: 'Hopes and aspirations may overleap frontier lines like sparks across a street ... no one would be surprised if constitutional changes in British India quickened the pace in the native states as well.'[73] The Montagu–Chelmsford recommendation was for all the important states, of which Kashmir was one, to have direct political relations with the Government of India since 'the trend of events' would inevitably draw the princely states still closer into the 'orbit of empire'. A consultative body was to be set up known as the Chamber of Princes.

As the Government of India deliberated on the future of British India, Pratap Singh was trying to reassert full power over his state. In October 1918 he made another request and, the following year, a few procedural changes were agreed. In 1920 he appealed to the British again, pointing out that it was 'high time' – after nearly thirty years – that the restrictions were removed. But he was also testing the patience of the Government of India by his persistent refusal to announce that his nephew would be his heir. When Hari Singh visited Europe after the war, as 'Mr A' he caused considerable notoriety because the husband of a woman with whom he had had relations resorted to blackmail. Pratap Singh used this as a further pretext to try and disclaim him as his heir. Although the maharaja later relented, he was still opposed to an official announcement. Given the prevailing conditions of political uncertainty in British India, the resident, Colonel Bannerman, believed that the Government of India should accede to his wishes:

I would urge that it should not be forgotten that the Maharaja of Kashmir is the leading chief of Northern India, that he has much influence with the Hindus throughout India and that he is highly respected ... I would also respectfully observe that we are not in the quietest of times and we need all the leading men we can get to rally round us. The support of the Maharaja of Kashmir was of the first importance to the Punjab in the time of the Mutiny and it would be a political disaster to alienate the Maharaja now.

The attention which Pratap Singh continued to focus on his 'spiritual heir', Raja Kumar Jagat Dev Singh, strengthened the demand of those who wanted to announce Hari Singh's accession. Colonel Bannerman, however, pointed out that it was not normal practise for an official announcement to be made when the ruler did not have a natural son, lest it would 'at once create two parties in the state' which would draw allegiance away and 'lead to the adoption by the declared successor of a too independent attitude'.[74] Against this the Government of India had to contend with 'Hari Singh's practical refusal to take any share in the state affairs, which is greatly to be deplored' and, it was believed, mainly due to his belief that he would not in the end become maharaja.[75]

On 4 February 1921 the maharaja was restored full powers, on condition only that the resident's advice would be accepted by the maharaja whenever it was offered. A new Executive Council was established, of which Hari Singh became a member, and the Kashmir Reforms Scheme was introduced. The maharaja also pointed to the progress of the state over the last thirty-six years: 'The revenues of the state have increased by leaps and bounds, different laws, rules and regulations ... have been brought into force with a view to add to the prosperity of my people.'[76] Communications were also improved. A road over the Banihal pass from Jammu was completed in 1915. Hospitals were opened and electricity introduced. But Colonel Windham, the resident, noted that, in his opinion, the maharaja intended to do all 'in his power to prevent the new council from working properly and being a success'.[77] The final epitaph on Pratap Singh's ability was provided by Sir John Wood, resident in 1923:

Experience has conclusively shown that His Highness, however good his intentions may be, cannot be trusted to give a right decision on any question of policy or administration without some sort of control. His inveterate habit of listening to the advice of the palace intriguers and even menial servants renders this control essential.[78]

As predicted by Montagu and Chelmsford, however, Kashmir could not be immune to 'the sparks across the street'. The Kashmiri Pandits were mounting a campaign against the continued presence of 'foreigners' in the administration. 'Their minds were full of the ideas of the onrushing tide of democracy in the West. They read with emotion about political movements of Turkey, Ireland, Egypt,' writes Prem Nath Bazaz. 'The spirit of independence revived and with it came the desire to turn out the outsiders and to fight for the freedom of the motherland.'[79] Throughout the 1920s the honorary secretary-general of the All India Muslim Kashmiri Conference, Syed Mohsin Shah, a Kashmiri lawyer, who had moved to Lahore in the early 1920s, was constantly writing to the resident, Sir John Wood, on behalf of the Kashmiri Muslims.

Amongst those who also gave vocal support to the Muslims was the influential and widely respected poet, Allama Sir Muhammad Iqbal. He first visited Kashmir in 1921 and put to verse his distress at the poverty of the people:

In the bitter chill of winter shivers his naked body
Whose skill wraps the rich in royal shawls.[80]

Leading Muslim newspapers in India continued to point to the progress of the Kashmiri Pandits at the expense of the Muslims: 'They till the land, feed the State, fill its coffers, they are invariably sent to the wall and the Kashmiri Pandit is placed at the helm of affairs to rule them with a rod of iron,' stated the *Muslim Outlook* in 1923.[81]

In the Spring of 1924 the workers of the state-owned silk factory demanded an increase in wages and the transfer of a Hindu clerk whom the workers alleged was extorting bribes. Established in the late nineteenth century, the factory employed about 5,000 workers, most of whom were Muslims. Although the workers were given a minimal wage increase, some of their leaders were arrested, which led to a strike. As later reported in a representation to the viceroy, Lord Reading: 'Military was sent for and most inhuman treatment was meted out to the poor, helpless, unarmed peace loving labourers who were assaulted with spears, lances and other implements of warfare.' The representation, signed by the two chief religious leaders, submitted to the viceroy, through Mohsin Shah, also referred to other grievances:

The Mussulmans of Kashmir are in a miserable plight today. Their education needs are woefully neglected. Though forming 96 per cent of the population, the percentage of literacy amongst them is only 0.8 per cent ... So far we have patiently borne the State's indifference towards our grievances and our claims and its high-handedness towards our rights, but patience has its limit and resignation its end ... the Hindus of the State, forming merely 4 per cent of the whole population are the undisputed masters of all departments.[82]

They also complained about the closure of certain mosques in Srinagar and the desecration of the Khanqah Bulbul Shah, which was claimed by the Hindus to be a Hindu shrine. When Lord Reading forwarded the representation to Maharaja Pratap Singh an enquiry was made, but the conclusion of the Kashmir Darbar was that the protesters were 'sedition mongers'. The signatories of the representation were reprimanded; some were banished from the state while others apologised. For its part, the Government of India saw no reason to interfere with the discretion of the Kashmir Darbar or the resident.[83]

By the time Pratap Singh died on 25 September 1925 he was, as Major Searle, assistant political agent in Chilas district, observed, 'a courteous tho' opium sodden old gentleman.'[84] Despite his initial dislike of the Executive Council, it continued to function until his death and relations between Pratap Singh and Hari Singh became less strained. Although Hari Singh's accession was not contested, the Government of India was at once alert to the implications of a change of leadership on British foreign policy. The day after the maharaja's death, J. P. Thompson, political secretary to the Government of India wrote to the foreign secretary, Sir Denys Bray:

> In view of the great importance of Kashmir as a frontier state – and its importance is probably greater than ever, owing to the growth of Afghan power[85] and the Bolshevik menace – I have thought it advisable to ascertain whether the restrictions which have been placed on the powers of the late Ruler from time to time, have been in any degree due to its geographical position.[86]

Although Thompson concluded that the control was in fact due to the 'personal defects' of the maharaja's character, considerable correspondence ensued between the resident and the Government of India as to how best the new maharaja could be persuaded to reaffirm 'the old confidential undertaking to keep the resident informed in regard to frontier matters and to accept his advice in respect of such matters.'[87] After rejecting the suggestion that Hari Singh's formal recognition as maharaja should be made dependent on reaffirming such an undertaking, the resident was told that it was not necessary to have any 'confidential undertaking' from the new maharaja in regard to foreign affairs, but that the maharaja should be informed that the government 'presumed' the conditions prevailing, both in Gilgit and on the Ladakh frontier, would continue unchanged. 'This position is believed to be the outcome not of any special undertaking given by the late maharaja but of the general political canon which lays it down that no Indian state can have any foreign relations.'[88] The new maharaja was to be allowed to return to the normal relationship with the Government of India, which any princely state enjoyed within the limitations imposed by treaty obligations, but at the same time, as the sub-continent moved slowly towards self-government, the British were not prepared to lose sight of the importance of Jammu and Kashmir as a 'frontier state'.

PART THREE

The Mirage of Independence

CHAPTER 8

Enter the Lion

'Wherever I looked, I saw a relentless struggle between the oppressor and the oppressed. I yearned to become their saviour and sacrifice my life in their cause.' Sheikh Mohammad Abdullah[1]

In the 1930s, as the Indian political leaders in British India became involved in the struggle to determine how they should become self-governing, the people of the state of Jammu and Kashmir began a campaign against the autocracy of the new maharaja. Of those who became politically active, the name of Sheikh Mohammad Abdullah is pre-eminent. An impassioned orator, he became known as 'Sher-i Kashmir' – the Lion of Kashmir. There were many other political leaders who played important roles, but Abdullah became the giant among them, both in appearance and on the political stage. His ideology was a fusion of socialist and humanitarian principles: 'Destiny had intertwined my future with the future of Kashmir. No one knew how the mysterious hand of God would unfold events, but the future was casting its ominous shadow on the present world of ideas and ideals.'[2] He did not, however, have universal support and, as the independence of the sub-continent came closer, differing ideologies and objectives competed for the loyalties of the people of Jammu and Kashmir.

The last maharaja

When Lieutenant-General His Highness Inder Mahander Rajrajeshwar Maharajadhiraj Sir Hari Singh succeeded to the throne, there was cautious optimism that he would prove a more effective ruler than his uncle. He had been educated at Mayo College in Rajputana and, writes Muhammad Saraf, 'the Western education had, it must be said to his credit, given him a better sense of public duty and it seemed for a while that he might succeed where others had failed, in cultivating the support of his people through a policy of good government.' But the peoples' enthusiasm for the new ruler was at once dampened by his lavish coronation costing millions of rupees. 'That such a huge amount should have been spent on celebrating his accession to the throne in a land where the great majority of people did not enjoy even one meal a day, was undoubtedly a poor demonstration of his being well-intentioned.'[3]

The alienation of the Kashmiris from their new ruler was heightened by the continuing presence of 'outsiders' in government service, which led to a movement known as 'Kashmir for the Kashmiris', sponsored by the more educated Kashmiri Pandits. In 1927 a law defining a 'Hereditary State Subject' was passed forbidding the employment of non-state subjects in the public services; they were also not allowed to purchase land. But, to the annoyance of the Kashmiris, the top positions were invariably filled by people from Jammu, especially the ruling class of the Dogra Rajputs, who headed all the departments of the state administration.

When the Pandits began to improve their status in government service, this caused further aggravation amongst the Muslims. Abdul Suhrawardy was a young boy from the rural districts, whose ambition in the 1930s was to become a gazetted officer in the Indian Civil Service. 'As I grew up I found that the Muslims were the underdogs. The Hindus were the privileged class because they belonged to the religion of the community of the ruler. Almost all the government officials occupying almost all the ranks from the lowest up to the highest were occupied by Hindus.'[4] The army was also exclusively reserved for the Dogras. No Muslim in the valley was allowed to carry a firearm and the only Muslims who were recruited into the army, normally under the command of a Dogra officer, were the Suddhans of Poonch and the Sandans from Mirpur. Culturally and linguistically distinct from the Kashmiris of the valley, the maharaja believed he could depend on them to suppress whatever trouble might arise in the valley.

The Lahore Muslim press had been consistently highlighting the condition of the Muslim Kashmiris and newspapers critical of the maharaja were sent into the state. In 1929 an even greater impact was made when Sir Albion Banerji a Bengali Christian, who had come to Kashmir in 1927 as a senior member of the Council, resigned on the grounds that he no longer wished to be associated with the maharaja's government:

> Jammu and Kashmir State is labouring under many disadvantages, with a large Muhammadan population absolutely illiterate, labouring under poverty and very low economic conditions of living in the villages and practically governed like dumb driven cattle. There is no touch between the Government and the people, no suitable opportunity for representing grievances and the administrative machinery itself requires overhauling from top to bottom to bring it up to the modern conditions of efficiency. It has at present no sympathy with the peoples wants or grievances.[5]

At the same time, small groups joined together to discuss their complaints. In 1929 Ghulam Abbas, one of the comparatively few educated Muslims from Jammu who had obtained a law degree in Lahore, reorganised the Anjuman-i Islamia into the Young Men's Muslim Association of Jammu, for the betterment of Muslims. He also looked after Muslim orphans and did social work. In Srinagar the Reading Room Party, comprising a number of graduates from Aligarh university, rose to prominence. Prem Nath Bazaz, Ghulam Abbas, Muhammad Yusuf Shah were all active in discussing their grievances. In 1931 Yusuf Shah succeeded his uncle as Mirwaiz in Srinagar. He used his position in the mosque to organise a series of meetings, which protested against the maharaja's government.

While Maharaja Hari Singh was being made increasingly aware of a new more vociferous discontent within his state, he was also actively participating in the discussions which the British had instigated to determine how best to answer the clamour for 'responsible' government throughout India. Following the recommendation of Montagu and Chelmsford in 1918 for a consultative body to be set up, the Chamber of Princes was instituted, which included 108 rulers in their own right and twelve representatives of 127 smaller states. When the first Round Table Conference met in the House of Lords in London from November 1930 to January 1931 to discuss the future of the sub-continent, all the princes, including Hari Singh, endorsed the statement of the Maharaja of Bikaner for an all-India federation. The starting point for their future relationship, he said, 'must be sought, not in the dead land of an impossible uniformity, but in an associated diversity.' A unitary state would be impossible and would 'crack under its own ponderability.'[6] Two further Round Table Conferences elaborated on the scheme for federation, which was eventually embodied in the 1935 Government of India Act.

1931 was personally an eventful year for Hari Singh. After three wives, and no children, he had married for the fourth time and this wife, Tara Devi, finally produced a son and heir. The pageantry of Karan Singh's arrival in Jammu after his birth in France was reminiscent of the French court before the revolution:

> My father and mother went through the town in an open horse-carriage, while I was driven behind in a car ... after five days the whole performance was repeated in Srinagar ... there was a staggering array of feasts, receptions, banquets, illuminations, free cinema shows, music performances, the distribution of sweets and sundry festivities.

For Hari Singh, this was the zenith of his rule. 'Almost immediately after the festivities were concluded the State was plunged into serious political turmoil, after which things were never again to be the same.'[7] It meant that Karan Singh, the long-awaited heir to the Dogra dynasty, never became maharaja.

Hari Singh responded to rising tension between the Muslims and Hindus with a proclamation on 9 July 1931.

> From time immemorial, all communities within the State have been living on terms of closest harmony and friendship with each other ... I am, therefore, greatly pained to see that quite recently, owing to external influences a changed and regrettable attitude is observable in certain sections in the cities of Jammu and Srinagar ... At the beginning of my rule, I announced to you, my people, that my religion is justice.[8]

But his well-meaning sentiments did not reflect the reality. Kashmir was already like a powder keg. The spark was provided by a butler in the service of a European, Abdul Qadir, who made an impassioned fiery speech calling for the people to fight against oppression.[9] When he was arrested, crowds mobbed the jail, and several others were also arrested. There was further protest from the crowd at which point the police fired at them. Twenty-one people died. Their bodies were carried in procession to the centre of the town. Hindu shops were broken and looted. From the somewhat safer enclave of the Church Missionary School, Canon Tyndale-Biscoe observed: 'It is remarkable how quickly blood begins to flow in the name of religion. Each party pretends that its god or gods has been insulted so has an excellent excuse to show its devotion to its deity by breaking somebody's head or looting the shops owned by those of the opposite religion.'[10] The government retaliated with further arrests. 'Our Dogra rulers unleashed a reign of terror,' recalled the young Sheikh Abdullah, who was amongst the many hundreds of young protesters arrested after the Abdul Qadir incident.[11]

The lion rises

Sheikh Abdullah was born in 1905 in Sura, a village on the border of the Srinagar valley, north of Hari Parbat. He was the youngest of five sons and five daughters. 'My father, Sheikh Mohammad Ibrahim, traded in shawls. He started off with a small business, but persistence and hard work turned it into a medium scale enterprise.'[12] Abdullah's father had died two months before his youngest child's birth. During Afghan rule, one of Abdullah's ancestors, who were Kashmiri Brahmins, converted to Islam. Noticing his obvious intelligence, his mother sent him to school. He attended Sri Pratap [SP] College in Srinagar and Islamia College in Lahore, and finally Aligarh Muslim University which he described as 'the nerve centre of Muslim unrest,'[13] from where he obtained a Master of Science degree. After completing his MSc, Abdullah wanted to go abroad for further studies. But he had passed the age limit imposed upon Muslims. He therefore took a job as a science teacher. Although Abdullah claims that he did not neglect his school duties, as his involvement in politics increased he was asked to resign. From then on he focused his energies entirely on politics. 'Thank God! The chains were broken and I could walk along my chosen path without any external hindrance. All my time was now committed to the fight for freedom.'[14]

Sheikh Abdullah had returned to the valley in 1930, just as the political turmoil in Kashmir was beginning. 'How could I have known that the nation was on the brink of an eruption. The trampled pride and hope of the people of Kashmir was like molten lava ready to flow. Nature fanned the embers of protest which were smouldering inside me. It was left to me to take the lid off the volcano's mouth.'[15] Like other graduates, he was a member of the Reading Room Party. 'The Reading Room Party served as a rendezvous where we discussed national issues and amongst other things, deplored the existing conditions. We wanted to open a window to the world to apprise it of the wretched conditions of Kashmir.'[16] Abdullah was also strongly influenced by the Sufi, Akhan Mubarak Shah, who preached love, tolerance and peace. He learnt to recite the Quran with tremendous resonance, which captivated audiences throughout his life. According to Bilqees Taseer, whose husband was principal of the Sri Pratap College in the early 1940s: 'The masses were too downtrodden, too ignorant to be awakened by mere politics. They followed him as a religious leader, who, in the early days, lived amongst them as one of them. This is how he was so successful in motivating them.'[17] After three weeks in jail following the Abdul Qadir incident, Abdullah was released. Together with several other prominent Muslim leaders, he toured the valley. 'I felt this was a golden opportunity to broaden and strengthen the popular base of our movement.'[18] Abdullah's speeches against the injustices of the maharaja's regime led to more periods of detention. In September 1931 he was arrested and kept in detention for ten months.

The events of 13 July 1931 did not go unnoticed in the rest of India and soon afterwards leading Muslims met at Simla and formed the All India Kashmir Committee to campaign for the redress of the grievances of the Kashmiri Muslims. At the Darbar in October 1931, celebrating his thirty-sixth birthday, the maharaja made another attempt at reconciliation by inviting all sections of the people to submit their grievances. Under pressure from the British resident, he appointed a commission, headed by Sir Bertrand Glancy, a senior officer in the Political Department of the Government of India, to inquire into the complaints of the people. Prem Nath Bazaz and Ghulam Abbas were amongst the co-members of the commission. In April 1932 Glancy presented his report. 'It is a document of great historical importance,' writes Prem Nath Bazaz 'as it established beyond doubt that real grievances existed which needed redress.'[19] 'The commission had recommended far-reaching reforms for the development of education, particularly, primary education,' said Abdullah. 'It had also suggested reforms in the appointment of government servants, as well as granting proprietary rights to the cultivators of government-owned lands. In addition it recommended setting up of industries to create employment opportunities.'[20]

A hallmark of Abdullah's personal struggle was his insistence that the fight was against oppression of all the poor, both Muslim and Hindu. He and Prem Nath Bazaz had resolved 'that the Kashmir Freedom Movement will be conducted on secular, progressive and democratic lines.'[21] While he and the other political leaders were in Srinagar Central Jail they had discussed the formation of a political party which they decided to call the 'Muslim Conference.' Released from prison in June 1932, Abdullah became President and Ghulam Abbas was the first general secretary. The inaugural session took place in October 1932. 'It was a unique gathering,' writes Saraf, 'especially in the sense that all Muslims, irrespective of their religious differences or social distinction, sat shoulder to shoulder on the same platform, with the common object of providing Muslims with a single political platform.'[22]

Abdullah had stated that the movement was not directed against the minorities. But his continuing emphasis on secularism eventually led to an internal disagreement, which also had some foundation in religious differences amongst the Muslims. Although he denied the allegation, Abdullah was accused of being a sympathiser of the Ahmadiyya sect whose followers are considered to have called into question the uniqueness of Prophet Muhammad. Several prominent Muslim leaders, including Mirwaiz Muhammad Yusuf Shah, broke away. The rift between Abdullah and Yusuf Shah distressed their Muslim well-wishers in British India. On behalf of the All India Kashmir Committee, in 1933, Muhammad Iqbal issued a poster, entitled 'A sincere appeal to the Mussulmans of Kashmir':

> You dumb Mussulmans of Kashmir, your misfortune is again taking an unlimited turn. It is only two years since you had started a national fight for your primary human rights and in that struggle the way you displayed your bravery and non-violence was such that no Indian community can present such an example, with the result that your surprising bravery and determination bowed down all the power of oppression under your feet, so much so that the Kashmiri government was obliged to admit that you were really oppressed.

The internal feud between Abdullah and the Mirwaiz now gave their enemies a 'golden opportunity'. The poster went on to say that clearly there were hot (extremist) and soft (moderate) parties, but with their combined efforts they could build up a nation. When the interests of moderation and extremism can work together, 'the national ship comes out of the whirlpool and anchors safety at a harbour of mutual object.'[23] Although the Government of India brought the poster to the Kashmir government's attention for containing 'considerable vilification' against the maharaja, it was not considered worth taking any legal action because it would give its author the opportunity of 'leading evidence in court in support of his main contention, which is that the Kashmir Government have promised reforms, but are apparently evading the fulfilment of their promise.'[24]

Glancy's recommendations had been supplemented by the Reform Conference, which proposed that a legislative assembly should be set up. Known as the Praja Sabha, it was to have seventy-five members, but, of its sixty non-official representatives only thirty-three were to be elected, leaving the maharaja with the majority vote. Abdullah was sceptical about the benefits of the assembly: 'What hopes can the people of this country have in this kind of representative Assembly where the dead weight of the official and nominated majority will always be ready to crush the popular voice?' he asked.[25] In 1934 a civil disobedience movement was mounted to press for the implementation of the reforms.

The first session of the Praja Sabha was held in October 1934. 'My comrades and I were fully aware that the proposed assembly was a hoax, but we wanted to use it as a forum to demonstrate that the Muslim Conference represented the majority of the population of the State,' said Abdullah. 'It was a strange assembly! All the legislative powers were in the hands of the Maharaja. He could also veto any act passed by the Assembly.'[26] But at least the Praja Sabha brought Muslims and non-Muslims together. In 1935 Sheikh Abdullah and Pandit Prem Nath Bazaz started an Urdu weekly newspaper known as *Hamdard* which later became a daily. Its first editor was Maulana Muhammad Masoodi who was to become a lifelong associate of Abdullah.

The empire speaks

By the early 1930s the British had once more become alarmed at the activities of the Soviet Union in Sinkiang, which they perceived threatened Gilgit directly. Even though much of their anxiety was without foundation, certain British officials, among them Olaf Caroe, the deputy secretary in the Indian Foreign Department, argued forcefully for resuming direct control over Gilgit. There was also the belief that so long as the British had maintained exclusive control over the maharaja's foreign affairs, as they had during the reign of Pratap Singh, they could be sure that the Jammu and Kashmir forces could be relied upon to act on behalf of the Government of India in an emergency over the northern frontier. But now that the maharaja was conducting his own foreign policy and did not appear to regard the frontier as 'sacrosanct' as the British, the time seemed right for a reassessment both of the costs of maintaining the agency and its direction. There had always been an uneasy relationship between the political agent, who was responsible for Punial jagir, the states of Hunza, Nagar as well as Yasin, Koh-Ghizar and Ishkoman and the wazar-i wazarat who controlled the tehsil of Gilgit and Astor.

In 1930 the resident, Lieutenant-Colonel Oglivie, prepared a detailed memorandum on the future of the Gilgit Agency in which he noted that in the past five years there had been a gradual erosion of the political agent's powers in Gilgit. The wazar-i wazarat had stopped the usual practice of meeting the political agent at a fixed hour once a week, and so had the local commandant of the Kashmiri troops. 'My own opinion is that if the political agent's position is so delicate that it can be undermined with such little difficulty, it is high time that other arrangements should be considered whereby the appointment should be placed on less fragile foundations.' Oglivie's suggestion was to withdraw the political agent, thereby relinquishing all British control of affairs in Gilgit in favour of the Kashmir government.[27]

The Government of India, however, was opposed to leaving complete control of the frontier districts in the hands of the maharaja. For financial reasons, British officials were also initially reluctant to consider taking over complete responsibility of the area itself. After over two years of discussion, the maharaja suggested that he would either take over responsibility for the

5. The Gilgit Agency, 1930
(Source: Charles Chenevix-Trench, *The Frontier Scouts*, London 1985)

defence of Gilgit, provided the dual administration of the political agent and
the wazarat was terminated; alternatively, he was prepared to hand over all
responsibility to the Government of India. Despite their financial concerns,
the British favoured the second alternative. The result of subsequent negotiations was the lease by the British of the Gilgit Agency north of the Indus
for a period of sixty years from 26 March 1935.

In 1935 the suggestion made at the first Round Table Conference for an
all-India federation was formulated in the Government of India Act. The
legislation provided for autonomous legislative bodies in the eleven provinces
of British India, as well as the creation of a central government which
would represent the provinces and the princely states. It also stipulated that
Muslim minorities would be protected. Although the princely states repres-

ented only a quarter of the population, they were given over a third of the seats in the federal legislature. This was, according to E. W. R. Lumby, a clear indication of the British intention that the princely states should form 'an element of conservatism, stability and loyalty to the British connection.'[28] The viceroy, Lord Linlithgow, invited the rulers of the Indian princely states to join the federation as provinces of British India. But, despite the princes' earlier support for an all-India federation, they raised various objections and all refused to enter it. 'Their status as sovereigns in their own States was to them supremely precious. Circumscribed though it had been by British paramountcy, they hated to yield any fraction of it to an India power, even if that power was to be partly themselves,' writes H. V. Hodson who became constitutional advisor to the viceroy in 1941.[29] According to Abdullah, the Muslim Conference believed that if Jammu and Kashmir were to join the federation it should be represented by its people and not the maharaja.[30]

The Government of India Act marked the beginning of the next stage in Britain's deliberations over how India should become self-governing. Amidst changing proposals, and the shifting attitude of the Indian National Congress Party and the Muslim League leaders, the idea of some sort of a federation remained a constant feature. As the largest and most northerly princely state, strategically located on the borders of China and the Soviet Union, the state of Jammu and Kashmir could have played a key role in future negotiations. But Hari Singh never seems to have given the future of his state, nor indeed the sub-continent, the consideration it deserved. When Sir Francis Wylie, a prominent Indian Political Service officer, visited the maharaja to explain the implications of the 1935 Act, he recalled how the discussions took place 'in the presence of a bored and sulky Hari Singh' and 'the whole matter took on, even for me, an air of complete unreality.'[31]

The first elections to the new provincial legislatures in British India took place in 1936. The Congress party, led by Jawaharlal Nehru and Sardar Patel, won in eight out of the eleven provinces. In Jammu and Kashmir the political leaders aimed at bringing about 'responsible' government under the nominal leadership of the maharaja. On 8 May 1936 the Jammu and Kashmir Muslim Conference organised Responsible Government Day, in which minority Sikhs and Hindus were also invited to participate. Abdullah, G. M. Sadiq, Mirza Afzal Beg, Bakshi Ghulam Muhammad and several others offered themselves for arrest. By 1937 the party had extended its influence to the working class who frequently took to the streets under the direction of Bakshi Ghulam Muhammad and Ghulam Muhammad Sadiq. Bakshi was becoming increasingly close to Sheikh Abdullah because of his links with the townspeople, especially the tonga drivers and boatmen. In the same way Mirza Afzal Beg added weight to Sheikh Abdullah's following because he represented the rural areas.[32]

Since his break with Mirwaiz Yusuf Shah, Abdullah's focus was entirely secular. On 26 March 1938 he addressed the Muslim Conference:

Like us, the large majority of Hindus and Sikhs in the state have immensely suffered at the hands of the irresponsible government. They are also steeped in deep ignorance, have to pay large taxes and are in debt and starving ... sooner or later these people are bound to join our ranks ... we must end communalism by ceasing to think in terms of Muslim and non-Muslims when discussing our political problems.[33]

As a Kashmiri Pandit active in the freedom struggle, Prem Nath Bazaz rejoiced at the trend towards secularism. 'The Freedom Movement had come out of the mire of communalism and was shining in all its brilliance in the high pedestal of Nationalism.'[34] At the end of August 1938 the political leaders once more took to the streets to protest against unemployment, high taxes, revenue demands and lack of medical facilities. Muslims, Hindus, Sikhs made common cause and went to jail together. 'Many Kashmiri Pandits fought shoulder to shoulder with Muslims and suffered equally with them,' writes Bazaz.[35]

As soon as they emerged from prison at the beginning of March 1939, they once more reiterated their commitment to secularism. 'The garb in the shape of the Muslim Conference has become outworn and threadbare,' said Ghulam Abbas at a special session of the Jammu and Kashmir Muslim Conference. 'Now we are in need of a Nationalist guise. The time has come when we should discard the old and decayed mantle and tear it to pieces.[36] The following day, on 11 June 1939 , the Muslim Conference finally changed its name to the 'National Conference'. Abdullah's adherence to nationalism brought him closer to Jawaharlal Nehru and the Indian Congress Party with its promises for a secular India. The first formal session of the newly constituted National Conference was held in the autumn of 1939. Jawaharlal Nehru sent a message: 'All the world is on the move and India must move with it, not separately or in isolation. India must attain her full freedom based on unity ... I hope that the Conference will view all these events that are happening in true perspective so that the people of Kashmir may attain their freedom in the larger freedom of India.'[37]

War and the 'New' Kashmir

On 3 September 1939, the viceroy, Lord Linlithgow, issued a proclamation that war had broken out between Britain and Germany and that there was a state of 'war emergency' in India. Congress politicians objected to their involvement in war without prior consultation with their representatives and used the issue of their co-operation with which to bargain for immediate independence. Mohammad Ali Jinnah and the Muslim League used their support to demand for representation in any decisions regarding the Muslims of India. The British were, however, in no position to grant what H. V. Hodson describes as 'mutually antagonistic' demands. The best they could offer was a consultative body, involving representatives of the political parties and of the Indian Princes. As an expression of their dissatisfaction, the Congress ministries, which had taken power after the 1936 elections, resigned. In March 1940 Nehru condemned a war 'for imperialist ends' to which the Congress could not in any way be party. He also affirmed that 'Congress would not admit the right of the Rulers of the Indian States or of foreign vested interests to come in the way of Indian freedom.'[38]

In March 1940 the Muslim League adopted the Lahore Resolution 'that the areas in which the Muslims are numerically in a majority, as in the north-western and eastern zones of India, should be grouped to constitute "independent states" in which the constituent units shall be autonomous and sovereign.'[39] Although it was not clear how such a proposal would be formalised, the demand for a separate homeland for the Muslims of the sub-continent had its roots in an emergent ideology, first proposed by a student, Chaudhuri Rahmat Ali in Cambridge in 1933 for the Muslims living in Punjab, North-West Frontier Province (Afghan Province) Kashmir, Sind and Baluchistan, to be recognised as a distinct nation, 'Pakstan' later called Pakistan. The scheme was drawn up for the Muslim delegates of the Round Table Conference, but since it would involve a large transfer of people, it was dismissed by the delegates as 'a student's scheme' which was 'chimerical' and 'impractical.'[40] The inclusion of predominantly Muslim Kashmir was, however, an early indication that there was already a body of opinion which believed that the princely state should become part of Pakistan, if and when it could be achieved. When alternative avenues for a federation of British India and the princely states had been exhausted, and partition of the sub-continent took place, this opinion held fast. Initially the demand for Pakistan was no more than an ideal. Mohammad Ali Jinnah, who cherished his own vision of Indian unity, kept the concept of Pakistan 'intentionally undefined', writes Ayesha Jalal. In this way, he was able 'to paint a thin veneer of solidarity and unanimity over interests which were neither solid nor unanimous.'[41]

As the war continued, both the Congress and the Muslim League continued to press for a plan for independence which would suit their varying objectives within a nominally united India. The entry of Japan into the war in 1941 and the threat of a Japanese invasion of the sub-continent did not inspire any of the political leaders to consider a compromise either with the British or amongst themselves. On 11 March 1942, four days after Rangoon fell to the Japanese, the British prime minister, Winston Churchill, announced that Sir Stafford Cripps, a member of the British war cabinet, would visit India with a 'draft declaration' on eventual independence after the war was over. But, faced with the possibility that Japan might be successful in invading India, there was little inclination amongst the political leaders to take Cripps' mission seriously. As Mahatma Gandhi was reported as asking, why accept 'a post-dated cheque on a bank that was obviously failing?'[42] The civil disobedience movement of the Congress politicians in British India, culminated in Gandhi's Quit India movement in August 1942 and the arrest of the leading Congress leaders. At the same time the Muslim League's demands for a separate homeland grew louder.

Pratap Singh had supported the war in 1914–18 with Kashmiri forces. In 1939 Hari Singh, who was one of the two Indian representatives in the Imperial War Cabinet, did the same. His military budget was increased from 35 to 76 lakhs and, in 1941, he went on a tour of the Middle East to meet the Kashmiri troops, who were engaged in the fighting and spent a considerable amount of time in Europe. Political activity was not, however, in abeyance. One of the most serious incidents against the war effort in Kashmir was the destruction of a silk weaving factory where parachute silk was being made. It followed a warning, which had not been received in time, that there would be damage to certain buildings 'in connection with the Congress agitation'.[43] Under the terms of the newly-introduced constitution in the state, the elected members of the legislative assembly were given a theoretical majority. But franchise was restricted and the maharaja still maintained control over the assembly. When the National Conference members threatened to resign, Hari Singh requested them to remain because the war meant fresh elections would not be possible.

By the end of 1943, India was comparatively calm and the acts of sabotage had decreased. The new viceroy, Field-Marshal Lord Wavell, who replaced Lord Linlithgow in October 1943, was committed to bringing the war to a successful conclusion against the Japanese. Politics came second. But, as British victory both in Europe and the Far East became assured, Wavell – described by H. V. Hodson as 'a brilliant soldier, with a strong artistic streak'[44] but lacking in diplomatic or political skills – became increasingly drawn into the difficult task of bringing independence to the sub-continent.

In the state of Jammu and Kashmir, Sheikh Abdullah busied himself with his plans for a 'New Kashmir' in what was one of the most advanced socialist programmes of its time. At the annual session of the National Conference at Sopore in September 1944, the members adopted the 'Naya Kashmir' manifesto. Abdullah promised a constitution which gave freedom, equality and democracy:

> To perfect our union in the fullest equality and self-determination, to raise ourselves and our children forever from the abyss of oppression and poverty, degradation and superstition, from mediaeval darkness and ignorance, into the sunlit valleys of plenty ruled by freedom, science and honest toil ... Women citizens shall be accorded equal rights with men in all fields of national life ... women shall be ensured rest, social insurance and education equally with men. The law shall give special protection of the interests of mother and child.[45]

Abdullah's progressive socialist thinking was reinforced by many of his advisers at this time. B. P. L. Bedi, whose Marxist leanings and those of his wife, Freda, were most apparent, drafted the manifesto for ' New Kashmir'. D. P. Dhar, also committed to socialism, had joined the National Conference as had the leftist sympathiser, G. M. Sadiq.

As Abdullah admits, initially 'New Kashmir' was opposed by 'reactionary' elements from amongst both the Hindus and Muslims. Inder Gujral, a Hindu from Jhelum, who was later to become India's foreign minister, describes how they succeeded in publishing the manifesto: 'Srinagar didn't have many printing presses in any case, and no printing press was willing to print it, so it was decided that the manuscript should be taken out. So I took it out to Lahore and there was a friendly proprietor, who had a printing press, but he was also afraid, and so he printed it at night.'[46]

Abdullah's choice

Abdullah's own position as the most dominant of the Muslim leaders in the valley, as well as the strength of his friendship with Jawaharlal Nehru, was a key factor in determining the future course of events.[47] Had Abdullah ever developed any understanding with Mohammad Ali Jinnah, or had, for example, Ghulam Abbas or another political figure taken Abdullah's place as a popular leader, the future of Kashmir could have been very different. But Abbas, born in Jullundur, was not a 'state subject' and, since he came from Jammu, he did not speak Kashmiri. His appeal amongst the valley Kashmiris was therefore reduced.

Abdullah is recorded as first meeting Nehru briefly in 1937. The following year, during a visit to Lahore, Nehru asked Abdullah to accompany him on a tour to the North-West Frontier Province. There Abdullah also met the Frontier leader, Abdul Ghaffar Khan. Although Muslims from Muslim majority areas, both Ghaffar Khan and Abdullah became secular supporters of the Congress party, led by Jawaharlal Nehru. In May 1940 Nehru, accompanied by Abdul Ghaffar Khan, visited Kashmir as much on a holiday as to strengthen their relations in what they perceived was their mutual struggle against communalism.

Those Muslims who were discontented with Abdullah's pro-Congress stance, especially the non-Kashmiri speakers, became staunch supporters of the Muslim League. In 1941 Ghulam Abbas broke with Abdullah and joined with Mirwaiz Yusuf Shah in reviving the Muslim Conference, which eventually came out in support of the movement for Pakistan. In Jammu the Muslims did not have the same majority status which they enjoyed in the valley. They were therefore liable to feel more threatened by the prospect of being governed by a Hindu majority.

Jawaharlal Nehru and the Congress Party had defined their position on the Indian states in August 1935: 'The Indian National Congress recognises that the people in the Indian states have an inherent right of Swaraj (independence) no less than the people of British India. It has accordingly declared itself in favour of establishment of representative responsible government in the States.'[48] On the other hand, Jinnah and the Muslim League made it clear that they did not wish to interfere with the internal affairs of the princely states. Despite Rahmat Ali's 1933 description of Kashmir forming part of Pakistan, Jinnah's main focus of attention remained with British India. 'We do not wish to interfere with the internal affairs of any State, for that is a matter primarily to be resolved between the rulers and the peoples of the States.'[49] Professor Zaidi explains Jinnah's policy on the grounds that he was a constitutional lawyer and was not willing to take any steps which went beyond his legal jurisdiction. Mohammad Ali Jinnah was also working single-handedly. 'Congress had Gandhi, Nehru, Patel, Menon. Jinnah was one man's political bureau all rolled in one. The League was not in a position to give the same attention to the future of the States as it gave to the British provinces.'[50] But Jinnah was not unconcerned by events within Kashmir. In 1943 he wrote to the viceroy, Lord Linlithgow, stating that he understood that 'the present situation is intolerable unless some responsible independent and impartial head of the Administration takes charge.'[51]

Abdullah's relationship with Jinnah never developed into anything beyond strained cordiality. They had first met in 1935 when Jinnah made a private visit to Kashmir which coincided with the Prophet's birthday. 'He spoke in English, and exhorted the Muslims, as the majority community, to respect the sentiments of the non-Muslims,' recorded Abdullah.[52] The two men remained in contact and, subsequently, Abdullah held discussions on the political situation with Jinnah in Delhi accompanied by Bakshi Ghulam Muhammad. However, when Jinnah returned to Kashmir nearly a decade later he and Abdullah had ideologically grown apart. Abdullah was critical of the 'two-nation' theory which asserted that there were two nations in the sub-continent, Muslims and Hindus. 'Jinnah had a very high opinion of himself and wanted to carve an eminent place for himself at the national level.'[53]

Jinnah's last visit to the state of Jammu and Kashmir took place in May 1944. 'When the frail but imperial figure of the leader passed through their rows,' writes Muhammad Saraf, who became a keen supporter of the movement for Pakistan, 'thousands of men and women were unable to control themselves as his very sight stirred up deep emotions resulting in tears trickling down their eyes. Many actually wept under the sheer weight of joy.'[54] Abdullah, G. M. Sadiq and Maulana Masoodi welcomed him on the outskirts of Srinagar. During his welcome address, Abdullah described Jinnah as 'a beloved leader of the Muslims of India'.

After being received by the leaders of the National Conference, Jinnah went on to address the Muslim Conference. He reaffirmed his belief in his non-secular Islamic platform and called upon all Muslims to join the Muslim Conference. 'If your objective is one, then your voice will also become one. I am a Muslim and all my sympathies are for the Muslim cause.'[55] Jinnah remained for nearly two months in the state. Whilst reaffirming the policy of the Muslim League not to interfere with the international administration of the state 'or the grave and serious issues that face the Maharaja and his government', he made it clear that 'we are certainly very deeply concerned with the welfare of the Mussulmans in the State.' Despite Abdullah's warm welcome, by the time Jinnah left, relations between the two men had soured. Jinnah maintained that Abdullah had 'indulged in all sorts of language of a most offensive and vituperative character in attacking me.'[56] Sheikh Abdullah's main criticism of Jinnah was directed towards Muslim League policy: 'Viewing the position from an all-India perspective, we find that Mr Jinnah has repeatedly declared that he does not extend his plans of Pakistan to the Indian States. Thus his conception of Islamic sovereignty halts at the customs barrier which divides our State from British India. Yet when it comes to giving advice, Mr Jinnah trespasses his own boundaries.'[57]

Towards the end of his stay Mohammad Ali Jinnah attempted to meet Hari Singh, who had recently returned from the war in Europe. 'Mr Jinnah sent him a letter welcoming him back and asking him for an appointment,' writes K. H. Khurshid, a young Kashmiri who was to become Jinnah's private secretary. 'This was politely turned down by the Maharaja on the pretext that he had various other commitments.'[58]

While he was in Kashmir, Jinnah had also recognised that the main problem facing the Muslim Conference in Kashmir was the absence of a 'presentable' Kashmiri speaking leader. 'Quaid-e Azam realised very early that unless the Party was able to approach Kashmiri speaking Muslims through a leader who could speak to them in their mother tongue, it was not possible to build up the organisation or effectively challenge the leadership of Sheikh Muhammad Abdullah.'[59] Attempts to find such a leader, including the suggestion that Ghulam Abbas learn Kashmiri, failed.

Writing in later life Abdullah recalled the outcome of Jinnah's visit: 'Jinnah's tour of Kashmir left him very bitter. He never excused the National Conference and its leaders, and we all know too well its traumatic consequences.'[60] According to Karan Singh, Jinnah 'had little use for Abdullah and his associates, partly because the Sheikh was not prepared to toe his line and partly because of Jinnah's messianic belief that he and his Muslim League were the sole guardians of Muslim interests in the sub-continent'.[61] Although, through intermediaries, subsequent efforts were made to open a dialogue between Jinnah and the Sheikh, the two men never met again. In his memoirs, Abdullah describes how he and his colleagues agonised over the choice between accession to India or Pakistan. 'If we were to accede to India, Pakistan would never accept our choice, and we would become a battleground for the two nations.'[62]

Once the war was over, the British Labour government under Clement Attlee initiated further steps towards giving independence to the sub-continent. In March 1946 Sir Stafford Cripps returned to India, as part of a three-man team, in order to propose a new Cabinet Mission plan. The objective was to try and reach agreement on the establishment of a constituent assembly which would draft the constitution of a self-governing but united India with safeguards guaranteeing the rights of minorities. Initially the Muslim League accepted the Cabinet Mission plan, with some reservations, but the Congress Party rejected it. While discussions continued in October 1946 an interim government was set up, made up solely of Indians. The announcement that full ruling powers would be returned to the rulers of the princely states left each of the 565 maharajas and nawabs with the responsibility of determining their own future.[63] The great majority had holdings of land constituting little more than a landed estate. Only twenty were of sufficient size for their rulers to be in a position to make serious decisions about their future, of which one was the state of Jammu and Kashmir.

Sheikh Abdullah objected to the decision being left to the maharaja who, he had consistently maintained, did not enjoy any support from the majority of the people. His message to Sir Stafford Cripps once again revived the issue of the sale of Kashmir to the Dogras a century earlier. 'Today the people of Kashmir cannot be pacified with only a representative system of governance. They want freedom. Total freedom from the autocratic Maharaja.' He therefore stated that at the termination of British rule Kashmir had the right to become independent. 'Ours is a unique land. Its physical beauty is unparalleled. Its strategic importance for military operations is undisputed, located as it is at the meeting point of the Chinese and Russian frontiers.'[64]

Mirroring Gandhi's Quit India movement of four years earlier, Sheikh Abdullah launched a Quit Kashmir Movement. 'The tyranny of the Dogras has lacerated our souls. The Kashmiris are the most handsome people, yet the most wretched looking. It is time for action. To end your poverty, you must fight slavery and enter the field of Jehad as soldiers.'[65] Abdullah's activities were once more courting the patience of the authorities. When he attempted to visit Nehru in Delhi, for the last time as a citizen of a princely state ruled by Maharaja Hari Singh, Sheikh Abdullah was arrested and put in prison. The prime minister, Pandit Kak, placed the state under martial law. G. M. Sadiq, D. P. Dhar, Bakshi Ghulam Muhammad went to Lahore where they remained until Independence in August 1947.

Abdullah's Quit Kashmir movement also came under criticism from his political opponents in the Muslim League who charged that he had begun the agitation in order to boost his popularity, which he was losing because of his pro-India policy. Prem Nath Bazaz, who had resigned from the National Conference in 1941 on the grounds that the party was no longer a 'revolutionary nationalist body',[66] accused him of opportunism. But as Mir Abdul Aziz, general secretary of the Muslim Students Union in Srinagar, noted, the Quit Kashmir movement gave a boost to the National Conference at the expense of the Muslim Conference:

A large section of the people was impressed by the stunt and they became National Conference-minded. At this time, according to my thinking, it was the duty of the Muslim Conference leaders either to jump into the Quit Kashmir movement headlong and get themselves finished or to denounce the Quit

Kashmir Movement as the Congress patronised it, and of course, with the help
of the local government, get a foothold in the political field of Kashmir. The
Muslim Conference did neither of the two things. In fact the Muslim Conference
leaders, including Abbas, were subconsciously won over by the Quit Kashmir
Movement.[67]

Mir Abdul Aziz also highlighted the difference of opinion existing between
the Muslim Conference members in Srinagar and those in Jammu. 'We can
carry on without interference of the Jammu leaders who have never helped
but have always spoiled our Muslim Conference.' But, as Alastair Lamb points
out, 'the relative quiescence of the Muslim Conference at this time undoubtedly did much to reinforce Jawaharlal Nehru's conviction (which was
to be such an important factor in the following year) that Sheikh Abdullah's
National Conference alone had any significant popular following in the State.'[68]

The leaders of the Muslim Conference were also taken into custody after
Ghulam Abbas led a 'campaign of action' similar to Jinnah's in British India.
Abbas and Abdullah were held in the same jail where they discussed in
night-long conversations the possibility of a reconciliation and resumption
of the common struggle. 'Both leaders recounted these conversations with
feelings of sadness and nostalgia. They seemed to share the belief that the
split in 1939 had been the beginning of all their troubles' writes Josef Korbel
who met the two men separately in 1948.[69]

In a dramatic gesture Nehru attempted to visit Kashmir on 24 July 1946
with the intention of defending Abdullah at his trial. Although he was refused
entry he stood at the border for five hours until finally he was allowed in,
only to be taken into protective custody. Karan Singh, the maharaja's son,
viewed his arrest as a turning point in relations between his father's government and the Indian National Congress Party. 'Here was the most charismatic
leader of the national movement for freedom ... the declared future Prime
Minister of the Indian Republic, and instead of welcoming him and seeking
his co-operation, we had arrested him.'[70] After his release, when Nehru tried
to visit Abdullah again, after the intercession of the viceroy, Lord Wavell, he
was able to enter the state and attend part of Abdullah's trial. The maharaja,
however, refused to meet him on the grounds of ill health.[71]

In January 1947, even though the main political leaders of both parties
remained in jail, the maharaja called for fresh elections to the legislative
assembly. The National Conference boycotted the elections with the result
that the Muslim Conference claimed victory. The National Conference,
however, said that the low poll demonstrated the success of their boycott;
the Muslim Conference attributed the low turnout to the snows and claimed
that the boycott was virtually ignored. The local Muslim Conference leaders,
however, continued to feel that they were not being given sufficient support
by the Muslim League and they blamed this on the League's policy of non-
interference in the internal affairs of the princely states. 'Muslims long for
the guidance of the League but they are dismayed – they complain of League's

"non-interference",' wrote Mohi-ud Din, a member of the Muslim Students Union to K. H. Khurshid to whom all correspondence to Jinnah was addressed. 'Pakistan needs Kashmir, and we need Pakistan. But the fight for it must begin now. Thus the policy of non-interference is beyond my understanding.'[72]

Shaukat Ali, the general secretary of the Muslim Conference who was imprisoned in Riasi sub-jail, also wrote to Khurshid on 24 March: 'What we are surprised about is the complete indifference and nonchalant attitude of the League *vis-à-vis* Kashmir ... you have been over-cautious not to offend the Princely order, so that they may support you, and not the Congress, in the future Indian Constitution-making, which they too have not done.' No volunteer, he complained, was sent to help with the January elections. 'Everybody has forgotten Kashmir. Look at the Congress and what they are doing for the National Conference – even if mingled with hypocrisy and window-dressing.'[73]

The maharaja's dilemma

'It has always seemed to me tragic that a man as intelligent as my father, and in many ways as constitutional and progressive, should have in those last years so grievously misjudged the political situation in the country,' writes Karan Singh. As Sheikh Abdullah increased his political following throughout the 1930s and 1940s, Hari Singh emerged as a helpless figure caught up in a changing world with which he was unable to keep pace. His son describes him as 'generally an enlightened ruler' who introduced reforms in the state far in advance of what other rulers had done in their states. But, he says, 'being a progressive ruler was one thing; coping with a once-in-a-millennium historical phenomenon was another.'[74] Much as the fate of Kashmir was shaped by the actions and convictions of Sheikh Abdullah, the maharaja's own role was fundamental in determining the future course of events.

Hari Singh had reacted to the freedom movement with cautious reforms, such as the Praja Sabha, which were designed to relieve that discontent without actually diminishing his own power. In 1944 the Praja Sabha had been given the right to nominate a panel of six, of which he would choose two people to join the Council of Ministers. For the first time a 'popular' element was introduced and those elected were Mirza Afzal Beg and Wazir Ganga Ram, a Muslim and Hindu respectively, who had achieved the greatest number of votes amongst the candidates. But the experiment was short-lived and the maharaja was soon challenged by both the National Conference and the Muslim Conference in their respective protest movements.

As Karan Singh also admits, his father was too much of a feudalist to be able to come to any real accommodation with the key protagonists in the changing order. He was also 'too much of a patriot to strike any sort of surreptitious deal' with the British. He was hostile to the Indian National

Congress, led by Gandhi, Nehru and Patel, partly because of Nehru's close friendship with Abdullah. Although the Muslim League supported the rulers' right to determine the future of their states, Hari Singh opposed the communalism inherent in the League's two-nation theory. Nor could he come to terms with the National Conference, because of the threat it posed to the Dogra dynasty. Thus, says Karan Singh, 'when the crucial moment came ... he found himself alone and friendless.'[75] Joining Pakistan would leave a substantial number of Hindus in Jammu as a minority (as well as Buddhists in Ladakh); joining India would go contrary to the advice given by the British that due consideration should be given to numerical majority and geographical contiguity. In retrospect, Karan Singh concluded that the only rational solution would have been to have initiated a peaceful partition of his state between India and Pakistan. 'But that would have needed clear political vision and careful planning over many years.'[76]

Furthermore, as ruler of one of the largest princely states, independence was an attractive option. For this utopian dream, Karan Singh partly blames the influence of Swami Sant Dev, a religious figure, who returned to Kashmir in 1946. The Swami encouraged the maharaja's feudal ambitions 'planting in my father's mind visions of an extended kingdom sweeping down to Lahore itself where our ancestor Maharaja Gulab Singh and his brothers Raja Dhyan Singh and Raja Suchet Singh had played such a crucial role a century earlier.'[77] It also meant that when critical decisions had to be made, the maharaja did nothing.

CHAPTER 9

Standstill in 1947

History seems sometimes to move with the infinite slowness of a glacier and
sometimes to rush forward in a torrent. Lord Mountbatten[1]

By 1947 the independence of the sub-continent was assured. How and when
still remained to be determined. On 20 February the British government
announced 'its definite intention to take necessary steps to effect the transference of power to responsible Indian hands by a date not later than June
1948.' The last attempt to keep the sub-continent together as a federation
had ended with the failure of the Cabinet Mission plan of 1946. Attempts
to bring together the political leaders of the Congress Party and Muslim
League were not succesful. The concept of Pakistan, 'the dream, the chimera,
the students' scheme', was to become reality.[2]

An indication of the shape which might constitute 'Pakistan' was provided
by the viceroy, Field-Marshal Lord Wavell, in 1946. Known as the 'Breakdown
Plan', his suggestion had been to give independence to the more homo-
geneous areas of central and southern India whilst maintaining a British
presence in the Muslim majority areas in the north-west and north-east.
Once agreement had been reached on final boundaries, the British would
withdraw. Part of the inspiration behind the plan was to demonstrate how,
by creating a country on the basis of Muslim majority areas only, Mohammad
Ali Jinnah would be left with a 'husk', whereas he stood to gain much more
by keeping the Muslims together in a loose union within a united India, as
proposed by the Cabinet Mission plan.[3] Although the 'Breakdown' plan was
finally rejected by the British government in January 1947, it had been the
subject of serious consideration in the Cabinet in London, by the governors
and in the viceroy's house, both before and after the failure of the Cabinet
Mission plan. The significance of the plan in the context of future events
is that long before the British conceded that partition along communal lines
was inevitable, there was already a plan in existence showing the geographical
effect such a partition would have on the sub-continent.

In March 1947, Lord Wavell was replaced as viceroy by Rear-Admiral
Lord Louis Mountbatten, whose brief from Prime Minister Attlee was 'to
obtain a unitary government for British India and the Indian States, if
possible.'[4] Soon after his arrival, Mountbatten made a gloomy assessment of
trying to revive the Cabinet Mission plan: 'The scene here is one of unrelieved

gloom … at this early stage I can see little common ground on which to
build any agreed solution for the future of India.'[5] Although his initial
discussions were not supposed to convey to the Indian political leaders that
partition was inevitable, by the end of April Mountbatten had concluded
that unity was 'a very pious hope'[6]

On 3 June the British government finally published a plan for the partition
of the sub-continent. On 18 July the Indian Independence Act was passed,
stating that independence would be effected on an earlier date than previously
anticipated: 15 August 1947. As Mountbatten's press secretary was to note:
'Negotiations had been going on for five years; from the moment the leaders
agreed to a plan, we had to get on with it.'[7] The sense of urgency was
heightened by civil disturbances and riots between the communities, which
were to reach frightening proportions in several areas, particularly in Punjab,
which bordered the state of Jammu and Kashmir.

Lobbying for accession

Although the Cabinet Mission plan was rejected, the recommendations for
the future of the 565 princely states, covering over two-fifths of the sub-
continent, with a population of 99 million, became the basis for their future
settlement. In a 'Memorandum on States' Treaties and Paramountcy' it was
stated that the paramountcy which the princely states had enjoyed with the
British Crown would lapse at independence because the existing treaty
relations could not be transferred to any successor. The 'void' which would
be created would have to be filled, either by a federal relationship or by
'particular political arrangements' with the successor government or governments, whereby the states would accede to one or other dominion.[8]

The state of Jammu and Kashmir had unique features not shared by
other princely states. Ruled by a Hindu, with its large Muslim majority it was
geographically contiguous to both India and the future Pakistan. In view of
a potential conflict of interest, there was 'pre-eminently a case for the same
referendum treatment that the Frontier received,' writes W. H. Morris-Jones,
constitutional adviser to Mountbatten. The North-West Frontier Province,
with its strong Congress lobby, led by Khan Abdul Ghaffar Khan, opposed
partition and favoured India. The decision was therefore put to the people
in a referendum. (The Congress party boycotted the referendum since the
option of an independent 'Pashtunistan' was not included, and the Muslim
League won an overwhelming majority.) A referendum in the state of Jammu
and Kashmir would, says Morris-Jones, have been 'a carefully considered
option – if only the States problem had been where it should have been in
June, high on the Mountbatten agenda' – which it was not. By the time
Mountbatten put forward the idea of a reference to the people in October,
it was too late. 'He was no longer Viceroy and so no longer in a position to
see it through as an integral part of the partition operation.'[9]

In hindsight, Sir Conrad Corfield, who was political adviser to the viceroy from 1945–47 also believed that, instead of listening to the advice of the Indian Political Department, Mountbatten preferred to take that of the Congress party leaders. Corfield had suggested that if Hyderabad, second largest of the princely states, with its Hindu majority and Muslim ruler, and Kashmir, with its Hindu ruler and Muslim majority, were left to bargain after independence, India and Pakistan might well come to an agreement. 'The two cases balanced each other ... but Mountbatten did not listen to me ... Anything that I said carried no weight against the long-standing determination of Nehru to keep it [Kashmir] in India.'[10]

Although Jawaharlal Nehru's family had emigrated from the valley at the beginning of the eighteenth century, he had retained an emotional attachment to the land of his ancestors. This was reinforced by his friendship with Abdullah and the impending changes in the sub-continent. In the summer of 1947 Nehru planned to visit the valley in order to see Abdullah in prison. But, given the troubled situation, Mountbatten was reluctant for either him or Gandhi to go there and decided to take up a long-standing invitation from Hari Singh to visit Kashmir himself.

On 18 June the viceroy flew to Srinagar. He had with him a long note prepared by Nehru, which, on the basis of Sheikh Abdullah's popularity in the valley, made out a strong case for the state's accession to India:

> Of all the people's movements in the various States in India, the Kashmir National Conference was far the most widespread and popular ... Kashmir has become during this past year an all-India question of great importance ... It is true that Sheikh Abdullah's long absence in prison has produced a certain confusion in people's minds as to what they should do. The National Conference has stood for and still stands for Kashmir joining the Constituent Assembly of India.

Nehru also pointed to the influence which the maharaja's prime minister, Ram Chandra Kak, had over him. Nehru held Kak responsible for the maharaja distancing himself from the National Conference and the possibility of joining the dominion of India. Most significantly, he made it clear to Mountbatten that what happened in Kashmir was:

> ... of the first importance to India as a whole not only because of the past year's occurrences there, which have drawn attention to it, but also because of the great strategic importance of that frontier State. There is every element present there for rapid and peaceful progress in co-operation with India.

He concluded by reaffirming Congress's deep interest in the matter and advising Mountbatten that, but for his other commitments, he would himself have been in Kashmir long ago.[11]

Although Pakistani accounts suggest that from the outset Mountbatten favoured Kashmir's accession to India, in view of his close association with Nehru, Mountbatten contended that he just wanted the maharaja to make up his mind. 'My chief concern was to persuade the Maharaja that he should decide which Dominion Kashmir should join, after consulting the wishes of his people and without undue pressure from either side, especially the Congress Leaders.'[12] He also brought the message from the Congress leaders that, if the maharaja were to decide in favour of Pakistan because of his Muslim majority population, they would not take it 'amiss'.[13]

During Mountbatten's short stay in Kashmir, the maharaja gave the viceroy very little opportunity to discuss the accession. As noted by his son, Karan Singh: 'Indecisive by nature, he merely played for time.'[14] Instead of taking advantage of Mountbatten's visit to discuss the future of the state, he sent Mountbatten on a fishing trip. Captain Dewan Singh, the maharaja's ADC, confirmed that Hari Singh had no intention of succumbing to any pressure: 'He told Mountbatten that he would consult with his people and meet with him the next day. The meeting was scheduled for 11 o'clock, but ten minutes before, the Viceroy was informed that the Maharaja was not feeling well. In fact the Maharaja did not want to meet Mountbatten again.'[15] On Mountbatten's return, his press secretary, Alan Campbell Johnson, noted that: 'Mountbatten had seen for himself the paralysis of Princely uncertainty.' The maharaja was 'politically very elusive'.[16]

Mountbatten believed, however, that he had succeeded in giving the maharaja some sound advice, which he hoped he would follow in due course. He suggested that the maharaja was not to join either of the constituent assemblies until the Pakistan Constituent Assembly had been set up and the situation was a bit clearer. He also advised that the maharaja should sign 'standstill' agreements with both India and Pakistan. Nehru was not pleased by the results. 'There was considerable disappointment at the lack of results of your visit,' he later wrote to the viceroy.[17]

When Lord Hastings Ismay, Mountbatten's chief of staff, visited Kashmir soon afterwards he received the same treatment as the viceroy: 'Each time that I tried to broach the question, the Maharaja changed the subject. Did I remember our polo match at Cheltenham in 1935? He had a colt which he thought might win the Indian Derby! Whenever I tried to talk serious business, he abruptly left me for one of his other guests.'[18] 'The Maharaja was in a Micawberish frame of mind, hoping for the best while continuing to do nothing,' observed former constitutional advisor V. P. Menon. 'Besides he was toying with the notion of an "independent Jammu & Kashmir"'.[19]

Despite the assurances given by Mountbatten to Hari Singh that the Congress leaders would not regard it as 'an unfriendly act',[20] if, given his Muslim majority population, he eventually acceded to Pakistan, it is clear that Nehru in particular had strong reasons for wanting the state of Jammu and Kashmir to accede to India. Furthermore, if the Muslim majority of the State of Jammu and Kashmir, under the popular leadership of Sheikh Abdullah, were to accede to India it would disprove the validity of Mohammad Ali Jinnah's two-nation theory.

Nehru was also supported by the formidable presence of Sardar Patel, who wrote to the maharaja on 3 July: 'I wish to assure you that the interest of Kashmir lies in joining the Indian Union without any delay. Its past history and traditions demand it, and all India looks up to you and expects you to take this decision.'[21] Sardar Patel's position in charge of the States Ministry in India, which he assumed on 5 July, gave him a unique platform from which to guide India's policy towards the states. He was to be assisted by V. P. Menon who already had intimate knowledge of the workings of the Government of India. Patel and Menon's influence persuaded Mountbatten to ensure adherence of the States before the lapse of British paramountcy, rather than leave them free to negotiate their future relationships with the successor states in what might potentially become turbulent conditions afterwards. Sardar Abdur Rab Nishtar and Mr Ikramullah were in charge of the States Ministry for Pakistan.

On 25 July, Mountbatten informed the Chamber of Princes that although their states would 'technically and legally' become independent, there were 'certain geographical compulsions' which could not be avoided. He therefore urged the princes to enter into 'standstill' agreements with the future authorities of India and Pakistan in order to make their own arrangements.[22] Although most of the states were too small to consider surviving on their own and geography determined their allegiance, three out of the 565 held back from taking any decision: Hyderabad, Junagadh and the state of Jammu and Kashmir.

When, at the end of July, Mountbatten heard that Nehru was once more planning to go to Kashmir he was not pleased: 'I called upon him as a matter of duty not to go running off to Kashmir until his new Government was firmly in the saddle and could spare his services.'[23] Mountbatten was obviously irritated by Nehru's insistence that he go to Kashmir and considered that a visit by Gandhi would be preferable, provided he did not make any inflammatory political speeches. In a confidential note to Colonel Wilfred Webb, the resident, Mountbatten had written: '[Nehru] is under very great strain and I consider that a visit by him to Kashmir at this moment could only produce a most explosive situation; whereas if His Highness can be persuaded to handle Gandhi tactfully, I believe there is a good chance that his visit could be passed off without any serious incident.'[24]

As Nehru persisted in attempting to visit Kashmir, Mountbatten continued to try and dissuade him. He noted that both the maharaja and his prime minister, Ram Chandra Kak, 'hate Nehru with a bitter hatred and I had visions of the Maharaja declaring adherence to Pakistan just before Nehru arrived and Kak provoking an incident which would end up by Nehru being arrested just about the time he should be taking over power from me in Delhi.' Mountbatten had also heard how, during a meeting with Patel, 'Nehru had broken down and wept, explaining that Kashmir meant more to him at the time than anything else.' After considerable correspondence between the

Congress leaders and the viceroy over whether Nehru or Gandhi would visit Kashmir the issue was finally resolved by Sardar Patel, who believed that neither should go but that in view of Pandit Nehru's great mental distress if his mission in Kashmir were to remain unfulfilled, he agreed that one of them must go. Mountbatten noted that Patel bluntly remarked: 'It is a choice between two evils and I consider that Gandhiji's visit would be the lesser evil.'[25]

The Congress leaders' interest in Kashmir evidently disturbed the future leaders of Pakistan. The sub-continent was in the midst of a deep communal and political crisis. Yet both Nehru and Gandhi had insisted on visiting Kashmir. No Muslim leader visited the princely states of Hyderabad or Junagadh, nor did they visit Kashmir. Nehru and Gandhi were both known to be opposed to the maharaja making any declaration of independence. In addition the princes of Patiala, Kapurthala, and Faridkot from east Punjab visited Hari Singh in the summer, as well as the president of the Indian National Congress, Acharya J. B. Kripalani. Why so many visitors, all of whom must surely have had a vested interest in the advice they gave?

Gandhi finally left for Srinagar on 1 August. Muhammad Saraf was amongst those who protested at his arrival in Baramula. 'The biggest, noisiest demonstration was organised by me against Gandhi. Even some glass panes of his car were broken by the demonstrators.' In the event, Gandhi's visit passed off without any serious incident. But Saraf believed that during his meeting with the maharaja and the maharani, he persuaded the maharaja to accede to India.[26] 'Before his departure from Delhi the "Apostle of Truth" announced that his tour was absolutely non-political,' writes Shahid Hamid, private secretary to Field-Marshal Auchinleck. 'In reality it was to pressurise the Maharaja to accede to India and to remove Kak.'[27]

The Muslim Conference in Srinagar, whose leaders remained in prison after their 1946 agitation, was also perturbed by the potential impact of the pro-India lobby in Kashmir. 'The trouble was that whereas the Congress said that the people of the States will decide the future, the Muslim League was continuing to stress that the rulers will decide.' says Mir Abdul Aziz.[28] In a state like Hyderabad, ruled by the Muslim nizam, there was a clear political advantage in supporting the ruler, despite its location in the heart of India, but with Jammu and Kashmir, the Muslim League was obliged to rely on the wisdom of Hari Singh. 'I have no doubt that the Maharaja and the Kashmir Government will give their closest attention and consideration to this matter and realise the interests not only of the Ruler but also of his people,' Jinnah had declared in July 1947. 'Wisdom demands that the feelings and sentiments of the Muslims who form 80 per cent of the population should not be ignored, much less hurt.'[29]

Unlike the Congress leaders, Jinnah had also endorsed the right of the princely states to remain independent: 'If they wish to remain independent and wish to negotiate or adjust any political or any other relationship such as commercial or economic relations with Pakistan, we shall be glad to discuss with them.'[30] He was not alone in this view. Sir Walter Monckton, adviser to the government of Hyderabad, believed that provided the princely states were 'fairly treated' they had 'a sounder hope of survival than the brittle political structure of the Congress party after they have attained inde-pendence.'[31]

The Boundary Commission

An extraordinary feature of the partition of the sub-continent, which was effected on the day of its independence from British rule, is that the details were not officially revealed in advance. Lord Ismay explained that, in his opinion, the announcement was 'likely to confuse and worsen an already dangerous situation.'[32] There were, however, enough areas of concern in the border districts to arouse the interest of Hindus, Muslims and Sikhs as to where exactly the partition would be effected.

The Partition Plan of 3 June 1947, established under the Indian Independ-ence Act, envisaged two Boundary Commissions, consisting of four High Court judges each, two nominated by Congress and two by the Muslim League. The chairman was to hold the casting vote. The man entrusted with that post was a British lawyer, Sir Cyril Radcliffe, who arrived in India for the first time on 8 July 1947. The objective of what came to be known as the Radcliffe Award was to divide the provinces of Punjab in the west and Bengal in the east, leaving those Muslim majority areas in Pakistan and those with Hindu majorities in India. There was, however, a loose provision that 'other factors' should be taken into account, without specifying what they might be. Radcliffe had just five weeks to accomplish the task.

Since the state of Jammu and Kashmir adjoined British India, the partition of the sub-continent was relevant insofar as where the existing lines of communication would fall. Of the main routes by which Kashmir could be reached, two roads passed through areas which could be expected to be allocated to Pakistan: the first via Rawalpindi, Murree, Muzaffarabad, Baramula and thence to Srinagar – the route so treacherously undertaken in winter by Sher Singh, when he was governor of Kashmir in the 1840s; the other route went via Sialkot, Jammu and the Banihal pass. A third route, which was no more than a dirt track, existed via the district of Gurdaspur, which comprised the four tehsils of Shakagarh, Batala, Gurdaspur and Pathankot. A railway line from Amritsar passed through Gurdaspur tehsil and on to Pathankot. Another railway line went from Jullundur as far as Mukerian; from there the journey could be continued directly to Pathankot on another unsurfaced track via Bhangala by crossing the Beas river by ferry. From Pathankot the route carried on to Madophur, across the Ravi river to Kathua in the state of Jammu and Kashmir.

Under the 'notional' award provided in the first Schedule of the Indian

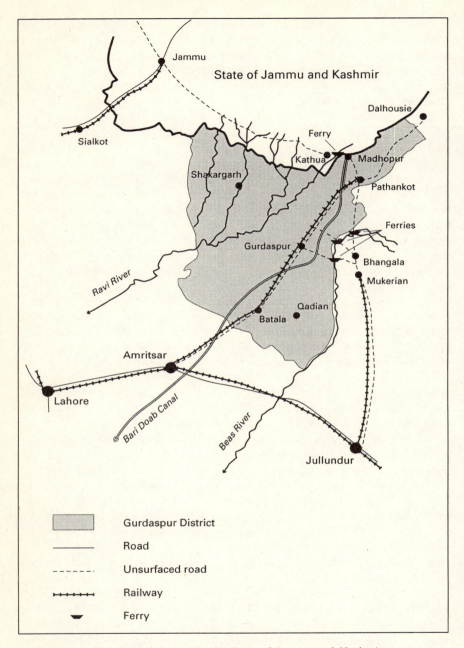

6. Gurdaspur District and Access to the State of Jammu and Kashmir
(Source: Royal Geographical Society Collection. Published under the direction of the
Surveyor-General of India, revised 1937)

Independence Act, all of the Gurdaspur district, with a 51.14 per cent Muslim majority had been assigned to Pakistan, which meant that all these routes would have fallen under the control of Pakistan. At his press conference on 4 June, in answer to a question regarding provisional and final demarcations, Mountbatten, however, suggested that the Boundary Commission would be unlikely 'to throw' the whole of the Gurdaspur district into the Muslim majority areas.[33] Of Gurdaspur district's four tehsils, one, Pathankot, was predominantly Hindu. Subsequently, the revised Mountbatten plan referred to the basis for partition by area rather than by district. The future Pakistanis soon became concerned by the prospect of a departure from the 'notional' award giving all of Gurdaspur district to Pakistan to one where part of Gurdaspur would be allocated to India. Chaudhri Muhammad Ali, one of the two joint secretaries on the Partition Council, suggested that it was 'highly improper' for Mountbatten to be commenting on the likely award. According to his account, his suspicions were confirmed when, upon instructions from Jinnah, he visited Mountbatten's chief of staff, Lord Ismay, on 9 August to talk about Gurdaspur. At first Ismay did not appear to understand Chaudhri Muhammad's concern. 'There was a map hanging in the room and I beckoned him to the map so that I could explain the position to him with its help. There was a pencil line drawn across the map of the Punjab.' The line followed the boundary along the Ravi river, which Jinnah had heard was to be drawn, allocating three of the four tehsils in Gurdaspur district to India. 'Ismay turned pale and asked in confusion who had been fooling with his map.'[34] Ismay, however, does not refer to this incident in his memoirs.

In the final award the three tehsils of Batala, Gurdaspur and Pathankot went to India. A memorandum prepared by the minister of state, which included Radcliffe's observations after he returned to England, reported that the reason for changing the 'notional' award regarding Gurdaspur was because 'the headwaters of the canals which irrigate the Amritsar District lie in the Gurdaspur District and it is important to keep as much as possible of these canals under one [i.e. Indian] administration.'[35] Wavell, however, had made a more significant political judgement in his plan, submitted to the secretary of state, Lord Pethick-Lawrence, in February 1946: 'Gurdaspur must go with Amritsar for geographical reasons and Amritsar being sacred city of Sikhs must stay out of Pakistan ... Fact that much of Lahore district is irrigated from upper Bari Doab canal with headworks in Gurdaspur district is awkward but there is no solution that avoids all such difficulties.' Wavell had also noted the problem this would create by leaving Qadian, the holy city of the Ahmadiyyas, in India, but the interests of the Sikhs were considered to be paramount. 'The greatest difficulty is position of Sikhs with their homelands and sacred places on both sides of the border. This problem is one which no version of Pakistan can solve.'[36] The Boundary Commission was supposed to be working in absolute secrecy and Radcliffe's award has always been presented as entirely original, even though in its final form, apart from the

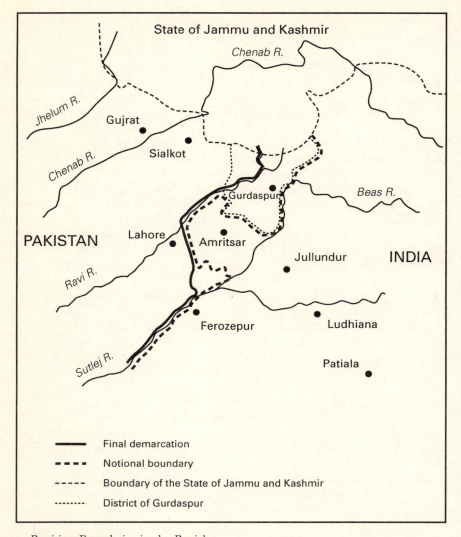

7. Partition Boundaries in the Punjab
(Source: Nicholas Mansbergh, (ed.) *The Transfer of Power*, 1942–47, Vol X11, London, 1983)

award of the Chittagong Hills in Bengal, which Wavell gave to India and Radcliffe awarded to Pakistan, the two plans are remarkably similar. Wavell, however, emphasised more strongly the British fear of upsetting the Sikhs as a key factor in determining the award of Gurdaspur to India.

It is also clear from correspondence emanating from the viceroy's house that the element of secrecy was selective. Mountbatten had chosen not to announce the partition plan until after independence in order not to 'mar' the celebrations, but this did not mean that advance information could not be given to the governors 'so that the best dispositions might be made of military forces and police.'[37] On 8 August Sir George Abell, Mountbatten's private secretary, who had also worked under Wavell and had been in London to present the 'Breakdown Plan' to the Cabinet in January 1947, wrote to Stuart Abbott, secretary to Sir Evan Jenkins, the governor of the Punjab, a 'top secret' letter: 'I enclose a map showing roughly the boundary which Sir Cyril Radcliffe proposes to demarcate in his award.'[38] Lord Ismay also asked for 'such advance information as could be given me of the award, so that the military and civil authorities directly concerned with law and order might make their plans, and if necessary redistribute their forces.' He did not address his request to the Boundary Commission 'with whose proceedings I had nothing whatever to do, but to the Viceroy's house.'[39] When this letter became public a few months later, it merely increased Pakistani suspicions that the viceroy and his staff were well aware of the disposition of the award. And if they were aware of it, might they also, for their own reasons, seek to alter it?

The suspicions created in the minds of the Pakistanis by the award of three tehsils of Gurdaspur to India were compounded by the issue of the 'salient' of the Ferozepur and Zira tehsils. In the map of the Radcliffe award, which Abell sent to Abbot, the salient, which protruded beyond the notional boundary into the Sikh heartland, was marked as part of Pakistan and, for once, did not accord with Radcliffe's preference for keeping Pakistan to the west of the Sutlej, but was theoretically designed to give a more equitable share of control over the canal headworks. A day after Abell sent his letter to Abbott, together with the map, the first serious massacre by Sikhs of prominent Muslim bureaucrats on the 'first Pakistan special' train which was shifting members of the government from Delhi to Karachi on 9 August occurred. Sometime after this date the boundary was finalised with the salient as part of India. Although the reason for its eventual inclusion in India was most probably in order to take into account the interests of the militant Sikhs rather than to deprive Pakistan of territory, sensitive as the Pakistanis were, it was not easy for them to rationalise the logic of draft awards which went in their favour, on the basis of Muslim majorities, only to be removed because of 'other factors.' 'It is very strange that other factors should have worked consistently in favour of India and against Pakistan,' commented Chaudhri Muhammad Ali.[40] Ironically, Wavell had not awarded the salient to Pakistan in the first place, probably because, as with the award of Gurdaspur, he was more concerned about the Sikhs.

The departure from the 'notional' award to Radcliffe's division of Gurdaspur between the two Dominions has created considerable bitterness, not only because of the loss of territory, but because of the growing realisation that India was thereby assured of access to the state of Jammu and Kashmir. Although the future of the princely states was a separate issue from the division of the Punjab and Bengal, for which purpose the Boundary Commission was instituted, Mountbatten himself had made the connection between Jammu and Kashmir and the award of the Boundary Commission. Kashmir, he said, 'was so placed geographically that it could join either Dominion, provided part of Gurdaspur were put into East Punjab by the Boundary Commission.[41] V. P. Menon, who Wavell had described as the 'mouthpiece' of Sardar Patel,[42] was thinking along the same lines: Kashmir 'does not lie in the bosom of Pakistan, and it can claim an exit to India, especially if a portion of the Gurdaspur district goes to East Punjab.[43]

Had the whole of Gurdaspur District been awarded to Pakistan, according to Lord Birdwood, 'India could certainly never have fought a war in Kashmir.'[44] Birdwood maintained that even if only the three Muslim tehsils had gone to Pakistan 'the maintenance of Indian forces within Kashmir would still have presented a grave problem for the Indian commanders, for their railhead at Pathankot is fed through the middle of the Gurdaspur tehsil.' 'Batala and Gurdaspur to the south,' said Chaudhri Muhammad Ali 'would have blocked the way'.[45] The fourth route which passed through Hindu Pathankot tehsil, would have been much more difficult to traverse. Although it did provide geographical access, the railway at the time extended only as far as Mukerian and it required an extra ferry coming across the river Beas.

The Indian journalist, M. J. Akbar, interprets the award as a simple piece of political expediency on the part of Nehru. 'Could Kashmir remain safe unless India was able to defend it? Nehru could hardly take the risk. And so, during private meetings, he persuaded Mountbatten to leave this Gurdaspur link in Indian hands.'[46] This seems an over-simplification, given the other issues at stake, especially concern for the Sikhs. But in view of inadequate explanations and selective secrecy surrounding the Radcliffe award, the belief amongst Pakistanis that there was a conspiracy between Mountbatten and Nehru to deprive Pakistan of Gurdaspur has held fast. Mountbatten and his apologists repeatedly denied any prior knowledge of the award or any discussions with Sir Cyril Radcliffe. Christopher Beaumont, secretary to Radcliffe, asserts, however, that in the case of Ferozepur (although not over Gurdaspur) Radcliffe was persuaded to give the Ferozepur salient to India.[47] Alan Campbell-Johnson, however, maintains that Beaumont based this allegation on the proceedings of a meeting at which he was not present and about which he was not briefed.[48] When Professor Zaidi questioned Radcliffe in 1967, he said that he had destroyed his papers, in order 'to keep the validity of the award.'[49]

Stories of bad relations between Mountbatten and Muhammad Ali Jinnah also added fuel to the Pakistani argument that Mountbatten was not well disposed towards Pakistan and hence not willing to see Kashmir go to the new Dominion. 'He talked about mad, mad, mad Pakistan,' says Professor Zaidi.[50] As Morris-Jones relates, Mountbatten had assumed that he would continue as governor-general of the two dominions. 'When Jinnah, after long consideration, told him in July that the first Governor-General of Pakistan would be Jinnah himself, the hope of a common Head of State was blasted and Mountbatten took it as a shattering blow to his own pride. As far as I can see from the records, that was the only moment in all the months of frustrating negotiations when the Viceroy lost his temper; on his own account he exploded in fury at Jinnah and stormed out of the room.'[51]

Pakistani apprehension about the intentions of both the Indians and the British arose from their long-standing feeling that neither Britain nor India wanted nor expected Pakistan to survive. They therefore wanted Kashmir in order to gain a strategic advantage over Pakistan and put pressure on Pakistan's north-eastern border. Possession of Kashmir would also give control of the headwaters of the important rivers which watered the plains of the Indus valley. 'The object of grabbing Kashmir was to encircle Pakistan militarily and strangle it economically,' writes Suhrawardy. 'India would have, through Gilgit, a common border with Afghanistan, then openly hostile to Pakistan and the only country in the world which opposed Pakistan's admission as member of the UN. Pakistan would get sandwiched and with the active support of India and Afghanistan, the Pukhtoonistan stunt backed by the Frontier Gandhi, Abdul Ghaffar Khan, would be used for military intervention.'[52] Anti-Pakistani feeling stemmed, believed Suhrawardy, from India's contention expressed in the Congress Resolution of 5 June 1947: 'Geography and mountains and the sea fashioned India as she is, and no human agency can change that shape or come in the way of her final destiny.' The resolution went on to say that once 'present passions' had subsided 'the false doctrine of two nations will be discredited and discarded by all.'[53] Every move on the part of India was therefore interpreted by the future Pakistanis as being part of this long-term strategy.

Independence?

In 1947, only the maharaja and a few close associates may have entertained the idea of remaining independent. Mountbatten was most unreceptive to this third possibility. In a long letter to the Earl of Listowel, dated 8 August, he wrote:

> The Indian Dominion, consisting nearly of three-quarters of India, and with its immense resources and its important strategic position in the Indian Ocean, is a Dominion which we cannot afford to estrange for the fate of the so-called independence of the States. I have no doubt that you will agree with me that we should leave no stone unturned to convince the Indian Dominion that although we had to agree to the plan of partition, we had no intention to leave it balkanised or to weaken it both internally and externally.

In addition, he did not want the reputation of Britain to suffer because the situation regarding the states was not fully resolved at independence:

If we leave the States without association with one or the other of the two
Dominions, there will be plenty of justification for the allegations against us
that while we unilaterally terminated all treaties and agreements, we took no
steps for the safety and security of the States from either internal troubles or
external aggression.[54]

But the maharaja's prime minister, Ram Chandra Kak, a Kashmiri Brahmin
described by Karan Singh as 'the one man who had the intellectual capacity
to make some coherent effort towards an acceptable settlement',[55] was also
believed to be the main force behind the maharaja's reluctance to join India.[56]
On the eve of independence, with obvious pressure from Delhi, the maharaja
replaced his prime minister with a retired army officer. Mountbatten saw this
as a sign that the main obstacle against accession to one or other dominion
was now out of the way. He was pleased to note on 16 August, after the
'sacking' of Kak, that the maharaja now talks of holding a referendum to
decide 'whether to join Pakistan or India, provided that the Boundary
Commission give him land communication between Kashmir and India.'
Mountbatten went on to observe with obvious, but misplaced, relief: 'it
appears therefore as if this great problem of the States has been satisfactorily
solved within the last three weeks of British rule.'[57]

Mountbatten was, however, precipitate in his analysis. When the sub-
continent became independent from British rule on 14–15 August, for the
first time since Yaqub Shah Chak submitted to Akbar in 1589, the state of
Jammu and Kashmir was independent. It remained so for seventy-three days.
On 12 August, in an exchange of telegrams, Hari Singh made a 'standstill'
agreement with Pakistan. The objective was to ensure that those services
which existed for trade, travel and communication would carry on in the
same way as they had with British India. Pakistan therefore retained control
of the rail and river links, which were used to float timber down the Jhelum
river to the plains. India did not, however, sign a standstill agreement. V. P.
Menon's explanation is revealing given the interest Congress had shown in
Kashmir in the months preceding independence: 'We wanted to examine its
implications. We left the State alone ... moreover, our hands were already
full and if truth be told, I for one had simply no time to think of Kashmir.'[58]
That India did not sign a standstill agreement with the state of Jammu and
Kashmir has merely added to the suspicion amongst Pakistanis that the Indian
government was already engaged in making its own arrangements for
Kashmir's future and did not consider a standstill agreement to be a necessary
part of those plans. The standstill agreement signed with Pakistan, says Abdul
Suhrawardy, was really 'a camouflage to hide the real designs and lull Pakistan
and her supporters into a false sleep of satisfaction.'[59]

In the state of Jammu and Kashmir there were staunch Muslim League
supporters who believed they would become part of Pakistan at independence
and when freedom came at midnight on 14 August they rejoiced. The
Pakistani flag was hoisted on most of the post offices until the government

of the maharaja ordered that they should be taken down. All pro-Pakistani newspapers were closed. Muhammad Saraf was in Baramula, where the flag remained flying until dusk: 'It was a spectacle to watch streams of people from all directions in the town and its suburbs swarming towards the Post Office in order to have a glimpse of the flag of their hopes and dreams.'[60] Those whose hopes were dashed at not becoming part of Pakistan set in train a sequence of events which was rooted in their past disappointment.

Revolt in Poonch

Of the 71,667 citizens of the state of Jammu and Kashmir who served in the British Indian forces during World War II, 60,402 were Muslims from the traditional recruiting ground of Poonch and Mirpur.[61] After the war, the maharaja, alarmed at the increasing agitation against his government, refused to accept them into the army. When they returned to their farms, they found 'not a land fit for heroes, but fresh taxes, more onerous than ever,' writes the British pacifist, Horace Alexander. 'If the Maharaja's government chastised the people of the Kashmir valley with whips, the Poonchis were chastised with scorpions.'[62] Throughout his reign, Hari Singh had been working to regain control of Poonch. As a jagir of Gulab Singh's brother, Dhyan, although a fief of the maharaja, Poonch had retained a degree of autonomy. Friction between the maharaja and the Raja of Poonch had remained ever since Pratap's adoption of Kumar Jagat Dev Singh as his spiritual heir. After a lawsuit, the maharaja had succeeded in dispossessing the rajah and bringing the administration of Poonch in line with the rest of the state of Jammu and Kashmir. This move was not welcomed by the local people. 'There was a tax on every hearth and every window,' writes Richard Symonds, a social worker with a group of British Quakers working in the Punjab: 'Every cow, buffalo and sheep was taxed, and even every wife.' An additional tax was introduced to pay for the cost of taxation. 'Dogra troops were billeted on the Poonchis to enforce the collection.'[63]

In the Spring of 1947, the Poonchis had mounted a 'no-tax' campaign. The maharaja responded by strengthening his garrisons in Poonch with Sikhs and Hindus. In July he ordered all Muslims in the district to hand over their weapons to the authorities. But, as communal tension spread, the Muslims were angered when the same weapons appeared in the hands of Hindus and Sikhs. They therefore sought fresh weapons from the tribes of the North-West Frontier who were well known for their manufacture of arms. This laid the basis for direct contact between the members of the Poonch resistance and the tribesmen who lived in the strip of mountainous 'tribal' territory bordering Pakistan and Afghanistan. In the belief that the maharaja had passed an order to massacre the Muslims, a thirty-two year-old Suddhan, Sardar Mohammed Ibrahim Khan, collected together the ex-soldiers amongst the Suddhans. 'We got arms from here and there and then we started fighting the Maharaja's army.' In about two months he says he had organised an army of about 50,000.[64]

The transfer of power by the British to the new Dominions of Pakistan and India on 14–15 August brought no respite to the troubled situation which the maharaja now faced as an independent ruler. Unrest in Poonch had turned into an organised revolt against the Dogras, which was reminiscent of the rebellion led by Shams-ud Din in 1837. Amongst the activists was a young landowner, Sardar Abdul Qayum Khan, who came from Rawalakot:

> Unlike many other people who believed that the partition plan would be implemented with all sincerity of purpose, I thought that perhaps India would like to obtain Kashmir and that is why the armed revolt took place. Against the declared standstill agreement, the maharaja had started moving his troops along the river Jhelum. It was an unusual movement which had never happened before and I could see that it had a purpose of sealing off the border with Pakistan. In order to thwart that plan, we rose up in arms.[65]

Qayum Khan withdrew to the forests outside Rawalakot, from where the message of rebellion was spread throughout Poonch and south to Mirpur. The close links with their neighbours on the western side of the Jhelum river meant that the border was impossible to seal and the maharaja's government attributed the trouble in Poonch to infiltration from Pakistan. 'Intelligence reports from the frontier areas of Poonch and Mirpur as well as the Sialkot sector started coming in which spoke of large-scale massacre, loot and rape of our villagers by aggressive hordes from across the borders,' writes Karan Singh. 'I recall the grim atmosphere that began to engulf us as it gradually became clear that we were losing control of the outer areas.' He records how his father handed him some reports in order to translate them into Dogri for his mother. 'I still recall my embarrassment in dealing with the word "rape" for which I could find no acceptable equivalent.'[66]

The Pakistani government, however, believed the uprising in Poonch was a legitimate rebellion against the maharaja's rule, which was gaining increasing sympathy from the tribesmen of the North-West Frontier, who were also sympathetic to the troubles in the Punjab. On 23 September, George Cunningham, governor of the North-West Frontier Province noted: 'I have offers from practically every tribe along the Frontier to be allowed to go and kill Sikhs in eastern Punjab and I think I would only have to hold up my little finger to get a lashkar of 40,000 to 50,000.'[67]

Poonch was also undoubtedly affected by events in neighbouring Jammu. Whereas the valley of Kashmir was protected by its mountain ranges from the communal massacres which devastated so many families in the weeks following partition, Jammu had immediate contact with the plains of India and, as a result, was subject to the same communalist hatred which swept throughout the Punjab and Bengal. According to Pakistani sympathisers, whilst deliberating over accession, the maharaja was undertaking a systematic purge of Muslims. 'Certain it is that the Maharajah's government was using its Dogra troops to terrorise many Muslim villages in the neighbourhood of Jammu,' wrote Horace Alexander. 'Later in the year, I myself saw villages near Jammu that had been completely gutted.'[68]

Ian Stephens, editor of *The Statesman,* Calcutta, noted the situation in Jammu: 'Unlike every part of the state, Hindus and Sikhs slightly out-numbered Muslims, and within a period of about 11 weeks, starting in August, systematic savageries ... practically eliminated the entire Muslim element in the population, amounting to 500,000 people. About 200,000 just disappeared, remaining untraceable, having presumably been butchered or died from epidemic or exposure. The rest fled to West Punjab.'[69] There they reported that these atrocities had been perpetrated 'not only by uncontrolled bands of hooligans but also by organised units of the Maharaja's army and Police.'[70] In September, the outgoing chief of staff of the Jammu and Kashmir State Forces, Major-General Scott, had informed the maharaja that the situation was becoming difficult for his army to control on its own.

Manoeuvres

In the weeks following independence, despite the signature of the standstill agreement with Pakistan, political manoeuvring was taking place on all sides. Both Pakistan and India were actively trying to determine events so that Kashmir would accede to their respective Dominions. India retained the upper hand and despite the maharaja's dislike for Nehru, he communicated more regularly and amicably with the Indian leaders than with those in Pakistan. Although he had rejected Mountbatten's suggestion of retaining military links with either India or Pakistan, on 13 September he requested the Government of India for the loan of an Indian army officer to replace Major-General Scott as his commander-in-chief.

Prime Minister Nehru and Sardar Patel, who had become minister for Home Affairs, corresponded regularly in order to determine how Kashmir could be secured for India. 'One of the most interesting revelations of the Patel papers when they began to be published in 1971,' writes Alastair Lamb 'was the extent to which this powerful Congress politician had directly involved himself in all planning directed towards an eventual Indian acquisition of the State of Jammu and Kashmir.'[71]

Clear steps were being taken to improve communications with India, by telegraph, telephone, wireless and roads. On 27 September *The Pakistan Times* reported: 'the metalling of the road from Jammu to Kathua is also proceeding at top speed. The idea is to keep up some sort of communication between the State and the Indian Union, so that essential supplies and troops could be rushed to Kashmir without having to transport them through Pakistani territory.'[72] A boat bridge was also being constructed over the Ravi river near Pathankot, which would improve the access from Gurdaspur. In addition, there were reports that the Kashmir government was constructing an all weather road linking the valley of Kashmir with Jammu via Poonch instead of the Banihal road which was impassable in winter. In Pakistan it was widely believed that India was preparing to announce Kashmir's accession to India in the autumn. The Pakistani government alleged that India had violated the standstill agreement, because they had included Kashmir within the Indian postal system. As evidence, they produced a memorandum, dated 1 September 1947, signed by the director-general of Postal Telegraph, New Delhi, in which towns in the State of Jammu and Kashmir were listed as part of India.[73]

The Indian leaders were equally anxious about Pakistani moves. The armed raids from Pakistani territory into the state and disturbances in Poonch led the Indians to believe that there would be a full-scale Pakistani incursion before winter.: 'I understand that the Pakistan strategy is to infiltrate into Kashmir now and to take some big action as soon as Kashmir is more or less isolated because of the coming winter,' Nehru wrote to Patel on 27 September.[74] Nehru therefore suggested to Patel that the maharaja should 'make friends' with the National Conference, 'so that there might be this popular support against Pakistan.' Nehru had hoped that the maharaja could be persuaded to accede to India before any invasion took place and he realised that accession would only be more easily accepted if Abdullah, as a popular leader, were brought into the picture.

Two days after this letter, on 29 September, Abdullah, who had been in prison since his Quit Kashmir movement in 1946, was released from jail. His letter pledging allegiance to the maharaja was widely publicised. But he also repeated his pre-independence rhetoric: 'When I went into prison, I took a last look at undivided India. Today it has been broken into two fragments. We the people of Kashmir must now see to it that our long-cherished dream is fulfilled. The dream of freedom, welfare and progress.'[75] At the beginning of October Dwarkanath Kachru, the secretary of the All-India States Peoples' Conference, visited Srinagar with the objective of convincing Abdullah of the merits of joining India. He reported back to Nehru that 'Sheikh Abdullah and his close associates have decided for the Indian Union.' The decision, however, was not to be announced. The objective of the Kashmir National Conference 'is the attainment of people's sovereignty with the Maharaja enjoying a constitutional position.' This, explained Kachru:

> … would be the main factor determining the position of the Conference in the matter of accession … The threat to Kashmir is real and unless the Congress takes up a strong stand and forces the Maharaja to come to some agreement with the National Conference, Kashmir is doomed and there will be nothing to prevent the conquest of Kashmir by the Muslim League leaders and private armies.[76]

A copy of this report was passed on to Sardar Patel and he responded to Nehru: 'We are giving the Kashmir government as much assistance as possible within the limited resources available. There are all sorts of difficulties in our going all out to assist the State.'[77]

The Pakistani leaders were also actively trying to turn the situation in their favour, at the same time as being criticised by the Kashmiri government for the armed raids and a 'blockade' of the border. Immediately after Abdullah's release, he was visited by Dr Muhammad Din Taseer, a friend of Abdullah's and former principal of Sri Pratap College in Srinagar but now a Pakistani citizen. He was accompanied by Anwar-ul Haq, district magistrate, Rawalpindi, who was deputed to find out why essential supplies, including sugar, salt, petrol, kerosene, oil and cloth were being held up at Sialkot and Rawalpindi. The allegation from the Kashmiri side was that because they were not being transported into Kashmir, the Pakistanis were not honouring the terms of the standstill agreement and that it was tantamount to a blockade to force the state to accede to Pakistan.

The Pakistani government, however, maintained that this arose because of the troubled situation within Kashmir. Haq concluded that the lorry drivers were too frightened to make the journey because Sikhs and Hindus were attacking Muslims. After some investigation, the British High Commission concluded that there may have been obstructions which were overlooked, perhaps even encouraged, by some low grade officials.[78] But, from the Indian perspective, the allegations of the blockade were evidence of Pakistan's intended 'aggression' towards Kashmir and added fuel to the argument that an invasion was imminent.

While Anwar ul Haq was holding discussions with the concerned authorities about the supplies, Taseer met with Sheikh Abdullah. 'When Taseer returned in the evening, he told me he had a very fruitful discussions with Sheikh Abdullah and he had agreed to meet Quaid-i Azam.' But the Sheikh was also playing for time. The Punjab was on fire. 'So I felt I had to be very careful about taking any decision concerning Kashmir,' he told Bilqees Taseer, recalling his earlier conversation with her husband in 1947. 'I also believed that any decision made had to be that of the Kashmiri people themselves, i.e. as regards joining Pakistan, because not merely those of the present generation would be affected by such a decision but also generations to follow.'[79] In his memoirs Abdullah noted: 'I firmly told him that the time to decide had not yet arrived. Both countries are caught in a vortex.'[80] He agreed, however, to meet Mohammad Ali Jinnah in Lahore after he had first visited Delhi.

In the meantime, Abdullah sent his 'trusted lieutenant', G. M. Sadiq back to Lahore with Dr Taseer for further discussions. Bakshi Ghulam Muhammad was already there. Ghulam Muhammad Sadiq was anxious to ensure acceptance of the condition that no non-state subject would be allowed to purchase property in Kashmir (as was the case in pre-independence times). On the assumption that Kashmir would eventually go to Pakistan there were stories of wealthy Pakistani feudals making enquiries about buying land.

The Pakistani government was also pursuing diplomatic channels with the maharaja and his government. Liaquat Ali Khan, the prime minister of Pakistan, had sent a representative to Srinagar 'to try and lead the Kashmir Prime Minister towards accession to Pakistan. He said that for three or four days he was succeeding, but that then the new Prime Minister arrived and told him to clear out.'[81] The new prime minister, who had arrived in Srinagar on 15 October, when the state was 'on the chessboard of power politics', was Mehr Chand Mahajan.[82] An Indian judge, he had been one of the Hindu representatives on the Boundary Commission. In an exchange of telegrams, the Kashmir Government offered an impartial inquiry into the allegations made against Pakistan; otherwise, Prime Minister Mahajan stated that the Government of Kashmir would be obliged to ask for 'friendly assistance' from the state's other neighbour, India. The Pakistani government accepted the idea for an impartial inquiry, but on 18 October Mahajan sent another telegram to Mohammad Ali Jinnah again threatening to ask for 'friendly' assistance unless the Pakistanis acceded to their request to stop the alleged armed infiltration into Poonch, the blockade of the border, as well as continuing propaganda against the maharaja. This time, however, there was no mention of the impartial inquiry.

Jinnah responded to Mahajan's telegram, by sending a telegraphic message to Hari Singh deploring the 'tone and language' adopted by Mahajan. He also outlined numerous complaints against the maharaja's government. He noticed the more favourable treatment given to Sheikh Abdullah since his release at the end of September, and to the National Conference, compared with the Muslim Conference whose leaders, including Ghulam Abbas, remained in detention:

> The real aim of your Government's policy is to seek an opportunity to join the Indian Dominion through a coup d'état by securing the intervention and assistance of that Dominion ... I suggest that the way to smooth out the difficulties and adjust matters in a friendly way is for your Prime Minister to come to Karachi and discuss the developments that have taken place, instead of carrying on acrimonious and bitter telegrams and correspondence.[83]

At the same time Sardar Patel continued to correspond with the Kashmiri government. Mahajan had already requested arms and ammunition from India to deal with the growing unrest within the state. On 21 October, Patel once again encouraged Mahajan to enlist the support of Sheikh Abdullah: 'It is obvious that in your dealings with the external dangers and internal commotion with which you are faced, mere brute force is not enough ... It is my sincere and earnest advice to you to make a substantial gesture to win Sheikh Abdullah's support.'[84] Mahajan noted Patel's views but replied that 'the situation in the state at the present moment is such that one cannot get a single moment to think of politics.'[85] He urged Patel to send arms and ammunition at once to assist with the worsening situation which the Kashmiri government insisted was aided by Pakistan. 'No raids could take place if the Pakistani authorities wished to stop them.'[86]

As both India and Pakistan continued to court the old rulers of the state of Jammu and Kashmir and the new, such diplomatic initiatives were brought to an immediate halt when news was received that a large number of raiders from the tribal territory of Pakistan's North-West Frontier province had crossed the borders and were heading for Kashmir. G. M. Sadiq returned from Lahore to Delhi. According to Faiz Ahmed Faiz, chief editor of *The Pakistan Times* and an old friend of Sadiq's, when news of the tribal invasion reached Lahore, 'we could see that everything was lost.'[87] The 'jihad' of the tribesmen came in the wake of two months of nominal standstill, when, behind the scenes amidst a deteriorating law and order situation, India and Pakistan were both independently planning for the state of Jammu and Kashmir to accede to their respective dominions. 'There ended the opportunity of Kashmir's accession to Pakistan,' said Faiz. 'The rest is history.'[88]

CHAPTER 10

Jihad

Death and destruction were fast approaching Srinagar, our smug world had collapsed around us, the wheels of destiny had turned full circle. Karan Singh, October 1947[1]

For over two months after the independence of the sub-continent from British rule, the maharaja had attempted to remain independent. While the Government of Pakistan and the state of Jammu and Kashmir were engaged in their war of words over the deteriorating law and order situation, India's rulers were offering moral and the promise of material support to the beleaguered maharaja. The invasion of large numbers of tribesmen from the North-West Frontier of Pakistan into Kashmir forced a decision on him. In order to receive military assistance from India, Hari Singh was obliged to accede to the Indian Dominion. But would he have eventually done so anyway? Under what circumstances might he have acceded to Pakistan? Could he have ever remained independent? In addition, was the 'holy war' into Kashmir instigated by Pakistan or was it an extension of the internal troubles already existing in the maharaja's state?

The road to war

Claims and counterclaims of aggression within the state of Jammu and Kashmir persisted throughout September. Whereas the maharaja and his government stated that the attacks came from armed raiders across the border in Punjab, the Pakistanis insisted that there was an indigenous rebellion within the state which was an extension of the political opposition to the maharaja which had been going on since the 1930s. Predictably, the discontented Poonchis had crossed the border to Pakistan for help. 'One day someone introduced me to Sardar Ibrahim,' writes Akbar Khan, a junior army officer who was in Murree in September 1947. 'As yet he [Ibrahim] was not prominent enough to be known in Pakistan. Most of the recognised leaders of the pro-Pakistan Muslim Conference were still in jail in Kashmir. Ibrahim, like many others passionately stirred, had come across the border in search of help for his people.'[2] 'I was almost the only person left to take decisions,' recalls Ibrahim. 'You can imagine the precarious position of a young man.'[3]

Ibrahim Khan had requested 500 rifles 'if they were to liberate themselves.'

Akbar Khan describes how the commander-in-chief of the fledgling Pakistani army and other senior officers, who were British, were not to be taken into confidence regarding any plan to assist the rebels. Through an indirect source, Ibrahim Khan succeeded in getting 4,000 rifles. 'Further weapons, Frontier made or from abroad, could be obtained depending on the money available.' Akbar Khan subsequently wrote out a plan, called 'Armed Revolt in Kashmir'. The main objective was to focus on strengthening the Kashmiris themselves internally. Discussions with the prime minister, Liaquat Ali Khan, who was clearly aware of their plans were so 'informal' that Akbar Khan deduced 'there was complete ignorance about the business of anything in the nature of military operations.'[4] It was also known to George Cunningham, the governor of the North-West Frontier, that a Punjabi called Khurshid Anwar, 'something in the Muslim National Guard' had been in Hazara district 'organising what they call a three-pronged drive on Kashmir.'[5]

As the politicians deliberated, a large contingent of tribes from the North-West Frontier headed for Kashmir. 'I am afraid the Kashmir situation is going to be a serious crisis,' noted George Cunningham in his diary on 20 October. 'Heard this morning that 900 Mahsuds had left Tank in lorries for the Kashmir front ... about 200 Mohmands are also reported to have gone.'[6] They were soon to be joined by Wazirs, Daurs, Bhittanis, Khattaks, Turis and some Afridis from Tirah as well as Swatis and men of Dir. At dawn on 22 October 1947, they crossed the Jhelum river into Kashmir. 'My own position is not too easy, ' wrote Cunningham. 'If I give my support to the movement, thousands more will flock to it and there may be a big invasion; if I resist it, I have to bear the brunt if the movement fails through lack of support.'[7] Prior to independence, the British had only succeeded in maintaining an uneasy peace with the tribesmen by paying subsidies to the chiefs and keeping frontier posts at their various 'forward' positions along the North-West Frontier. But after the British withdrew in August 1947, in Pakistan's 'new-born, unorganised state,' writes Ian Stephens, in the midst of the Kashmir imbroglio, the government was still formulating its relationship with the tribes.[8]

The general belief amongst Pakistanis is that the tribesmen were incited to a 'holy war' by the stories of atrocities which fleeing Muslims brought with them to the market places of Peshawar. 'I was assured by a man in authority in Peshawar that the corpses of Muslims killed by the Dogras had been paraded through the Peshawar streets by men who called on the people to support a "jihad" against the infidels in power in Kashmir and in India,' recalled Horace Alexander after his visit to the North-West Frontier in 1947.[9] A number of Kashmiri Muslim families from Poonch were also settled in the Rawalpindi and Jhelum districts of the Punjab. In addition, the chief minister of the North-West Frontier Province, Khan Abdul Qayum Khan was a Kashmiri from Poonch. In the weeks to come, his officials assisted with the supply of petrol, which was scarce, as well as the provision of grain and transportation to tribal volunteers.[10]

Although Liaquat Ali Khan knew of the plan for tribesmen to invade Kashmir, to date there is no evidence that Mohammad Ali Jinnah was involved in the discussions. 'So far I have not come across that evidence,' says Professor Zaidi, editor of the Jinnah papers:

> I promise and I declare that the moment such evidence comes to light, it shall not be suppressed. The Pathan tribesmen moved against the wishes of the then Federal government. I personally know that for sure and there was nobody to stop them. When they went there, they went without any proper planning and co-ordination. It was all a confusion and the blame on Pakistan that they had deployed them on a defined objective is baseless.[11]

Muhammad Saraf, who had come to Lahore after leaving Baramula in August 1947 states, however, that the tribal invasion was undertaken with the know-ledge of the Pakistani leaders in order to enhance the efforts of the local Kashmiris. 'It may be stated emphatically that it took place with the blessings of the Quaid-i Azam, Mohammad Ali Jinnah, and Mr Liaquat Ali Khan.'[12]

K. H. Khurshid, Jinnah's private secretary disagrees:

> I left Karachi on October 1, 1947. My last meeting with the Quaid-e Azam was on September 30, 1947. We discussed Kashmir for two hours. We discussed everything and the Quaid-e Azam told me: "Please convey to our leaders in Kashmir that I do not want to create any trouble for the maharaja at the moment. I want them to remain calm and we shall deal with the situation later on as it arises.[13]

According to George Cunningham, on the basis of information given to him by the defence secretary, Iskander Mirza on 26 October: 'Apparently Jinnah himself first heard of what was going on about 15 days ago, but said "Don't tell me anything about it. My conscience must be clear."' Cunningham does not, however, refer to Jinnah either ordering or having any knowledge of a specific invasion plan. All British Officers, he said, were kept out of the discussions 'simply not to embarrass them.'[14]

Indian accounts maintain that the whole operation into Kashmir was instigated at the highest level in Pakistan. Code named 'Gulmarg', they believed that it was masterminded by Akbar Khan, who used the pseudonym General Tariq in memory of the Berber general who crossed the straits of Gibraltar to invade Spain in the eighth century.[15] The raiders, said V. P. Menon, 'have free transit through Pakistani territory. They are operating against Kashmir from bases in Pakistan. Their modern military equipment could only have been obtained from Pakistani sources; mortars, artillery and mark V mines are not normally the kind of armament which tribesmen possess.'[16] Menon estimated that about 5,000 tribesmen, travelling in two to three hundred lorries, crossed into Kashmir.

The first real opposition the tribesmen encountered was at Muzaffarabad, where a battalion of Dogra troops was stationed. They succeeded in capturing the bridge between Muzaffarabad and Domel and, on the evening of 23

October, they captured Domel. Over the next two days they took Garhi and Chinari. Their main column proceeded on towards Uri, where according to their 'commander' Khurshid Anwar, they encountered 'the first Sikh Regiment of Patiala State.'[17] No one has confirmed when the Patiala state forces arrived, but Alastair Lamb considers the presence of such 'exotic forces' as a covert operation, which, since the Maharaja of Patiala's accession to India, meant they were in fact forces which came under the control of the Indian Union.[18] At Uri, Brigadier Rajinder Singh, who had succeeded Scott as chief of staff of the state forces, was killed. 'He and his colleagues will live in history,' writes V. P. Menon 'like the gallant Leonidas and his three hundred men who held the Persian invaders at Thermopylae.'[19]

The tribesmen carried on along the Jhelum river road, the traditional route traversed by their forbears, the Afghans, towards Baramula, the entry point into the valley, where the road led directly to Srinagar. At Mahura there was a large power house and a power failure temporarily plunged Srinagar into darkness, creating a sense of impending doom.[20] Sheikh Abdullah returned to the limelight by organising the defence of the city. His heroic efforts, however, became tarnished with allegations that Hindu and Sikh refugees were being armed by the Kashmiri government and encouraged to kill those whose loyalty to Abdullah and the National Conference was dubious.[21]

The flight of Hari Singh

On October 24, Maharaja Hari Singh made an urgent appeal for help to the Government of India. As he waited for the Indian response he attempted to carry on his duties. 'Incredibly enough,' writes his son, Karan Singh, 'the annual Durbar was held in Srinagar as usual ... in the beautiful hall of the city palace on the Jhelum with its richly decorated papier maché ceiling.'[22] Although the maharaja had wanted to cancel it, Prime Minister Mahajan said that to do so would create panic amongst the people.

In Delhi, Lord Mountbatten, governor-general of India, was attending a buffet dinner in honour of the foreign minister of Thailand, when Prime Minister Nehru informed him that Kashmir was being invaded by large numbers of Pathan tribesmen. Although the Indian government had been talking about an incursion from Pakistan, the actual invasion took them by surprise. The following day, 25 October, the Defence Committee of the Cabinet met, chaired by Lord Mountbatten. 'The most immediate necessity,' writes Alan Campbell-Johnson, Mountbatten's press secretary, 'was to rush in arms and ammunition already requested by the Kashmir Government ... .' Mountbatten contended, however, 'that it would be the height of folly to send troops into a neutral State, where we had no right to send them, since Pakistan could do exactly the same thing, which could only result in a clash of armed forces and in war.' He urged therefore that the legal formalities regarding accession should be completed but that it should only be temporary, prior to 'a referendum, plebiscite, election or even, if these methods were impracticable, by representative public meetings.'[23] As a first step towards popular government, Nehru wanted provision to be made for Sheikh Abdullah in the maharaja's government. According to Nehru's biographer, Sarvepalli Gopal, at the meeting, neither Nehru nor Patel 'attached any importance' to Mountbatten's insistence on temporary accession.[24]

The sequence of events from the moment the maharaja requested help from the Government of India on 24 October to the time when Indian troops arrived on 27 October has been a subject of debate ever since. The official account relies heavily on the memoirs of V. P. Menon who, at the Defence Committee meeting, was instructed to 'fly to Srinagar immediately in order to study the situation on the spot and to report to the Government of India.' When he reached Srinagar airfield on 25 October Menon recorded: 'I was oppressed by the stillness as of a graveyard all around. Over everything hung an atmosphere of impending calamity ... The Maharaja was completely unnerved by the turn of events and by his sense of lone helplessness. There were practically no State forces left and the raiders had almost reached the outskirts of Baramula.'[25] Menon first met Prime Minister Mahajan, and then went to the maharaja's palace. Menon gives no details of their discussions, but merely states that their first priority was to get the maharaja and his family out of Srinagar. Captain Dewan Singh, the maharaja's ADC, recalls: 'Menon said to the maharaja: "It would be foolhardy for you to stay in Srinagar when the raiders are so near. They could capture you and get any statement from you." So, on the advice of Menon, he left Srinagar and came to Jammu.'[26]

Karan Singh was with his parents as they fled from Srinagar:

> The subsequent events are a jumble in my mind – the servants frantically rushing around ... It was bitterly cold as the convoy pulled out of the palace in the early hours of the morning. The raiders were pouring in from across the border, pillaging, looting and raping as they came, and there were rumours that the road to Jammu had been cut and that we were likely to be ambushed on the way ... All through that dreadful night we drove, slowly, haltingly, as if reluctant to leave the beautiful valley that our ancestors had ruled for generations. Our convoy crawled over the 9,000 ft Banihal Pass just as first light was beginning to break.

According to Victor Rosenthal, Hari Singh's friend and confidant, the departing maharaja did not speak at all throughout the journey. Only as he arrived at his palace in Jammu that evening, he said: 'We have lost Kashmir.'[27] In the years to come, Hari Singh's flight from Srinagar was used by his critics as a reason for stating that he had no right to take the decision to accede to India because he was no longer in control of his state.

As the maharaja departed from Srinagar on the treacherous journey to Jammu, V. P. Menon went to the State Guest House to have 'a little rest'.

But he did not sleep because, as he relates, 'just as I was going to sleep,' the prime minister telephoned to say that it was unsafe to stay any longer in the city. Both Mahajan and Menon went to Delhi 'at first light' on the morning of 26 October, arriving at Safdarjung airport at about 8 a.m. Menon went straight to a meeting of the Defence Committee, which, according to Mahajan began at 10 a.m.[28] Mahajan went to rest at the house of Baldev Singh, the defence minister. At 12.45, Baldev Singh came to say that the decision had been taken to send two companies of Indian troops to Srinagar. As related by Menon, 'soon after the meeting', in the company of Prime Minister Mahajan, he took a plane to Jammu.

The Instrument of Accession

On arrival in Jammu, Menon found the palace 'in a state of utter turmoil with valuable articles strewn all over the place.' The maharaja was still asleep. 'I woke him up and told him what had taken place at the Defence Committee Meeting. He was ready to accede at once.' He then composed a long letter to the governor-general describing 'the pitiable plight of the State and reiterating his request for military help.' His letter requesting accession is full of regret. 'I wanted to take time to decide to which Dominion I should accede … whether it is not in the best interest of both the Dominions and my State to stay independent, of course with cordial relations with both.' But the tribal invasion had forced a decision upon him. And Mountbatten's insistence on accession before assistance had pushed him a step further than he may necessarily have wanted to go. Menon's meeting in Srinagar on the evening of 25 October had made Hari Singh understand the logic of accession which had not been present in his earlier requests for 'friendly assistance'. 'Naturally, they cannot send the help asked for by me without my state acceding to the Dominion of India. I have accordingly decided to do so and I attach the Instruments of Accession for acceptance by your government.' The maharaja further stated that it was his intention 'to set up an Interim Government and ask Sheikh Abdullah to carry the responsibilities in this emergency with my Prime Minister.'[29]

Menon is also amused to note that at the end of their meeting the maharaja told him that 'he had left instructions with his ADC that if I came back from Delhi, he was not to be disturbed as it would mean that the Government of India had decided to come to his rescue and he should therefore be allowed to sleep in peace; but if I failed to return, it mean everything was lost and, in that case, his ADC was to shoot him in his sleep.'[30] Captain Dewan Singh recalls the atmosphere at the time as: 'Very gloomy. Jammu was on fire'.[31]

With both the letter and the Instrument of Accession, Menon returned 'at once' to Delhi. Sardar Patel was at the airport and they both went to a meeting of the Defence Committee that evening. 'There was a long discussion

K. Rumbold.
I have not shown to Sir A. Carter
283

OFFICE OF THE HIGH COMMISSIONER
FOR THE UNITED KINGDOM.
6, ALBUQUERQUE ROAD,
NEW DELHI.

POL.
1512
1947

TOP SECRET.   27th October, 1947

My dear Carter

      Developments in Kashmir have been so rapid during the last two days that I have thought it as well to put them down shortly in diary form. A copy is enclosed herewith.

2.   I am dictating this at 4.00 p.m. while awaiting a copy of Mr. Nehru's reply to the message which I delivered to him this morning from Mr. Attlee. There are persistent rumours that Kashmir has acceded to the Indian Union, and I think that I shall receive confirmation of this very soon. I have received definite information that ten aircraft were sent off early this morning from Delhi to Kashmir loaded with troops and arms. I telephoned to Mr. V.P. Menon's office a few minutes ago but was told that he had not yet returned from Jammu.

3.   As you will see from the diary, I have kept Sir L. Grafftey-Smith fully informed regarding developments here, and I am sending him a copy of this letter with its enclosures.

Yours sincerely

(A.C.B.-SYMON)

P.S.   I have been in touch with Iyengar who confirms that Kashmir has requested accession to the Indian Union. This has been accepted provisionally by the Government of India. A final decision will be taken in the light of the wishes of the people. This, Iyengar says, is in accordance with the declared policy of the Government of India.

(A.C.B. SYMON)

Sir Archibald Carter, K.C.B.,K.C.I.E.,
Commonwealth Relations Office,
LONDON, S.W.1.

REC. POL. DEPT.
[...] 47
INDIA OFFICE

Alexander Symon's Letter to Sir Archibald Carter. (A note at the top indicates that Carter may not have seen this letter.)

at the end of which it was decided that the accession of Jammu and Kashmir should be accepted, subject to the provision that a plebiscite would be held in the state when the law and order situation allowed.[32] The precedent was Junagadh, which was Kashmir in reverse: a Muslim ruler, whose accession to Pakistan the Indians were disputing on the grounds that the majority of the people were Hindu.

In his letter dated 27 October accepting the maharaja's accession to India, Mountbatten once more stated that the accession should be confirmed by a reference to the people 'consistently (sic) with their policy that, in the case of any State where the issue of accession has been the subject of dispute, the question of accession should be decided in accordance with the wishes of the people of the State.'[33] Future commentators, however, point out that the strength of this recommendation was reduced by the fact that he did not indicate the holding of a plebiscite was itself a condition of aid. 'One must ask,' wrote Josef Korbel, who was a member of the first United Nations Commission which visited the sub-continent in 1948, 'whether Mountbatten was not at this point more interested in the principle of accession than in the final determination of the will of the Kashmiri people by plebiscite.'[34] On the morning of 27 October, 300 troops of the First Sikh Battalion were airlifted to Srinagar. Prime Minister Mahajan describes how, after he had heard that the army had landed, he flew with Menon to Jammu to get the maharaja's signature on certain supplementary documents about the accession.[35] 'As we landed at Jammu, the brigadier of the state forces met me. He felt considerably relieved by the arrival of the Indian army in Srinagar.'[36]

The official version of events leading up to the signing of the Instrument of Accession does not, however, always correspond with individual accounts. In numerous publications it has been maintained that Menon first reached Jammu on 26 October but, writes Alastair Lamb, 'it is at this point that the hitherto established narrative diverges dramatically from the facts.'[37] Menon intended to return to Jammu on 26 October, but it appears he was not able to do so. And would Hari Singh have been there to receive him?

The maharaja left Srinagar 'in the early hours of the morning' of 26 October or, as Mahajan confirms, at 2 a.m. The journey at night in winter by road from Srinagar to Jammu could be expected to take at least sixteen hours.[38] The convoy of cars only reached the Banihal pass 'as first light was beginning to break'. They also made a stop at Kud, a small settlement 60 miles from Jammu. 'The maharaja finally reached Jammu 'the next evening' recalls his son, Karan Singh,[39] and had already gone to sleep before Menon arrived. But Menon states that on the evening of 26 October he was back in Delhi meeting with the Defence Committee. When, therefore, could he have met the maharaja on 26 October? Menon also says that Mahajan accompanied him to Jammu on 26 October but Mahajan makes no mention of this visit and, in fact, states that he was not prepared to go to Jammu 'till I got news from my aerodrome officer at Srinagar that the Indian forces had

landed there.' Mahajan also recollects that 'around dinner time' on the evening
of 26 October Nehru sent a message that the following day 'with Mr V. P.
Menon, I should fly to Jammu to inform the Maharaja' of the decision of
the Cabinet meeting that military aid was to be given.[40] Menon does not
mention this visit. Mahajan describes how the deputy prime minister left for
Delhi on 24 October with a letter of accession, but Menon does not refer
to this.[41] Nor, as the key witness does he corroborate Mahajan's statement
that an Instrument of Accession was in fact signed in Srinagar. If the
Instrument of Accession had been signed before the maharaja left Srinagar,[42]
why was it necessary for Menon to relate that it was signed the following day
when he returned to Jammu?

And what of the meeting between Alexander Symon, acting British high
commissioner in Delhi, and Menon on the evening of 26 October? In a
much quoted passage, Lapierre and Collins relate how as Symon and Menon
sat down to have a drink, 'an enormous smile' spread across Menon's face.
'Then he pulled a piece of paper from his jacket pocket and waved it gaily
towards the Englishman. "Here it is," he said. "We have Kashmir. The bastard
signed the Act of Accession. And now that we've got it, we'll never let it
go."'[43] Symon's diary of events for 26 October, as reported in a 'top secret'
letter to Sir Archibald Carter at the Commonwealth Relations Office in
London, tells a different story:

> 3.30 p.m. In view of the importance of establishing contact [with Mr V. P.
> Menon] without delay, I went to the Willingdon aerodrome at once to try and
> see him before the aeroplane took off [for Jammu]. I was told that the aeroplane
> was leaving from Palam aerodrome to which place I went at once. I found Mr
> Menon on the point of returning to Delhi because he had left it too late for the
> aeroplane to reach Kashmir before nightfall. I arranged with Mr Menon to see
> him at his house about 5 p.m.

When Symon went to meet Menon, Menon told him that

> ... he would leave next morning for Jammu and would be returning by lunch-
> time next day ... In reply to my enquiry as to the form of aid which the
> Government of India were considering affording to Kashmir, he said that he
> could not tell me anything definite except that the Government of India were
> determined "at all costs" to prevent the raiders from spreading East and South.

In his covering letter to Carter, dictated at 4 p.m. on 27 October, Symon says
that he 'telephoned to Mr V. P. Menon's office a few minutes ago but was
told that he had not yet returned from Jammu.'[44] In a letter dated 27 October
Nehru wrote to the maharaja stating that V. P. Menon 'returned from Jammu
this evening and informed me of the talks there. He gave me the Instrument
of Accession and the Standstill Agreement which you had signed, and I also
saw your letter to the Governor General of India'[45] In defence of the Indian
position that the Instrument of Accession was signed on 26 October, B. G.
Verghese states that 'there is no contradiction between what V. P. Menon

stated and Mahajan subsequently wrote in his memoirs,' but a careful study of the relevant sources does not inspire such a confident dismissal.[46]

What is significant about this sequence of events is not so much that Menon may not have been able to reach Jammu on 26 October, but that the Indian government found it necessary to maintain in official accounts that he did in order to support their argument that the maharaja acceded to India before Indian troops were sent to Srinagar. 'By early 1948 the place of the 26 October Instrument of Accession in the armoury of Indian advocacy had been well established,' writes Alastair Lamb. Had the maharaja in fact acceded in Srinagar before he left for Jammu, it would not have been necessary to maintain that Menon returned to Jammu on 26 October. But the absence of a signed Instrument of Accession prior to the official arrival of Indian troops on 27 October would have reduced the strength of the Indian claim to be assisting a state which had acceded to India. Accession before intervention gave the Indians the legal right to be in Kashmir, including the ability to control the circumstances for the holding of a plebiscite. It also 'enabled India to reject any Pakistani proposal for simultaneous withdrawals on both sides.'[47] Why also was the Instrument of Accession not published in the 1948 White Paper? 'It would certainly have been the documentary jewel in India's Kashmiri crown,' writes Lamb, who doubts the authenticity of the 'Instrument', dated and signed by both the maharaja and Mountbatten, which appears in Sardar Patel's edited correspondence, published in 1971. 'There the matter must rest until fresh documents surface to justify a firmer verdict one way or another.'[48]

At the time, the belief that the state of Jammu and Kashmir had acceded to India before Indian troops were sent prevailed. Whether or not the Instrument of Accession was signed before or after Indian troops landed, the maharaja had agreed to accession in principle upon the terms outlined by Mountbatten. Unhappy as Hari Singh sometimes became with the state's accession to India, he never suggested that he had not signed an Instrument of Accession before Indian troops landed nor that he had never signed one. Alexander Symon went on to become high commissioner in Pakistan and subsequently in India, but he never published his diary of events of 26 and 27 October. Despite Pakistan's protestations, India maintained that from 26 October 1947 the state of Jammu and Kashmir was a part of Indian territory, and therefore that their action in sending in troops to assist in the defence of the state against the Pathan raiders was legitimate.

Mountbatten's insistence on accession before assistance has, however, also been questioned. As Joseph Korbel noted, the Indian government had already promised arms and weapons to counter the spreading rebellion in Poonch; although, these had not arrived, there was no demand then for accession to be a condition upon receiving assistance. Despite Mountbatten's fear of a full scale war, involving British officers on opposing sides, how could he have reasoned that it was necessary for Jammu and Kashmir – technically an independent country – to accede first before receiving military assistance? Why was no appeal made to the United Nations for assistance at that time? And why did no one suggest getting in touch with the Pakistani government in Karachi for consultation?[49] No convincing explanation has been offered: 'It is hard to understand why Mountbatten attached such importance to immediate accession,' concludes Philip Ziegler, Mountbatten's official biographer. 'If there had been no accession, the Indian presence in Kashmir would have been more evidently temporary, the possibility of a properly constituted referendum have become more real. By exaggerated legalism the Governor-General helped bring about the result he most feared: the protracted occupation of Kashmir by India with no attempt to show that it enjoyed popular support.'[50]

As the politicians deliberated in Delhi the tribesmen continued their attack. On 27 October they reached Baramula, which they ransacked, killing a large number of the local people. They also attacked St Joseph's Franciscan convent killing five people of which three were Europeans in addition to one nun. Father Shanks, one of the survivors, described how 'the tribesmen – great, wild, black beasts they were – came shooting their way down from the hills on both sides of the town.'[51] The traditional view suggests that, had they moved on quickly, they could have reached Srinagar and taken possession of the airfield, which could have prevented Indian troops from landing.

From Major Khurshid Anwar's account, as narrated in *Dawn* newspaper, it appears, however, that the tribesmen were never in a position to take the airport. They only reached Baramula the day the Indian troops landed and, before proceeding to Srinagar, they had first to take Pattan, by which time the Indian air force had arrived. 'Here they encountered air bombing by Indian Union planes and machine-gunning by fighters. The tribesmen lost heavily in transport, vehicles and ammunition.' On 31 October they captured Pattan, but it was considered 'absolutely impossible to proceed on the straight road to Srinagar.' Although Anwar and a small group of men detoured round to reconnoitre the airport they found that at Achhgam, about a mile from the airfield, three battalions of the Kumaon Regiment were stationed there. 'Major Anwar and his men, acting on the principle "discretion is the better part of valour" withdrew.' In early November there were skirmishes on the outskirts of Srinagar but by this time the Indian air offensive was launched in full strength. On 10 November, Anwar was seriously wounded.[52] 'In the last two days there has been a considerable withdrawal of tribesmen from Kashmir,' noted Cunningham on the same day. 'They seem to have taken a knock on the outskirts of Srinagar on the night of 7th and came right back to Uri the next day.'[53] Although the tribesmen continued to operate on the Poonch front, Cunningham estimated that they numbered, at most, about 7,000.

Of all the actions of the first Kashmir war the invasion of the tribesman, especially the ransacking of Baramula, has been most widely condemned. Brigadier L. P. Sen, veteran of the Burma Campaign in World War II, who was commanding the 161th Infantry Brigade, recalled his arrival in Baramula: 'Everywhere one looked ... there were signs of pillage, arson or wanton destruction ... out of a population of 14,000 at least 3,000 had been slain.'[54] Ian Stephens, known for his pro-Pakistani sympathies, however, described the murders at St Joseph's convent as 'a bad but secondary episode, soon inflated out of all proportion by Indian propaganda aimed at countries of the Christian West'.[55] Muhammad Saraf, a recent graduate from St Joseph's, applauded the tribal invasion, even though, because of it, India persisted in condemning Pakistan for its 'aggression': 'I believe the tribal attack wasn't wrong. It led to the liberation of Azad Kashmir and the Northern Areas, over 32,000 square miles of territory.'[56] Prem Nath Bazaz, a Kashmiri Pandit disillusioned with Sheikh Abdullah and still opposed to the autocracy of the maharaja, believed the motives of the tribesmen should be considered. 'They wanted to liberate Kashmir from the tyranny of the Maharaja and nationalist renegades. And we should not forget that some members of the Indian army did no less of looting and molesting.'[57] A note of the Commonwealth Relations Office concluded: 'whatever errors have been committed by both sides since the trouble started, the basic cause was the action of the Hindu ruler in suppressing popular agitation in favour of Pakistan.'[58]

Attempting dialogue

The maharaja lost no time in thanking Mountbatten for sending the troops: 'It was the most momentous and quick decision ever taken by politicians in India,' wrote Mahajan.[59] Mountbatten's major concern, however, was to prevent an inter-Dominion war. British officers were still on active duty in both the Pakistani and Indian armies. Field-Marshal Auchinleck was supreme commander-in-chief of both forces, theoretically to assist with the division of the former Indian army. When, after the accession, Jinnah summoned General Gracey, his acting commander-in-chief, and ordered Pakistani troops to be moved at once into Kashmir, after the Indian troops had landed Auchinleck prevailed upon him to withdraw the order. 'The Auk said that under the orders of His Majesty's Government he had no option but to withdraw the British officers if the border was violated,' recorded Shahid Hamid, his private secretary. 'He was enforcing the orders in the literal sense, without appreciating the extenuating circumstances. But then the Auk was no politician.'[60] George Cunningham met with Mohammad Ali Jinnah soon afterwards and noted:

> Jinnah said that Auchinleck had just told him that, in the event of war between the two Dominions, all B.Os [British Officers] in both armies would at once stand down. He held that he had a good moral and constitutional case for intervening by force, just as India had ... Kashmir had turned down every approach Pakistan had made to them, and the lives of Muslims in all Kashmir were at stake. But he realised the Pakistan army was weak at present.

Although Jinnah was not convinced that the decision was right, Cunningham concluded that 'in his own mind, he had really ruled out the possibility of sending troops in to fight.'[61] When Sir Frank Messervy, commander-in-chief of the Pakistani Army, came back from England he visited Delhi before returning to Rawalpindi. He was surprised 'to find Mountbatten directing the military operations in Kashmir' writes Cunningham. 'M. B. is daily becoming more and more anathema to our Muslims, and it certainly seems as if he could see nothing except through Hindu eyes.'[62] 'The mantle of Governor-General fell from him and he assumed the garb of Supreme Commander,' commented a member of Mountbatten's staff to Chaudhri Muhammad Ali.[63]

On 1 November Mountbatten flew to Lahore to meet Jinnah and Liaquat Ali Khan. Nehru was 'indisposed' and declined to attend the meeting. Mountbatten related the outcome of his discussions with the Pakistani leaders in a long note to Nehru. Jinnah's 'principal complaint was that the Government of India had failed to give timely information to the Government of Pakistan about the action that they proposed to take in Kashmir.' The telegram, which he had received, informing him that Indian troops were being landed, arrived after the event and 'it did not contain any form of appeal for co-operation between the two Dominions in this matter.'

Pakistan's position was that the accession of the state of Jammu and Kashmir to India was based on 'fraud and violence' and therefore was not 'bona fide'. Mountbatten countered that the maharaja was 'perfectly entitled to accede to either Dominion; since the violence had come from the tribes for whom Pakistan was responsible, it was clear that he would have to accede to India to obtain help against the invader.' Jinnah however repeatedly asserted that it was India, who had committed the violence by sending troops to Srinagar. 'I countered as often with the above argument, thereby greatly enraging Mr Jinnah at my apparent denseness.' At this meeting, Mohammad Ali Jinnah did not respond enthusiastically to the suggestion of a plebiscite. When Mountbatten asked him what were his objections, he replied: 'With the troops of the Indian Dominion in military occupation of Kashmir and with the National Conference under Sheikh Abdullah in power, such propaganda and pressure could be brought to bear that the average Muslim would never have the courage to vote for Pakistan.' At this point, Mountbatten suggested inviting the UNO to send observers 'to ensure that the necessary atmosphere was created for a free and impartial plebiscite.' Jinnah, however, appeared despondent about the future, maintaining that India was out 'to throttle and choke the dominion of Pakistan at birth and that if they continued with their oppression there would be nothing for it but to face the consequences.'[64] His fears were later echoed in Liaquat Ali Khan's telegram to Nehru. 'India never wholeheartedly accepted the partition scheme but her leaders paid lip service to it merely in order to get the British troops out of the country.. India is out to destroy the state of Pakistan.'[65]

In a radio broadcast on 4 November the Prime Minister of Pakistan asserted that it was a 'dishonest rewriting of history to present the rebellion of the enslaved people of Kashmir to the world as an invasion from outside just because some outsiders had shown active sympathy with it … it was not Kashmir but a tottering despot that the Indian government and their camp followers were trying to save.'[66] The Indians, however, made much of Sheikh Abdullah's presence in Delhi at the time of the accession, stating that he 'had been pressing the Government of India on behalf of the All Jammu and Kashmir National Conference for immediate help to be sent to the state to resist the tribal invasion.'[67]

Nehru and Patel were clearly sensitive to the repercussions which the developing situation in Junagadh would have in Kashmir. Unlike Kashmir, the small state of Junagadh was surrounded by Indian territory and had no geographical contiguity with either wing of Pakistan, other than a 300-mile sea link. When the Nawab of Junagadh, Sir Mahabatkhan Rasulkhanji, acceded to Pakistan, the Indian government resisted his decision, calling for a plebiscite to determine the will of the people. Indian troops had invaded Junagadh at the end of October, at the same time as the Kashmir crisis erupted. On 7 November Sir Shah Nawaz Khan Bhutto, the Prime Minister of Junagadh, resigned, effectively accepting the Indian position pending the outcome of a plebiscite. It was eventually held on February 1948, when the majority Hindu population voted overwhelmingly in favour of India. The same principle could therefore be applied to Kashmir in reverse; Nehru therefore insisted that Sheikh Abdullah, as a popular Kashmiri leader, should be publicly associated with the Indian action and brought into the state government.

Rebellion in Gilgit

On 5 June 1941 the Resident of Gilgit, Lieutenant-Colonel D de M. S. Frazer had been informed that, in the opinion of the secretary of state, although Hunza and Nagar were under the suzerainty of the Kashmir state, they were not part of it, nor were Chilas, Koh Ghizar, Ishkoman and Yasin. The British argument was based on the terms of the Treaty of Amritsar which stated that the limits of the territories 'shall not be at any time changed without concurrence of the British Government'. Although Gopalaswami Ayyangar, the prime minister, provided a detailed rebuttal to this assertion, it was rejected. In its deliberations, the Government of India conceded that their decision would be most 'unpalatable' to the maharaja and even admitted that it had not been officially announced earlier in order not to hinder Kashmir's war effort. When the figures for the 1941 census were compiled, the government purposely listed the populations for these areas separately from those of the state.[68] Nonetheless, when the partition plan was announced on 3 June 1947, the Gilgit Agency was returned to the maharaja's control. 'The retrocession of Gilgit was accepted by the Maharaja with jubilation', writes V. P. Menon.[69]

Brigadier Gansara Singh was sent by the maharaja to take control of the area. After independence, the Gilgit Scouts had remained under the command of a British officer, Major William Brown, whom Cunningham described as 'a quiet self-confident Scot'. His second-in-command, Captain Jock Mathieson, was based in Chilas. After Brown heard that the maharaja had acceded to India, he met with the governor and urged him to ascertain the wishes of the Muslim Mirs and Rajas regarding the accession to India. Gansara Singh appears not to have taken Brown's advice, whereupon Brown warned him that he may have to take his own measures to avoid bloodshed. 'With these words to his senior officer, writes Charles Chenevix-Trench, 'Willie Brown crossed the Rubicon.'[70] On the night of 31 October, Brown put into operation a daring plan code-named 'Datta Khel'.

'Bright moonlight lit up the parade ground. The platoons moved out from the barrack rooms in single file and the men passed a Holy Koran lying on a table. In turn, they placed their right hands on the book and swore by Almighty God that they would be faithful to the cause of Pakistan,' recalled Willie Brown. A platoon of Scouts proceeded to the governor's house to take him into protective custody. Other platoons went to take over the key locations. 'Reports started coming in. The Post Office had been taken, the Gilgit Bridge held, the bazaar cleared and the curfew imposed. In the early hours of 1 November, after holding out through the night, Governor Gansara Singh surrendered. As Brown was to discover, amongst the rebels, whilst openly supporting Pakistan, there was a secret plan to set up an independent republic of Gilgit-Astor, which claimed the backing of 75 per cent of the Scouts. As the only non-Muslim, Brown was in no position to dissuade them and went along with their plans to set up a provisional government. He succeeded, however, in sending a telegram to the Chief Minister of the NWFP, Khan Abdul Qayum Khan: 'Revolution night 31st to 1st Gilgit Province. Entire pro Pakistan populace has overthrown Dogra regime. Owing imminent chaos and bloodshed Scouts and Muslim State Forces taken over law and order.'[71]

Whereas Pakistani commentators concur that the rebellion had the full support of the people, India still regards the operation as a coup by the Scouts which did not have popular support. 'Whatever the sentiments of the populace, the only person in authority who had unequivocally declared in favour of union with Pakistan was Willie Brown himself. Union with India had been repudiated, but except for shouting slogans, none of the Provisional Government had done anything to promote union with Pakistan,' writes Chenevix-Trench.[72] Brown himself realised the gravity of his position: 'I had contracted to serve the Maharaja faithfully. I had drawn his generous pay for three months. Now I had deserted. I had mutinied … My actions appeared to possess all the ingredients of high treason. Yet I knew in my own mind that I had done what was right.' On 2 November, after outmanoeuvring the pro-independence group and securing the approval of the mirs and rajas for accession to Pakistan, Brown relates how the Pakistani flag was raised on the old tower in the Gilgit Scout Lines. 'A great cheer went up. Allah o Akbar. Pakistan Zindabad.'[73]

Brown's action had taken the British government by surprise. 'The fate of Gilgit appears to rest with Major William Brown. Who is Major William Brown?' asked a Commonwealth Relations official. The only information they had managed immediately to discover was that he was twenty-four years old.[74] In 1994, Major Brown was given a posthumous award by the Government of Pakistan for the part he played in the rebellion, and his wife, Margaret Brown, travelled to Islamabad to accept the award on his behalf. The political future of the region, however, remains unresolved because Gilgit and its neighbouring states, which include the former kingdoms of Hunza and Nagar, who signed Instruments of Accession to Pakistan on 18 November 1947, have never been formally accepted as part of Pakistan pending a resolution of the future of the entire state. As part of the Northern Territories, together with Baltistan, they remain under Pakistani administration without the same rights and privileges as the other provinces enjoy under the Constitution of Pakistan. 'They liberated themselves,' commented Muhammad Saraf, 'but they don't enjoy the fruits of freedom.'[75]

Brown held Gilgit for over two weeks until, on 16 November, Muhammad Alam arrived to take control of Gilgit as political agent and, the following day, the Pakistani flag was raised over the Agent's house in Gilgit. On 12 January 1948, Brigadier Aslam Khan took over command of the Scouts from Brown. Under the pseudonym of 'Colonel Pasha' Aslam Khan also played a leading role in command of the local Azad forces, which comprised Kashmiris opposing the state's accession to India and Pathan tribesmen. Throughout the war, Brigadier Gansara Singh remained a prisoner of the Pakistanis. According to Aslam Khan's son, his father made special arrangements for Gansara Singh to receive tea and soap.[76] In 1949 Gansara Singh was exchanged for K. H. Khurshid, Jinnah's former private secretary, who had also become active in the 'Azad' Kashmir struggle against the Indian government and was later to become its president. Aslam Khan's father, Brigadier Rahmatullah Khan, who had been in the maharaja's service and placed under arrest during the war, was also given in exchange.

The fight continues

At the end of November Liaquat Ali Khan went to Delhi to meet Nehru, which Cunningham described as 'a hopeful sign'. 'We all felt at the time that there was every possibility of an amicable settlement' recorded V. P. Menon.[77] But hopes of an early peace were dashed when, soon after the meeting, the Defence Committee of the Indian Cabinet met. As Mountbatten noted: 'This was one of the most disastrous and distressing meetings it has ever been my lot to preside over. It appeared that all the efforts of the last few days

towards reaching an agreement on Kashmir were to come to naught.' The
Indian leaders were informed that additional tribesmen were entering Kashmir
and committing 'the most ghastly atrocities'.[78] In December, under pressure
from Mountbatten, the two prime ministers met again in Lahore. Mountbatten
subsequently reported how 'the conversation circled round the means of
attaining the object on which both sides were agreed – namely the holding
of a fair and impartial plebiscite ... what was to be the first step? ... The
talk went on, round and round, on the whole very friendly, but with occasional
outbursts, such as when Pandit Nehru flared up and declared that the only
solution was with the sword.'[79] From a British perspective the stakes were
high for both India and Pakistan. 'A severe tribal reversal might have repercussions on the North-West Frontier, as well as in Afghanistan since the whole
Kashmir dispute had assumed a strong Islamic aspect.' A reversal for India
would cause a 'loss of face'.[80]

Allegations that Pakistani soldiers were assisting the local forces from the
start circulated widely. Pakistani officers, 'conveniently' on leave from the
army were 'certainly fighting' alongside the Azad forces,' reported the British
high commissioner in January 1948.[81] On 13 January 1948 *The Times* (London)
reported: 'That Pakistan is unofficially involved in aiding the raiders is certain.
Your correspondent has first hand evidence that arms, ammunition and
supplies are being made available to the Azad Kashmiri forces. A few Pakistani
officers are also helping to direct the operations. And however much the
Pakistani government may disavow intervention, moral and material support
is certainly forthcoming.'[82] 'It was desirable that some trained personnel should
be available for the organisation and co-ordination of the whole effort,'
writes Akbar Khan. 'No Army officers could be taken for this, but we had
in Pakistan some of the senior ex-Army officers of the Indian National
Army.'[83] With the Pakistan army barely in existence, whatever support was
limited and the real importance was not so much in numbers but in terms
of their expertise. Khurshid Anwar was said to be 'very bitter against the
Pakistan government for not having rendered any assistance to the tribesmen
in their heroic bid to capture Srinagar.'[84]

In May 1948, on General Gracey's advice, the regular Pakistani army was
finally called upon to protect Pakistan's borders. Despite Indian denials there
was sufficient concern that the intervention of the Indian army in Kashmir
would not be limited to Kashmir and would ultimately be directed towards
Pakistan. Gracey was also concerned about the tribesmen. 'An easy victory
of the Indian army, particularly in the Muzaffarabad area, is almost certain
to arouse the anger of tribesmen against Pakistan for its failure to render
them more direct assistance and might well cause them to turn against
Pakistan.' Technically, however, Pakistani forces should avoid 'until the last
possible moment' a clash with the Indian army. They were to remain behind
the local Azad forces and prevent a break through to the Pakistani borders
by the Indians.[85] As future commentators were to observe, 'with the Army

HQ at Rawalpindi and the seat of the government at Karachi, there was hardly any politico-military cohesion in the war ... war direction was ding-dong at the least and many opportunities were missed.'[86]

In an effort to circumvent Indian defences in the valley, the Azad irregulars and Gilgit Scouts had moved towards Baltistan and Ladakh. Skardu was besieged and fell to their forces. Dras and Kargil, strategically located on the 200 mile track across the Zojila pass between Srinagar and Leh were also captured in May. Central Ladakh was therefore cut off from the most easily accessible land route. The Ladakhis, who were not anxious to be 'liberated' by the Azad forces, sent an urgent appeal for help to the Indian General Thimmayya's headquarters in Srinagar. The Indian air force flew in Gurkha reinforcements and hastily constructed an airstrip at Leh which, at 11,500 feet, remains the world's highest civil landing strip. 'You follow the Indus river to the landing strip,' explained an Indian Airlines pilot in 1995. 'If you can't see the river, you can't land.'[87]

As the Azad forces converged on Leh, Nehru was writing to Patel: 'This is of no great military significance and we can recapture all the lost ground. But it is irritating that on the map, a huge province may be shown as under the enemy.' He also admitted that the maharaja's State Forces in Ladakh and Skardu in Baltistan had behaved 'in a most cowardly and disgraceful manner. They had not only run away at the slightest provocation but have handed over our weapons and ammunition to the enemy.'[88] Throughout the summer, the Indian leaders were frustrated at their lack of progress in the war, despite pouring in men and money. 'Like Oliver Twist, the military commanders always ask for more and their estimates of requirements are constantly changing,' observed Sardar Patel. The extent of Indian military assistance also raised the question of what was to become of the maharaja's State Forces. Patel was reluctant to merge them with the Indian army because 'if and when any question of withdrawal of these Indian forces comes about, this autonomous existence would enable us to maintain friendly forces on the spot.' If, however, they were merged with the Indian army, the Indian government risked being asked to withdraw them, when the time came for the holding the plebiscite.[89] The prolonged fighting was also taking a more serious toll on the Indian resources than they had at first anticipated: 'The military position is none too good,' On 4 June Patel confided to the former prime minister of Jammu and Kashmir state, Gopalaswami Ayyangar, who was India's representative at the UN. 'I am afraid our military resources are strained to the uttermost. How long we are to carry on this unfortunate affair, it is difficult to foresee.'[90] At the same time, however, the Indian leaders were also focusing their attention on the state of Hyderabad in central India which, like Junagadh, with a Muslim ruler and a Hindu majority population, was Kashmir in reverse. On 11 September 1948 Indian troops invaded Hyderabad; the Muslim nizam was deposed and this large state became part of India. It was also the day Muhammad Ali Jinnah died.

While Kargil was out of their control, the Indians succeeded in making use of an alternative land route to Leh, from Marali in east Punjab through the 16,200 ft Barahacha pass. Thousands of porters and mule convoys brought up supplies. But the Indians believed that in order to safeguard the Ladakhis, they would have to recapture Kargil and re-open the much shorter land route. In October 1948, General Thimmayya launched a counter-offensive. Using tanks, unprecedented at such a height over the Zojila pass, the Indian forces reoccupied Kargil and, on their third attempt, took the pass. Pakistan took pride in the fact that its 'irregular' militia, armed with nothing but their personal weapons, inflicted nearly 1,000 casualties and withstood the Indian attack for nearly two months.

Pakistani army movements on the Poonch front were in preparation for a push towards Jammu. 'The overall plan,' writes Major-General Sher Ali Pataudi, who was sent to the Kashmir front in mid-July, 'was to cut the Line of Communication of the Indian forces in the Mehndar Valley and Poonch area and then pose a threat towards Jammu. If the surprise created panic, as was expected, then I would move towards Jammu with my entire regular Army force reserve and Armour and then see what happened.'[91] During the fighting, Pataudi, like so many others, found that he encountered his former comrades in arms across the battle lines. 'The Indian commander, Atma Singh, was a buddy of mine. He said "For God's sake, let's stop. I said: "I can't until I get the orders." We were great friends and we had to fight each other. It was a tragedy.'[92] As it happened, the plan to strike at Jammu was never put into effect.

Enter the UNO

Lord Mountbatten's belief, and that of the British government, that the UN would be able to perform some useful role in resolving the Kashmir dispute made it one of the first major issues with which the newly founded world body was to deal. Mountbatten had first suggested the use of the UN during his 1 November 1947 meeting with Mohammad Ali Jinnah in Lahore. The talks between Nehru and Liaquat Ali Khan in Lahore in December 1947 reinforced his belief that an intermediary was necessary: 'I realised that the deadlock was complete and the only way out now was to bring in some third party in some capacity or other. For this purpose I suggested [not for the first time] that the United Nations Organisation be called in.'[93] Prime Minister Liaquat Ali Khan had agreed to refer the dispute to the UN, including measures to stop the fighting and arrange a programme for the withdrawal of troops. But India was not prepared to deal with Pakistan on an equal footing. When the two prime ministers met again in Delhi towards the end of December, Nehru informed Liaquat Ali Khan of his intention to refer the dispute to the UN under article 35 of the UN Charter, which provided for any member 'to bring to the attention of the Security Council a situation whose continuance is likely to endanger the maintenance of international peace.' The Pakistani prime minister was unhappy with the accusatory tone of the reference 'but supposed he would have to accept it, since the earlier the UN was brought in the better it would be.'[94] On 31 December 1947 Nehru wrote to the UN secretary-general:

> To remove the misconception that the Indian government is using the prevailing situation in Jammu and Kashmir to reap political profits, the Government of India wants to make it very clear that as soon as the raiders are driven out and normalcy is restored, the people of the state will freely decide their fate and that decision will be taken according to the universally accepted democratic means of plebiscite or referendum.[95]

In January 1948 the Kashmir issue was debated in the Security Council of the United Nations, at Lake Success, New York, with representations from the Indian and Pakistani delegates. Much to the annoyance of the Indians, Sir Zafrullah Khan made a bold speech lasting five hours in favour of Pakistan's position and against the continuing rule of the Dogras over the Kashmiris: 'What is not fully known is the depths of misery to which they have been reduced by a century of unmitigated tyranny and oppression under Dogra rule until it is difficult to say which is the greater tragedy to a Kashmiri: his life or his death.'[96] The Indian government also believed that the Security Council, under the guidance of the British delegate, Philip Noel-Baker, was ignoring India's complaint and giving equal consideration to Pakistan's position.[97]

V. Shankar, private secretary to Sardar Patel, noted:

> The discussions in the Security Council on our complaint of aggression by Pakistan in Jammu and Kashmir have taken a very unfavourable turn. Zafrullah Khan had succeeded, with the support of the British and American members, in diverting the attention from that complaint to the problem of the dispute between India and Pakistan over the question of Jammu and Kashmir. Pakistan's aggression in the State was pushed into the background due to his aggressive tactics in the Council as against the somewhat meek and defensive posture we adopted to counter him.[98]

Sardar Patel believed that by referring the dispute to the UNO 'not only has the dispute been prolonged, but the merits of our case have been completely lost in the interaction of power politics.'[99] On 20 January, the Security Council passed a resolution which established a commission, to be known as the United Nations Commission for India and Pakistan (UNCIP), to investigate the facts of the dispute and carry out 'any mediatory influence likely to smooth away difficulties.'[100] Deliberations were temporarily halted with news of the assassination of Mahatma Gandhi on 30 January.

A further resolution was adopted on 21 April 1948 which called on the Government of Pakistan 'to secure the withdrawal from the State of Jammu and Kashmir of tribesmen and Pakistani nationals not normally resident therein who have entered the State for the purposes of fighting'; the Government of India was requested to reduce its forces to the minimum strength, after which the circumstances for holding a plebiscite should be put into effect 'on the question of the accession of the State to India or Pakistan.'[101] The United Nations Commission for India and Pakistan, of which Josef Korbel was a member, was instructed to depart without delay for the sub-continent. On their return, a further resolution on 13 August 1948 adopted unanimously by UNCIP outlined arrangements for the cessation of hostilities and once more restated that a final decision on the future status of the Jammu and Kashmir 'shall be determined in accordance with the will of the people.'[102]

In October 1948 Nehru was in Paris as a member of the Indian delegation to the UN General Assembly. On the first anniversary of the arrival of Indian troops in Srinagar, he wrote to Patel:

> So far as Kashmir is concerned, I think it is generally recognised that our case is a good one; nevertheless this business of a plebiscite and the conditions governing it fills peoples' minds. Of course people cannot get rid of the idea that Kashmir is predominantly Muslim and therefore likely to side with Muslim Pakistan. They say that if it is agreed that there should be a plebiscite, why is there any difficulty in having a cease-fire and truce.

Nehru was already talking about partition of the state on lines 'previously talked about, i.e. Western Poonch, etc., Gilgit, Chitral, most of Baltistan etc. to go to Pakistan.' But this suggestion was not acceptable to Liaquat Ali Khan who, as prime minister, was the main Pakistani spokesman after Mohammad Ali Jinnah's death in September 1948.[103]

The ceasefire was finally imposed on 1 January 1949, signed by General Gracey on behalf of Pakistan and General Roy Bucher, who was shortly to hand over to General Cariappa, on behalf of India. It was the last document signed by two Englishman on behalf of the respective Dominions to whom the British had granted independence sixteen months earlier. The line was to be monitored by a United Nations Military Observer group (UNMOGIP). On 5 January 1949, UNCIP once more affirmed that, when the truce agreement had been signed, the question of the accession of the State of Jammu and Kashmir to India or Pakistan would be decided through 'the democratic method of a free and impartial plebiscite.'[104]

From a Pakistani perspective, the ceasefire came when the Indians were militarily in the ascendancy. 'We all knew that ceasefire had to come,' writes Akbar Khan 'but its acceptance a month earlier would have left Poonch in our hands as a hostage. Or after the relief of Poonch – non agreement to cease fire for another month or two would again have enabled us to counter balance the Indian advantage.'[105] 'The ceasefire was imposed on us at a time when it suited the enemy most,' writes Colonel Abdul Haq Mirza, who fought as a volunteer from October 1947. 'Four months of operational period was

allowed to the Indians to browbeat the ill-equipped Mujaheddin and to bring
back vast tracts of liberated territories in their fold. Perhaps on signal from
the enemy "high command," the UN protection was arranged to safeguard
Indian interests. That was what people thought and said of the ceasefire in
Kashmir.'[106] Major-General Pataudi admits that the justification for accepting
the ceasefire was 'that in Lahore our troops were thin on the ground and the
risk was too great.' He believed, however, that had the full plan been put
into operation, he could have reached Jammu 'within 24 hours and into
Pathankot and Gurdaspur in the next 24 hours and that would have created
such a shock for the Indians that they would not have dared to move in
strength against Lahore.'[107]

After General Atma Singh's action in Poonch and that of General
Thimmayya in Ladakh the Indians were clearly in a better position than they
had been earlier in the year and had also benefited from the use of air
power, which advantage the Pakistanis did not have. But they too maintained
that the decision to impose a ceasefire was taken without consulting their
military commanders. They had not, for example, been able to re-capture the
Haji Pir pass on the Uri-Poonch road, which they believed gave the Pakistanis
a strategic advantage. Baltistan and Gilgit remained under Pakistani control.
From a political perspective, however, V. P. Menon believed that when the
ceasefire came into force, 'the initiative was definitely in our favour along the
entire front.'[108] Uppermost in British policy objectives was to secure a ceasefire
while their own officers were still in charge and able to control the situation,
lest the fighting escalate into full-scale war. The ceasefire line divided Poonch,
leaving Poonch city on the Indian held side. Although the Indians had retaken
Kargil, Skardu remained on the Pakistani side and the unofficial frontier
extended north-east to the indeterminate frozen wastes of the Siachen glacier.
Approximately one-third of the entire state was under the control of Pakistan.

India's 'truth'

'The roots of the Kashmir dispute are deep,' concluded the third and final
report of UNCIP, which made three visits to the sub-continent between
1948 and 1949. 'Strong under currents, political, economic, religious – in
both Dominions have acted, and do act, against an easy and prompt solution.
It is imperative that a settlement of the Kashmir issue be reached.'[109] But the
respective positions of India and Pakistan, which the Commission outlined,
did not make for an easy solution and the terms of article 35, under which
India had referred the issue to the UN, did not give the UN any mandate
to impose a solution, only to make recommendations. Then as now, the
Indian government considered itself to be in legal possession of the state of
Jammu and Kashmir by virtue of the Instrument of Accession of October
1947 signed by the maharaja and the then governor-general, Lord
Mountbatten. This basic premise constituted the legality of India's presence

in the state and of her control over it. The assistance which Pakistan gave to the tribesmen, who invaded the state, was, according to the Indians, therefore a hostile act and the involvement of the Pakistani regular army was an invasion of Indian territory. India maintained that her armies were in Kashmir as a matter of right; her control of the defence, communications and external affairs of the state was as a direct consequence of the act of accession.

Pakistan, accordingly, was regarded as having no *locus standi* in Kashmir. Since India was responsible for the security of the state, the problem of demilitarisation had to take into account the importance of leaving in the state sufficient Indian and state forces to safeguard the state's security. From an Indian perspective, the plebiscite, to which Nehru had agreed, would be to confirm the accession which was, in all respects, already complete. As the UN Commission reported: 'the cardinal feature of India's position is her contention that she is in Kashmir by right, and that Pakistan cannot aspire to equal footing with India in the contest.' Pakistan was illegally in Kashmir and had no rights in the matter. The Azad forces should be disbanded and disarmed because they constituted forces which were in revolt against the government of the state.

Pakistan's 'truth'

The Pakistani position was based on the contention that the accession of the state of Jammu and Kashmir to India was illegal and, therefore, there was no basis whatsoever for India's contention that the legality of the accession was 'in fact and law beyond question'. The state of Jammu and Kashmir had executed a Standstill Agreement with Pakistan on 15 August 1947 which debarred the state from entering into any kind of negotiation or agreement with any other country.

Furthermore, Pakistan maintained that the Maharaja of Jammu and Kashmir had no authority left to execute an Instrument of Accession on 26 October 1947 because the people had successfully revolted, had overthrown his government and had compelled him to flee from Srinagar, the capital. The act of accession was brought about by violence and fraud and as such it was invalid from the beginning. The maharaja's offer of accession was accepted by the Governor-General of India, Lord Mountbatten, on the condition that as soon as law and order had been restored, the question of the accession of the state would be decided by a reference to the people.

Pakistan also believed that the Azad movement was indigenous and spontaneous, as a result of repression and misrule by the maharaja's government. The tribal incursions were likewise spontaneous and arose as the result of reports of atrocities and cruelties perpetrated on the Muslim peoples of Kashmir and East Punjab. The entry of Pakistani forces into Kashmir was necessary in order to protect its own territory from invasion by Indian forces, to stem the movement of large numbers of refugees driven before the Indian army into Pakistan, and in order to prevent the Government of India from presenting the world with a *fait accompli* by taking possession of the entire state by force. 'It is Pakistan's opinion that her action in lending assistance to the people of Kashmir is far less open to criticism than was India's intervention at the request of an autocratic ruler. Pakistan considers herself as having equal status with the Government of India and entitled as a party to the dispute, to equal rights and considerations.'[110]

CHAPTER 11

Special Status

Kashmir has always been special. It came to India in 1947 in special circumstances and with special protection of its autonomy ... something that Indian political parties often forget. Tavleen Singh[1]

The Instrument of Accession, which formed the basis of Jammu and Kashmir's future relationship with India, accorded the state a special status which was not granted to other former princely states. Legally, India's jurisdiction only extended to external affairs, defence and communications. It was anticipated that the accession would be confirmed by reference to the people, under the auspices of the United Nations. In the years to come, the Indian government sought to integrate within the framework of India, what it controlled of the original princely state of Jammu and Kashmir, known also as the state of Jammu and Kashmir. The will of the people, however, was never ascertained in a such a manner as to make them feel that the issue was finalised. The history of what happened to the state's 'special status' partially explains events in the present day.

Demise of the Dogras

Hari Singh had demurred from acceding to India before partition because he wanted an assurance that he would retain authority within his state. 'Nehru wanted him to quit and hand over power to Sheikh Abdullah,' said the maharaja's former ADC, Captain Dewan Singh.[2] When, after the invasion of the tribesmen, Hari Singh finally acceded to India his bargaining power was greatly reduced. Nonetheless the Instrument of Accession specified a number of safeguards to his sovereignty:

Nothing in this Instrument shall be deemed to commit me in any way to acceptance of any future constitution of India ... (Clause 7)

Nothing in this Instrument affects the continuance of my sovereignty in and over this State ... ' (Clause 8)[3]

For Hari Singh the hardest part about the accession was having to deal not only with the prime minister of India, Jawaharlal Nehru, with whom he had little rapport, but also with the man who had so consistently opposed him for over twenty years, Sheikh Abdullah. Nehru believed that 'in the peculiar circumstances of Kashmir with its Muslim majority it was absolutely essential both for national and international reasons for Sheikh Abdullah to be fully involved in the government of the State.'[4] On 13 November 1947, Nehru wrote to the maharaja: 'The only person who can deliver the goods in Kashmir is Sheikh Abdullah. He is obviously the leading popular personality in Kashmir ... Full confidence must be placed in him ... I would suggest to you to keep in close personal touch with him and deal with him directly and not through intermediaries.'[5] The maharaja did not always take kindly to Nehru's suggestions, especially regarding Sheikh Abdullah and, in general, he communicated more freely through Sardar Patel with whom he had a better understanding. Patel was less committed to Abdullah's socialist programmes than Nehru and he made it clear that the maharaja's rights and privileges should be respected.

Nehru, however, continued to attach importance to 'popular' leadership. On 1 December, he wrote to Mahajan, who remained as prime minister:

> From our point of view, that is India's, it is of the most vital importance that Kashmir should remain within the Indian Union ... But however much we may want this, it cannot be done ultimately except through the goodwill of the mass of the population. Even if military forces held Kashmir for a while, a later consequence might be a strong reaction against this.[6]

Sheikh Abdullah's first political role in the government of the state of Jammu and Kashmir was as head of the Emergency Administration. His long years in opposition to the maharaja meant he had neither the training nor the skills of an administrator. Communication between Hari Singh and Abdullah remained tense. 'My father,' wrote Karan Singh, 'belonged to the feudal order and, with all his intelligence and ability, was not able to accept the new dispensation and swallow the populist polices of Sheikh Abdullah. The Sheikh, on the other hand, while a charismatic mass leader and a superb orator in Kashmiri, was imbued with a bitterly anti-Dogra and anti-monarchical attitude.'[7] 'Practically in all matters,' complained Mahajan to Patel, Abdullah 'is ignoring and bypassing H. H. and is daily showing increasing communal tendencies.'[8]

Sheikh Abdullah's programme for the 'New Kashmir' envisaged that the maharaja would be no more than a figurehead. In explaining his revolutionary land reforms, he condemned the 'special rights and privileges of the Maharaja', who had been granted all cultivated land as his personal property when Kashmir was sold to Gulab Singh by the British in 1846. This meant that most of the 2,200,000 acres of cultivable Kashmiri land still belonged either to the maharaja or to jagirdars and small landlords called chakdars, who were Jammu Hindus. The Muslim peasants who tilled the land had no security of tenure and had, in the past, been obliged to migrate to India during the winter season or starve. Abdullah's land reforms put the maximum land holding at 22.75 acres; the rest was reserved for tenants. There was to be no compensation for the break-up of the huge landholdings of the rich.

Abdullah and Hari Singh also argued over the distribution of government departments and the appointment of Muslims to more senior positions. They disagreed on the creation of a Home Guard, which would mean providing the Muslims of the valley with weapons. Mahajan came under attack for diverting weapons destined for the Home Guard to the pro-Hindu RSS. The maharaja was also held responsible for financing the Praja Parishad, a Hindu nationalist organisation based in Jammu. The personal hostility which had existed between the two men in pre-independence days persisted. Sheikh Abdullah condemned Hari Singh openly for leaving for Jammu on the night of 25/26 October. He also charged him with being responsible for atrocities against Muslims and he was angry that his reforms were being obstructed.

Antipathy between Abdullah and Mahajan made their relationship almost unworkable, to the extent that by December 1947 Mahajan was threatening to resign if only the maharaja would let him go. 'The administration here is on Hitlerian methods and is getting a bad name and the sooner I am out the better, as I do not in the least wish to be associated with gangster rule. There is no rule of law at all,' he wrote to Sardar Patel on 11 December.[9]

On 31 January 1948, as the war continued and Kashmir was discussed in the Security Council at the UN, the maharaja wrote a long letter to Sardar Patel, outlining his grievances:

> Sometimes I feel that I should withdraw the accession that I made to the Indian Union. The Union only provisionally accepted the accession and if the Union cannot recover back the territory and is going eventually to agree to the decision of the Security Council which may result in handing us over to Pakistan then there is no point in sticking to the accession of the State to the Indian Union.

He even suggested leading his own troops into battle against the tribesmen, with the Indian forces as volunteers: 'I am tired of my present life and it is much better to die fighting than watch helplessly the heartbreaking misery of my people.'[10] Both Nehru and Patel were opposed to cancelling the accession and Patel wrote a short letter to Hari Singh saying that 'a counsel of despair is entirely out of place.'[11] But Hari Singh's position was to become weaker.

On 2 March 1948 Mahajan finally resigned as prime minister. Sheikh Abdullah was installed in his place and the rift with Hari Singh deepened. Nehru, who invariably took Abdullah's side, was worried about the effect a show of strength by the maharaja would have both locally and abroad. 'Any impression which the people or the Security Council may get that the Maharaja is still strong enough to obstruct or oppose the people's representatives will weaken our case very greatly and come in the way of our winning the people of Kashmir to our side.'[12] Nehru wrote to Patel how unpopular the maharaja was 'with almost everyone he meets, including foreigners'.[13] A particular embarassment was Hari Singh's refusal to let his stud farm outside Jammu be used for a relief camp for the 40,000 refugees.

'Meanwhile children are dying in the Jammu streets. You can imagine the public reaction to this.'[14]

Abdullah also conflicted with the maharaja over the future of the Jammu and Kashmir State Forces, of which Hari Singh remained commander-in-chief. Abdullah believed that as prime minister he should be the C in C. Alternatively, administrative control should be handed over to the Indian Army, (which ultimately it was). Hari Singh's continued absence from Srinagar was not only resented but meant that communication with Abdullah was minimal. As his prestige declined, the maharaja tried to retain the vestiges of his former glory by reminding Patel about the necessary gun salutes for Hindu festivals and his birthday, which was on 27 September: 'Therefore early instructions may very kindly be issued.'[15]

As relations continued to deteriorate between the maharaja and Sheikh Abdullah, with the Sheikh asking for Hari Singh's abdication, Sardar Patel was obliged to suggest to the maharaja that a holiday away from the state would be beneficial for all concerned and in May 1949 he invited the maharaja and maharani to come to Delhi. Their son, Karan Singh, relates : 'The Sardar told my father gently but firmly that although Sheikh Abdullah was pressing for his abdication, the Government of India felt that it would be sufficient if he and my mother absented themselves from the State for a few months.' Karan, who had just turned eighteen would be appointed regent.

> My father was stunned. Although rumours to the effect that he might be pushed out of the State had been in the air for some time, he never believed that even the Sardar would advise him to adopt this course. He emerged from the meeting ashen-faced ... my mother went to her room where she flung herself onto her bed and burst into tears.[16]

In less than two years after signing the Instrument of Accession, in which Hari Singh had asserted that he would continue to enjoy 'the exercise of any powers, authority and rights now enjoyed by me as Ruler of this State,' he was obliged to relinquish control. Initially he saw his absence as only temporary: 'I should like to be assured that this step is not a prelude to any idea of abdication. I should like to make it clear now that I cannot entertain the latter idea even for a moment.' he wrote to Patel on 6 May.[17] But only his ashes ever returned to Kashmir, brought by his old ADC, Captain Dewan Singh, who served him loyally to the end. According to Dewan Singh, the former maharaja did not miss the beauty of the valley nor the mountains: 'He was a person with a very great common sense and a very long vision, so once he'd been asked to go out, it was a bit too small a thing for him to think of these mountains.'[18] He died in Bombay in 1962. First as regent, then as sadar-i-riyasat, his son Karan Singh remained involved in Kashmiri affairs. But the Dogra dynasty, founded by Hari Singh's great-grandfather a century earlier, was gone.

Abdullah in charge

For the Lion of Kashmir, the years since 1947 had heralded his trans-formation from vehement political activist against Dogra rule in the princely state of Jammu and Kashmir to prime minister of that part of the state which India retained militarily after the tribal invasion. For over thirty years, until his death in 1982, whether in jail or in office, Sheikh Abdullah dominated the Kashmiri political scene. His immense popularity in the valley was founded on his long struggle against the Dogras. Although a religious man he was not communal and initially his progressive socialism was welcomed by both Hindus and Muslims. He appealed directly to the poor people and con-sequently was disliked by the upper classes of both communities. To supporters of the Muslim Conference who represented the interests of those Muslims favouring accession to Pakistan, his secular stance amounted to a betrayal of the Muslim community. To the Hindu aristocrats who were the inevitable victims of his sweeping land reforms his socialist policies had communist and communal overtones favouring Muslims.

The departure of both of his parents from the state left Karan Singh, on the threshold of his own political career, 'poised between the weight of the past and the burdens of the future.'[19] It was up to this eighteen-year-old, supported by Nehru, with whom, unlike his father, he had close relations, to create a harmonious relationship with Abdullah, now at the height of his power. 'In all my actions I had to try and steer a middle path between appearing subservient to the Sheikh on the one hand and offending him and Jawaharlal on the other.'[20]

The ceasefire with Pakistan had been in force since January and Sheikh Abdullah was intent upon pushing ahead speedily with his plans for his 'New Kashmir'. 'As soon as the boom of guns died down we set about putting our state in order.'[21] Encouraged by his stature as prime minister, Abdullah had been happy to profess his allegiance both to Nehru and India. 'We have decided to work with and die for India,' he had said at a press conference after he became prime minister in 1948.[22] His programme of land reforms was designed to benefit the peasants and 'further consolidated the peasantry's ties with India,' writes M. J. Akbar, 'because they understood – and Abdullah told them so – that such reform would never be possible in a Pakistan which protected feudalism and landlordism.'[23]

Although overtly Abdullah was loyal to India, he never lost sight of what has become known as the 'third option' – that of independence. When he visited the United States as one of India's representatives at the UN in January 1948, he spoke openly in favour of Kashmir's accession to India. But in private, he met Warren Austin, the US representative at the UN. According to a telegram sent to the US Secretary of State, Austin reported that Abdullah had been anxious to point out 'that there is a third alternative, namely, independence ... he did not want his people torn by dissensions between Pakistan and India. It would be much better if Kashmir were independent and could seek American and British aid for the development of the country.' Austin, however, assured the secretary of state: 'I, of course, gave Abdullah no encouragement on this line and am confident when he left he understood very well where we stand on this matter.'[24] Whatever conversations Abdullah had with various American individuals, official US policy favoured the incorporation of all the princely states in either India or Pakistan lest the subcontinent become 'balkanised', which might destabilise the area and work against US interests.

While the Sheikh was in the US he also met with part of the Pakistani delegation in a hotel in New York, including Dr Taseer, who was acting as an adviser to Sardar Muhammad Ibrahim Khan, the president of 'Azad' Jammu and Kashmir – that part of the former princely state, which lay to the west of the ceasefire line, under Pakistani control – and Chaudhri Muhammad Ali, now secretary general of the Government of Pakistan. When they asked Abdullah what he saw as a solution for Kashmir, he replied:

> Only this, that Kashmir should be an independent state, free from both India and Pakistan. This should be a solution which should be acceptable to all, a face saving solution. Afterwards, if Kashmir has become an independent state, it will naturally be closer to Pakistan, firstly because of a common religion and secondly, because Lahore is near and Delhi is far off. Such a solution cannot be harmful to Pakistan.

When Chaudhri Muhammad Ali protested that India would plot against this scenario, Abdullah told him to 'put some trust in the Kashmiris, they will not join in conspiracies against Pakistan and be bought over.' His parting words were to warn them 'that the time will come when you will have to admit that Kashmir should be an independent country but by that time, it will not be possible. If you leave this problem hanging fire now, you will be the losers.'[25]

The restrictive nature of Hari Singh's accession to India meant that total integration with India could not take place without a new agreement and, until such time, Kashmir would retain its special status. Sheikh Abdullah was as insistent as Hari Singh had been that New Delhi had no right to extend its jurisdiction in Kashmir beyond the three areas agreed in the Instrument of Accession, namely, foreign affairs, defence and communications. This special status was now proposed as an article in the Indian Constitution, drafted first as article 306–A and then finalised as article 307. 'This article ' said N. Gopalaswami Ayyangar, who moved the article in India's Constituent Assembly in October 1949, 'proposes a special status for Kashmir because of its special circumstances. The State is not in a position to merge with India. We all hope that in future the State of Jammu and Kashmir will get over the hurdles and completely merge with the Union, like the rest of the states.'[26] In the final revised draft, the clause relating to the Fundamental

Rights and Directive Principles was omitted. 'Little did the State leaders realise,' write Teng and Kaul, 'that they had vested the government in the State with unrestricted authority, and, whoever had the government in hand, would assume dictatorial powers and powers which could be operated absolutely.'[27] From an Indian perspective, another unsatisfactory feature of Kashmir's relations with the Union of India was its initial economic isolation, effected through tariff barriers which provided much needed revenue at the expense of economic progress.

At a political level, Sheikh Abdullah was also beginning to pursue his own course. 'He seems to act independently of us and is extremely critical of, if not hostile to, us,' Patel wrote to Nehru on 27 June 1950. Sheikh Abdullah had also remained in touch with his former associates, who were now based across the ceasefire line in Pakistani-controlled Azad Kashmir. 'In particular, Sheikh Sahib's manoeuvres to have a separate talk with Ghulam Abbas fill me with misgivings.'[28] Patel was particularly worried about 'the attitude of Sheikh Sahib, his failure to deal with the communist infiltration in the State and the dissensions within the National Conference. It appears that both the National Conference and Sheikh Sahib are losing their hold on the people of the valley and are becoming somewhat unpopular.'[29]

Included in Article 370 was the provision for a Constituent Assembly with 100 seats, a quarter of which were reserved for representatives from the part of the state retained by Pakistan. In 1951 Kashmir's first post-independence elections were held in which Sheikh Abdullah and the National Conference won seventy-five unopposed seats, mainly because the election was boycotted by the Praja Parishad. Pakistan protested that the holding of an election would prejudice the outcome of a plebiscite. Abdullah, however, was still publicly giving his support to eventual accession with India. In a memorable speech on 5 November 1951, at the first session of the Jammu and Kashmir Constituent Assembly, he examined the variables for Kashmir's future accession to India, Pakistan or independence. Eventually he came down on the side of India, because of what its secularism meant for Kashmiris:

> After centuries, we have reached the harbour of our freedom ... once again in the history of this State, our people have reached a peak of achievement through what I might call the classical Kashmiri genius for synthesis, born of toleration and mutual respect ... The Indian Constitution has set before the country the goal of a secular democracy based upon justice, freedom and modern democracy ... Pakistan is a feudal state in which a clique is trying to maintain itself in power ... from August 15 to October 22, 1947 our State was independent and the result was that our weakness was exploited by the neighbour with invasion.[30]

Abdullah's primary concern was that the Congress ideals of equality for all communities should not give way to religious intolerance. Yet, soon afterwards, in a speech in Jammu which disturbed the Hindus, he criticised India for its

communalism. 'No one can deny that the communal spirit still exists in India
... if there is a resurgence of communalism in India, how are we to convince
the Muslims of Kashmir that India does not intend to swallow up Kashmir?'[31]

In July 1952 Abdullah succeeded in reaching a consensus with the
government in New Delhi on a number of issues which came to be known
as the Delhi Agreement: article 370 was accepted; Kashmir was to be allowed
its own flag, but the Indian flag would be supreme; Kashmiris would be
citizens of India; the President of India would be the head of state of the
whole of India, including Kashmir; the governor of Jammu and Kashmir
(sadar-i-riyasat) would be elected by the state legislature (as opposed to
nominated from Delhi) but he could not assume office without the consent
of the president of India. Suspicions, however, remained on both sides.
'Communal elements did not like the Delhi agreement,' writes Abdullah.
'Some newspapers went to the extent of writing that instead of Kashmir
acceding to India, in fact, India had acceded to Kashmir.'[32] The people of
Jammu were unhappy with their own obvious loss of political power.
'Accession of the state to India and the dawn of democracy for the people
of Jammu,' writes Balraj Puri 'as such meant the transfer of power from a
Jammu-based ruler to a Kashmiri-based leadership.'[33] Puri had personally
written to Nehru on the eve of the Delhi Agreement, warning of the growing
deterioration of the internal relations between the different regions.

Discontent in Jammu and Ladakh

Throughout the early years of independence, the people of Jammu found it
hard to reconcile themselves to government from Srinagar. 'Jammu and
Kashmir, which were united in 1846, are not known to have been mutually
well adjusted regions of the state they comprise,' writes Balraj Puri. 'The
political and administrative set up after 1947 was as conducive to regional
tensions as the one it had replaced.' Secessionist sentiments in the valley
were fed by communalism in Jammu which in turn was provoked by the
fears aroused by the secessionists.'[34] The numerical superiority of the valley
over Jammu was nominal: 53 per cent of the population in the valley,
compared with 45 per cent in Jammu. But the latter's share in the new power
structure was marginal.[35]

When Abdullah had first addressed the Hindus of Jammu in November
1947, he surprised them by his tolerance. 'The man so far regarded as an
enemy of Hindus almost hypnotised every soul in his audience, by calling
for communal peace in the name of the Hindu Dharma, Lord Krishna and
Gandhi.'[36] But in the years to come communal tensions were exacerbated by
Sheikh Abdullah's reforms. His revolution was not only social but economic.
Those who had been oppressed were mainly the Muslim peasants. Those
who were affected by his revolutionary land reforms were Hindus. The Praja
Parishad, based in Jammu, had influential supporters as well as links with

other pro-Hindu organisations throughout India. In Delhi Nehru also had to contend with extremist elements anxious to derail his secular policy. Politics at the centre were also passionately nationalistic and Kashmir's separate status was tolerated, at best, on sufferance. In October 1951 orthodox Hindus launched the Jana Sangh, led by Shyama Prasad Mookerjee, which aimed at abrogating article 370 and fully integrating Jammu and Kashmir into the Indian Union. The Praja Parishad saw the National Conference not only as a Muslim communal party, but also as 'a cover for the extension of communist ideology'.[37]

In February 1952 there was violence in the streets of Jammu and curfew was imposed for seventy-two hours. Alarmed by the significance of the Delhi Agreement, the Praja Parishad used the slogan: 'One President, one Constitution, One Flag'. They disliked the use of the distinctive titles, sadar-i-riyasat and prime minister, as opposed to those of governor and chief minister used by the other states. Claiming that they could not tolerate Jammu and Ladakh 'going to the winds'[38] the Parishad leaders accused Sheikh Abdullah of preventing the merger of the state of Jammu and Kashmir with the Indian Union. In November the Praja Parishad leader, Prem Nath Dogra, and one of his associates were detained by Abdullah. In February 1953 Dr Shyama Prasad Mookerjee wrote to Abdullah: 'You are developing a three-nation theory, the third being Kashmiris. These are dangerous symptoms.'[39] When Dr Mookerjee attempted to go to Jammu, he was arrested at the border. His death in detention, from a heart attack, fuelled suspicions of foul play. Right wing elements never forgave the Sheikh for crushing their movement.

The Ladakhi people, of Tibetan origin, who lived in virtual isolation, had escaped the trauma of communal riots and massacres at the time of partition. During the war, when the raiders captured Kargil and threatened Leh, relations between the two communities of Buddhists and Muslims became tense, although their long tradition of goodwill enabled them to withstand the strain.[40] When Sheikh Abdullah took over as prime minister, he too recognised the spiritual qualities of Ladakh's Buddhist community. 'Kashmir has always been the cradle of love, peace humanism and tolerance, which was created by Buddhism and which flourished in the valley for about a thousand years.'[41] Yet the Buddhists of Ladakh resented Abdullah's centralising tendencies. They neither wanted to join with Pakistan nor did they want to be governed by Srinagar.

The Ladakhis soon came to realise that Sheikh Abdullah had little knowledge or understanding of their way of life. Jawaharlal Nehru had himself realised that, in depending on Sheikh Abdullah as a political leader in Jammu and Kashmir, it might be difficult to keep together the multi-racial empire created by Gulab Singh in the previous century. In 1949 the Buddhist Association of Ladakh had sent a memorandum to Nehru suggesting that Ladakh be integrated with Jammu in some way, either to become an Indian state in its own right or as part of east Punjab totally separate from Sheikh Abdullah's administration in Kashmir. Although this plan was never put into practice, the Ladakhis remained restive under control from Srinagar. Before China's annexation of Tibet, the head Llama had suggested secession and union with Tibet; their spiritual allegiance was to the Dalai Llama in Lhasa, so too might be their political future. But after the communists took over Tibet in 1950, they lost the contact dating back seven centuries, which had influenced both their spiritual and cultural lives.

Abdullah's land reforms threatened the wealth of the Buddhist monasteries. In 1952 Kushak Bakula, the Abbot of Spituk Monastery, and regarded as the head Llama of Ladakh, declared that once power had been transferred from the maharaja to the National Conference 'the constitutional link, which tied us down to the state, was shattered and from that time we were morally and juridically free to choose our own course, independent of the rest of the state.'[42] There was still potential friction with the Muslim minority community in Kargil, who had traditionally controlled the Ladakhi economy, especially the supply of pashmina wool for weavers in Kashmir. Like Jammu, the people of Ladakh saw money poured into the valley at their expense. And, as Balraj Puri points out, 'the spectre of plebiscite' also haunted the people of Jammu and Ladakh. The fear of a pro-Pakistani verdict as well as the prevarication of the Kashmiri leaders over accession, made them suggest the possibility of a zonal plebiscite, which option Sheikh Abdullah refused to consider.[43]

The plebiscite and the United Nations

One of the reasons why Sardar Patel had impressed upon Hari Singh the need to absent himself from Srinagar for a 'few months' in 1949 was because of the 'complications arising from the plebiscite proposal then being actively pursued in the United Nations.'[44] UNCIP's visit to the sub-continent had laid the groundwork for demilitarisation and plebiscite, but as Joseph Korbel noted at the time, and their reports indicated, there was very little common ground other than the agreement in principle to hold a plebiscite. After their mission they recommended that the entire problem be turned over to one man, because the members of the commission were themselves divided. In 1949, General A. G. L. McNaughton, the Canadian president of the Security Council, was appointed as an 'informal mediator' in order to establish a plan for demilitarisation prior to the holding of a plebiscite. Although Pakistan agreed to his proposals, India did not. On 27 May 1950 the Australian jurist, Sir Owen Dixon, arrived in the sub-continent, as the one-man successor to UNCIP. Dixon's commitment in trying to resolve the problem was not lost on the Indians. Patel wrote to Nehru that Dixon was working to bring about an agreement on the question of demilitarisation. 'If we are not careful, we might land ourselves in difficulties because once demilitarisation is settled, a plebiscite would be, as it were, round the corner.'[45] Patel, however, did not live to see the outcome of the negotiations towards plebiscite. Regarded as the 'iron man' of the Indian government, who had so profoundly influenced India's policy towards the princely states, he died on 15 December 1950.

After three months of extensive discussions, Dixon made a number of suggestions, condemned by Nehru as an 'Alice in Wonderland business of vague proposals':[46] firstly, that there should be a zonal plebiscite region by region, and that the existing government should be replaced with an administrative body of UN officers; alternatively, that areas which would unquestionably vote for Pakistan or India would be allocated to the respective countries, with a plebiscite in the valley; that the state should be partitioned, with a plebiscite in the valley or, finally, that the country be divided along the ceasefire line. Yet again the question of demilitarisation was the sticking point, causing Dixon to conclude:

> I became convinced that India's agreement would never be obtained to demilitarise in any such form or to provisions governing the period of the plebiscite of any such character, which would in my opinion permit the plebiscite being conducted in conditions sufficiently guarding against intimidation and other forms of influence and abuse by which the freedom and fairness of the plebiscite might be imperilled.

Without such demilitarisation, the local 'Azad' and regular Pakistani forces were not prepared to withdraw from the territory they had retained. Dixon's final suggestion was to leave India and Pakistan to negotiate their own terms. 'So far the attitude of the parties has been to throw the whole responsibility upon the Security Council or its representatives of settling the dispute notwithstanding that except by agreement between them there was no means of settling it.' Dixon also noted the strange features of the problem:

> The parties have agreed that the fate of the state as a whole should be settled by a general plebiscite but over a considerable period of time, they have failed to agree on any of the preliminary measures which it was clearly necessary to take before it was possible to set up an organisation to take a plebiscite.[47]

The UN's decision to postpone further discussion of Kashmir unleashed a storm of protest in Pakistan.

The issue was briefly taken up by the Commonwealth, when, in January 1951, at a meeting of Commonwealth prime ministers, Robert Menzies, the Australian prime minister, suggested that Commonwealth troops should be stationed in Kashmir; that a joint Indo–Pakistani force should be stationed there, and to entitle the plebiscite administrator to raise local troops. Pakistan agreed to the suggestions, but India rejected them. In particular India was unhappy that Pakistan, whom India considered to be the aggressor, was placed on an equal footing. In March, the Security Council once again discussed Kashmir, and once more observed that India and Pakistan had accepted the resolutions of 13 August 1948 and 5 January 1949, affirming that the future of the state of Jammu and Kashmir was to be decided through 'the democratic method of a free and impartial plebiscite.'[48] The proposal, formulated by Britain and the United States, also suggested that in case of failure to reach agreement, arbitration might be considered. Pakistan accepted this recommendation, but Nehru responded by stating that he would not permit the fate of four million people to be decided by a third person. Korbel, who had continued to observe developments, was critical of India's stance: 'One could have expected that a country of such undisputed greatness led by a man of Nehru's stature and integrity would have reacted more favourably to such a valid, and under the Charter of the United Nations, the recommended technique of international co-operation.'[49]

When Dr Frank Graham, Dixon's successor as UN representative for India and Pakistan, visited the sub-continent in the Spring of 1951 he arrived in an atmosphere of extreme tension. Graham's brief once more was to try and effect demilitarisation, prior to the plebiscite. Yet again the two countries could not agree on the number of troops remaining in Kashmir. By the summer there was a significant concentration of Indian troops along the borders of western Pakistan and genuine concern that the two countries might again resort to war.

The Pakistani establishment was obviously also reviewing its policy regarding Kashmir. In January 1951 Ayub Khan took over as commander-in-chief of Pakistan's army. Two months later the newly appointed chief of general staff, Major-General Akbar Khan, 'hero' of the Kashmir war, was arrested with several others for plotting a 'coup'. Their alleged objective was to overthrow the government, replace it by a military dictatorship, favourable to Moscow instead of London and to move into Kashmir. Known as the Rawalpindi Conspiracy Case, the struggle for power between Akbar and Ayub was 'a tussle between two divergent perspectives on the Kashmir dispute within the Pakistani defence establishment,' writes Ayesha Jalal.[50] It also demonstrated that there was a body of opinion in Pakistan which believed that the Soviet Union might be a better ally than the British, who it was believed had failed to make good their promises of supplying arms and ammunition to Pakistan and consequently enabled India to achieve a *fait accompli* in Kashmir.[51]

In October 1951 Liaquat Ali Khan was assassinated by an unidentified gunman at a time when, speaking *ex tempore*, it was believed he was about to make a bid for support from the Muslim world.[52] Tension between India and Pakistan remained. Nehru's New Year message in 1952 warned of full scale war if Pakistan accidentally invaded Kashmir. Kashmir Day on 24 October 1952 was celebrated in an atmosphere of hostility towards the UN for its failure to solve the Kashmiri problem. And, as Korbel observed, the continuing uncertainty was matched by 'profound political changes in Kashmir which are not only dimming hope that an impartial plebiscite will be held' but also endangering peace and democracy. For a short while, there appeared to be a genuine dialogue between Nehru and Muhammad Ali Bogra, prime minister of Pakistan. In June 1953 they discussed Kashmir informally with Nehru in London, where they were both present for the coronation of Queen Elizabeth II. Nehru held talks with Bogra in Karachi. Soon afterwards Bogra visited Delhi and together they discussed the naming of a plebiscite administrator with the view to holding a plebiscite in the whole state. 'We have to choose a path which not only promises the greatest advantage but is dignified and in keeping with our general policy,' Nehru wrote to Bakshi Ghulam Muhammed on 18 August 1953.[53] But Pakistan's reluctance to consider a different nominee, other than the American Admiral Nimitz, whom India did not accept, stalled the whole proceedings. Such an opportunity never arose again. 'It is one of those ironies of history that just when India appeared to be willing to settle the Kashmir dispute, the prime minister of Pakistan allowed the opportunity to be frittered away,' writes Gowher Rizvi.[54]

The Western powers, most significantly the United States, were also reappraising their policy towards India and Pakistan. Initially, American liberals saw India 'in a romantic haze', writes Sam Burke. But the United States' failure, most demonstrably over Korea, to enlist India's support in the fight against communism and Nehru's commitment to a policy of 'non-alignment' finally alienated the US from India and brought them closer to Pakistan. 'To the Americans the main problem of the day was communism, to Nehru it was colonialism,' writes Burke. 'Americans viewed socialism as the road to communism; Nehru looked upon capitalism as the parent of imperialism and fascism.' Pakistan, however, took a different view of communism from that of India, which meant that the United States was prepared to look more favourably on Pakistan's position on Kashmir. This support was demonstrated in the UN, when both Britain and the United States voted for resolutions which were acceptable to Pakistan.

Pakistan's signature of a Mutual Defence Assistance Agreement with the United States in May 1954 and acceptance of American aid was regarded by India, as upsetting the sub-continental balance of power. Before the agreement was signed, Nehru had written to Muhammed Ali Bogra:

> If such an alliance takes place, Pakistan enters definitely into the region of the cold war. That means to us that the cold war has come to the very frontiers of India ... It must also be a matter of grave consequence to us, you will appreciate, if vast armies are built up in Pakistan with the aid of American money ... All our problems will have to be seen in a new light.[55]

As an Indian journalist was to observe, however, Pakistan's acceptance of Western support ensured its survival. 'India held the pistol at the head of Pakistan, until, in 1954, the American alliance delivered the country from the nightmare.'[56] In September Pakistan joined SEATO and the following year the Baghdad Pact (later called CENTO), whose other members were Turkey, Iran and the United Kingdom.

Initially, the Soviet Union abstained from voting when a resolution was passed regarding Kashmir in the Security Council and, through the Communist Party of India, was supportive of Kashmir's own nationalist stance. But, as relations deteriorated between the Soviet Union and its former allies in the Second World War, the Russians began to maintain that the British were using the Kashmir issue to keep control of both Dominions. In 1952 the Soviet representative at the Security Council said that the purpose of the United States and Britain was to convert Kashmir into a protectorate under the pretext of rendering assistance through the United Nations.[57] At the end of 1955 Nikolai Bulganin and Nikita Khrushchev stopped at Srinagar, where their visit marked a new phase in Indo–Soviet relations. They stated that the people of Kashmir had clearly already decided to join India. 'We are so near that if ever you call us from your mountain tops we will appear at your side,' said Khrushchev.[58]

Outside the forum of the UN, Chinese leaders had been evolving their own strategy towards the state of Jammu and Kashmir. In the early 1950s, like the Soviet Union, China maintained that the issue was being exploited by the UK and the US for their own 'imperialist' objectives, for which purpose they were using the UN. Even when the Soviet Union began to favour the Indian position, China remained neutral. Nehru, however, was interested in forming a special relationship with China. 'It was essential for the success of his programme of a resurgent Asia, from which western influence would have to be eliminated, that India and China, the two largest Asians, should march hand in hand,' writes Sam Burke.[59] In support of this objective, for reasons of 'realpolitik rather than morality,' Nehru was prepared to overlook Chinese actions in Tibet. China was, however, also moving towards confrontation with India because of disagreements over the demarcation of borders in the Aksai Chin area of Ladakh, which was one of three disputed areas along the 2,500 mile frontier. Unobserved by India, between 1956 and 1957 the Chinese had constructed a road in this inhospitable uninhabited north-eastern corner of Ladakh, rising to an altitude of 16,000 ft, which provided a direct link between Tibet and Chinese territory in Sinkiang province. By the time Indian patrols encountered Chinese vehicles using the road in 1958 their presence was already an accomplished fact. Nehru hoped to resolve any untoward border incidents by quiet diplomacy, but resentment amongst the Indian people at continued Chinese encroachments along the border was high.

In the late 1950s, as Indian and Chinese forces began to clash along their disputed frontier, Pakistan started a dialogue with China. In 1957, Po Yi-Po, chairman of the Chinese Economic Commission, arranged for a team of Chinese officials to visit the Hunza and Gilgit valley, which had long-standing contact with China because of the traditional Chinese relationship with the Mir of Hunza. Two centres were opened by Peking in Hunza and Gilgit for promoting 'good feeling' between China and Pakistan.[60] Zulfikar Ali Bhutto, who was Ayub Khan's minister for Fuel and Natural Resources 'recognised this simmering conflict between India and China as a major source of potential diplomatic advantage for Pakistan if properly exploited,' writes Stanley Wolpert.[61] In 1960 Bhutto became minister for Kashmiri Affairs. He led the Pakistani delegation to the UN and for the first time broke ranks with the established United States' position regarding China's membership of the UN. Instead of vetoing the proposal, Pakistan abstained. From India's perspective, writes Louis Hayes, the growing Sino–Pakistani co-operation constituted 'a vice, with Indian-held Kashmir in the middle'.[62] Discussions subsequently began to build a motorised road from Rawalpindi through the Khunjerab pass to China which would be visible proof of the growing link between the two countries.[63]

By the late 1950s, the United Nations had ceased to be a viable forum for the resolution of the Kashmiri dispute. In 1957, Dr Gunnar Jarring, the Swedish president of the Security Council, visited the sub-continent in order to assess the situation in Jammu and Kashmir. He stated that for the time being the present demarcation line must be respected and that the use of force to change the status quo must be excluded. The UN Security Council subsequently passed a resolution expressing its concern over 'the lack of progress towards a settlement of the dispute' shown by Jarring's report.[64] In 1962 Dr Graham returned again to the sub-continent. But the draft resolution, reminding the parties of the principles contained in their earlier resolutions calling for a plebiscite, was not adopted. For the first time, instead of abstaining, the Soviet Union voted against the resolution. 'It is now quite unrealistic to demand a plebiscite,' stated the Soviet representative 'just as, in the words of the representative of India, obviously no one would now demand a plebiscite in Texas, Ohio or any other state in the United States of America.'[65] But, even though the United Nations had failed to ensure that the plebiscite was held, the idea in principle of a referendum to ascertain the wishes of the people was handed down to a new generation of Kashmiris. That the plebiscite was agreed upon in a world body, such as the United Nations, meant that those Kashmiris who were opposed to union with India came to expect international support for what they perceived to be their right of self determination.

Azad or occupied Kashmir?

While India always refers to the part of the state under Pakistani administration as 'Pakistan-occupied Kashmir' or PoK, Pakistan refers to it as Azad Kashmir. Officially, the name used by Pakistan is 'the Azad government of the state of Jammu and Kashmir' which signifies that, in the opinion of Pakistan and the Azad Kashmiris, 'freedom' [i.e. from Indian control] should eventually extend to include the whole state. Technically, this narrow strip of mountainous land, covering some 5,134 square miles, is as much part of the

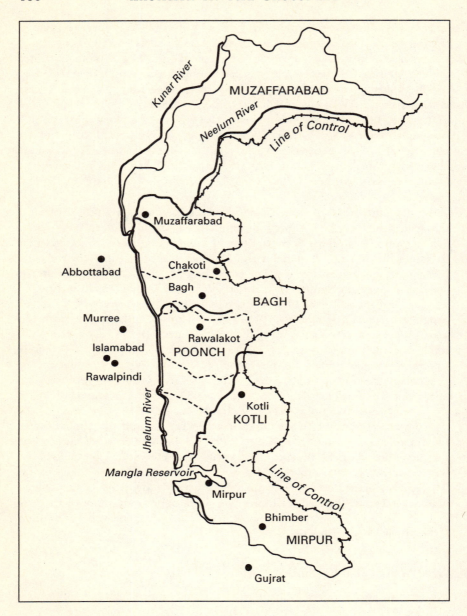

8. The Azad State of Jammu and Kashmir
(Source: *Azad Kashmir at a Glance*, Azad Government of Jammu and Kashmir, 1993)

state of Jammu and Kashmir as the valley, as is the approximately 27,000 square miles of the Northern Areas, which included the former Gilgit Agency and Baltistan. In the midst of the tribal invasion of 1947, on 24 October, the rebel Kashmiris had set up a government in exile. Sardar Ibrahim Khan was confirmed as president. The Azad Kashmir government described itself as a 'war' council whose objective was the liberation of the rest of the state of Jammu and Kashmir, as well as administration of that part of the state which was already under their control. A cabinet was formed with ministers appointed for Mirpur, Poonch, Kashmir valley, and Jammu. Despite the representation provided for the Kashmir valley, there was no one to speak for the valley. 'This reflected the fact that in the 1930s and 1940s the Valley Muslims had tended to support Sheikh Abdullah's National Conference Party,' writes Leo Rose.[66] The Muslims of Jammu, Poonch and Mirpur supported the Muslim Conference. But 'the government had practically nothing to do as the liberated territory was still in a state of disorder and confusion which was quite natural in the circumstances,' writes Muhammad Saraf, who had settled permanently in Pakistan once he realised that he would not be able to return to the Indian-administered side of the state.[67] In an attempt to assert its legality, on 3 November, the Azad Kashmir government leaders appealed to several heads of state, including Clement Attlee, Harry Truman, Joseph Stalin, and Chiang Kai-Shek, through the secretary-general of the UN, Trygve Lie, to recognise its formation. But the status of Azad Kashmir has never been legally defined in international terms. It is neither a sovereign state nor a province of Pakistan. In its resolution of 13 August 1948, UNCIP referred to it as territory to be 'administered by the local authorities under surveillance of the Commission'.

Once the ceasefire came into operation in January 1949, the Azad government's initial role of a government in exile, with its seat in Muzaffarabad, was soon overtaken by the demands of having to administer the land to the west of the ceasefire line, on a day to day basis. Initially the Gilgit Agency, comprising Gilgit, Hunza, Nagar, as well as Baltistan came under the administration of Azad Kashmir, but in 1949 Pakistan took over their direct administration.

When Ghulam Abbas was released from in jail in March 1948, he too went to Pakistan and became active in the Azad Kashmir government. At first he was appointed to look after the refugees, of whom there were estimated to be 200,000 in addition to the indigenous population of 700,000. Mir Abdul Aziz was just one of the thousands who fled. 'Actual warfare was going on. I came on foot, three hundred miles, I walked through snow. I lost all my toenails because of frost bite.'[68] Some refugees went to the main cities in Pakistan, most remained in Sialkot, Gujrat and Gujranwala. Others trekked back to their homes in Mehndar and Rajauri after the 1949 Ceasefire.

In 1950 an ordinance, 'Rules of Business of the Azad Kashmir Government,' was passed to serve as a basic law. Full executive and legislative powers

were vested in the 'Supreme Head of State', which, in effect, was the Muslim
Conference Party, which had the power to appoint the president, members
of the Council of Ministers, as well as the chief justice and other judges of
the Azad Kashmir High Court. The supreme head's absolute authority was,
however, checked by the Ministry of Kashmir Affairs (MKA) of the
Government of Pakistan, set up in 1948 and headed by a joint secretary.
'The Kashmiris, of course, were very skilful at exploiting and manipulating
some of the poor, well meaning Joint Secretaries, but there were limits on
how far this could be done,' writes Leo Rose.[69] Initially, the Muslim
Conference was also subordinate to Pakistan's Muslim League. As the only
political party in Azad Kashmir, the Muslim Conference, of which Ghulam
Abbas remained president, was, observed Josef Korbel 'no more democratic
than its opposite number, the National Conference.'[70] But relations between
Ghulam Abbas and Sardar Ibrahim Khan were strained. As a Jammu Muslim,
Abbas did not have any cultural affinity with Ibrahim, a Suddhan from
Poonch. Although they attempted a compromise, while Ibrahim was president
and Abbas was supreme head of the Azad Kashmir government, Azad
Kashmir effectively had two parallel administrations running at the same
time. Disagreements, however, between Ibrahim and Abbas continued until
eventually Ibrahim was dismissed as president in May 1950. The reaction in
Poonch amongst the independent-minded Suddhan community was defiant,
with the result that in the early 1950s the Azad government was not able to
function in large areas of Poonch.

Under the terms of the agreement, Pakistan was to retain control of
defence, foreign policy, negotiations with the UNCIP, as well as publicity in
foreign countries and in Pakistan, co-ordination of arrangements for the
refugees, publicity regarding the plebiscite and all activities within Pakistan
regarding Kashmir, such as transport and procurement of food. The Azad
Kashmir government retained control of the administration, local publicity,
development of economic resources within its territory, as well as the daily
running of the state. The Muslim Conference was allotted specific functions,
which related to the organisation of publicity and political activities in the
entire state of Jammu and Kashmir, as well as organisational work for the
plebiscite. Its objective remained the unification of the state of Jammu and
Kashmir and unification with Pakistan. Unlike the National Conference, its
leaders did not raise the objective of independence. When Ian Stephens, the
British journalist and former editor of *The Statesman*, visited Muzaffarabad in
1953 he noted the strange paradox, that although the government of Sheikh
Abdullah in Srinagar may have been politically stronger, the Azad Kashmir
government had more trained Muslim officials, many of whom had come
from Srinagar in 1947.[71]

In the early years, the Azad Kashmiris continued to press for firmer
action from the Pakistani government to assist their development. One of
the poorest areas of the former princely state, with the exception of the area

around Muzaffarabad and the more fertile region around Mirpur, extending north from the Punjab plains, there was no land reform comparable to the reforms enacted by Sheikh Abdullah in the valley. Although the old feudal system was abolished, living conditions were only just bearable. There was a desperate need for schools, hospitals, doctors and nurses. In May 1954 Ibrahim protested against bribery, corruption and embezzlement, as well as accusing the minister of Kashmiri Affairs in Pakistan of proposing 'to colonise' Azad Kashmir.

Partly because of its truncated nature and its general poverty, Azad Kashmir remained an adjunct to Pakistani politics, at times used as a launching pad for initiatives into the valley, at others, a poor relation, which, because of Pakistan's claim to the whole of the state of Jammu and Kashmir, the Pakistani government never found itself in a position to acknowledge as a province of Pakistan. At the same time, Azad Kashmir remained dependent on Pakistan for its economic survival. The Azad Kashmiris were as much waiting for the plebiscite as their counterparts in the valley in order to resolve their status, which the Pakistani government was obviously anxious to ensure would go in favour of accession to Pakistan, if and when the plebiscite were held. But, while they waited, Azad Kashmir become a semi-autonomous unit in its own right. 'This new-born baby,' writes Muhammad Saraf, who later became chief justice of the Azad Kashmir High Court 'whom so many of the leading politicians were afraid to own at the time of its birth, has, over the years, got transformed into a huge structure, with all the paraphernalia of a modern State, from a flag down to town committees.'[72] And so long as 'Azad Jammu and Kashmir' existed, an alternative formula other than integration within the Indian Union presented itself to the Kashmiris across the ceasefire line. Although at times critical of Azad Kashmir, Sheikh Abdullah had kept in touch with its leaders. 'There can be no doubt,' writes Alastair Lamb 'that the prospect of a deal between Sheikh Abdullah and Azad Kashmir for what might be called an "internal settlement" of the Kashmir question caused great anxiety in New Delhi; and it was certainly a contributing factor in Sheikh Abdullah's downfall in 1953.'[73]

Abdullah under arrest

By 1953 Nehru and Abdullah had grown apart. Suspicions about Abdullah's true commitment to India had festered. Abdullah had also become dis-illusioned with India's secularism. Although he remained opposed to the two-nation theory, contrary to his earlier expectations, Pakistan was proving viable and there were some useful comparisons to be made. His speech in Jammu in 1952 pointed to specific areas of dissatisfaction: 'I had told my people that their interests were safe in India, but educated unemployed Muslims look towards Pakistan, because, while their Hindu compatriots find avenues in India open for them, the Muslims are debarred from getting

Government service.'[74] He also objected to discrimination against Muslims in the central departments as well. 'Muslims were almost entirely debarred from working in postal services. Instead of striving for secularism, the officers of this department did just the opposite.'[75]

Despite the Sheikh's earlier allegations that Pakistan was the aggressor against the state in 1947, he began to talk about India and Pakistan in the same terms. His meeting with Adlai Stevenson in May 1953 in Srinagar was viewed with alarm. As reported by the *Manchester Guardian*, Stevenson had stated that the best status for Kashmir could be independence both from India and Pakistan.[76] Although the Americans denied any interference in Kashmir's affairs, the Indian government believed that the US preference for an independent Kashmir was encouraging Abdullah to think likewise. On 13 July 1953, the anniversary of 'martyr's day' following the arrest of Abdul Qadir in 1931, Abdullah stated that it was not necessary for Jammu and Kashmir to become an appendage of either India or Pakistan.[77] In addition, there were also allegations that Abdullah was running a one-party state. Even the land reforms could be side-stepped by those with influence, who used the names of family members to increase their holdings. By 1953 the government had to admit that the co-operatives, which had been set up to help the peasants, had collapsed because of corruption and poor administration.

On 8 August, Sheikh Abdullah was dismissed as prime minister after five years in office and put under arrest. Abdullah's sense of indignation at his dismissal is clear from his memoirs, written many years after the event: 'How did a patriot, praised by Jawaharlal Nehru and Mahatma Gandhi for his straightforwardness, turn into an enemy of the country?'[78] Abdullah's procrastination in confirming the Instrument of Accession was not, however, serving India's objective of consolidating its hold on Kashmir. 'From a position of clearly endorsing the Accession to India, he had over the last few months moved into an entirely different posture,' writes Karan Singh who, as sadar-i-riyasat, signed the letter of dismissal.[79] Although Nehru knew of Abdullah's impending dismissal, he appears to have deliberately distanced himself from the precise circumstances, leaving it to the 'men on the spot' who knew best.[80]

Sheikh Abdullah's role as prime minister of Kashmir from 1948–53 has come under scrutiny ever since. Was Abdullah still the secular nationalist who had been let down by India's own ambitions to integrate Kashmir as part of India? Or was he charting his own course for Kashmir in order to retain the autonomy promised by the Instrument of Accession and enshrined in article 370 in order to safeguard the interests of his fellow Kashmiris? Or was he working towards the independence of Jammu and Kashmir, as Nehru came to believe? 'I really cannot explain his new attitude except on the uncharitable assumption that he has lost grip of his mind,' Nehru wrote.[81] Such a remark, however, says Nehru's biographer, Sarvepalli Gopal, demonstrates the 'total failure of communication' between the two men who had worked so closely for over twenty years. B. N. Mullik, the Indian Intelligence Bureau chief, was probably more accurate in assessing that Abdullah was looking for a semi-independent status. India would protect him while he would benefit economically from the tourist industry and other sources of Kashmiri wealth, free from interference from what he had come to regard as the Hindu-dominated government in New Delhi.[82]

Abdullah's thinking at that time was also assessed in *The Times* of London:

> The Sheikh has made it clear that he is as much opposed to the domination of India as to subjugation by Pakistan. He claims sovereign authority for the Kashmir Constituent Assembly, without limitation by the Constitution of India, and this stand has a strong appeal to Kashmiris on both sides of the Ceasefire line and if his movement of purely Kashmiri nationalism was to gain ground, it might well oblige India, Pakistan and the United Nations to modify their view about what ought to be done next.[83]

Ian Stephens met Abdullah just before his arrest. He described the Sheikh as 'a Kashmiri patriot: full of zeal to improve his countrymen's plight; preoccupied with the Vale, the centre and motive of his whole political life; little concerned with the rest of the subcontinent's affairs.' Stephens, whose sympathies lay with Pakistan, went on to note that: 'it emerged from what he said that he did not at first take the idea of Pakistan seriously, nor expect her, when eventually created, to survive. Many others, better placed misjudged likewise.'[84]

Abdullah's downfall was only made possible by the support given to Delhi by some of the Sheikh's most trusted associates, G. M. Sadiq and Bakshi Ghulam Muhammad, who had been with Abdullah since the 1930s. Bakshi, from a poor family, with little education, had risen to prominence as Abdullah's right hand man. But in the post-independence years he had begun to make his own way. From 1948 to 1950 he had developed a special relationship with Sardar Patel and Karan Singh, which meant that, when the time came, he acquiesced in the Sheikh's dismissal. Only Mirza Afzal Beg was not prepared to go along with the plan. In the early hours of the morning on 9 August, Bakshi was sworn in as chief minister. Sheikh Abdullah did not return to political office until 1975 after an absence of twenty-two years, by which time he was seventy years old.

Bakshi the builder

'No one, except perhaps he himself in his secret thoughts,' writes Bilqees Taseer, 'could have dreamt then that the time would come when he, an eighth class pass student, would rise to such heights that he would intrigue to topple the Lion of Kashmir in 1953 and take his place for a reign of ten years of dictatorship and corruption.'[85] The outcry at Sheikh Abdullah's arrest was not sufficient to destabilise Bakshi's new government. The right wing was content because of his moves against the Praja Parishad movement; the leftists had been alarmed at Abdullah's meetings with US politicians. Even the Communist Party of India, which had initially given its support to Abdullah, had become disenchanted. The Pakistanis, however, reacted angrily at Abdullah's dismissal, despite their earlier criticism of the Sheikh's pro-India stance. Karachi went on strike and the government of Pakistan announced the cancellation of their August independence day celebrations.[86]

Bakshi, however, had a substantial package to offer the people of Kashmir, which included salary rises for all government servants and workers. Known as Bakshi the Builder, he also managed to secure funds for economic development, building and road construction. From 1947 to 1953 the Indian government had invested 100 million dollars in the state and built 500 primary schools. During Bakshi's tenure they undertook the construction of a one and a half mile long tunnel under the Banihal pass.[87] Still bitter at his dismissal, Sheikh Abdullah later described how 'lavish amounts of money were distributed by India to appease the Kashmiri Muslims'. He complained that Bakshi was distributing 'largesse' to his supporters, as well as 'filling his own coffers'.[88] Abdullah did, however, concede that some positive developments took place while Bakshi was in office: for the first time a medical college and a regional engineering college were set up. From primary to university level, education was made free. Kashmiris were economically better off in the 1960s – especially when compared with those in Azad Kashmir or as they had been in the days of the maharaja.

Part of Bakshi's brief was to finalise the details of Kashmir's accession to India. In 1954 the Constituent Assembly formally ratified the accession of the state of Jammu and Kashmir, which was intended to legitimise the Instrument of Accession, signed by Hari Singh in 1947. This measure was also meant to end all discussion of a plebiscite. On 13 April 1954 the customs barrier between Kashmir and the rest of India was lifted. President Rajendra Prasad made the first official visit by a president of India to the state of Jammu and Kashmir. Still under arrest, Sheikh Abdullah watched anxiously as the Constituent Assembly set about framing a constitution for the state of Jammu and Kashmir. His request to attend the session was refused. He therefore argued that the Constituent Assembly was not in a position to ratify the Instrument of Accession, since, without him and his supporters, it no longer represented the will of the people.

On 26 January 1957 the state of Jammu and Kashmir approved its own Constitution, modelled along the lines of the Indian Constitution; Abdullah described the introduction of the Constitution as a direct repudiation of the Indian commitment to a plebiscite under United Nations supervision. His protests and those of the United Nations Security Council, however, went unheeded. The next step was elections for a legislative assembly. Throughout this period the Constituent Assembly also functioned as a state legislature. In March 1957 elections were held and Bakshi was elected as prime minister

with a majority of sixty-eight seats. The elections caused a split in the National
Conference – G. M. Sadiq led a breakaway group, which included D. P. Dhar
and Mir Qasim, to launch the Democratic National Conference. On 9 August
1955, two years after Sheikh Abdullah's dismissal, Mir Afzal Beg had also
launched the All Jammu and Kashmir Plebiscite Front. Each year, 9 August,
was observed as a 'black day' by Front activists.

After over four years in prison, Abdullah was released in January 1958.
Soon afterwards he issued a statement to the press, in which he began to talk
once more about the plebiscite and the right of self-determination for the
people of the state. 'Expression of the will of the people through a plebiscite
is the one formula which has been agreed upon by the parties concerned,
and in a mass of disagreements about details, this common denominator has
held the field so far.'[89] He also stated that Bakshi could 'shout from the top
of the Banihal pass' that Kashmir's accession to India was 'final and
irrevocable' but his government was composed of 'goondas, opportunists
and thieves.'[90] The Indian authorities regarded his provocative statements as
the result of contacts with Pakistan, by whom they alleged he was being
financed. After only four months of freedom, Sheikh Abdullah was arrested
in April and detained again for six more years.

This time the charge brought against him, along with twenty-five other
co-defendants, including Mirza Afzal Beg, was of conspiracy. Abdullah's re-
arrest created an angry reaction in Pakistan, where the leading Kashmiri
activists, Muhammad Saraf, Sardar Qayum Khan, Ghulam Abbas decided to
launch a Kashmir Liberation Movement (KLM) by crossing the ceasefire
line. Their slogan was 'Kashmir Chalo' – 'Let's go to Kashmir'. But the
Pakistani government, headed by President Iskander Mirza, did not wish to
provoke India by supporting the attempt to cross the ceasefire line. Hundreds
of activists were arrested in Azad Kashmir, including Ghulam Abbas.
Muhammad Saraf pointed to the irony that Abbas, who had championed the
cause of Kashmir's accession to Pakistan was in a Pakistani jail, while his old
colleague, Sheikh Abdullah, who had supported Kashmir's accession to India,
was under detention in India. With considerable optimism, Saraf believed
that had the Pakistani government permitted them to cross the ceasefire line,
it would have attracted world-wide attention, which would have 'brought
home not only to the leaders of India, but also to those of the world, the
urgency of solving the Kashmir issue in accordance with justice.'[91]

During Abdullah's conspiracy trial the prosecution examined 229 witnesses
and exhibited nearly 300 documents. Abdullah continued to protest his
innocence whilst looking at the larger interests of the people of Kashmir. 'It
is a small matter as to what happens to me,' he said in a court appearance
in 1961. 'But it is no small matter that the people of Jammu and Kashmir
suffer poverty humiliation and degradation ... My voice may be stifled behind
the prison walls, but it will continue to echo and ring for all times to come.'[92]
Although he had raised the issue of plebiscite and self-determination again,

Abdullah did not, however, renounce his allegiance to India. 'My comrades [in jail] felt that we could not continue to hitch our wagon to a country in which we were treated so badly. I told them that we were wedded to certain ideals, so long as India propagated those we could not snap our ties.'[93] On 25 January 1962, the special magistrate committed all the accused to the Court of Sessions for trial, which dragged on for another two years.

Bakshi's government was not popular. Although he allowed the nominal existence of other political parties, their leaders were arrested indiscriminately and public meetings were banned. The 'Peace' Brigade was used to victimise opponents of the government. Foreign journalists were not welcome in the state. Stephen Harper, a reporter for the *Daily Express* wrote:

> I had scarcely arrived in Srinagar, the capital, last week when a mob swarmed around my car. They shouted "Murder him – we don't want British reporters here!" Car doors and canopy were ripped off. Hands grabbed and tore at my clothes. Little baskets of charcoal – carried around for heat were poured over me and burned my face.[94]

Political dissent was crushed. 'The common man, under Bakshi's tyrannical rule, was denied even basic civil liberties,' noted Mir Qasim, a former associate, but now a political opponent. 'The government agents forced hot potatoes into the mouths of their opponents, put heavy stones on their chest; and branded them with red hot irons.'[95] Various newspapers critical of the government were banned, including the *Voice of Kashmir*, edited by Prem Nath Bazaz, who had moved to Delhi. The elections in 1962 were so evidently rigged, that Jawaharlal Nehru commented: 'In fact, it would strengthen your position much more if you lost a few seats to bona fide opponents.' All that could be said of Baskhi's government was that the people had more freedom than under the maharaja. 'It is true that political liberty does not exist there in the same measure as in the rest of India. At the same time, there is much more of it than there used to be.'[96]

'So far as the economic and social life of the Kashmiris is concerned,' writes Prem Nath Bazaz, who visited the valley in the early 1960s, 'I have no doubt that they are grateful to India for the little progress they have made ... but political persecution and suppression of free opinion coupled with harassment by the goonda element is, besides making them sullen and resentful, neutralising the good effects of the benevolent attitude of the Union government.' He also believed that the accession issue had not gone away. 'To make Kashmir's accession to India everlasting, it is essential that the Kashmiris should feel convinced that economically as well as politically they will enjoy freedom by remaining as part of the great Indian nation.' He also noted that whereas Sheikh Abdullah guarded Kashmir's autonomy, 'to curry favour with the Indian public opinion' Bakshi Ghulam Muhammed 'made inroads into it.' With some foresight to the future deterioration of relations he concluded: 'Before long when India wakes up, as it must some day, in the near future, if not today, it may be too late. No liberalisation of policy may be able to repair the damage.'[97] On 3 October 1963 Bakshi was one of many cabinet ministers and chief ministers who agreed to resign under the terms of the plan put forward by K. Kamaraj, the chief minister of Madras, who suggested that he and some other chief ministers might resign in order to do party work. Bakshi Ghulam Muhammed was replaced by Khwaja Shamsuddin. Subsequently, a one-man commission, under Mr Justice Ayyangar, enquired into charges of corruption and misuse of power by Bakshi. Initially 77 charges were brought against him, of which 38 were referred to the commission. Ayyangar ruled that fifteen were proved.

The ten-year period of Bakshi Ghulam Muhammad's rule is noted for the steady erosion of the special status with which Kashmir had begun its relationship with India. Some of the changes appeared to be cosmetic, but they increased suspicions amongst Kashmiris that the state of Jammu and Kashmir was being made to conform with the other states in India. Shortly before his resignation, Bakshi Ghulam Muhammed had announced that the head of the Kashmir state would, in future, be called chief minister rather than prime minister, which would conform with the other states of the Indian Union and that the sadar-i-riyasat would be known as the governor. The jurisdiction of the Supreme Court and the Election Commission of India was also extended. Throughout most of this period, Sheikh Abdullah was in prison, but his influence and that of his supporters kept alive not only the issue of the plebiscite but also of Kashmir's 'special status'.

PART FOUR

Vale of Tears

CHAPTER 12

Diplomacy and War

The talks between India and Pakistan resemble badminton. The arrangement was to talk a few days first in Pakistan, now a few days in India. The thing is to get the shuttle back in the other court. John Kenneth Galbraith[1]

India's basic advantage lay in the fact that she was already in occupation of what she wanted. If Pakistan wished to change the status of the disputed territory, it was for her to do something about it and risk seeming belligerent. Outsiders are prone to treat the maintenance of the status quo as peace and its disturbance by either side, even for good reasons, a move toward war. Sam Burke[2]

Throughout the 1960s the Kashmiri issue continued to cause concern at an international level. In October 1962 the unresolved dispute between India and China over their Himalayan border erupted when the Chinese overran Indian outposts and moved troops into the North-East Frontier Area (N–EFA) and Ladakh. Although the immediate crisis between India and China ended when, on 21 November, the Chinese declared a unilateral ceasefire, the Indians, who had shown themselves particularly ill-equipped for such high altitude fighting, still felt vulnerable over their long-term security. Nehru, who had earlier shunned military assistance as signifying 'practically becoming aligned to that country', was now prepared to accept it. In a much quoted passage, he admitted that through his policy of non-alignment: 'We were getting out of touch with reality in the modern world and we were living in an atmosphere of our own creation.'[3] He was even prepared to talk in terms of a tacit air defence pact with the United States in case the Chinese resumed their offensive.[4] In return, however, the Indian government was obliged to submit to political pressure from Western countries for talks with Pakistan regarding a resolution of the Kashmir issue.

Endless talks

At the end of November 1962 both Britain and the United States sent missions to New Delhi, led respectively by Duncan Sandys, the secretary of state for Commonwealth Relations, and Averell Harriman, the assistant secretary of state for Far Eastern Affairs in order to determine what military help India might need. The Americans and British were also anxious to reassure Pakistan regarding the extent of any military assistance to India. In a statement on 20 November President John Kennedy said: 'In providing military assistance to India, we are mindful of our alliance with Pakistan. All of our aid to India is for the purpose of defeating Chinese communist subversion.'[5] The Anglo–American team also wanted to initiate bilateral talks between India and Pakistan to help them resolve their differences, in order to present a united front against the threat from communist China.

Pakistan, under President Ayub Khan, who had assumed power in a military coup, ousting Iskander Mirza in 1958, was, however, not convinced that such solidarity would work to Pakistan's advantage. Not only did the Pakistanis mistrust the Indians, but they were angered that India, which had so consistently pursued a policy of 'non-alignment' should receive weapons from the West, which the Pakistanis had been permitted only after joining the two Western military alliances, CENTO and SEATO; in addition, Pakistan had been obliged to allow the Americans to install surveillance equipment on Pakistani soil, which had displeased the Soviets and potentially impaired Pakistan's relations with the Russians. The grant of military equipment appeared to have put India on the same level as Pakistan, who was supposed to be America's 'most favoured ally'.

The Indian government also reacted less positively to the talks because the Pakistani government was already engaged in its own separate negotiations with the Chinese to demarcate the common boundary between China and northern Kashmir. Even before the Sino–Indian war, Krishna Menon, the Indian defence minister, had stated in the UN Security Council in June 1962 that any agreement was in 'total violation of any rights of authority Pakistan may possess, for Pakistan has no sovereignty over the state; it is not Pakistan's to trade away or to negotiate about.'[6]

Sandys and Harriman were, however, able to use the Indians' desperate need for weapons to persuade Nehru to meet Ayub in order to try and resolve the Kashmir problem. 'Dependent on the United States and Britain for military assistance, India could not refuse to talk to Pakistan,' writes Nehru's biographer, Sarvepalli Gopal.[7] Lord Mountbatten was once more back in Delhi with Sandys in order to prepare the ground for the talks. By this time, according to Philip Ziegler, Mountbatten believed that the only solution was for Kashmir to be independent and demilitarised. 'When Nehru pleaded how dangerous any change of the present balance in Kashmir might be for the large Muslim minority in India, Mountbatten replied that he was never one to stir up sleeping dogs unnecessarily, but that this dog was already awake and barking.'[8] Nehru's cabinet ministers were unreceptive to the proposal. In their joint statement, issued on 29 November, announcing the talks, Ayub Khan and Jawaharlal Nehru merely announced that a renewed effort should be made to resolve outstanding differences between the two countries on Kashmir and other related matters.

The first round of talks over Jammu and Kashmir between India and Pakistan was held at the end of December 1962. During this, and subsequent meetings various proposals were put forward. Whereas India suggested the ceasefire line should become the international boundary, with a few minor realignments around Poonch, the Pakistanis wanted to draw the boundary far to the east, giving themselves the whole state with the exception of south-eastern Jammu. Out of a total area of over 84,000 square miles India was to be left with less than 3,000 square miles.

After the second round of talks came the official signing of the Sino–Pakistan Border Agreement, which soured an already tense atmosphere. Zulfikar Ali Bhutto, who had taken over as foreign minister in January 1963 after the death of Muhammed Ali Bogra, went to Beijing to meet with his Chinese counterpart, Chen Yi, for the ceremony on 2 March 1963. Although the Pakistanis claimed to have gained 750 square miles of land, the Indians believed they had ceded 2,700 square miles of what they regarded as 'Indian' (because it was Kashmiri) territory.[9] The Pakistanis countered the allegation, stating that the agreement was provisional pending a proper boundary treaty once the Kashmiri dispute had been resolved. China's agreement to the negotiations was interpreted as public acceptance of Pakistan's position that the status of Jammu and Kashmir had not yet been finalised.

Another of Pakistan's proposals, supported by Britain, was to inter-nationalise the valley so that Indian troops could be withdrawn and replaced by forces of other countries; after six months the wishes of the people were to be ascertained. This was, however, writes Gopal 'a suggestion which even the Americans saw to be impractical, as it played into the hands of the Chinese, who would work on any Asian and African powers concerned.'[10] Sir Morrice James, the British high commissioner in Pakistan, believed 'the right course would be for India and Pakistan each to accept that the other should have a substantial position in the Vale, and the Indian government could not be expected to give up Ladakh.' The proposal was designed 'to permit clearly defined arrangements for sovereignty, political freedom, the free movement of people, the development of tourism, and economic development.'[11] Initially, this solution was favoured by President Kennedy, who urged the Indian government to make such proposals 'which will be proof positive to the Pakistanis that you genuinely seek a settlement by signalling a willingness to give Pakistan a substantial position in the Vale.'[12] In April 1963 Walt Rostow was sent by President Kennedy to India and Pakistan to assess the prospects for agreement between the two countries. But he did not find 'a driving determination to settle the quarrel' on either the Indian or the Pakistani side.[13]

After six rounds of talks, which were held intermittently until May 1963, and in which Bhutto and Swaran Singh, the Indian foreign minister, were the principal negotiators, a joint communiqué was issued which stated that with regret no agreement could be reached on a settlement of the Kashmir dispute. Whereas during the talks the two sides had discussed the possibility of partitioning the state, in their public statements this suggestion was rejected.[14] The Indian government proposed that both countries should seek only peaceful methods to settle their differences and that neither should seek to alter the status quo in Kashmir. Bhutto did not endorse the 'no war' declaration but gave the assurance that Pakistan did believe in peaceful methods. 'To have promoted the 1962–3 Indo–Pakistan talks and seen them fail, had thus served the useful purpose of showing that further efforts of the kind would not succeed.' commented Sir Morrice James.[15]

From the Indian point of view, due to her vulnerability over China, the 1962–63 talks were one of the rare occasions when they were obliged to depart from their established position over Kashmir: that discussion in some way implied that the status of Jammu and Kashmir was in doubt. The Pakistanis mistakenly hoped that Britain and the United States would withhold the promised weapons to India in return for a more favourable outcome for Pakistan over Kashmir, but it is unlikely that Nehru would have yielded to such a threat. By 1962 possession of the best part of Kashmir was both politically and psychologically too important, particularly when the Indian public were still reacting to their army's defeat by the Chinese.[16]

After the talks Nehru went to Srinagar where he noted how China's attack on India had given the Pakistanis an opportunity to revive the Kashmir issue. But, he said: 'Pakistan is mistaken if it thinks it can intimidate us because we are facing this threat from the Chinese.' The new relationship between China and Pakistan meant, however, that the Pakistanis also felt inclined to speak from a position of strength: 'Attack from India on Pakistan today is no longer confined to the security and territorial integrity of Pakistan,' said Zulfikar Ali Bhutto in Pakistan's National Assembly in July 1963. ' An attack by India on Pakistan involves the territorial integrity and security of the largest state in Asia.'[17] He also made the dramatic statement: 'Kashmir is to Pakistan what Berlin is to the West' and warned that, since the conflict threatened peace and security of the world, 'it was an issue hanging heavily on the conscience of mankind.'[18]

Amongst the Kashmiris watching as Pakistan and India discussed their future were those who were discontented with the status quo, but not yet in a strong enough position to do anything about it. One of this older generation of activists was Amanullah Khan. Born in Astor near Gilgit and educated in Srinagar, he and some colleagues reacted to the discussion on the partition of Kashmir by forming an organisation called the Kashmir Independence Committee. 'We suggested that if there has got to be some sort of deviation from plebiscite, from the right of self-determination, it should not be the division of Kashmir, it should be the independence of the whole state.'[19] The talks failed and the Committee was later disbanded. But, says Amanullah Khan, it was the first time the Kashmiri nationalists in exile in Pakistan began to think seriously about independence.

In October 1963 the Government of Pakistan once more referred the question of Kashmir to the Security Council and, in the Spring of 1964, the issue was debated for the 110th time in fifteen years. On his way to New

York, Bhutto announced that Pakistan was prepared to discuss the issue a thousand times in order to see that it was settled 'in an honourable manner'.[20] But, in view of the Soviet veto, there was little the United Nations could do. The president of the Security Council expressed the concern of all the members that 'two great countries which have everything to gain from re-establishing good relations with each other and whose present disputes, particularly that centring upon Jammu and Kashmir, should be settled amicably in the interest of world peace.'[21]

Politics in the vale

In mid-winter, on a freezing cold night in late December 1963, an event of extraordinary significance had occurred in the valley. The most sacred Muslim relic in Kashmir, the strand of hair from the beard of the Prophet, the Mo-i Muqaddas, was stolen from the mosque at Hazratbal. Word of the theft spread throughout the city and thousands marched through the streets of Srinagar, demanding that the thieves should be caught and punished. A 'Sacred Hair Action Committee' was set up by the outraged Kashmiris, which tempor-arily united pro and anti-Abdullah factions. The Sheikh's son, Farooq, and Mirwaiz Maulvi Farooq, jointly protested at the theft.

Chief Minister Shamsuddin was slow in taking the initiative, and Nehru dispatched his Intelligence Bureau chief, B. N. Mullik, to take steps to recover the relic. While he set about the delicate task of locating it, the anger of the people spread into the countryside. In order to diffuse fears of communal strife, on 4 January Karan Singh arrived in Srinagar and visited Hazratbal. He organised prayers in the temples for the return of the sacred relic. Later that evening the mosque was cleared of policemen and officials. It has never been revealed who stole the holy relic, but Mullik succeeded in tracking down the thieves and arranging for the relic to be returned quietly to the mosque that evening.

From the Pakistani perspective, the tremendous Islamic fervour which manifested itself throughout the state over the missing relic seemed to be a sure sign that all was not well with the so-called secularism espoused by the current rulers of Kashmir. Muslim disturbances in Srinagar were accompanied by protests from Hindus at the theft of holy objects from temples in Jammu. As unrest increased, the government crushed the demonstrations by force, killing several people. As a reaction there were riots against Hindus in East Pakistan, which in turn resulted in communal outbreaks in some towns in India. The tense atmosphere was only relieved when, at the beginning of February 1964, a panel of holy men examined the relic and judged that it was the original.

Soon after the return of the sacred relic, Shamsuddin was replaced as chief minister by Ghulam Muhammad Sadiq. The atmosphere in the valley changed considerably. Prem Nath Bazaz described an 'altogether different political climate'. People were able to express their political views freely, hooliganism was dying down and corruption decreased.[22] At the same time Bazaz felt that it was necessary to maintain the momentum of liberalisation. 'I found that after restoring the civil liberties of the Kashmiris, the Sadiq government was inclined to rest on its oars, thinking that the people should remain beholden for what had already been done for them.'[23]

The accession issue, however, was still unresolved in people's minds. In addition, Abdullah's conspiracy case had dragged on for nearly six years and his continuing detention was proving embarrassing to the Government of India. 'Sheikh Abdullah on Trial but India in the Dock' was just one of many newspaper headlines at the time.[24] On 8 April 1964 Abdullah was honourably acquitted and released from Jammu Central jail. 'Falsehood has a rotten core. Their vile accusations were fully exposed before the public and the case became a joke.' wrote Abdullah.[25] He immediately went on the offensive: 'We have to win hearts and if we fail in this regard we cannot be ruled by force,' he said two days after his release.[26] But the Indian government continued to maintain that the accession of the state of Jammu and Kashmir to India was 'full final and complete.'[27] 'Whatever be the grandiose delusions and dreams Abdullah now nourishes, New Delhi must leave him and his supporters in no doubt that accession is an accomplished fact and that only some of the processes of integration remain to be completed,' stated an editorial in the *Indian Express*.[28] 'Sheikh Abdullah is now a demagogue at large, and he is plainly engaged in secessionist political activity,' said *The Times of India*, Bombay.[29]

At the highest level, however, the ailing prime minister of India, Jawaharlal Nehru, was no longer prepared to share these misgivings about his old friend. 'His attitude to Abdullah at this time was a blend of guilt at having allowed him to have been kept so long in detention and of concern at the consequences of his activities,' writes Sarvepalli Gopal.[30] After his release, Abdullah went to stay with Nehru in Delhi:

> Panditji expressed his deep anguish and sorrow at the past incidents. I also became very emotional and told him that I was glad to have convinced him that I was not disloyal to him personally or to India ... I implored him to take the initiative in resolving the Kashmir problem. Panditji agreed and asked me to visit Pakistan and try to persuade the President, Ayub Khan, to enter into negotiations with his Indian counterpart.[31]

For the first and last time in his life, Sheikh Abdullah went to Pakistan. Before he left he issued a press statement: 'We are faced with an alarming situation. If we fail to remedy it our future generations will never pardon us ... The Kashmiri problem is a long-standing bone of contention.'[32]

When Abdullah arrived in Rawalpindi, he received an enthusiastic welcome from a crowd estimated to be half a million. 'There was much excitement in Pakistan about the first ever visit of Sheikh Abdullah – the Lion of Kashmir,' writes Altaf Gauhar, Ayub Khan's minister for information. 'His critics preferred to call him the "leopard of Kashmir" who had finally changed his spots. What was India's game in allowing Sheikh Abdullah to visit Pakistan?'[33] According to Gauhar, the official view was that Sheikh Abdullah should be given a warm but not effusive welcome and an elaborate programme was drawn up 'so that he could see for himself the progress Pakistan had made since independence.'[34]

Although the personal rapport between the Kashmiri leader and the Pakistani president was good, Ayub Khan was obliged to reject Abdullah's suggestion of a confederation. 'Any kind of confederal arrangement would undo the partition and place the Hindu majority in a dominant and decisive position in respect of confederal subjects, i.e. foreign affairs, defence and finance.'[35] Abdullah later said that the idea of confederation was only one proposal among many and that the purpose of his visit was specifically so that both parties 'should abstain from rigid attitudes and sympathetically consider each other's viewpoint.'[36] At a press conference, he declared that a solution of the Kashmiri problem must satisfy the wishes of the Kashmiri people and depended on friendship between India and Pakistan. He also stated that it must not give either side a sense of defeat.[37] Ayub Khan agreed to consider any solution which met Pakistan's minimum conditions. He also accepted the invitation to come to Delhi to meet Nehru in the middle of June.

The day the news of the proposed meeting was announced was 27 May. Sheikh Abdullah left for Muzaffarabad. But his visit was cut short by the sudden news that Jawaharlal Nehru, aged seventy-four, had died. In one of those mysteries of history, the Indian prime minister left unfinished whatever he might have been able to do for Kashmir in the last days of his life. Bhutto travelled with Abdullah to Delhi for Nehru's funeral, and discussed Kashmir with the Sheikh, who, according to Stanley Wolpert's account, advised Bhutto to hold to requesting a plebiscite for the entire state whilst suggesting that partition below the Chenab river might be a realistic solution. Bhutto was apparently 'elated' by the Sheikh's 'flexibility', since during his talks with Ayub, Abdullah had insisted that partition was not possible.[38] But further proposed talks did not materialise. According to Abdullah, Nehru's successor, Lal Bahadur Shastri, was keen to finish Nehru's work, but 'he did not have the strength to bring his colleagues round to his viewpoint.'[39] Furthermore, the Indian government was continuing to pass measures designed to strengthen Kashmir's links with India.

The Presidential Order passed by the Indian government on 21 December 1964 enabling the president to govern the state of Jammu and Kashmir directly was bitterly resented by opponents of India's increasing control. So too was the announcement on 9 January 1965 that the local National Conference party would be dissolved and that the Indian National Congress party was to establish a branch in Kashmir. 15 January 1965 was observed as a Protest Day.

In February 1965 Abdullah decided 'to fulfil the tenets of Islam which have been ordained for all Muslims – the performance of Haj.'[40] He and a small party which included his wife and Mirza Afzal Beg, planned to visit some other Islamic countries, as well as Britain and France. In Algiers, Abdullah met Chou-en Lai, China's prime minister and, according to his memoirs, they discussed China's agreement with Pakistan over the northern frontier of Gilgit. The Chinese premier stated: 'At present, Gilgit is under the control of Pakistan and, therefore, we entered into an agreement stipulating that the agreement shall remain valid only as long as Gilgit is under the control of Pakistan.' Abdullah says that he sent a summary of his conversation to the Indian ambassador to China, but news of Chou en Lai's invitation to Abdullah to visit China upset the Indian authorities. Abdullah had also written an article in a US quarterly magazine in which he suggested that India, Pakistan and the Kashmiris should find a solution which would concede to the Kashmiris 'the substance of their demand for self-determination but with honour and fairness to both Pakistan and India.'[41] When he returned to India in May 1965 Abdullah was arrested. He was interned in Tamil Nadu at Otacamund, 2,000 miles away from Kashmir. Afzal Beg was imprisoned in Delhi. Begum Abdullah was also interned in Delhi. Protests in the valley against the arrests were crushed. 'A vilification campaign was started against us under a well-planned conspiracy with a view to distorting our image and creating a psychological environment in which harsh measures may be used against us.'[42]

In Pakistan Ayub Khan was coming under increasing domestic pressure to take some initiative over Kashmir. During the July Presidential campaign, when he was opposed by Muhammad Ali Jinnah's sister, Fatima, Ayub had stressed his role as the defender of Kashmir. He was also being pressed by the 'Azad' Kashmiris, who claimed to have a force of 20,000 trained men in order to mount an Algerian-type struggle to liberate their 'brothers'. On the military front, time was also running out. In April 1963 the Indian defence ministry had announced that the strength of the army would be doubled. The following September, the Indian government gave further details of the expansion of the Navy, Army and Airforce, made possible by the assistance of the UK, the USA and the USSR.[43]

Armed conflict

Internationally, Pakistan was beginning to emerge from its political dependence on the United States. Ayub Khan's successful visit to China in March 1965 had considerably enhanced his domestic standing. 'The people felt elevated by the knowledge that China had become Pakistan's friend and ally against India,' writes Altaf Gauhar.[44] When President Johnson cancelled Ayub Khan's scheduled visit to the United States,[45] Ayub Khan at once accepted an invitation by the Russians to visit the Soviet Union, making the first ever visit by a Pakistani head of government to Moscow. According to Gauhar, who accompanied the president, Ayub Khan had a frank conversation with Prime Minister Alexei Kosygin about Kashmir. He pointed out that by using the veto, the Soviet Union was 'bailing India out' in the UN Security Council. The Soviets were upset at the recent U2 episode when an American espionage plane, launched from the Badaber base in Pakistan, had been shot down over Soviet territory. What began, however, as a cool exchange of views was, according to Gauhar, described by Kosygin at the end of their meetings as 'a turning point which will lead to further exchanges of views and to big decisions in the interest of our two countries.'[46] A trade treaty was signed as well as a credit agreement on oil prospecting. But while Ayub Khan was still in Moscow he received a cable from Islamabad indicating the movement of Indian troops into the disputed territory of the Rann of Kutch.

Distant from Kashmir, the Rann of Kutch affair preceded the outbreak of formal hostilities between India and Pakistan in their second war over Kashmir in September 1965. This tract of land, equivalent in size to the valley of Kashmir, separates Sind in Pakistan from Kutch in India. Inhabited mainly by flamingos and wild donkeys, during the monsoon it is flooded; at other times of the year it is dry and desolate (which is the meaning of the word 'rann') Ever since partition, Pakistan had been contesting the boundary between Sind and Kutch. In the spring of 1965 a clash between border patrols escalated into fighting between the regular armies. When Indian forces withdrew, leaving behind them 40 miles of marshland, the Pakistanis were jubilant. A ceasefire was mediated in the name of the British prime minister, Harold Wilson, facilitated by the two British high commissioners in Islamabad and Delhi, Morrice James and John Freeman. Agreement was finally reached on 30 June 1965, which provided for arbitration. A year later Pakistan was awarded the northern half of the Rann. 'The Pakistanis thus gained more by accepting Western mediation between India and themselves than they would have achieved alone,' writes Morrice James.[47] The significance of this affair is that it undoubtedly encouraged the Pakistanis in their assessment that the Indian army, still suffering from the after effects of its defeat by the Chinese, and not yet bolstered by its planned expansion, was inferior to their own.

The conclusion which Morrice James believes President Ayub Khan, Zulfikar Ali Bhutto and Aziz Ahmed, Ayub's expert on Indian affairs, drew from the Rann of Kutch affair was as follows: if the Kashmir dispute could be reactivated by stirring up a rebellion in the Indian-held section, a critical situation would arise which would be sufficient to oblige the western countries to intervene. India might then be pressurised to submit the dispute to mediation, which if successful might lead to a more favourable solution to Pakistan than the status quo. They also deduced that after the Rann of Kutch affair the morale of the Indians was low.[48] 'For all his realism and prudence,' writes Altaf Gauhar 'Ayub's judgement did get impaired by the Rann of Kutch in one respect. His old prejudice that the "Hindu has no stomach for a fight" turned into belief, if not a military doctrine, which had the decisive effect on the course of events.'[49] Viewed from across the ceasefire line, the valley of Kashmir appeared ripe for revolt. The theft of the holy relic from Hazratbal in 1963 had demonstrated the intense Islamic feeling amongst the Muslims of the valley.

The headquarters for what came to be known as 'Operation Gibraltar' were based at Murree under Major General Akhtar Hussain Malik. Malik was in command of several task forces, named after famous generals drawn from Muslim history: Tariq, Qasim, Khalid, Salahuddin, Ghaznavi, and Nusrat, which would advance across the ceasefire line into Kashmir and attack specific targets. The initiative, however, was not without risk. The Indian army was three times the size that of Pakistan and there was no guarantee that India would not invade Pakistan across the international frontier. In addition, writes Major-General Shahid Hamid, 'the Army was not trained or ready for the offensive; some 25 per cent of the men were on leave. There was little time to make up for this deficiency in our planning and the crisis created a series of isolated battles.'[50]

The objective was for Salahuddin force to assemble in Srinagar on 8 August; the next day – the 12th anniversary of Sheikh Abdullah's arrest in August 1953 – supporters of the Plebiscite Front had planned to hold a strike against Abdullah's recent arrest. The Pakistani strategists therefore believed that the discontented population would support their invasion. After seizing the radio station and Srinagar airport, a Revolutionary Council would issue a declaration of 'Liberation', proclaiming it was the only legitimate government of Jammu and Kashmir. In an additional operation, known as Grand Slam, lines of communication were to be attacked in the Poonch/ Nowshera district; possession of Akhnur Bridge across the Chenab river would isolate the state of Jammu and Kashmir from the rest of India, trapping the Indian army in the state as well as the forces facing the Chinese in Ladakh.

No contact, however, appears to have been made in advance with the Muslim political leadership in the valley. Contrary to Pakistani intelligence information, the valley was not ripe for revolt. 'Pakistani commandos, armed to the teeth, would appear as liberators in the middle of the night only to create panic and terror,' writes Altaf Gauhar.[51] On 5 August, a shepherd boy reported to the police the presence of some 'strangers' in Tanmarg who had offered bribes in return for information. He led the police directly to Salahuddin's base camp. 'Pakistan at this stage had little mass support in the valley and that is why this ingenious plan failed to take off,' writes the Indian Major-General Afsir Karim. 'In fact no one was quite sure what was going on. Pakistan kept denying its "involvement" at the top of its voice and called it a local uprising - but there was no local uprising.'[52] Kashmiri anger demonstrated over the missing sacred relic did not, at this stage, mean that the people were prepared to throw their lot in with the Pakistanis and fight

India. With the exception of Ghaznavi, the forces were not able to make any impact on the Indian positions.

The Indian prime minister, Lal Bahadur Shastri, was also under pressure from his military advisers to take decisive action. On 16 August a crowd of over 100,000 marched on the Indian parliament in Delhi to demonstrate against any weakness over the state of Jammu and Kashmir.[53] The Indian counter-offensive was more far reaching than the Pakistanis had anticipated. For ostensibly defensive reasons, in order to close the points of entry from the infiltrators, they attacked Pakistani positions in the Kargil sector, as well as in Tithwal and Uri-Poonch. Their operation against the Haji Pir Pass on 28 August left the Pakistani forces dangerously exposed.

Despite the setback to Operation Gibraltar, of which Ayub Khan appears to have been unaware, General Muhammed Musa, the commander-in-chief, was 'urging Bhutto to obtain Ayub's approval' to launch Operation Grand Slam.[54] Musa had been appointed by Ayub, writes Major-General Shahid Hamid, 'though quite aware of his limitations. His chief virtue was that he would never challenge his leader's authority or position. On the other hand, Musa played it safe, and always toed the line.'[55] On 29 August President Ayub Khan sent Musa a 'top secret' order 'to take such action that will defreeze the Kashmir problem, weaken India's resolve and bring her to a conference table without provoking a general war.'[56] Under Malik's leadership, Operation Grand Slam was launched on 31 August. The objective was to move in from Bhimber and cut off Indian lines of communication along the Pathankot road from Jammu to Srinagar via the Banihal pass, much as was planned in 1947. Once Pakistani forces reached Akhnur, they had only to take the bridge across the Chenab river in order to reach the city of Jammu. 'At this point, someone's prayers worked,' writes the Indian journalist M. J. Akbar. 'An inexplicable change of command took place.'[57] Hussain Malik was replaced by Major-General Agha Mohammad Yahya Khan.

Gauhar describes the details of Grand Slam as still being shrouded 'in a haze of confusion, indecision and loss of communication.'[58] The operation was based on the assumption that the Indian forces were exposed, but they had in fact been building up their defences and the Pakistani troops were not able to make the swift breakthrough they had envisaged. Furthermore, the Pakistanis had crossed a small section of the international frontier between Sialkot and Jammu, which was an open provocation for the Indian forces to extend the war. Although the view both in India and even amongst 'sensible army officers' in Pakistan was that Malik's sudden replacement led to the failure of Grand Slam, Gauhar maintains that Malik had already lost all credibility after Gibraltar. 'The truth is that General Malik was a broken man because he knew better than anyone else that his mission had failed.'[59] Once Ayub Khan was aware of the failure of Operation Gibraltar and realised how vulnerable the Pakistani forces were, the task of winding up the operation was given to Major-General Mohammad Yahya Khan.

In addition, the assessment, supported both by Bhutto and Aziz Ahmed, that the Indians were in no position to attack across the international frontier was also disproved. At first light on 6 September two columns of the Indian army marched towards Lahore which lay only fourteen miles from the international border. 'Astonishingly the Pakistanis were taken by surprise,' records Morrice James. 'Their troops had not been alerted and were asleep in their barracks. Some of them left with their weapons for the front line in their pyjamas for want of time to put on battle-dress.'[60] A third column crossed into West Punjab towards Sialkot, north-east of Lahore. The Indian air force also bombed Pakistani air bases. The sub-continent was set for all out war. Both Britain and the United States, who were the main suppliers of weapons to both sides, announced a halt in military aid until peace was restored. During the war, Russia continued to supply military equipment to India, but remained ostensibly neutral. Muslim countries, with the exception of Malaysia, promised assistance and moral support to Pakistan. The Arab summit conference commended the principle of self-determination and requested India and Pakistan to settle their differences according to the UN resolutions.[61]

Once again the United Nations was drawn into trying to bring about a ceasefire. On the basis of information provided by the UN Military Observer Group, which had been monitoring the ceasefire line for the past sixteen years, Secretary-General U Thant repeatedly appealed to the governments of India and Pakistan to return to their original positions along the ceasefire line. On 4 and 6 September the Security Council had adopted resolutions calling for a ceasefire and on 9 September U Thant visited first Pakistan and then India in an attempt to get the two sides to stop fighting. When Morrice James met Ayub Khan on 7 September he found him 'visibly depressed', saying that the ceasefire 'must be a purposeful one that would open the door to a settlement of the Kashmir dispute.'[62] India refused to negotiate and Pakistan was running out of ammunition. With the capture of Khem Karan, an Indian village across the border, the Pakistani counter-offensive against Amritsar looked as if it might temporarily succeed. But on 11 September India opened the floodgates of its dams trapping nearly 100 Pakistani tanks and Khem Karan, became, according to Gauhar, 'a graveyard of Pakistani tanks ... for Pakistan the war was over'.[63]

Before finally being drawn to the negotiating table, Ayub Khan turned to the Chinese. On 4 September the Chinese foreign minister, Chen Yi, had met Bhutto in Karachi and supported Pakistan's 'just action' in repelling the Indian 'armed provocation' in Kashmir.[64] Further statements in support of Pakistan followed, warning against Indian intrusion into Chinese territory. On 16 September the Chinese issued an ultimatum accusing India of building up military works on the boundary of the Chinese-Sikkim frontier. Unless these were dismantled and the Indians agreed to refrain from further raids, they were warned that they would have to face the consequences.[65] The

British and Americans viewed the entry of China into the diplomatic war of words with increasing alarm and as a potential prelude to intervention and the escalation of the war. The British prime minister, Harold Wilson, issued a statement promising the assistance of both the United States and United Kingdom to India if the Chinese intervened in the war.[66]

How close this intervention could have become is related by Altaf Gauhar, who describes Ayub Khan's secret visit to Beijing on the night of 19 September, when he met Prime Minister Chou en Lai. According to Ayub's verbatim account to Gauhar, the Chinese premier gave the Pakistani president an offer of unconditional support on the understanding that Pakistan realised it would have to be prepared for a long war in which some cities like Lahore might be lost. Ayub Khan was not prepared to undertake a protracted war and returned to Pakistan as secretly as he had come, without taking up the Chinese offer.[67] Moreover, he knew that the Army and Air Force were opposed to prolonging the conflict. As Shahid Hamid noted: 'All planning was based on a short, sharp encounter and ammunition and reserves were organised accordingly.'[68] Subsequently, the Chinese backed down on their aggressive stance towards India. The precise nature of India's alleged 'military installations' on the border was never established.

On 20 September, the UN Security Council passed a strongly worded resolution, for the first time in its history, 'demanding' that a ceasefire should take effect on 22 September. Bhutto flew to New York to address the Security Council on the night of 22 September. Pakistan's official position was still not conciliatory towards India and, in a speech, whose rhetoric was thrilling to the Pakistanis back home, he warned that Pakistan would wage a war for 'a thousand years, a war of defence.'[69] But the opportunity for Pakistan to fulfil its declared objectives had now passed.

The ceasefire came into force at midday on 22 September on the under-standing given to Ayub Khan, by both the British and Americans, that they would do their best to settle the political problem between India and Pakistan which had caused the current conflict.[70]

Tashkent

Once the cease-fire was put into effect an uneasy truce prevailed. Neither the United States, preoccupied with Vietnam, nor Britain were in a position to pressurise India to negotiate a settlement over Kashmir which would be favourable to Pakistan. India was certainly not going to give up through diplomacy what Pakistan had failed to secure in war. Swaran Singh, the Indian foreign minister, had declared in the General Assembly that Kashmir was an integral part of India and that its future was not negotiable.[71] Bhutto's veiled threats in the General Assembly and the Security Council that Pakistan would have to withdraw from the UN unless the ceasefire was made conditional on a resolution of the plebiscite issue went unheeded.

In January 1966 Indian and Pakistani delegations met in Tashkent where the Soviet prime minister, Alexei Kosygin, acted as unofficial mediator. Ayub and Shastri accepted a declaration in which both countries reaffirmed their commitment to solving their disputes through peaceful means. They also agreed to revert to their positions prior to 5 August 1965. Within hours of the close of the negotiations, on 10 January 1966, Shastri died of a heart attack. He was succeeded as prime minister by Jawaharlal Nehru's daughter, Indira Gandhi. Ayub Khan returned to Islamabad having accepted a return to the status quo which was far removed from Pakistan's declared war aims. While the Tashkent declaration noted the existence of the Kashmir dispute, it effectively put the issue into cold storage.

In Pakistan the controlled press did not allow criticism of Tashkent and 'continued to beat the patriotic drum as if the war with India was still going on,' writes Morrice James.[72] The 'spirit of Tashkent' was taken to symbolic extremes with the banning of the popular – but anti-Russian – James Bond film, 'From Russia with Love'.[73] But there was discontent beneath the surface. Those who had been led to believe that Pakistan was poised for victory, could not understand the necessity of the ceasefire. In early 1966 there were student riots in the colleges and universities. In Lahore the police opened fire on a group of demonstrators and two students were killed. Once the true significance of the ceasefire and Tashkent were apparent the people reacted against their President. 'The feeling of let-down and frustration was particularly strong amongst the people who lived in the areas of the Punjab around Lahore and Sialkot, where over the years many Kashmiris had settled,' writes Morrice James. 'For them Ayub had betrayed the nation and had inexcusably lost face before the Indians.'[74]

What is significant about the 1965 war from a Pakistani perspective is that, despite its failure to achieve its objectives, undoubtedly based on wrong assessments and policy decisions, the belief that the incursion was morally justifiable prevailed both in the rhetoric of the politicians, especially Zulfikar Ali Bhutto, and in subsequent recollections of the war. Pakistan's war dead are still referred to as 'martyrs' to the cause of freedom. When Bhutto was accused of adventurism and aggression, he replied: 'If support to the struggling people of Jammu and Kashmir constituted aggression against India, then all those countries like China, Indonesia, and others who unstintedly supported the cause of the Kashmiris were committing aggression against India.'[75] This conviction, so evident in 1965, was incompatible with the Indian position that by launching an invasion into the valley, the Pakistanis were effectively attacking India.

The war which Bhutto so enthusiastically supported had failed, but he emerged as the most popular politician in Pakistan precisely because he had pursued a much more vigorous – and therefore domestically more popular – line against India. He had also skilfully managed to disassociate himself from a regime which was becoming unpopular, and he succeeded in sweeping the political ground from beneath Ayub Khan's feet in a movement which had mass appeal.[76] In 1967 he formed his own political party, the Pakistan Peoples Party, which had a radical programme of socialist reform. In 1968, Ayub was replaced by General Yahya Khan, Malik's successor in operation 'Grand Slam'. His mandate was to hold elections and return the country to civilian rule. The issue of Kashmir was temporarily set aside as domestic politics in East and West Pakistan held centre stage.

Valley reaction

Although there had been no large scale uprising of the Kashmiris of the valley to coincide with Pakistan's invasion in 1965, there was evidence of the beginnings of political dissent amongst the younger Kashmiris, which meant the movement for plebiscite and self-determination would, as the older pro-Pakistan activists hoped, be carried on to the next generation. 'The greatest headache of the politically alert sections of my generation was how to get the new generation – our children – involved in the struggle for the State's accession to Pakistan,' writes Muhammad Saraf. Most were young children, some not even born in 1947, and many of their politically active parents, like Ghulam Abbas, Muhammad Saraf, and others had opted for Pakistan. In addition, under the influence of Sheikh Abdullah, although they might not be happy with the erosion of their 'special status', large sections of the population still supported accession to secular India and no longer looked to acceding to Pakistan under military dictatorship: 'In my estimation martial law had badly affected the liberation movement,' says Justice Abdul Majeed Mallick. 'The liberation movement primarily rested on the principle of the right of self-determination. When the first martial law was enforced in 1958, the Indian government snubbed Pakistan by saying "when you don't have fundamental rights in Pakistan, how can you have them in Kashmir?"'[77]

However, when Selig Harrison toured Kashmir in July, he reported that he found the people were solidly hostile to Indian rule and that it was only the presence of twelve Indian army brigades which kept the movement for self-determination contained.[78] Despite its adherence to a secular platform, Muslims believed that some elements inside the state, supported by the pro-Hindu Jana Sangh (which had merged with the Praja Parishad), wanted to reduce the majority Muslim preponderance by forcing them to leave. In the late 1960s fires in Muslim areas left many Muslim families homeless; activists hostile to the Indian government regarded the occurrence of these fires with suspicion as part of a plan to make Kashmir into a majority Hindu state. Ever sensitive of the incursion of outsiders into the state, they objected to 'citizenship' certificates being awarded to non-Muslims who had settled in the valley. In October 1969 a bill making evacuee property available to non-Muslim refugees was adopted by the Srinagar Assembly. With the opening of a University in Srinagar in 1948, however, and free education, a new generation of educated graduates emerged. Since there was virtually no industry in Kashmir, large numbers remained unemployed.

G. M. Sadiq, the chief minister, was becoming increasingly aware of the problem of the educated unemployed. In 1968 he met Prime Minister Indira Gandhi to explain the rising discontent in the state. In the presence of Inder Gujral, he told her: 'India spends millions on Kashmir but very little in Kashmir. If I were to tell you that the law and order situation requires one more division of the army, you would send it, without the blink of an eye, but if I ask you to set up two factories, you will tell me twenty reasons why it cannot be done and therefore what do our youth do?' Gujral subsequently acted as convener for a Committee of Ministers of State to deal with Kashmir:

> But I confess with a great deal of regret and dismay, that our achievements were very marginal. We succeeded in setting up two factories, but we were unable to make any dent on unemployment. Some progress was made in agriculture, but that was not much of an achievement because agriculture and fruits were growing in any case. Most of the concessions which were given were utilised by the industries more in the Jammu area, but hardly anything in Kashmir. The major failure is that we should have concentrated more on public sector investment. Apart from the merits and demerits, public sector investment encourages the private sector. And since in Kashmir disquiet was there all the time, for one reason or the other the private sector was very reluctant to invest.[79]

Nevertheless Dharma Vira, a civil servant, recalled how much better off the Kashmiris were in this period compared with their conditions under the maharaja. 'Then I saw people coming in large numbers, in tatters, saying: "God give us food". But today the standard of living has changed. It is Indian money that has produced that change.'[80] He attributed the current distress of the Kashmiri people to the greed of their leaders.

Algeria's successful struggle against France and the Vietnamese resistance against the United States, were beginning, however, to show the Kashmiri nationalists in exile in Pakistan that there might, after all, be a way to change the status quo. In 1965 Amanullah Khan, Maqbool Butt, and several others had joined together to form a political party in Azad Kashmir. 'One day they came to my house to discuss not only the formation of the party but also sought my participation,' recalls Muhammad Saraf.[81] 'We could not agree because I insisted that the Party should have, as its political goal, the State's accession to Pakistan.' The party was to be called the Plebiscite Front (as distinct from the Plebiscite Front formed in the valley). The armed wing, which gained greater notoriety, was called the Jammu and Kashmir National Liberation Front (NLF). 'We said there can't be freedom unless we shed our own blood as well as that of the enemy.' said Amanullah Khan.[82] As Butt later recounted: 'Interestingly, Amanullah Khan and several others in my group had seen eye to eye with my proposal favouring an Algerian type struggle to free Kashmiris from Indian occupation.'[83] Butt, who had first come to Pakistan in 1958, crossed back secretly to the valley in June 1966. For four months he trained local workers for sabotage and set up secret cells.

In September 1966 Butt clashed with the Indian army during an exchange of fire in Kunial village, near his hometown of Handwara; a co-worker was killed as well as an Indian army officer. As the group captain of what was called the 'OID' (Operations against Indian Domination) Butt and several others were charged with sabotage and murder. Detained in the women's jail in Srinagar, Butt defended his actions in the armed struggle:

> I could not reconcile to the new political set-up brought about in Kashmir after Sheikh Abdullah's dismissal and arrest in 1953. The Sheikh's successor, Bakshi Ghulam Muhammad, had, much against the wishes of the average Kashmiri, added some more laws to the armoury of repression. Any citizen could be detained in prison for five years at a stroke and Bakshi's government was under no obligation to inform the detainee about the grounds of detention. The helpless victim could be rearrested after release and detained for another term of five years.[84]

Butt and another activist were sentenced to death in September 1968, but, before the sentence was carried out, they escaped from the jail and fled across the ceasefire line to Azad Kashmir. 'It created a sensation and electrified the people who rejoiced on their brilliant escape,' writes Saraf. 'Can there be any better proof of Kashmiris innate hatred against India than the fact that for one month they were sheltered, transported and guided by their people and safely entered Azad Kashmir in January 1969?'[85]

Sheikh Abdullah had been released from jail in 1968. In support of his release, Jai Prakash Narain, Nehru's old socialist friend and co-worker of the freedom movement had written to Mrs Gandhi in 1966:

> We profess democracy, but rule by force in Kashmir ... the problem exists not because Pakistan wants to grab Kashmir, but because there is deep and widespread political discontent among the people ... Whatever be the solution, it has to be found within the limitations of accession. It is here that Sheikh's role may become decisive. Why do I plead for Sheikh's release? Because that may give us the only chance we have of solving the Kashmir problem.[86]

After his release, Abdullah revived his association with Prem Nath Bazaz who had frequently visited him in jail. They participated in two conventions, held in 1968 and 1970, to ascertain peoples views on Kashmir. In his inaugural speech, Jai Prakash Narain stressed that no government in India could accept a solution to the Kashmir problem which placed Kashmir outside the Union. He also encouraged the Kashmiri leaders to enter into a dialogue with the Indian government. In the June 1970 Convention, the Sheikh again stressed the need for freedom and self-determination of the Kashmiri people. When Ved Bhasin, editor of the *Kashmir Times*, pointed out the Kashmiri leadership's *volte face*, Abdullah countered with the assertion that it was not he who had gone back on his commitment, but Nehru, who had kept him in prison and failed to honour the commitments he had made to the Security Council.[87]

After 1970 the security situation in the valley deteriorated. Although protests and demonstrations were common, a new phenomenon of systematic violence had emerged. The Indian authorities blamed the frequent acts of sabotage on a group known as Al Fatah, which supposedly was working in the interests of Pakistan. But neither its membership nor real allegiance was clear. In January 1971 an Indian airlines plane, 'Ganga', en route from Srinagar to New Delhi, was hijacked by two Kashmiri youths armed with a hand grenade (subsequently discovered to be made of wood) and a pistol. The plane was diverted safely to Lahore, the twenty-six passengers were allowed to leave and it was subsequently blown up. The hijacking created tremendous euphoria in Pakistan, where disappointment over the failure of the 1965 war still lingered. Crowds numbering hundreds of thousands gathered at Lahore airport. Maqbool Butt came into the limelight by meeting the hijackers and claiming responsibility for the hijacking. The two Kashmiris were at first treated like heroes, but later, under pressure from India, they were arrested by the Pakistani authorities. Subsequently, Pakistan argued that the hijacking was a 'sting' operation planned by Indian intelligence.[88] A direct consequence was the Indian ban of overflights between West and East Pakistan, which strained relations between the two wings prior to the outbreak of war later in the year.

Maqbool Butt's dealings with the hijackers were regarded as a demonstration of his commitment to the Kashmir freedom struggle and no proceedings were taken against him in Pakistan or Azad Kashmir. But when he returned again to the valley in the 1976, he was caught and imprisoned for the murder of a bank clerk. This time he did not manage to escape and was kept in prison. After Butt's re-arrest, Amanullah Khan moved to England. 'We changed the name of the National Liberation Front, because I could not run an organisation in England which had a constitution which had armed struggle as an objective.' The organisation was changed to Jammu and Kashmir Liberation Front (JKLF), and for ten years Amanullah Khan operated out of Birmingham. 'I used to shuttle between London, New York, Paris, Amsterdam, Berlin, just projecting Kashmir at an international level. That used to pinch the Indians a lot.'[89]

War and Simla

In 1971 President Yahya Khan held the promised elections in East and West Pakistan, but their outcome was traumatic. The overall victory by the Awami League in East Pakistan, led by Sheikh Mujib ur Rahman, was challenged by Bhutto and his Peoples Party, who had won a majority in the West. Bhutto suggested handing over power to the majority parties of both wings. But after the breakdown of negotiations, Sheikh Mujib began to call for an independent country for the Bengalis, Bangladesh. 'An eager India interfered,' writes M. J. Akbar.[90] Relations had been deteriorating steadily between India and Pakistan throughout 1971, and the third war between the two countries led to the break-up of Pakistan as created in 1947. The Pakistani army's severe repression of the secessionist movement caused a reaction in India. 'Humanitarian feelings were the main motivating force behind this outcry,' writes Indira Gandhi's biographer, Inder Malhotra, 'but many Indians also saw in the heart-rending situation an opportunity to cut Pakistan down to size.'[91] Indira Gandhi's role in the creation of Bangladesh is a matter of pride for Indian citizens and hatred for Pakistanis, who still hold India responsible for the dismemberment of their country. On 16 December 1971, in what was a humiliating defeat for Pakistan, the Pakistani army surrendered to India at Dacca race course. India retained 94,000 prisoners of war, mainly Pakistani soldiers. The Indians had also occupied about 5,000 square miles of Pakistani territory in Sind, including that part of the Rann of Kutch which they had lost to Pakistan as a result of the 1965 arbitration. 'The Indian government's attitude after the war,' says former Indian foreign secretary, J. N. Dixit, 'disproved the theory of those who still believed that India was opposed to the existence of Pakistan. Had India wanted to dismember Pakistan completely, the army could have marched straight on to Rawalpindi.'[92] Although the war was not extended to Jammu and Kashmir, it remained a stumbling block to complete normalisation of relations. In an open letter to President Richard Nixon, Indira Gandhi wrote: 'We do want lasting peace with Pakistan. But will Pakistan give up its ceaseless yet powerless agitation of the last 24 years over Kashmir?'[93]

At the end of June 1972, Indira Gandhi met Zulfikar Ali Bhutto, who had become Pakistan's new president, at Simla.[94] As the Indian White Paper on the war acknowledged, Pakistan was 'economically shattered and psychologically bruised while India was feeling the euphoria of triumph.'[95] It appeared that Indira Gandhi could have achieved any political objective she wanted. Most of the Simla agreement related to restoring peace between the two countries in the aftermath of war. The clause relating to Jammu and Kashmir in the Simla agreement is inconclusive:

> In Jammu and Kashmir, the line of control resulting from the cease-fire of December 17, 1971 shall be respected by both sides without prejudice to the recognised position of either side. Neither side shall seek to alter it unilaterally, irrespective of mutual differences and legal interpretation. Both sides further undertake to refrain from threat or the use of force in violation of this line.

Both governments further agreed to meet again 'at a mutually convenient time in the future' to discuss further the modalities of '... a final settlement of Jammu and Kashmir and the resumption of diplomatic relations.'[96] Noticeable by its absence from the clause relating to Kashmir was any mention of plebiscite.

T. N. Kaul, who was part of the Indian delegation at the plenary meeting at Simla, recorded his conversation with Zulfikar Ali Bhutto:

> At Tashkent, when you were Foreign Minister, you said that Kashmir is the root cause of all our differences. Today, you, the President, have the opportunity of reaching a final settlement of the Kashmir question peacefully and bilaterally. Will you do it?" He smiled and replied. "You are correct, Mr Kaul, about what I said at Tashkent. But there I did not represent a defeated country while today I do; if I accept any settlement of Kashmir here I shall be accused by my people of having given in to pressure."[97]

The Indians, however, gained the impression from their discussions with Bhutto that once he returned home he would prepare the ground for an eventual settlement.

The Pakistanis were in no position to press for any favours and Bhutto's political opponents alleged that he had in fact secretly agreed to the status quo as a permanent solution. When he was on trial for conspiracy to murder in 1978, what he called the 'canard' of the secret clause was raised. 'If the Simla agreement had contained a secret clause about Kashmir, it would have been revealed long ago,' he responded.[98] He also stated that there was no legal difference, as some commentators were suggesting, in changing the name of the ceasefire line into the line of control: 'The ceasefire line is a line of control and the line of control is a ceasefire line. They are interchangeable terms.'[99]

Yet still the idea persisted of a secret resolution of the dispute. In April 1995 a former secretary of Mrs Gandhi, P. N. Dhar wrote in *The Times of India* that Bhutto had agreed that the ceasefire line should become the international border.

> Bhutto agreed not only to change the ceasefire line into a line of control, for which he had earlier proposed the term 'line of peace', but also agreed that the line would be gradually endowed with the 'characteristics of an international border' ... An important feature of the proposal was that neither country was gaining or losing territory on account of the war. It also did not involve any transfer of population from one side to the other. Kashmiris as an ethnic community were left undivided on the Indian side. The line of control was, therefore, an ethnic and linguistic frontier. In fact, in 1947, at the time of the partition, it was also an ideological frontier, being the limit of the political influence of Sheikh Mohammad Abdullah and his National Conference party.[100]

J. N. Dixit, who was also present at Simla, concurred with Dhar. The idea of converting the ceasefire line into a line of control and subsequently an international border was 'conceptualised in such a manner that it would have resulted in the Jammu and Kashmir dispute being resolved.'[101] Muhammad Saraf believes that Bhutto convinced Mrs Gandhi that it was not possible to solve all the problems between India and Pakistan at once: 'Bhutto was a very clever man. He said to Mrs Gandhi, "You keep your options open, and

I will keep mine open more. They named the ceasefire line the line of control but that made no difference.' Saraf also believes that the Indians did not want to see another military dictatorship in Pakistan, which might have arisen had Bhutto been forced to settle Kashmir. 'It was preferable to have Mr Bhutto and make a compromise.'[102]

Most of those directly involved at Simla have died. P. N. Haksar, the chief negotiator, aged 82 in 1995, took pride in recalling the part he played in drafting the clause relating to Kashmir. 'It is too simplistic to say that Bhutto reneged on any promises he had made on Kashmir. The idea was to try and restore mutual trust and confidence in order to put Indo–Pakistani relations on a durable basis of peace.' Step-by-step all differences were to be resolved and Kashmir was part of this procedure. He also countered the suggestion, as had Bhutto, that by changing the name of the ceasefire line to the line of control (sometimes also called the 'line of actual control') this was a de facto recognition that it was equivalent to an international border. 'The ceasefire was imposed by the UN, which was a multilateral organisation; the line of control demonstrated the new bilateralism of the relationship.' Haksar believed, however, that the Pakistani army would not let go of its power, which prevented the bilateral relationship from developing.[103]

Commentators in India today also believe that Indira Gandhi lost the opportunity of her political career to settle the Kashmir issue once and for all. 'Even more outrageously than at Tashkent, the advantage gained by the Indian army was lost by its civilian masters,' writes Ajit Bhattacharjea 'India's iron lady and her advisers let the opportunity slip ... An official spokesman fended off criticism by asserting that it would not be correct to doubt Bhutto's bona fides. India would have to pay heavily for yielding to flattery.'[104] Rather than the two leaders entering into a secret agreement, it is much more likely that Bhutto managed to convince Indira Gandhi that he could not survive politically the announcement of a settlement of Kashmir as well as the severance of Pakistan's eastern wing. 'Mrs Gandhi felt that Mr Bhutto wanted to open a new chapter and a period of reconciliation and friendship will start. She went along some way to help Mr Bhutto's political standing in Pakistan,' says Girish Saxena, who was present in Simla as a member of RAW, India's Research and Analysis Wing. No further negotiations over Kashmir ever took place while he was alive. But, says Saxena, 'although Mr Bhutto made noises, he never did anything significant on the diplomatic front to unsettle Simla or to disturb the arrangements on the line of control. He did not proceed further to cement the outcome of the agreement and what was decided; he kept the whole thing fluid.'[105]

From his base in the United Kingdom, Amanullah Khan noted Bhutto's speech to the National Assembly after his return from Simla:

> They said to me: 'settle Kashmir if you want (sic) prisoners of war.' I said 'I cannot'. They said 'at least settle the principles.' If I settle the principles it means settlement, that is what I told them, because there is only one principle and that

is self-determination ... If the people of Jammu and Kashmir want their independence, if they want to be liberated from the Hindu yoke, if they want to be a free people in fraternity and friendship and comradeship with Pakistan, they will have to give the lead and we will be with them. Even if the Simla agreement is broken, even if we jeopardise all our relations with India, I tell you, Sir, on the floor of this House with solemn commitment of the people of Pakistan that if tomorrow the people of Kashmir start a freedom movement, if tomorrow Sheikh Abdullah, or [Mirwaiz] Farooq or others, start a people's movement, we will be with them, no matter what the consequences.[106]

Subsequently, without any further commitments other than those expressed in the agreement, Bhutto secured the release of the prisoners of war and the 5,139 square miles of territory.

Despite Bhutto's rhetoric, from what Farooq Abdullah heard during his visit to Pakistan in 1974,[107] he also concluded that the Kashmir issue was resolved. 'The entire bureaucracy of Pakistan and Bhutto's secretary himself told me that a final solution has been arrived at; there can be nothing more. What we (the Pakistanis) have got (in Kashmir) we are keeping, what they have got they are keeping, and that is how it is.'[108] Farooq Abdullah also said that this information was confirmed to him in conversations he had with D. P. Dhar. 'Bhutto had made it abundantly clear to Mrs Gandhi that the line of actual control will become the border; that over the years he would be able to convince his people what is India's is India's and what is ours is ours.'[109] Stanley Wolpert argues that Bhutto never meant to close off the Pakistani claim to Kashmir. 'He had needed the agreement primarily to prove to the rest of the world – doubting London, as well as sceptical Washington and Moscow – that Pakistan remained in the "great game".'[110] The absence of any formal declaration one way or the other left the situation subject to change, depending on the political circumstances in India, Pakistan and within the state of Jammu and Kashmir. Besides, as the Kashmiris on both sides of the line of control were to observe, the Simla agreement had been negotiated without their participation.

Within Azad Kashmir, in addition to his support for the Kashmiris across the line of control, Bhutto is remembered as the first Pakistani leader to introduce reforms and investment. 'It was not until the 1970s and Zulfikar Ali Bhutto that the Pakistani government began to take an interest in us,' said an Azad Kashmir government official in 1994. 'Money was poured in and our conditions improved.'[111] Until then the economy was at subsistence level. In 1947 there were 256 metalled and fair-weather roads. By 1977 these had been increased to 939. In 1947 there were no hospitals and only six high schools. By 1977, there were eleven hospitals and 136 high schools.[112] During his 1974 visit to Muzaffarabad, however, Farooq Abdullah remarked on his return to India, that the best way to assure the Kashmiris in the valley that they were better off under India, was for them to visit AJK and see how poor the region was.[113]

Until the 1970s, Azad Jammu and Kashmir operated under the basic democracy system first introduced by Ayub Khan in 1960 and amended in 1964 and 1968 to accommodate the demands both of the local Azad Kashmiris and the refugee committee, who wanted greater representation. But although the local councils had limited powers, their funds were scarce and they remained dependent on Pakistan. The 1970 Azad Kashmir Government Act, passed under President Yahya Khan, instituted a presidential system of government, which, in theory, provided for a fully democratic system. When Bhutto framed the 1973 Constitution in Pakistan, which substituted a parliamentary system of government for the presidential one, the same system was also introduced for Azad Kashmir. As in Pakistan, the prime minister was the chief executive and the president a titular head. Nonetheless, the Azad Kashmir Council in Islamabad continued to exercise considerable jurisdiction over the affairs of Azad Kashmir. What was most significant, however, was that although Azad Kashmir remained administratively apart from the rest of Pakistan, according to Leo Rose, who made a detailed study of Azad Kashmir politics in 1989, this was the first time Pakistan 'assumed a direct and open institutional role in the governance of Azad Kashmir' in the wake of the Simla agreement. In fact, Rose interprets the Simla Agreement as 'a first step in the actual accession of Azad Kashmir into Pakistan, in form as well as fact.'[114]

The Kashmir accord

Bhutto's vocal support of the Kashmiris right of self-determination could not hide the fact that Pakistan's position over any further initiatives in Kashmir was greatly weakened. The failure of the 1965 war, which Bhutto had blamed on Ayub, and Pakistan's defeat and the emergence of independent Bangladesh in 1971 left those Kashmiris who would have preferred the state to be joined to Pakistan with little hope for the future. G. M. Sadiq had died in office in the middle of the 1971 war. He was replaced as chief minister by a former colleague, Syed Mir Qasim, president of the Jammu and Kashmir Congress Party formed in 1965 out of the former National Conference.

Sheikh Abdullah had wanted to participate in the forthcoming elections in the state but, in January 1971, the Plebiscite Front had been banned and Abdullah was externed from the state. The Indian government still associated the Front with the activities of the terrorist group Al Fatah. Abdullah was scathing over the ban: 'Over a million politically conscious members of the outlawed Plebiscite Front were conveniently removed from the field to clear the path for a walk-over for the Congress. The door of democratic processes have thus been banged on the real representatives of the people.'[115] In the absence of any serious opposition, when elections were held in March 1972 Mir Qasim won with a comfortable majority. The Jamaat-i Islami, with its pro-Pakistani leanings, won five seats and the Jana Sangh, won three. Mirwaiz

Mohammad Farooq, who had founded his own Awami Action Committee in 1964, alleged rigging and manipulation. Mir Qasim protested at the time that the elections were 'the freest and fairest'[116] but in his memoirs he put the exclusion of the Plebiscite Front and Abdullah in the context of a proposal to hold talks with Sheikh Abdullah in order to try and resolve the ongoing conflict between New Delhi and the Kashmir state: 'If the elections were free and fair, the victory of the [Plebiscite] Front was a foregone conclusion. And, as a victorious party, the Front would certainly talk from a position of strength that would irritate Mrs Gandhi who might give up her wish to negotiate with Sheikh Abdullah. That in turn would lead to a confrontation between the centre and the Jammu and Kashmir government.'[117]

After the elections Mir Qasim began to relax a number of restrictions on his opponents. In April 1972 Begum Abdullah was allowed to return to the state, political prisoners were released and, in June, the externment order on Sheikh Abdullah was lifted as well as those on Mirza Afzal Beg and G. M. Shah. The ban on the Plebiscite Front was also lifted, which once more gave Sheikh Abdullah a political platform. Referring to the recently signed Simla agreement, he stated that neither India nor Pakistan could discuss the fate of the state of Jammu and Kashmir without the participation of the Kashmiris. Whilst noting Bhutto's remarks on self-determination, he nonetheless pointed to the absence of any comment on the situation in Azad Kashmir, where the people might also like the same right of self-determination. He had also begun to shift emphasis by pressing for greater autonomy within the Indian Union rather than drawing attention to the unheld plebiscite. 'There is no quarrel with the Government of India over accession; it is over the structure of internal autonomy. One must not forget that it was we who brought Kashmir into India; otherwise Kashmir could never have become part of India.'[118] When Zulfikar Ali Bhutto once more called for the self-determination of the Kashmiri people, Abdullah spoke against any intervention in the internal affairs of the state. In a series of negotiations, which lasted for over a year, Indira Gandhi chose to capitalise on Abdullah's more favourable stance towards India.

In his memoirs, Abdullah justifies his agreement to what came to be known as 'the Kashmir accord': 'We only wanted Article 370 to be maintained in its original form ... Our readiness to come to the negotiating table did not imply a change in our objectives but a change in our strategy.'[119] Abdullah wanted the clock to be put back to pre-1953 before his dismissal by Nehru, but Mrs Gandhi did not make many concessions. There were to be no fresh elections; Abdullah was to be elected chief minister by Congress. 'Forgetting my past experiences I agreed to co-operate with the Congress, but soon regretted my decision.'[120]

Details of the six-point accord were announced by Mrs Gandhi in the Indian Parliament on 24 February 1975. 'Mrs Indira Gandhi was at her best that day,' writes M. J. Akbar. Her recognition of Abdullah's status as the leader of secular Kashmir, 'was Indira Gandhi's finest achievement. She did not put the clock back. But she picked it up and wound it again; and it was because of her that Kashmir saw a wonderful decade of freedom and peace. There was great joy in the nation at the news.'[121] Although Kashmir's special status, enshrined in article 370 of the Indian Constitution was retained, the state was termed 'a constituent unit of the Union of India.' The Indian government was able 'to make laws relating to the prevention of activities directed towards disclaiming, questioning or disrupting the sovereignty and territorial integrity of India or bringing about cession of a part of the territory of India from the Union or causing insult to the Indian national flag, the Indian national anthem and the Constitution.'[122] This effectively gave India control in the areas which mattered most. There was to be no return to the pre-1953 status. The titles of sadar-i-riyasat and prime minister, evidence of Kashmir's special status, were not to be re-utilised. Instead, as with all other states they were to remain as governor and chief minister. Commentators at the time believed that the issue of plebiscite and self-determination could now be laid to rest. The accession of the state of Jammu and Kashmir by the autocratic maharaja in 1947 had been confirmed by Sheikh Abdullah, a popular leader, who nearly thirty years after the accession, still commanded majority support in the state. From an Indian standpoint, the movement for self-determination virtually came to an end with the 1975 accord.[123]

Pakistan was less than happy with the accord. Tension had once more increased between India and Pakistan after India's first nuclear explosion in May 1974, resulting in a steady determination on behalf of Pakistan's leaders to acquire nuclear capability. In June the Pakistani politicians intensified their cry for a liberated Kashmir in protest at the ongoing negotiations prior to the conclusion of the Kashmir accord. When the accord was announced it was termed a 'sell-out' and Zulfikar Ali Bhutto called for a strike throughout Pakistan on 28 February 1975. Bhutto also stated that the accord had violated the terms of Simla and the UN requirements for a plebiscite. The Chinese government also voiced its disapproval.

Within the state of Jammu and Kashmir, Mirwaiz Maulvi Farooq believed that Abdullah had relinquished the Kashmiris' right of self-determination. Throughout 1974 there had been clashes between his Awami Action Committee and the Plebiscite Front. The Jana Sangh in Jammu and Delhi protested against the accord. As always opposed to the special treatment meted out to the valley in preference to Jammu, Jana Sangh supporters wanted article 370 to be abrogated and the whole state included in the Indian Union, like all the other states. Abdullah, however, was not going to be the pliant tool, which perhaps the Indian government hoped he would be in his old age. In April 1975 he talked about a merger with Azad Kashmir.[124] Although both he and Mirza Afzal Beg had assumed power as independent candidates in staged by-elections under the auspices of the Congress party, they rejected the suggestion of a formal alliance with the Congress party. M. J. Akbar attributes this to personal rivalries between the outgoing chief minister, Mir Qasim, and Muhammad Mufti Sayeed, a prominent Congress minister. When they both realised that there was to be no place for them or their relatives in a coalition government, they dissuaded Abdullah from contemplating the idea.[125] Akbar, however, does not provide any documentary evidence for this assertion. Mir Qasim took up a more prestigious position in Mrs Gandhi's cabinet and committed himself to working for Congress–National Conference co-operation.[126]

For the first two years of Abdullah's administration, only he and Beg were officially in the government. Although the National Conference, which had lain dormant for so many years, was revived out of what remained of the Plebiscite Front, it was not represented in the legislative assembly, which was controlled by the Congress. Abdullah therefore made use of his own family to support him – his wife, Begum Abdullah, his two sons, Farooq and Tariq, and his son-in-law, Ghulam Muhammad Shah. This led to allegations of corruption and nepotism. Prem Nath Bazaz, who remained, as ever, a critical commentator on events, described Sheikh Abdullah's new administration as 'democracy through intimidation and terror.'[127] The visual high-point of Abdullah's return to power was reached in October 1975, when Indira Gandhi, by now ruling India under Emergency powers, visited Srinagar. Her progress on Dal lake by boat, propelled by turbaned oarsmen was reminiscent of the visits of the Mughal emperors. People lined the banks and cheered. Her presence in Srinagar was, however, a powerful reminder to the people of Kashmir's reinforced links with the government at New Delhi, led by a prime minister who had curtailed civil liberties throughout India, muzzled the press and arrested her political opponents.

In March 1977 Mrs Gandhi lost the general election to the Janata party in India. The two year Emergency had greatly reduced her popularity. 'When it became obvious that the Janata Party would form the government at the Centre, the leaders of the State Congress party conspired to capture power in Kashmir,' writes Abdullah. 'A petition was submitted to the Governor declaring that they had lost confidence in me.'[128] Moraji Desai, the new prime minister, dissolved the State Assembly and called for fresh elections, which gave Sheikh Abdullah the opportunity of re-establishing his political credentials in his own right. P. S. Verma comments that these 1977 elections were 'relatively free from the vices of rigging and other related irregularities' and attributes this to the fact that the Congress Party was out of power in Delhi and Janata was still in its infancy. Thus no official patronage from Delhi was forthcoming. The Sheikh, still the National Conference's biggest asset, suffered a severe heart attack in 1977. He was not able to campaign extensively and his candidates had to rely on his taped speeches. Rumours persisted that he had already died, so when he appeared lying on a stretcher and raised his right hand to show that he was alive, the crowds cheered. His statements referring to the Kashmiris as a *qaum* (nation) were not lost on the people. Maulvi Farooq, who had consistently adopted a pro-Pakistani stance, lost credibility amongst his traditional sympathisers, by campaigning for the Janata party, as did the Jamaat-i Islami.

Abdullah was also not beyond playing the Pakistani card to his advantage in order to gain support. There was in addition a theatrical side to the campaigning. Mirza Afzal Beg used to carry a lump of Pakistani rock salt (as opposed to Indian sea salt) in his pocket wrapped in a green handkerchief. As his speech reached its climax, he would take out the salt with a dramatic gesture and exhibit it to his audience, 'indicating thereby that if his party won, Pakistan would not be far away.'[129] The National Conference contested all 75 seats and won 47, of which 39 were in the valley. The Jamaat-i Islami won only one seat compared with the five it had won in 1972. At the age of 72, Abdullah once more braced himself to meet the challenge of the future.

Confident of his new mandate, the Sheikh once more began to speak out assertively and relations with the ruling Janata party in Delhi became strained. On 23 May 1977 Abdullah threatened to secede from the Union unless the people were accorded their place of honour in terms of the safeguards guaranteed to them under Article 370 of the Constitution and he warned of an 'explosive situation'. When Mrs Gandhi returned to power in 1980, Abdullah continued to make provocative declarations about Kashmiris not being the slaves of either India or Pakistan. But it is doubtful that at this stage in his life, his rhetoric was designed to do anything more than assure Kashmiris of the importance of their Kashmiriyat – their cultural identity – without envisaging any significant change to the now established status quo.

At the same time, Abdullah was confronted by new problems in the state, whose political character had changed since he was last in power in the early 1950s. Opposition to the Kashmir accord continued and a new educated class was being drawn into the political arena. 'Our education taught us that the accord is not the resolution of the Kashmir dispute' said a Kashmiri journalist, who was editing a daily newspaper in Srinagar in 1975.[130] 'Our youth awoke and realised that we can't any longer be the slaves of India.' 'We Muslims feel we have been deprived of something,' said Ali, a carpet dealer, in 1981. 'We haven't been allowed to join India or Pakistan of our own free will. Rather we have been forced to be with India.'[131] Kashmir still depended on tourism and despite economic progress there was no real industry in which middle class Kashmiris could feel they had a stake. Increasingly, the Kashmiri youth moved not towards communism or socialism, but back to the fundamentals of their respective religions. Muslims, Hindus, Sikhs, Buddhists were all reasserting their cultural and religious identity which was in total contradiction to the secularism which the Indian government had espoused since independence. Although Sheikh Abdullah made some attempt to accommodate the regional sentiments in the state by granting a small degree of autonomy to the component parts of Jammu, Ladakh and the valley, the numerical superiority of the valley meant that its voice was predominant. Abdullah's political opponents also criticised his government for discrimination and lack of performance.[132]

Within the valley, some of the young Muslims were attracted to the schools run by the Jamaat-i Islami, who gained inspiration from the growing fundamentalist movement, which had affected Muslim countries of the Middle East. Some young Kashmiris also joined the Jamaat-i Tulba, a youth organisation set up by the Jamaat-i Islami. In 1975 Sheikh Abdullah had ordered the closure of the Jamaat schools. He later banned a convention of the Jamaat-i Tulba planned to be held in Srinagar in 1981. The Sheikh's reaction to the Muslim influence in the schools of the Jamaat demonstrated his concern, but the Jamaat-i Islami had only won one seat in the 1977 elections and did not appear to be a significant political force. Neither he nor anyone else could have predicted the growth in support for the Islamic movement, which came in later years, especially after the Iranian revolution in February 1979. This resurgence could not have been more dramatically demonstrated by the Afghan resistance to the Soviet invasion of Afghanistan in 1979: 'A small nation with a small population, with limited resources and weapons rose in revolt against the Soviet onslaught in Afghanistan, to the extent that the Soviet Union ultimately disintegrated into fragments,' says Azam Inquilabi, a teacher in Srinagar at this time. 'Out of that five Muslim states emerged as independent states. So we got inspired, if they could offer tough resistance to a super power in the east, we too could fight India.'[133]

CHAPTER 13

An Explosive Situation

History has seen such times, when the crime was committed by a moment, but the punishment was suffered by centuries. Sheikh Abdullah, 1981[1]

It is a thin line between bravado and despair. Farooq Abdullah, 1989[2]

The decade of the 1980s began peacefully for the valley of Kashmir. Its fame as an idyllic place for a holiday attracted foreigners from far and wide, who brought in welcome currency and left laden with traditional Kashmiri handicrafts. Sheikh Abdullah's charismatic presence as chief minister was in marked contrast to the personalities of those who had preceded him. His accord with Indira Gandhi in 1975 and his subsequent electoral victory in 1977 meant that the government of New Delhi was temporarily restrained from controlling Kashmiri affairs from the centre. Pakistan, under the military dictatorship of General Muhammad Zia-ul Haq since 1977, after the over-throw of Zulfikar Ali Bhutto,[3] was preoccupied with the war in Afghanistan. It did not appear that Zia's Kashmiri policy would be much different from that of Zulfikar Ali Bhutto. Pakistan's options were to be kept open.

Under the surface, however, disaffection was present. Sheikh Abdullah was not popular in Jammu or in Ladakh and the Islamic groups, which had opposed the accord, were gaining support in the valley. As the Sheikh's health began to fail and, in 1981, he settled the succession on his son, Farooq, a new era of violence began.

Crown of thorns

Farooq Abdullah, unlike his father, had not been schooled in the politics of the freedom movement. He had spent most of his adult life in Britain, where he had trained as a doctor. In a ceremony which dazzled the people, who had assembled in Iqbal Park in Srinagar, on 21 August 1981, Sheikh Abdullah appointed his untested progeny as president of the National Conference:

This crown that I am placing on your head is made of thorns. My first wish is that you will never betray the hopes of your *qaum* [nation]. You are young, Dr Farooq Abdullah, young enough to face the challenges of life, and I pray that God gives you the courage to fulfil your responsibilities to these people whom I have nurtured with such pride, and to whom I have given the best years of my life.[4]

Farooq's words of response were greeted with a roar of approval: 'I will give my life before I play with the honour of this community.' But as Indian journalist Tavleen Singh observes: 'He was his father's son but not his father and he was not capable of taking them seriously except then, on that tumultuous day, for that moment, when the event and the overwhelming response of the people made him seem like a bigger man.'5

Although Sheikh Abdullah was able to hand over the office, he could not pass on the experience to his son. As subsequent events were to show, his rise to power came too easily. 'In happier times,' writes Ajit Bhattacharjea 'Farooq Abdullah could have proved an ideal leader for Kashmir. Tall, handsome, engaging, and forthright, he attracted crowds easily, making them believe that he would lead them out of the uncertainty, intrigue and corruption that darkened the last days of his father.' But he was also impulsive, gullible, easy-going and a novice in administration and politics.'6 'He liked the attention, the fun that went with power, and he liked the atmosphere of a feudal court that surrounded his father, says Tavleen Singh. 'He was also both surprised and delighted by the adulation of the people and the society hostesses in Delhi.'7

For the time being, however, Kashmir's future seemed assured. Secession appeared no longer to be an issue and there were not many Kashmiris talking about the plebiscite. The tourists continued to come. Hotels were opened along the Boulevard facing Dal lake. Food grain and fruit production increased, as well as income from Kashmir's world famous handicrafts. 'Kashmir's economic boom gave it an atmosphere of permanent festivity, forcing the opposition politicians, who continued to remain suspicious, to keep their pessimism to themselves. Sheikh Abdullah was too powerful, too popular to touch.'8

On 8 September 1982 the 'lion of Kashmir' died. After his death even those who had opposed the Sheikh politically praised his conviction. Shahnawaz Khan Niazi, an old friend who migrated to Pakistan, describes what he believed Sheikh Abdullah represented for a large majority of the people.

> Sheikh Abdullah was a total idealist and his only interest was the best deal he could get for Kashmir and his Kashmiris. His often repeated statement to me was that destiny had played an important role, that circumstances were such that they did not permit him to come to an understanding with Pakistan. Every small opportunity he got to make a point or establish the separate identity of the Kashmiris he took.9

For those who were able to see through the shifts from India to Pakistan to independence and back again, of all their leaders, Sheikh Abdullah best personified the spirit of Kashmiriyat. At times, safeguarding Kashmiriyat meant independence; at others, when Delhi was prepared to loosen the reins of control, it meant autonomy within the Indian Union. Since Kashmiriyat included both Muslims and Hindus, he had opted for the secularism of India, which Jawaharlal Nehru had promised in his early speeches.

Yet critics, such as Sardar Abdul Qayum Khan, who had risen from being a 'mujahid' of the 1947 war to become first president and later prime minister of Azad Jammu and Kashmir, believe that Sheikh Abdullah was a 'stooge' of the Indian government. 'He had no *locus standi*; he was a nonentity. He was a quisling boosted by the power of the Indian Congress Party.'[10] Qayum condemned Abdullah's accord with Indira Gandhi in 1975 as 'getting power through the back door' and had little sympathy with an old man who, perhaps, after so many years wanted peace. Amanullah Khan acknowledged the Sheikh's contribution in the early years of the independence struggle against the Dogras. But in later years he held the Sheikh ' mainly responsible for the trials and tribulations of the Kashmiris. He trusted in Nehru far more than he should have done.'[11]

At Sheikh Abdullah's funeral all the shades of dissatisfaction and disappointment in him were forgotten. 'The grief, as the cortège passed,' writes Tavleen Singh, 'burst out like an uncontrollable wave. The salutation – our lion – was on everyone's lips. People wept, they chanted dirges and mouthed melancholy slogans ... for that day the man Kashmir remembered was not the Sheikh who had been chief minister for five years but the man who, for nearly thirty years, had symbolised Kashmir's identity.'[12] There is a certain irony in the present day that his marble tomb overlooking Dal lake, close to the Hazratbal mosque, is protected by Indian soldiers against desecration by the sons of those Kashmiris whose cause he had championed.

The Sheikh's legacy

Once Sheikh Abdullah was gone, in a climate of renewed assertion of religious identity, it was impossible to prevent the rise of communalist tendencies. During the period following his death, mistakes were made both by the state government and in Delhi, which changed the course of events and renewed the demand not so much for Kashmiriyat or union with Pakistan, but for *azadi*, freedom – for the people of the valley from what they perceived to be not secular, but Hindu-dominated, India.

Famed as the 'disco' chief minister, who enjoyed riding around Srinagar on his motor bicycle, the first problem which Farooq Abdullah inherited from his father was the Jammu and Kashmir Grant of Permit for Resettlement bill. Before his death the Sheikh had put forward a bill which enabled anyone who was a citizen of Kashmir before 14 May 1954 or a descendant to return to Kashmir, provided he swore allegiance both to the Indian and Kashmiri constitutions. As a refugee from the valley, Mir Abdul Aziz, a Muslim Conference supporter and political opponent of Abdullah's since the 1930s, believed it was 'the only good thing Sheikh Abdullah did.' In Delhi the bill, which had been passed by the Legislative Assembly, but still required assent from the governor to become law, aroused fears that Pakistani sympathisers and agents could cross the border and create trouble in the valley. Yet Abdullah was obliged to follow through a measure introduced by his father. He was also aware of the sensitivities of many of the Hindus and Sikhs in Jammu, who had been settled on the land of many of the Muslims who had left.

The Government of India was dissatisfied that an issue concerning citizenship, which it regarded as within its domain, was being dealt with in the state. 'What Abdullah did to save his skin and please his Indian masters was that he referred it to the Supreme Court of India for advice. So it has been kept in cold storage without any action,' says Mir Abdul Aziz.[13] He compared the situation with that of the many Indians and Pakistanis who have been to the UK in time of political strife, but, who are not prevented from returning to their respective countries when they want to do so. Farooq Abdullah, however, was already beginning to realise the need to balance the needs of Kashmiris with the demands of the government in Delhi.

In domestic affairs, however, Farooq Abdullah did not demonstrate the same caution. His attempts to eradicate corruption were greeted enthusiastically by the people. But, asks, M. J. Akbar, 'was it totally wise to drop all the "stalwarts" of his father's ministry after publicly calling them corrupt?'[14] His brother-in-law, G. M. Shah, married to his sister Khalida, was just one stalwart who was not included in the chief minister's cabinet. Abdullah scheduled elections for June 1983 in order to obtain an endorsement from the people. Indira Gandhi, however, wished to establish her Congress(I) Party[15] standing in the valley and requested an alliance between the Congress and the National Conference. 'They thought probably I would be a mere puppet and would go the way they wanted me to go.'[16] Abdullah refused the alliance, believing that the people of Kashmir would resent it. Instead, he offered to put up weak candidates in a few constituencies in order to allow Congress to win some seats. Mrs Gandhi did not accept this proposal and exponents of her subsequent actions believe that she never forgave Abdullah.

Tavleen Singh, who was covering the elections for the Indian press, witnessed the extraordinary interest the prime minister took in the campaign. 'Mrs Gandhi seemed to be staking her own *izzat* [honour] on winning. After whirlwind tours of Jammu, she descended on the valley with all the pomp and paraphernalia that accompanies prime ministers on such visits.'[17] During her interviews in the valley, Tavleen Singh asked whether the plebiscite was an issue. 'Almost everywhere the answer was an emphatic no. People said that the past was dead and they were participating in this election as Indians.'[18] Farooq Abdullah was popular, but the people were really voting in his father's memory.

The politics of the campaign between the National Conference and the Congress Party led to animosity on both sides. 'The electioneering set a new record in viciousness which often degenerated into "downright vulgarity",' writes Indira Gandhi's biographer, Inder Malhotra.[19] Abdullah reached an agreement with Mirwaiz Maulvi Farooq, whose uncle's feud with the Sheikh in 1932, had caused a lasting split amongst the Muslims. 'The pro-Pakistani *bakra* [goat][20] lay with the Abdullah lion arousing suspicions in Delhi,' writes M. J. Akbar.[21] In Jammu, the Hindus feared that the more numerous Muslims of the valley were, once more, uniting against them on the basis of religion. Abdullah also made the mistake of bowing to pressure from his family to include some Shah supporters amongst the candidates he fielded, whose reputations were questionable.[22] So too was their loyalty to Abdullah. Despite mistaken predictions by Indira Gandhi's advisers and some sections of the press that she would defeat Abdullah, the National Conference won forty-six seats out of seventy-five. Congress won only two seats in the valley. In Jammu, where the Congress Party had campaigned vigorously, it obtained twenty-four seats. Both the right wing Bharatiya Janata Party (BJP), favouring Hindu interests, and the Jamaat-i Islami, promoting those of the Muslims, failed to win any seats.[23] Tavleen Singh describes the 1983 elections as the first 'real' elections and that it seemed the Kashmir issue was over.[24]

Almost as soon as the election results were announced, the Congress began to campaign against Farooq Abdullah, alleging that the elections had been rigged. But, as Tavleen Singh noted, 'in that summer of 1983 there was no turmoil in the valley despite Congress attempts to create it. The Congress had an important ally in the national press and in retrospect I would go so far as to say that the press was the main reason why the alienation of Kashmir began.'[25] With the advice of her kitchen cabinet, which Singh describes as more like 'a mediaeval court in which nearly every decision was taken personally by Mrs Gandhi,' the Prime Minister of India set about subverting the elected government of Kashmir.[26] 'Indira seemed determined not to let him rule in peace because the abusive election campaign and Farooq's victory had made her angrier with him than ever before,' writes Malhotra.[27]

Abdullah also played into Mrs Gandhi's hand. Instead of confining himself to the politics of Jammu and Kashmir, he entered the national stage by discussing regional autonomy with the leaders of Andhra Pradesh, Karnataka, West Bengal and Tamil Nadu, in preparation for the launching of an anti-Congress alliance in the 1984 general elections. He also met with the Akali Dal in the Punjab, where a violent separatist movement amongst the Sikhs was ultimately to cost Indira Gandhi her life. In October 1983 he hosted a three-day opposition conclave in Srinagar involving fifty-nine state leaders from seventeen different regional parties. 'All this was anathema to Indira Gandhi,' writes Ajit Bhattacharjea. 'Always insecure, she now felt gravely threatened.'[28]

Mrs Gandhi did not appreciate Abdullah's independent line, reminiscent of tactics so often employed by his father. The Sheikh, however, had never challenged the Congress Party outside Kashmir as was clearly Farooq Abdullah's intention. Gandhi gave a clear warning that what she termed 'anti-national' – i.e. pro-regional autonomy – sentiments would not be tolerated. Over the next few months she set about destabilising those states which were exhibiting such tendencies. 'The hook-or-crook methods used to try and break the governments of Karnataka, Andhra and Kashmir,' writes M. J. Akbar 'were a blot on the very concept of a federation. Farooq Abdullah, for his sins, was at the top of the hit list.'[29]

Part of the strategy was to depict Farooq Abdullah as being 'soft' on Pakistan. In October 1983 much was made of a cricket match held in Srinagar between India and the West Indies. The Indian team was booed by the assembled crowd, and supporters of the Jamaat-i Islami waved their green party flags, which resembled, but were not identical to the Pakistani flag. 'For Delhi, this was heaven-sent material for propaganda. The Pakistani flag was fluttering freely in Farooq's reign,' writes M. J. Akbar.[30] On 28 October Mufti Muhammad Sayeed, the Congress leader in Kashmir, announced that Farooq had lost his hold on the administration. A crowd in Jammu protested against the failure of the government. Throughout the valley, small demonstrations, clearly orchestrated by the Congress, led to arrests. Farooq's self-defence fell on deaf ears.

'At this point, there was no Pakistani hand visible in the valley at all,' writes Tavleen Singh, 'but charges of Pakistani involvement were openly bandied about by Congress leaders.'[31] The kidnapping in February 1984 of Ravindra Mahtre, the assistant high commissioner in Britain, provided another opportunity to implicate Abdullah. The kidnappers requested a £1 million ransom and the release of several prisoners held in India, including Maqbool Butt, who was awaiting execution in Tihar jail after India's re-introduction of the death penalty. The Kashmir Liberation Army (KLA), believed to be associated with Amanullah Khan's JKLF, was held responsible for the kidnapping and subsequent murder of Mahtre. Farooq Abdullah's alleged connection with the kidnapping was that he had met Amanullah Khan in 1974 when, at the request of his father, during the discussions prior to the 1975 accord he had visited Muzaffarabad; this visit, nearly ten years earlier, was now given a sinister interpretation to add fuel to the argument that Farooq Abdullah could not be trusted. When Butt, described by Ajit Bhattacharjea as 'a colourful double agent used both by India and Pakistan',[32] was executed on 11 February a strike was held in Srinagar and some other towns of the valley to mourn his death, which again demonstrated to New Delhi the potentially subversive leanings of the state of Jammu and Kashmir.

Farooq Abdullah also had enemies within the state. Ghulam Muhammad Shah had never accepted his brother-in-law's ascent to the top position. A long time political supporter of the Sheikh, he had regarded himself as the natural successor. As relations between the two deteriorated, in October Farooq expelled G. M. Shah from the National Conference; Shah retaliated with the formation of the Awami National Conference Party. 'The air became filled with rumours of dirty deals and vast quantities of money being spent on National Conference malcontents to persuade them to join G. M. Shah's breakaway faction.'[33] A willing conspirator in the plan to topple Farooq, Shah brought together thirteen discontented members of the National

Assembly, including those of his supporters to whom Farooq had given seats. Combined with the twenty-six seats won by the Congress, they could claim a simple majority in the Legislative Assembly. Braj Kumar Nehru the governor and cousin of the prime minister, could have been ideally placed to acquiesce in a drawing-room dismissal of Farooq. Yet, despite provocation by Abdullah's high-handed style of government, Nehru insisted that the dissident members establish their majority in the Legislative Assembly. In early 1984 he was asked to resign and was later transferred to Gujerat. The new governor was Shri Jagmohan, a bureaucrat, who had stood by Indira Gandhi during the 1975–77 Emergency.

At the beginning of June, Mrs Gandhi's Operation Blue Star in the Punjab was put into action with the storming of the Golden Temple against the Sikh extremists of the Akali Dal led by Sant Jarnail Singh Bhindranwale. In the aftermath, Punjab was in turmoil. Yet with supreme confidence the plan for Farooq's dismissal was put into action. Soon after Blue Star, Gandhi visited Ladakh. On her return she summoned several newspaper editors, including Inder Malhotra. 'She made no secret of her conviction that Farooq's continuance as chief minister of Kashmir was bad for the state and the country. This shook most of us. After what had happened in Punjab it was hardly prudent to embark on a clash course in Kashmir.'[34]

On the national stage, because of his meeting earlier in the year with Bhindranwale, Farooq was charged with secretly supporting the Sikh separatists and of permitting them to train in the state of Jammu and Kashmir. Vehement denials from Farooq and members of his government could not silence the uproar in Delhi which reached a crescendo at the end of June. On 28 June, Governor Jagmohan received a letter signed by the thirteen members of the Kashmir Legislative Assembly, stating that they had withdrawn their support from the government of Farooq Abdullah. Delhi now had sufficient ammunition against Farooq and, what he later called Operation New Star, was put into action. G. M. Shah and his supporters were summoned to the governor's residence in the Raj Bhavan in Srinagar in the early hours of the morning on 2 July. In an operation which Jagmohan claimed was totally unplanned, yet took place with clockwork precision, Farooq was ousted and later replaced by his brother-in-law. 'With unaccustomed speed,' writes Ajit Bhattacharjea 'a contingent of the Madhya Pradesh armed police landed in Srinagar early next morning, suggesting that they had been alerted a day or more earlier.'[35] The army was also standing by. Jagmohan carried through his role as Mrs Gandhi's 'hatchet man'[36] with conviction. 'I was very anxious to prevent violence in the streets. Kashmir crowds are easily excitable. They soon get hysterical. It is immaterial whether they support or denounce a particular cause.'[37]

Jagmohan informed Farooq that he had 'lost the confidence' of the majority of the members of the Legislative Assembly. Tavleen Singh, who was covering the story, describes the deposed chief minister as reacting 'with the emotionalism of a schoolboy rather than the maturity of a politician.'[38] In an indignant document entitled 'My Dismissal' Farooq later pointed to the blatant compliance of Jagmohan:

> He was a direct party to the conspiracy but various trappings were given a dramatic touch to make it appear a natural political event ... The Governor's action in dismissing my government was invalid in law. The Raj Bhavan was not the place to test my majority that day; it should have been tested on the floor of the House.[39]

Farooq also pointed to Congress attempts to 'play up' his alleged links with the JKLF and gave the background to his visit to Muzaffarabad in 1974 when he was still living in England. 'Since negotiations were going on between Sheikh Abdullah and Mrs Gandhi for a probable accord, they wanted the feelings of the people of Pakistan-occupied Kashmir to be known first hand and to be conveyed to my father by me.' He also denied the accusations that he was in any way linked with pro-Pakistani organisations. 'As far as pro-Pakistan elements are concerned, they have been there all along since 1947. They did not appear all of a sudden during my regime or because of me.'[40]

Unfortunately for Abdullah, his plausible defence served only to set the record straight on paper. With the weight of Delhi behind Abdullah's brother-in-law, and contrary to Jagmohan's own preference for Governor's rule to be imposed first, G. M. Shah was appointed chief minister. In retrospect, had Farooq been more adept at convincing Delhi of his loyalty to India before, rather than after the event, had the power seekers in his party been less easy to exploit, had Indira Gandhi been less insecure and had she worked through the National Conference, as Nehru had done, rather than insist on a Congress presence in the valley, Farooq may have been able to maintain a workable relationship with the centre at the same time as focusing his attention on material improvements for the people of Kashmir. The fact that the prime minister of India was willing and able to set Abdullah aside for what essentially were personal reasons demonstrated the lack of regard she and the government of Delhi had for Kashmir's so-called special status. As Mir Qasim wrote: 'Mr Jagmohan's unconstitutional act was another nail in the coffin of the Kashmiri's faith in Indian democracy and law.'[41] 'The clock has been put back thirty years,' said Tavleen Singh. 'Kashmir has been reminded that no matter how much it feels that it belongs to the mainstream of India, no matter how often its chief minister asserts that he is Indian, it will always be special, always be suspect.'[42]

Farooq's dismissal touched off a wave of protest. Shah's government was unpopular from the outset. His past record as a minister under Sheikh Abdullah was 'far from savoury,' writes Inder Malhotra 'and even his best friends were not willing to vouch for his probity.' Under his chief ministership, the government sank 'to the lowest depths of corruption and capriciousness.' Why then did Mrs Gandhi allow him to be installed? 'The more one explores this question the more convinced one is that she was virtually blinded by her intense dislike of Farooq.' As Malhotra writes, 'According to Arun Nehru, a cousin of Rajiv Gandhi and a member of Mrs Gandhi's 'kitchen cabinet', 'Indira puphi (aunt) asked us to get rid of Farooq at all costs and we did.' The installation of G. M. Shah appears to have been so that Farooq's dismissal seemed to have been instigated by the Kashmiris and not New Delhi.[43]

All thirteen defectors were sworn in as cabinet ministers, which meant Shah was in no position to gain further supporters from amongst the National Conference by offering them places in his cabinet. 'The government made money like there was no tomorrow and given the uncertainty of the situation there may well not have been,' says Tavleen Singh.[44]

Mrs Gandhi's assassination in October 1984 by her Sikh bodyguards in revenge for Operation Bluestar removed the architect of Farooq's dismissal. But the memory of betrayal remained, not necessarily because of what happened to Farooq Abdullah personally, but because of what his dismissal signified for Kashmir. Apologists on behalf of the Indian government, like Jagmohan, have argued long and earnestly in support of their actions. But no amount of self-justification can hide the fact that Abdullah's drawing-room dismissal merely confirmed what Kashmiris had long suspected: that despite their 'special status', no one could remain in power in Srinagar if they did not have the support of Delhi. This lesson was not lost on Farooq Abdullah. When he returned to power in 1987 it was at the head of a Conference–Congress alliance.

Rajiv Gandhi, who became prime minister after his mother's assassination, made it a policy to attempt to accommodate regional forces, not only in Kashmir, but also in the Punjab and Assam. Despite the role he may have played in Farooq's dismissal, their personal relationship was better than that between Farooq and Mrs Gandhi. After less than two years in office, G. M. Shah was dismissed on 7 March 1986 in the wake of severe communal riots which the state government had been unable to control. The army was called out and people were advised to remain indoors for fear of getting shot. Indefinite curfew had been imposed, which gave G. M. Shah the name 'Gul-e Curfew' (the Curfew flower). After Shah's dismissal, Jagmohan took advantage of Kashmir's 'special status' by assuming exclusive power, a privilege reserved under Article 370 for an elected sadar-i riyasat, not a nominated governor:

> I feel the burden of the challenges. But I am a bit elated too. I have an opportunity to show the nobler, the purer, the more radiant face of power. I can now demonstrate how government can function in a poor and developing country, how a person, inspired by a higher purpose can serve as a model administrator, how domination of the elites can be done away with.[45]

He took steps to clean-up both the administration and the city of Srinagar. Muslims, however, found that they were being excluded from key jobs and that there was a general onslaught on Muslim culture and identity, both through the educational curriculum and socially. They objected to the prevalence of alcohol readily available in numerous bars in Srinagar. The Muslim political parties had called for peaceful strikes (*hartals*) in the valley to challenge the power of Delhi. Many were arrested. Azam Inquilabi, general secretary of the Mahaz-i Azadi (Independence Front) was detained in 1985 and his services as a teacher were terminated for his alleged involvement in 'subversive' activities. Shabir Ahmed Shah was also arrested. A veteran activist who had begun his political career in 1968 at the age of fourteen when he was arrested for demanding the right to self-determination he was now leader of the People's League.

Instead of ordering fresh elections in the state of Jammu and Kashmir, Rajiv Gandhi insisted on a Conference-Congress alliance. This time Abdullah, who had spurned the alliance with Mrs Gandhi five years earlier, agreed to it. He seemed to have realised that Kashmir would never be able to prosper unless it had the open backing of Delhi. After six months of discussions, in November 1986, Rajiv reappointed Farooq as chief minister in an interim National Conference–Congress coalition government. The election was scheduled for the following year. But Abdullah was already beginning to pay the price for bowing to Delhi. 'Overnight, Farooq was transformed from hero to traitor in the Kashmiri mind,' writes Tavleen Singh. 'People could not understand how a man who had been treated the way he had by Delhi, and especially by the Gandhi family, could now be crawling to them for accords and alliances.'[46] He 'was charged with betraying his father's fifty-year legacy of pride,' says M. J. Akbar. 'It created a vacuum where the National Conference had existed, and extremists stepped into that vacuum. Kashmiriyat had become vulnerable to the votaries of violence and Muslim hegemony, both injuring Kashmir and perverting Kashmiriyat.'[47] Later Farooq Abdullah admitted that the 1986 accord was his most serious political mistake.

Rise of MUF and militancy

Amongst those who entered the political vacuum were the collection of political parties which organised themselves in September 1986 to form the Muslim United Front to contest the election. Under the dominance of Sheikh Abdullah the National Conference had retained its secular character. But the party was now split between Abdullah's supporters and those of G. M. Shah, and with Jagmohan demonstrating a decidedly pro-Hindu bias within the administration, MUF had considerable appeal.

A key component of MUF, led by Maulvi Abbas Ansari, was the Jamaat-i Islami; founded in 1942, the party had first fielded candidates in the 1972 elections and again in 1977, but its main impact was felt not in politics but, as Sheikh Abdullah had realised, in the mosques and schools.[48] Delhi analysts believed that the Jamaat's strength lay in 'funds from abroad' and overlooked the genuine appeal which the party was beginning to have. At least ten other smaller Islamic parties joined MUF. In addition, Abdul Gani Lone's People's Conference and G. M. Shah's Awami National Conference held discussions with MUF. Maulvi Farooq's Awami Action Committee also expressed solidarity with MUF. Although subsequently they argued amongst each other, the potential combination of so many opposition parties presented the first real challenge the National Conference had faced since it had returned to active politics after Sheikh Abdullah's 1975 accord.

MUF's election manifesto stressed the need for a solution to all outstanding issues according to the Simla agreement. It also assured the voters that it would work for Islamic unity and against political interference from the centre. As the candidates, dressed in white robes, were presented to the people at Iqbal Park on 4 March, slogans were raised: 'The struggle for freedom is at hand and what do we want in the Assembly; the law of the Quran.'[49] Farooq Abdullah became unnecessarily alarmed by MUF's electoral strength. Before the election, several MUF leaders were arrested as well as a number of election agents.

When the election was held on 23 March 1987, there was nearly 75 per cent participation, the highest ever recorded in the state, with nearly 80 per cent overall voting in the valley.[50] The Conference–Congress alliance claimed sixty-six seats; Congress won five out of the six seats in the valley which their candidates had contested. *The Times of India* described the victory of the alliance as 'heartening from a non-partisan point of view.'[51] MUF had expected to win ten out of the forty-four seats they had contested, but they won only four. Even so, Balraj Puri commented that the election results reflected 'a phenomenal increase in the strength of fundamentalist forces in the Kashmir valley.'[52] The Bharatiya Janata Party (BJP) secured two seats of the twenty-nine seats it contested. Although this was an insignificant number, the subsequent rise of the BJP in India gave a new impetus to Hindu communalism, which aroused suspicions amongst the Muslims of Kashmir regarding their status within secular India.

Despite national jubilation at the Conference-Congress victory, there were widespread charges of rigging. 'Votes were cast in favour of the Muslim United Front, but the results were declared in favour of the National Conference,' says Mir Abdul Aziz, who was observing events from Pakistan. To this day, Farooq Abdullah denies all charges of rigging. 'My own law minister lost his seat. If there had been rigging would I not have ensured that he retained his seat?'[53] His critics however maintain that Abdullah did panic; if his law minister did not win, it was because he was one of the candidates Abdullah did not want to win. 'The rigging was blatant,' writes Tavleen Singh. 'In the constituency of Handwara, for instance, Abdul Gani Lone's traditional bastion, as soon as counting began on 26 March, Lone's counting agents were thrown out of the counting station by the police.'[54]

The Muslim United Front supporters were angered at their lack of electoral success. 'That manipulation of the election disappointed the Kashmiris,' says Mir Abdul Aziz. 'They said that "we were trying to change the political framework by democratic and peaceful methods, but we have failed in this. Therefore we should take up the gun." That was one of the reasons for the militancy. The people of Kashmir got disgusted and disappointed and disillusioned.'[55] Educated but unemployed, their grievances were fuelled by events both within and outside the valley. They were also the ones who considered themselves economically deprived because they were neither part of the bureaucracy nor the elite. Alienated youth found a ready outlet for their frustration in one or other of the politico-religious organisations. At the same time the broader MUF alliance fell apart. The People's Conference and Awami National Conference did not adhere to the Jamaat's emphasis on promoting a 'theocratic state'. Jamaat supporters were also beginning to call for self-determination of the people of Kashmir. 'The Jamaat's accent was on secession,' said Abdul Gani Lone, leader of the People's Conference. 'We are looking for economic justice and a better deal from India.'[56]

The armed insurgency which gathered momentum after the 1987 election caught the rest of the world unawares. To most onlookers, Kashmir was a tourist spot, a place for rest and relaxation after a hot and exhausting trip through the hotter plains of India. Despite the political discontent at the outcome of the election, in 1987 it remained ostensibly calm. One of the conditions of the Rajiv–Farooq accord was a massive programme of state spending and initially Farooq appeared confident that, because of the accord, he would receive all the assistance he needed. But the promised package of Rs 1,000 crores was never received.[57]

Unwittingly, an impetus to the activities of the exiled Kashmiri nationalists in Pakistan was given by the deportation of Amanullah Khan from England. He had been arrested in England in September 1985 over a year after the murder of Mahtre, the Indian deputy high commissioner in 1984. The charge brought against him was possession of some illegal chemicals which the prosecution alleged could be turned into explosives. Khan protested that they were insecticides for his back garden. He was acquitted in September 1986 but was deported three months later despite appeals to the home secretary, Douglas Hurd, from several Labour members of parliament. Khan maintains that he and a Sikh extremist were traded off in return for India's purchase of some British helicopters.[58] The agreement for the purchase of the twenty-one Westland helicopters was announced on 24 December 1985 after three years of discussion. As the defence correspondent of *The Times* observed, the order was delayed for a year 'because of Indian resentment that the British government did not do more to restrain the activities of members of the Sikh community in Britain after the assassination of Mrs Gandhi.'[59]

Amanullah Khan took refuge in Pakistan from where he began to direct operations across the line of control. He had realised that, in order for his movement to gain momentum, he had to attract support from the valley. Four young Kashmiris were recruited and brought to Azad Kashmir. Known as the 'Haji' group, their names were Ashfaq Majid Wani, Sheikh Abdul Hamid, Javed Ahmed Mir and Muhammad Yasin Malik.[60] Malik's disaffection arose from the violence of his childhood:

> As a young boy of ten years old I remember while I was wandering on the roads of Srinagar city, sudden panic gripped the streets, people were running here and there for shelter and armed men in uniform were attacking the people, catching hold of just anybody on the roads and taking them into custody or beating them. I was terrorised.[61]

In May 1987 the first major act of violence was perpetrated against Farooq Abdullah when his motorcade was attacked on the way to the mosque.[62] Throughout the year sniper attacks became more common and, according to Tavleen Singh, there was evidence of increasing arms in the valley 'some time in that summer of 1987, once the bitterness of the stolen election had sunk in.'[63] Farooq Abdullah's domestic standing was further diminished by his attempt to locate some of the government departments permanently in either Jammu or Srinagar instead of shuttling them back and forward in winter and summer. His suggestion caused an outburst in Jammu, where the people went on strike in protest. Regional groups began calling for a separate state for the Jammu region. On 14 November 1987 the order was rescinded. Jammu rejoiced, but the valley was discontented. A strike was observed which paralysed life in the towns. The Bar Association was in the forefront of the agitation. Their associates believed that Abdullah had surrendered to Jammu and they demanded that Srinagar be made the permanent capital of the state. Although the agitation died down after about a week, Abdullah's critics protested that he had instigated the move in order to gain support for the National Conference from amongst the Kashmiri Muslims after the loss of popularity during the elections earlier in the year.

Throughout 1988 there were continuing disturbances which disrupted daily life with such frequency that Jagmohan, who was still the governor, made a detailed note of them in his diary.[64] In June, there were demonstrations in Srinagar against the sudden rise in the cost of electricity. The price increase annoyed people because supplies of electricity were at best erratic, but the government's response was unsympathetic. For the first time in over twenty-five years of activism, Amanullah Khan was able to talk convincingly about 'an armed struggle' in the valley. There were two bomb blasts which just missed the Central Telegraph office in Srinagar and the television station. In September there was an attack on the director-general of police, Ali Mohammed Watali. The JKLF claimed their first martyr, Ajaz Dar, who was killed during police firing. Although the early acts of sabotage did not cause much damage, they were a warning of what was to come. Resistance factions, whose adherents were called militants, proliferated under an array of names.

The JKLF, however, was singled out by the Indian authorities as being mainly responsible for the upsurge in internal disorder.

Anti-Indian feeling within the valley was mirrored by a surge of support for Pakistan. On 11 April 1988, young Muslims in Srinagar had forced shopkeepers to keep their shops shut in sympathy with all those who had been killed in an ammunition dump at Ojhri in Pakistan. The camp had been used as a depot for arms destined for the Afghan rebels. Mirwaiz Maulvi Farooq sent a condolence telegram to General Zia for the loss of life. Prayers were said in the Jama mosque.

A mourning procession was taken out in the streets of Srinagar which raised pro-Pakistani slogans, burnt buses and clashed with the police. The Gandhi Memorial College was ransacked. Hindu sympathisers were critical of the government, but for different reasons. The BJP accused the government of failure to take action against the protesters in time. The Panthers Party, formed in 1982, representing the Rajput community in Jammu, demanded Farooq Abdullah's resignation.

As India prepared to celebrate forty-one years of independence, anti-India slogans were raised in the valley. Pro-Pakistani supporters celebrated Pakistan's independence day on 14 August, but India's independence on 15 August was called a 'black day'. Two days later, on 17 August, General Zia-ul Haq was killed in a plane crash at Bahawalpur in Pakistan. His death was mourned in the valley, which led to disturbances. Eight people were reported to have been shot dead and at least thirteen wounded. Trouble between the Shias and Sunnis led to increased violence. 'An impression was created that the Shias in Pakistan felt happy at the death of President Zia-ul Haq. Some Shias in the valley were also accused of raising anti-Pak and anti-Zia slogans,' states P. S. Verma.[65] On 27 October – the anniversary of India's airlift into Srinagar in 1947 – there was a complete strike on what the protesters were now calling 'occupation day'. Whereas in 1947 the Pakistanis were deemed the invaders whilst the Indians were greeted as the liberators, by 1988 in the minds of the militants, the roles had been psychologically reversed.

The revenge factor

Pakistan could not fail to be aware of events in the valley. 'It was a tempting scenario,' writes Ajit Bhattacharjea, 'another chance to make up for the failures of 1947 and 1965, coupled with the desire to take revenge for the loss of Bangladesh in 1971, in which Indian infiltrators had played a role.'[66] Indian commentators maintain that as early as 1982, almost immediately after Sheikh Abdullah's death, General Zia had instigated a plan to train Kashmiri youth to launch an 'armed crusade' in the valley. But it did not meet with much success and it was not until the mid 1980s that the plan was again revived.[67] General Zia's official stand towards India on Kashmir was openly conciliatory. 'Pakistan's point of view is: let us talk. You can claim the whole of Kashmir,' he said in an interview with Indian journalist Rajendra Sareen in 1983. 'But maybe there is a *via media*. So let us talk at least. We are not in favour of resorting to force. But we are not in favour of being browbeaten by the Indian point of view that since there is a Line of Control, there is therefore no issue involved.'[68]

The perception, however, of Pakistan's early involvement in the growing militancy was fuelled by the Indian government's own propaganda machinery. K. Subramanyam, one of India's top defence specialists maintained that 'Operation Topac', named after Topac Amin, an Inca Prince who fought a non-conventional war against Spanish rule in eighteenth-century Uruguay, was established in Pakistan in April 1988 in order to nurture an indigenous insurgency. Widely publicised in the Indian Defence Review of July 1989, including reports of alleged instructions from General Zia to his army officers, Topac was denied by the Pakistani authorities. They countered that it was invented by the Research and Analysis Wing (RAW) of the Government of India, as a hypothetical exercise, a fact which Subramanyam later acknowledged.[69]

Such 'hypothetical' exercises did not help to improve the strained relations between the two countries. In the mid-1980s, the threat of war loomed with clashes between Indian and Pakistani forces on the Siachen glacier, one of the most northerly points of the state of Jammu and Kashmir, where, due to its 20,000 ft altitude, the line of control had never been clearly defined. Discussions in January 1986 between the two defence secretaries helped to diffuse the situation but sporadic fighting continued throughout 1987. In 1988 the Indian government introduced high altitude helicopters which gave their forces a strategic advantage.

The new administration of Benazir Bhutto, who had been elected prime minister of Pakistan in elections following General Zia's death in 1988, attempted to demonstrate concern over the deteriorating Indo-Pakistani relationship. Her meeting with Rajiv Gandhi in Islamabad soon after she became prime minister in December 1988 was widely seen as an opportunity for members of the new post-partition generation to resolve their differences. In early 1989 top-level talks were instituted. Two agreements were signed whereby the two leaders agreed not to bomb each other's nuclear installations and that they would respect the 1972 Simla accord signed by their parents. But Gandhi and Bhutto were both subject to their own domestic pressures, which did not give them the necessary latitude for any constructive policy reassessments. For Benazir Bhutto détente with India meant that her political opponents, of whom Nawaz Sharif, leader of the IJI (Islami Jamhoori Ittehad) was the most vociferous, alleged that she was pro-India in order to discredit her government at home. Rajiv Gandhi likewise faced difficulties over rapprochement with Bhutto at a time when Pakistan was being widely condemned in India for supporting the Sikh separatist movement. In August 1989, Bhutto, who had demanded that Indian troops should withdraw from

Siachen, demonstrated Pakistan's continuing interest in the region by making a personal visit to the glacier; given its immense altitude, the struggle for Siachen was perhaps symbolic, but the tensions between the two countries remained.

As the law and order situation deteriorated in the valley, Indian analysts continued to assert that the trouble was instigated by Pakistan. They argued that Pakistan's ISI - the Inter-Services Intelligence - which had been set up by General Zia-ul Haq and was known to have played a leading role in the war in Afghanistan, was also active in Kashmir. The alleged 'foreign hand' was, however, also a convenient scapegoat which prevented the Indian government from seeing the internal trauma within the valley. The grievances amongst the Kashmiris, which had been allowed to fester, the steady erosion of the 'special status' promised to the state of Jammu and Kashmir in 1947, the neglect of the people by their leaders, were clearly India's responsibility. Tavleen Singh believes that Kashmir would not have become an issue 'if the valley had not exploded on its own thanks to Delhi's misguided policies.' Over a period of time, 'the LOC would have been accepted as the border and we could have one day forgotten the dispute altogether.'[70] Instead, as the decade of the 1980s drew to a close, the valley of Kashmir became 'the explosive situation' of which Sheikh Abdullah had so often warned.

CHAPTER 14

Closure of the Vale 1990

> I will put it bluntly. Independence is out. And they have to come to terms with it. They must realise it. But having said that, everything else is open. Girish Saxena.[1]

As the insurgency in the valley gained momentum, the acts of sabotage increased in frequency and intensity. The police and security forces reacted violently, often at the expense of innocent civilians who were caught in the crossfire. Every youth in Kashmir came to be regarded as a potential militant. Reports of human rights abuses began to hit the headlines world-wide. Stories emerged of torture, rape and indiscriminate killing. Although the insurgents seemed to have no long-term strategy, they appeared to hope that the repression of the Indian authorities in the valley would attract international attention which would take note of what they believed to be their 'just cause' and oblige the Indian government to relinquish control of the valley.

Farooq Abdullah was being side-lined as a political force by the Muslim parties, nearly all of whom developed a militant wing, and the continuing bomb attacks gave ample proof of the extent to which their supporters were armed. Amongst several direct assaults, Neel Kanth Ganju, the retired sessions judge who had passed the sentence of death on Maqbool Butt, was fired upon. Firing across the line of control was occurring regularly and a dawn to dusk curfew was imposed in all the border districts. Oblivious of the time-bomb which was about to explode in the valley, holidaymakers flocked to spend their summer on a houseboat or trekking in the foothills of the Himalayas. It was estimated that in 1989 a record number of nearly 80,000 foreign tourists visited Kashmir in what effectively became the valley's last tourist season.

The insurgency begins

While peace was 'breaking out' after the downfall of the communist regimes in Eastern Europe, 1989 marked the real beginning of the insurgency. A strike was called for India's Republic Day on 26 January. It was the first of many *hartals* in 1989, which took up one-third of the year's working days.[2] Severe riots in Jammu between Sikhs and Hindus led to unruly mobs roaming the city while the police 'acted merely as passive spectators.'[3] The fifth

anniversary of Maqbool Butt's execution on 11 February was the occasion
for another strike. Two days later there was a massive anti-Indian demonstration against Salman Rushdie's *Satanic Verses,* which lasted nearly a week,
even though the government had banned the book. The whole of Srinagar
went on strike. When five people were reportedly killed in police firing, the
strike spread to other towns in the valley. In March there was violence
between Muslims and Hindus in Rajauri. And throughout 1989 there was
sporadic violence between Muslims and Buddhists in Ladakh. The Buddhists,
ever conscious of the dominance of the valley Muslims, raised slogans like
'Save Ladakh, Free Ladakh from Kashmir.'[4]

On 12 July 1989 Jagmohan relinquished his position as governor after five
years in office. In his memoirs he describes how since 1988 he had been
sending 'warning signals' to New Delhi about the 'gathering storm'. 'All
these clear and pointed warnings were, unfortunately, ignored.'[5] Jagmohan
was replaced by a retired general, K. V. Krishna Rao. A former chief of
army staff, Rao had considerable expertise in counter-insurgency, but none
in politics. Farooq Abdullah was criticised by his political opponents for
being unable to control the situation. 'The last symbol of secular Kashmiriyat
remained a lightweight,' writes Bhattacharjea, 'given to helicopter sorties over
the stricken valley; to elitist projects to attract tourists, while basic facilities
were ignored.'[6] Enforced *bandhs* and *hartals,* attacks on government offices,
bridges, buses, murder of police informers and intelligence officers all
contributed to the increasing paralysis of the government.

Part of the militants' strategy was to intimidate National Conference
activists in order to oblige them to disassociate themselves from the party,
ultimately leading to a complete breakdown of the political process. On 21
August, Mohammed Yusuf Halwai, a National Conference leader was killed
near his home in downtown Srinagar; shopkeepers downed their shutters 'in
fear, confusion and mild disapproval'.[7] A placard on Halwai's body identified
the JKLF as responsible for his death. The government was clearly being
outmanoeuvred by the militants in 'the battle for hearts and minds' to which
Farooq Abdullah repeatedly referred. 'They remain faceless and underground
and yet control Kashmir,' wrote Tavleen Singh on 27 August 1989. 'This is
the most frightening aspect of the current political situation in this troubled
valley. All of last week shops remained closed in Srinagar without anyone
being sure why except that there had been orders from "them".'[8]

Despite its waning popularity, the National Conference still managed to
organise a rally on the anniversary of Sheikh Abdullah's death on 8 September.
But the militants called for a strike which was observed in Srinagar and other
towns throughout the valley. Effigies of the Sheikh were burnt. A week later,
the first Kashmiri Pandit was murdered, the BJP leader, Tikka Lal Taploo,
who was also an advocate of the High Court. Then Neel Kanth Ganju, who
had escaped the earlier attack, was shot dead in broad daylight on 4
November. The Hindus, who for centuries had lived in harmony with the

Muslims, began to fear for their lives. There was a blackout on 14 November, Nehru's birthday, and on 5 December, Sheikh Abdullah's birthday.

Farooq Abdullah's response to the insurgency was described by Balraj Puri as more 'a sense of bravado rather than maturity'.[9] Stringent measures were adopted whether the protests were because of religious sentiments, pro-Pakistani feeling, economic grievances or civil liberties. Abdullah also attributed the alienation not so much to the 'rigged' 1987 elections, but to the failure of the government in Delhi to fulfil its promise to give the funds which were agreed at the time of Farooq's accord with Rajiv. 'We were unable to create jobs, to stop corruption. We were unable to provide factories and power generating stations. At each stage we were not given the help which we envisaged when we joined hands with the Congress.'[10] Too many Kashmiri youth were unemployed; a problem which Farooq understood but could not remedy. 'What can I do? There are 3,000 engineers looking for jobs even after we gave jobs to 2,000 in the last two years.' Nearly 10,000 graduates were unemployed. Amongst those with school leaving qualifications, unemployment was around 40,000 to 50,000. Allegations of corruption in the admissions procedure also alienated the people: 'Bright students could not get admission into colleges in the 1980s unless they paid bribes to politicians,' stated a lecturer at the University of Kashmir. 'This led to a loss of faith in the system and eventually the revolt.'[11] Individual students also corroborated this statement.

By 1989, a number of significant militant groups had begun to operate throughout the valley, mainly centred on the towns of Srinagar, Anantnag, Baramula and Sopore.[12] Their objective was either complete independence or unification with Pakistan. The Jammu and Kashmir Liberation Front, led within the valley by the core 'Haji' group, was the most prominent. True to its earlier objectives, its supporters were fighting for an independent state of Jammu and Kashmir as it existed in 1947. Several of the Muslim political parties, who had been components of MUF, had formed militant wings. The militant group, Al Baraq, had links with Abdul Gani Lone's People's Conference. Al Fateh, led by Zain-ul Abdeen, a former contestant in the 1987 elections, was the armed wing of one faction of Shabir Shah's People's League. Both parties had also come out in support of the independence movement. Another armed faction of the Peoples' League was Al Jehad. Additional groups aimed at the formation of a 'theocratic' state. On a less significant level, the Allah Tigers had demonstrated that their main concern was closing video shops and beauty salons because they were 'unislamic'. In the early days of the insurgency, the Hizb-ul Mujaheddin, based in Sopore and regarded as the militant wing of the Jamaat-i Islami, did not have widespread support within the valley. The official Hizb-ul Mujaheddin objective was reunification with Pakistan. The Harkat-al Ansar was also not yet part of mainstream militancy. Smaller groups believed to favour Pakistan were Hizbullah, Al-Umar Mujaheddin, Lashkar-i Toiba, Ikhwan-ul Mujaheddin,

Hizb-ul Momineen, Tehrik-ul Mujaheddin, as well as other numerous splinter groups.

Azam Inquilabi had transformed his Mahaz-i Azadi (Independence Front) into Operation Balakote. His objective was to create a united front between the rival groups to fight for the liberation of Kashmir from Indian rule. 'India and Pakistan must recognise our right to self-determination so that the two parts of Jammu and Kashmir be allowed to annex with each other. Then the people must be able to decide whether they want to remain free or join with Pakistan. We want to be able to determine our political future for ourselves.'[13] At the outset, the divisions between the groups remained below the surface; when one group called for a strike, the others complied.

Many of the militants were the disappointed political workers and traditional opponents of the National Conference in the 1987 elections. Young men aged between sixteen and twenty-five, they came from the towns of Srinagar, Anantnag, Pulwama, Kupwara and Baramula. Unlike their forbears who had campaigned for education and political rights in the 1930s, the majority were well-educated – doctors, engineers, teachers, policemen – who had become alienated by Indian government policies in New Delhi and lack of job opportunities. Their grievances were as much economic as political. Older militants, like Amanullah Khan of the JKLF, Ahsan Dar of Hizb-ul Mujaheddin and Azam Inquilabi of Operation Balakote, provided the motivation and historical context in which the struggle was being waged: 'We kept struggling for a peaceful resolution of the dispute, but failed,' said Inquilabi, 'so this young generation has opted for active resistance and it has gained momentum and it will continue to gain momentum come what may.'[14]

At the beginning of December 1989, Rajiv Gandhi lost the general election in India to his former finance minister, V. P. Singh. Although Kashmir was not an election issue, the new prime minister chose to try and win some support in the troubled state by appointing a Kashmiri Muslim, Mufti Muhammed Sayeed as India's first Muslim home minister, a position once held by Sardar Patel. Six days after he took office, on 8 December 1989, the JKLF made headline news with the kidnapping of the home minister's twenty-three-year-old daughter, Dr Rubaiya Sayeed, an intern at the Lalded Memorial Women's Hospital in Srinagar.

The kidnappers demanded the release of five militants, including JKLF leader, Sheikh Hamid, and the brother of Maqbool Butt, in return for her freedom. Farooq Abdullah, who was abroad at the time, returned to face mounting panic in the state. Journalists and bureaucrats became involved in the negotiations to free Rubaiya. Although the kidnapping of a young unmarried woman was giving the militants adverse publicity, the government at New Delhi was not prepared to risk any harm coming to the hostage and on 13 December the militants were freed; two hours later, Rubaiya Sayeed was also released unharmed. The released militants were taken out in a triumphant procession. Jubilant crowds rejoiced and danced in the streets of

Srinagar. The perceived weakness of V. P. Singh's government in negotiating with the militants raised their morale considerably. In an interview with *India Today* Mufti Muhammed Sayeed attributed the current alienation of the people to 'the mishandling of the situation by the previous [centre and state] governments ... the 1987 Assembly elections were rigged and the people lost faith in democratic institutions.'[15]

The frequent strikes through the year, targeted assassinations, bomb blasts and attacks on government property, culminating in the JKLF kidnapping, all contributed to the impression of increasing disorder. 'I was in the valley in late 1989,' recalled Dr Muzaffar Shah, president of the Kashmir Action Committee in Pakistan and a refugee from Baramula. 'I saw the whole thing simmering, about to burst; there was no administration. It had failed to stop the people coming on the streets; they took out demonstrations and called for strikes. Then the whole place burst open like a dam in 1990.'[16]

The return of Jagmohan

After the kidnapping of Rubaiya Saeed, New Delhi adopted a tougher approach. Shri Jagmohan was sent back to Kashmir as governor in place of General Krishna Rao, who had been in office for just over six months. 'The tragic irony of the situation was that I, who had been persistently pointing out that poisonous seeds were being planted, had to come back to face a thick and thorny harvest.'[17] Farooq Abdullah immediately resigned on the grounds that he could not co-operate with 'a man who hates the guts of the Muslims.'[18] As a supporter of the Indian Union, Abdullah shared none of his father's pretensions towards independence, and had no sympathy with the demands of the militants, whom he at times referred to as 'misguided youth'. But the accord with Rajiv Gandhi, the 1987 elections, alleged corruption of his government and subsequent inability to control the situation had all lost him popular support. Farooq, however, was also feeling injured: 'Someone told him after he resigned,' reported M. J. Akbar, ' that the people of Kashmir were unhappy with him. "Well," he replied, "I am unhappy with them too."'[19]

Jagmohan compared the administration, of which he was once more in charge, to 'a sprawling but lifeless octopus ... Frenzied chaos and savage anarchy gripped the valley'.[20] His return to full control of events in Kashmir on 19 January 1990 marked the beginning of a new intensity both in New Delhi's dealings with the Kashmiris and their response. His appointment was probably 'the worst mistake the central government could have made at the time,' writes Tavleen Singh. 'But there was nobody in V. P. Singh's newly-elected government who could have told him this.'[21] His government depended heavily on the extremist BJP whose supporters wanted to abrogate article 370 and integrate Kashmir within the Indian Union. The attempt to find a political solution to Kashmir's problem was put aside in favour of a policy of repression.

On the night of 19 January an intensive house-to-house search was carried out in an area where militants were believed to be hiding. Three hundred people were arrested, most of whom were later released.[22] Jagmohan claimed that the search had been ordered, before he resigned, by Abdullah whom he accused of abandoning the valley. The former chief minister denied this. The reaction from the people was unprecedented. 'The whole city was out. I was sleeping – it was midnight. I heard people on the road shouting pro-Pakistani slogans and Islamic slogans – "Allah o Akbar", "What do we want? We want freedom!"' recalls Haseeb, a Kashmiri medical student.[23]

The next day, as Jagmohan was sworn in as governor with the promise that he would treat the state like a 'nursing orderly' a large demonstration assembled in the streets of Srinagar to protest against the search the night before. In response, paramilitary troops gathered on either side of the Gawakadal bridge over the Jhelum river. When the unarmed crowd reached the bridge it was fired on from both sides of the river. The shooting has been called the worst massacre in Kashmiri history. Over a hundred people died, some from gunshot wounds, others because, in fear, they jumped into the river and drowned.[24] Farooq Ahmed, a mechanical engineer who was watching the demonstration, was wounded. Presumed dead, he was put into a lorry filled with bodies, until he was finally rescued by Kashmiri police and taken to hospital. 'I was fortunate, my back was just touched. Six bullets … but my head was safe, I was conscious also. I saw the bridge was completely full of dead bodies … there was chaos, people running here and there.'[25]

Whereas the Indian press played the incident down, the foreign press reported the massacre and its repercussions to the world. 'Thousands of Muslims, chanting "Indian dogs go home," "We want freedom" and "Long live Islam" marched through Srinagar and other towns, despite police "shoot-on-sight" orders,' reported the *Daily Telegraph*.[26] As a result, foreign correspondents were banned from the valley. A curfew was imposed indefinitely. Several other towns were put under curfew. Jagmohan stated that he had no information about bodies floating in the Jhelum river and failed to mention the incident in his memoirs. No public enquiry was ordered afterwards. 'With this incident,' writes Balraj Puri, 'militancy entered a new phase. It was no longer a fight between the militants and the security forces. It gradually assumed the form of a total insurgency of the entire population.'[27]

However, even as the insurgency was gaining in intensity in Kashmir, Indian television 'went overboard with live coverage of the mass movements against authoritarianism in East Europe and Central Asia, inanely oblivious of the tremendous impact each visual of a woman kissing the Quran and taunting a soldier was having on Kashmir,' writes M. J. Akbar.[28] In defiance of what came to be called 'crackdown' by the authorities, the people continued to come out on the streets: 'There were loudspeakers in the mosques, encouraging people to come out. Everyday, all day people were shouting slogans,' recalls Haseeb. '*Azadi, Azadi* … Allah-o Akbar – Freedom, Freedom,

God is Great' was broadcast from the minarets. With extraordinary optimism, the people believed they had won their struggle almost before it had begun. 'Even I was thinking within ten days, India will have to vacate Kashmir.'[29] Teachers, doctors, lawyers, civil servants, students all came out on the streets in protest. For the first time the Indian flag was not hoisted to celebrate India's Republic Day on 26 January, which was observed as a 'black day'. Those journalists already in Srinagar remained confined to their hotel rooms; their curfew passes were withdrawn; telephone and telex lines were cut.

Pakistan seemed to be taken unawares by events in the valley. 'Islamabad was as surprised as New Delhi by the sudden, dramatic outburst of sentiment for *azadi*,' writes Edward Desmond, the *Time* magazine correspondent.[30] Given the past history of Indo–Pakistani relations over Kashmir, the Pakistani government was bound to repeat its demand of the past decades: the Kashmiris should be allowed their right to self-determination under the terms of the United Nations resolutions. Benazir Bhutto made an assertive speech in Azad Kashmir pledging Pakistan's moral and diplomatic support to the 'freedom fighters'. Talks in January 1990 between Inder Gujral, the Indian foreign minister, and Sahibzada Yaqub Khan, the Pakistani foreign minister, did not reduce the continuing tension between the two countries. 'Yaqub Sahib came with a very hard message,' said Inder Gujral. The Indian foreign minister described his Pakistani counterpart as 'almost challenging the Indian state's authority on Kashmir, saying that nothing in the past was binding on them and the Simla agreement was not relevant.'[31] The Indian government also talked of the need to be psychologically prepared for war, claiming that 10,000 Kashmiri youth had gone to Pakistan to undergo training.[32] But, writes, Indian journalist Tavleen Singh, 'the moral support became military support only after thousands of Kashmiris had taken to the streets to demand *azadi*.'[33]

Jagmohan withstood what he termed the 'propaganda missiles' emanating from Pakistan. 'I persuaded myself that I had a national obligation to discharge. With all the frozen turbulence in my mind with all the millstones round my neck, and with my back badly wounded by the stabs from the rear, I proceeded ahead.'[34] Restrictions on the press, however, prevented genuine information from getting through to the valley. With the exception of foreign radio, the Kashmiris were obliged to rely on press releases issued from Jagmohan's office in Raj Bhavan. The same stories appeared in different newspapers with the same content under different by-lines.

On 13 February Lassa Kaul, the local director of Indian television, Doodarshan, was murdered by militants in Srinagar on his way home. Jagmohan explained the murder on the grounds that Kaul had incurred 'the wrath of the terrorists by showing on television programmes which they termed unislamic and forming part of what was labelled as cultural aggression by India.' The militants blamed the administration for pressurising Kaul into broadcasting pro-Indian government material, 'thus indirectly bringing about his death'.[35] The next day, employees of Doordashan resigned on the grounds that Jagmohan had ruined the credibility of the official media. 'The media,' says Ved Bhasin, editor of the *Kashmir Times* based in Jammu, 'was caught in the crossfire between the militants and the military.'[36] The pressure from both sides to slant stories or omit information meant that journalists found it impossible to function.[37]

When Jagmohan dissolved the State Legislative Assembly on 19 February he dispensed with the only avenue for political expression other than the mosque. He explained his actions to the home minister, Mufti Mohammed Sayeed: 'Without dissolution there was no moral legitimacy for the use of force on an extensive scale. Nor was it possible for me and the advisers to secure the obedience of our orders from local officials, who were constantly being fed with the impression that Dr Farooq Abdullah and his colleagues were coming back after the role of "butcher" has been played by the Governor.'[38] With the backing of Delhi, Jagmohan's strategy was to militarise the state. The local police were bolstered by a federal paramilitary unit, the Central Reserve Police Force (CRPF); their harsh methods were resented by the local police who temporarily went on strike. 'Unofficial estimates have it that nearly a lakh [100,000] of army, paramilitary and police personnel have been deployed in Kashmir in the past six weeks. If this is not war, what is it?' asked journalist, Shiraz Sidhva after a visit to the valley in February 1990. 'That the people are with the militants is quite clear. In the one month since the new administration has taken over, not one single militant has been captured.'[39]

At the end of February an estimated 400,000 Kashmiris marched on the offices of the United Nations Military Observer Group to hand in petitions demanding the implementation of the UN resolutions. It was reported as the largest demonstration the Kashmir valley has seen.[40] But the UN officials were obliged to point out that their presence in the valley was only to monitor the line of control. Nearly every day a procession of lawyers, women, teachers, doctors marched through the streets of Srinagar. On 1 March more than forty people were killed in police firing when a massive crowd, estimated at one million took to the streets. The continuing curfew led to severe shortages of food, medicines and other essential items. The hospitals were becoming so full of the victims of the insurgency that the name of the Bone and Joint hospital in Srinagar was changed to the Hospital for Bullet and Bomb Blast injuries.[41]

Driven by his own sense of personal mission, Jagmohan saw the insurgency as a movement, abetted by Pakistan, which had to be brutally crushed, even if it meant targeting virtually the entire population.

> Obviously, I could not walk barefoot in the valley full of scorpions – the valley wherein inner and outer forces of terrorism had conspired to subvert the Union and to seize power ... I must equip myself to face all eventualities. I could leave nothing to chance. A slight slip or error would mean a Tienamen Square or a Blue Star or a formal declaration of a new theocratic state with all its international embarrassment ...[42]

Farooq Abdullah accused the governor of unleashing a reign of terror on the people.

The government of New Delhi took some remedial steps to control the effects of the repression by appointing George Fernandes as minister for Kashmir who was well known both in India and in the rest of the world for his concern for human rights. Jagmohan regarded Fernandes's approach as impractical and he took an unsympathetic view of his interviews with 'unresponsive elements in the subversives' camp'. Fernandes, he said, 'gave no consideration to the fact that as long as the pro-Pakistani elements, intoxicated by past successes, had faith in their guns and bombs, no worthwhile political process could be initiated and those who responded to it, were most likely to be eliminated.'[43] Fernandes, however, believed in dialogue. 'I know these people. I have met with them – quite a few of them before they became militants, and many of them thereafter. One has to interact with them to get a sense of the kind of alienation that these young people have experienced.'[44]

The flight of the Hindus

In a mass exodus, at the beginning of March, about 140,000 Hindus[45] left the valley for refugee camps outside Jammu. The more affluent took up residence in their second homes in Delhi, but the vast majority were housed in squalid tents in over fifty camps on the outskirts of both Jammu and Delhi. Their story is as familiar as any the world over. Displaced from their homes because of a war over which they had no control, they too seemed to be caught in the crossfire – used as propaganda material by the Indian government to demonstrate that not only Muslims were suffering during the insurgency. 'In the wake of terrorism, we left the valley. We are living in a miserable condition' said Jawaharlal, who used to be a teacher in Kupwara, a small town near the line of control. 'We used to live in peace. The Kashmiri Muslims are our brethren. We have been living with them for centuries together; we shared their joy and sorrow. But the gun culture forced us to leave.' Living in unhygienic conditions, with insufficient food, Jawaharlal believed that the human rights of Hindus have also been violated. 'The Kashmiri Pandits are in a minority. Our rights must be safeguarded in the hands of the Muslim majority in the valley. We have left our hearths and homes. Our civil liberties have been curtailed. Only if the majority community invites us to go back, then can we return to the valley; otherwise it is out of bounds for us.'[46] Dr Pamposh Ganju of the Indo–European Kashmir forum says that since 1990 over 6,000 Hindus have died in the camps, because of poor conditions, compared with 1,500 Kashmiri Pandits who were killed during the early months of the insurgency.[47] (Indian government figures for murdered Hindus number less than 200 in 1989/90.)

There was and still is, however, a widespread feeling that the departure of the Hindus was not necessary and that Jagmohan, who had a reputation for being anti-Muslim dating back to the days of the Emergency, attempted to give the Kashmiri problem a communal profile by facilitating their departure in government transport. It was an allegation he strongly refuted:

> What can you say of a Committee which comes out with a proposition that it is not the fearsome environment, it is not the brutalised landscape, it is not the ruthless Kalashnikov of the marauders, it is not the bomb explosions and fires, it is not the threatening telephonic calls, it is not the hysterical exhortations for "Jihad" from hundreds of loudspeakers fitted on the mosques ... but the inducements of the trucks that have impelled the Kashmiris to abandon their homes and hearths in the cool and crisp Valley and to move to the hot and inhospitable camps of Jammu?[48]

After their flight, there were numerous reports of Muslim neighbours and friends looking after the houses of the Hindus. 'The property, houses, orchards owned by the Pandits have not been damaged in the last one year,' stated George Fernandes in October 1990.[49] Furthermore, says Balraj Puri, only 'a thorough independent enquiry ... can show whether this exodus of Pandits, the largest in their long history, was entirely unavoidable.'[50] Their departure meant that the militant groups, like the JKLF, who maintained that their objectives for the state included all the occupants of the former princely state, could no longer claim to represent the Hindus, who were drawn to the extremist Hindu parties, the BJP and Shiv Sena.

Two eminent jurists, V. M. Tarkunde, now in his eighties, and Rachinder Sachar, as well as the educationalist, Amrik Singh, and Balraj Puri, toured Kashmir in March and April 1990. They condemned both militants and Jagmohan for the deteriorating situation in the valley: 'The fact is that the whole Muslim population of the Kashmir valley is wholly alienated from India and due to the highly repressive policy pursued by the administration in recent months, especially since the advent of Shri Jagmohan in January 1990, their alienation has now turned into bitterness and anger.' Their report also condemned the militants for their tactics following the kidnapping and murder in April of the vice-chancellor of Kashmir University, Mushir-ul Haq, his secretary, Abdul Ghani, and the general manager of the Hindustan Machine Tools watch factory, H. L. Khera: 'The militants are strengthening the repressive machinery of the state by their activities and are providing a semblance of justification to the government to assume more and more arbitrary powers.'[51] In a sense, this was their strategy: the greater the repression by the Indian government, the more support the militants hoped to gain amongst the people, and consequently, the more international pressure could be brought to bear. But with foreign correspondents banned from the valley and top political activists under arrest, there was no dialogue to modify the stand taken either by the government or the militants.

Death of the Mirwaiz

Since his days of opposition to Sheikh Abdullah, arising out of his uncle Yusuf's feud in the 1930s, Mirwaiz Maulvi Farooq had been known for his pro-Pakistani sentiments. The Farooq-Farooq alliance with Abdullah in 1983 marked a short-lived shift in attitude; as Farooq Abdullah's own position was marginalised with the rise of the Muslim parties, Mirwaiz Farooq assumed the role of a respected elder, someone who, in the present crisis, both the government and the militants could approach. As chief preacher at the Jama Masjid in Srinagar, his religious influence was considerable. On 21 May he was shot dead at his home. Militants blamed Indian agents; the government of New Delhi blamed the militants, but not convincingly enough so no one believed them. His death shocked both groups. His teenage son, Omar, blamed 'those elements who were working against the interests of the Kashmiri movement' for his death.[52] Supporters of the state's accession to India observed how his reputation changed overnight with his death. 'Till he was shot dead ... he was considered a traitor and a secessionist,' writes Tavleen Singh. 'No sooner was he dead than he came to be instantly revered as a martyr and a moderate.'[53]

The repercussions after his death did even more damage to the government. During his funeral procession, as the crowd passed Islamia College, where the 69th battalion of the CRPF was quartered, some officers opened fire; the government claimed that it did so in retaliation for an attack on the security forces by a section of the crowd. Officially, the government acknowledged twenty-seven dead, but unofficial sources claimed as many as 100 died, possibly more.[54] The Mirwaiz's coffin was also pierced with bullets. Outrage at the murder turned into hysteria against the government.

When interviewed by the Punjab Human Rights Organisation, Satish Jacob, one of the BBC's correspondents in Delhi, described the militant groups as not being 'a wee bit sad about Maulvi's death. Not to the extent they pretended to be. All the show of sorrow is spurious.' In his opinion, the murder was carried out by the Hizb-ul Mujaheddin because Maulvi Farooq was a supporter of the JKLF On the basis of his own information, Jacob also said that the security forces were wholly at fault in firing on the funeral procession and that there was no evidence that there was any provocation prior to the firing or any one from the crowd fired. He estimated that forty-seven people died.[55]

The valley under Jagmohan was a closed war zone. When the Punjab Human Rights Organisation investigated Maulvi Farooq's death, they described 'a complete iron curtain' separating the Kashmir valley from the outside world. 'The regime of the curfew is all pervading. There are severe restrictions on outsider Indians seeking to enter the valley.'[56] In retrospect, it is surprising that the Indian government did not appreciate earlier the adverse effect of crushing the insurgency so indiscriminately. Although

Jagmohan's tenure as governor lasted less than five months, during this period, the alienation of the valley against the Indian government became almost total.

By the time he left Kashmir, Jagmohan's thinking had none of the qualities of the promised nursing orderly:

> Every Muslim in Kashmir is a militant today. All of them are for secession from India. I am scuttling Srinagar Doordarshan's programmes because every one there is a militant ... The situation is so explosive that I can't go out of this Raj Bhavan. But I know what's going on, minute by minute. The bullet is the only solution for Kashmir. Unless the militants are fully wiped out, normalcy can't return to the valley.[57]

Ashok Jaitley, a respected civil servant, who worked under Jagmohan, saw things differently: 'What Jagmohan did in five months they (the militants) could not have achieved in five years.'[58]

Saxena steps in

After Mirwaiz Farooq's death, Jagmohan was replaced as governor by Girish 'Gary' Saxena. He had spent seventeen years with RAW, India's intelligence agency, Research and Analysis Wing. On his assumption of office, he received a memorandum form ten senior civil servants, which included the signature of Ashok Jaitley. In their report, they attempted to give Saxena a realistic picture of the alienation of the valley due to mishandling by the authorities. Although Saxena is generally regarded as being more benign in his approach than Jagmohan, Tavleen Singh believes he was just more subtle. 'The last thing the new governor wanted to hear were any home truths about Kashmir.'[59] He did not adopt Jagmohan's overtly repressive tactics, but he was equally committed to crushing the insurgency through force.

Increasing reliance was placed on the border security forces to combat the insurgency, but, as Saxena later admitted, they were young boys not trained for the sort of duties they were called to discharge.

> Border security forces are trained to guard the borders, patrol and guard pickets, they are not trained for urban terrorism and guerrilla warfare. So they had to learn many things the hard way. A person can act in haste or in panic. This is more likely in a small outfit led by a junior officer. Suddenly he is subjected to machine gun fire or a rocket attack, there is a feeling that he or his party might be over run ... Because of a proxy war being conducted from across the border and sponsoring of terrorist violence on a large scale, it was at times difficult to ensure targeted measured responses by the security forces. There were occasions when there was overreaction or even wrongdoing.[60]

Like many Indians officials, Saxena firmly believed that Pakistan was waging its own 'proxy war' in Kashmir, not only by supporting the militants by giving them arms but also by allowing them to train in their territory. In

February 1990, Indian intelligence had disclosed over 46 camps throughout
Azad Kashmir, which they described as 'safe houses' where militants were
given weapons and explosives training.[61] In June 1990 *Financial Times* journalist,
David Housego travelled throughout Azad Kashmir and was shown Jamaat-
i Islami refugee camps which were:

> ... quite unlike the official camps of the local Azad Kashmir government where
> you see the familiar miseries of refugee life ... In the Jamaat camps, there are
> no women, children or older men. They are all young men coming from different
> towns and villages in the Valley ... their morale is high. They say that they are
> well looked after...they describe themselves as refugees. But stickers on the wall
> proclaim they are members of the Hizb-ul Mujaheddin.[62]

The Pakistani and the Azad Kashmir governments denied that they were
giving any material support to the militants. But the activities of the Jamaat-i
Islami and other militant sympathisers were obviously not restricted. 'There
are no training camps in Pakistan, of course, but insofar as Azad Kashmir
is concerned, this is part and parcel of the State of Jammu and Kashmir,'
says Azam Inquilabi.[63] 'We can establish military training camps there and we
have been doing it.' Justice Tarkunde assessed the training camps in the
context of the Kashmiris political struggle against the government of India:

> It is very likely that Pakistan has provided military training and arms to the
> militants in Kashmir. But it is not responsible for the disaffection of the people
> of the valley from the government of India. The cause of the Kashmir debacle
> is the initial denial of the right of self-determination and the subsequent anti-
> democratic policies pursued by the Indian government.[64]

In March 1990, John Kelly, assistant secretary of state for Near Eastern
and South Asian Affairs told a House Foreign Affairs subcommittee: 'We are
concerned at the recent flare-up of tensions between India and Pakistan
over Kashmir ... the United States thinks the best framework for a resolution
of this dispute can be found in the 1972 Simla Agreement.'[65] With the
weakening of the Indo–Russian relationship following the collapse of the
Soviet Union, as Indian commentators observed the United States was also
aware of the significant opportunities for developing stronger ties with India.
Indian military purchases from the United States increased from $56,000 in
1987 to $56 million in 1990.[66] Pakistan was, however, facing difficulties with
its relationship with the United States because of its nuclear programme. In
October 1990, under the terms of the Pressler Amendment, American military
supplies were cut off. At the same time, Nawaz Sharif, who replaced Benazir
Bhutto as prime minister after her dismissal in August 1990, was coming
under domestic criticism for his Kashmiri policy. Amongst some circles in
Pakistan it was believed that, regardless of statements to the contrary, the
US was favouring an independent Kashmir in order to be able to use it as
a base for American strategic objectives and that, by not taking a tough
enough stand on Kashmir, Nawaz was acceding to this objective. 'The

scenario which the West is trying to create here goes something like this,' said Mian Zahid Sarfraz, a former political colleague of Nawaz Sharif:

> If Kashmir can't be buried on Indian terms, then it should become an independent country rather than a part of Pakistan through a plebiscite as originally envisaged. But if Kashmir becomes independent or is given some such status, it will at best be a landlocked domain, an international protectorate doomed to remain under Indian control forever ... By accepting this US vision, Nawaz has forsaken national security.[67]

It was clear, however, that despite a certain ambivalence in Nawaz Sharif's statements, Pakistan's long-standing commitment to resolving the Kashmir issue on the basis of the UN resolutions, meant that the policy shift required to accommodate the 'third option' of an independent Kashmir was in fact not acceptable.

Repression and retaliation

For the Kashmiris, the familiar pattern of attacks by militants on specific targets, reprisals by the government, cordon and search operations to flush out militants and find weapons and the call by the militants for strikes, had become part of their daily life, with very little dialogue in between. Human rights organisations, although restricted in their access, condemned the violations of human rights. In 1991 Asia Watch stated that the government forces 'have also systematically violated international human rights law by using lethal force against peaceful demonstrators.'[68] Kashmir would disappear from the international news for a few weeks or months only to reappear again when a journalist reported on some fearful event.

Although Saxena encouraged the security forces to use restraint on the grounds that excesses won recruits to militancy, stories of brutality by the security forces continued to emerge, especially in rural areas, where control from the top was not so effective. There was also very little check on security forces' operations. The Armed Forces (Jammu and Kashmir) Special Ordinance, introduced in July 1990, provided the security forces with extraordinary powers to shoot and kill, search and arrest without a warrant, all under immunity from prosecution 'in respect of anything done or purported to be done in exercise of power conferred by this Act.' Soon after its introduction, the security forces were reported as going on 'a binge' of arson, burning shops and houses in retaliation for a recent ambush by the militants.[69]

One of the most serious allegations of excess which Governor Saxena faced happened in the small town of Kunan Poshpura. In February 1991 there were reports of fifty-three women being gang-raped, while the men were kept outside in the freezing cold or locked in houses and interrogated. 'What happened in Kunan Poshpura is seen as the greatest single atrocity by security forces,' wrote Christopher Thomas in *The Times*.[70] The soldiers were identified as members of the 4th Rajput rifles. Three separate inquiries concluded that the evidence of the women was inconsistent and, on the basis of these inquiries, the Indian government, asserted that the episode was 'a massive hoax orchestrated by terrorist groups, their mentors and sympathisers in Kashmir and abroad.'[71] The mission of the International Commission of Jurists which visited Kashmir in 1993, however, concluded that 'while mass rape at Kunan Poshpura may not have been proved beyond doubt, there are very substantial grounds for believing that it took place.'[72]

'Indian security forces tied up and shot seven men and boys, all members of the same Kashmiri Muslim family in this remote village at the weekend, in what seems to have been a calculated act of brutality to deter villagers from helping Kashmiri separatists,' wrote David Housego from Malangam in the Kashmir valley in April 1991. 'The apparently cold-blooded reprisals by the BSF against villagers they believed to be shielding militants or weapons is further evidence of breakdown in discipline among Indian forces in Kashmir.'[73]

In June 1991, Tony Allen-Mills reported how the inhabitants of Kulgam were subjected to indiscriminate firing in the streets in reprisal for a rocket attack on BSF barracks, when two soldiers were slightly injured:

> Abdul Hamid Wazi, a baker's assistant, saw soldiers pouring gunpowder on the outside walls of his house. They fired a shot and set the place alight. The thatched roof collapsed on him. Wazi jumped through the flames, badly burning his leg and face. By the time the soldiers' wrath was spent, twenty-eight shops and two houses had been torched, there were bullet holes in the mosque and several women claimed to have been raped.[74]

In 1991 Tim McGirk of *The Independent* generously assessed the combined strength of the main militant groups at 45,000 armed and trained fighters. Indian army and paramilitary were initially estimated to be 150,000.[75] Over time, these figures fluctuated both in reality and perception. The belief that 'half a million Indian troops' were stationed in Kashmir became an established fact in the opinion of all opposition groups. The Indian government maintained there were less militants and definitely less military.

After the JKLF's early successes, their leaders found that the Hizb-ul Mujaheddin was finding more support in Pakistan at their expense. Amanullah Khan complained that his recruits were being coerced to join the Hizb and other groups. In December 1991 at a press conference in Islamabad, Khan regretted that the pro-Pakistani Hizb was killing JKLF workers. The JKLF also accused pro-Pakistani supporters of providing clues to the Indian security forces regarding JKLF hideouts, which made them easier to catch. In 1992 Amanullah Khan made a much publicised attempt to cross the line of control in order to demonstrate that the JKLF did not recognise the line dividing 'the motherland of Kashmir.'[76] His first attempt, on 11 February 1992 – the eighth anniversary of Maqbool Butt's execution – was stopped by the

Pakistani authorities and twelve of the marchers were killed. Before Amanullah could make another attempt on 30 March, he was detained with 500 supporters. A third attempt in October also failed. Although thwarted in his objective, the publicity involved did boost his support and demonstrated that the JKLF was prepared to pursue its independent objectives in the face of opposition from the Pakistani government.

'The JKLF staged a comeback,' writes Balraj Puri 'and the slogan of *azadi* returned to the valley at the expense of pro-Pakistani sentiments.' Puri believes at this stage the Kashmiris began to shed many of their illusions about Pakistani support for their movement: 'If this process of disillusionment was not complete, it was due to the central government's failure to appreciate the basic aspirations of the Kashmiris and the repressive acts of the Indian security forces.'[77]

The government in New Delhi was undergoing its own convulsions. After less than two years in office, V. P. Singh was replaced as prime minister following elections in June 1991. His successor was Narasimha Rao, the new leader of the Congress party after the assassination of Rajiv Gandhi in May. Although the BJP no longer wielded the same influence on Kashmiri policy, Hindu communalism remained a factor during this period. It reached alarming proportions at the end of December 1992 with the destruction by Hindu extremists of the mosque at Ayodha in Uttar Pradesh, south of Nepal. 'After Ayodha,' commented one Kashmiri activist, 'we did not understand why the Muslims in India did not do like us and rise up against the Indian government.'

Under Saxena, the Indian government also worked to improve its intelligence gathering operation and counter-insurgency measures in the valley. Those militants who could not withstand torture under interrogation, were 'turned' and used as 'Cats' [Concealed Apprehension Tactics] to identify fellow militants. 'Operation Tiger,' launched in August 1992 was the first in a series of security forces operations code named 'Shiva', 'Eagle', 'Cobra'. Their aim was to suppress the various militant groups through a 'catch and kill' policy. One of the towns to suffer most at the hands of the security forces was Sopore. On 6 January 1993, at least forty-three people were killed and a whole section of central Sopore was burnt to the ground. It was considered to be the largest reprisal attack by the security forces during the insurgency. 'The incident marked a watershed, forcing state and central government forces to acknowledge for the first time that the BSF forces responsible had retaliated against the town's civilian population after two of their forces were injured and subsequently died in a militant attack.' According to Asia Watch, witnesses reported seeing the BSF soldiers pour gasoline on to rags, set them alight and toss them on to houses and shops. Witnesses also stated that the BSF prevented fire fighters from putting out the blaze.[78]

Every so often during the Indian government's war against the insurgents, as with Mirwaiz Maulvi Farooq, a well known person was killed which attracted more attention and generally caused more embarrassment to the Indian government. Even the death of a militant could be the occasion for a huge funeral procession, which of itself was a manifestation of anti-government feeling. On 18 February 1993 Dr Farooq Ashai, chief orthopaedic surgeon at the Bone and Joint hospital in central Srinagar, was killed while returning home in his car with his wife and daughter. A respected doctor, his death caused an outcry. His widow, Dr Farida Ashai, recounted how the only shooting which took place were the three shots fired at their car. 'It was a deliberate killing. Instead of reaching home, he reached the graveyard.'[79] Although the government maintained that there was cross-firing, his family believed he was killed because of his known association with foreign journalists and human rights representatives. He also acted as a spokesman for injured civilians in Kashmir. 'Because he was an expert in bullet injuries, so he was also frequently sought out by militants.'[80] His students later erected a monument in his memory outside the hospital to their beloved teacher '... eminent surgeon, efficient intellect, humanist patriot fell to the bullets of security forces.'

Governor Saxena maintained that because there had been cross firing, the incident was not deliberate. 'It is very unlikely that anyone could have had an inkling that this car was carrying Dr Ashai. So there was no motivation and this incident shook us all up because he was a highly respected law-abiding man.'[81] But the perception persisted that the security forces had once more taken the law into their own hands.

In March another renowned doctor, Dr Abdul Ahad Guru, a heart surgeon, was shot in Srinagar. A known sympathiser of the JKLF, dubbed by Jagmohan as one of 'the unresponsive elements in the subversives' camp', it was suggested he had been shot by members of the Hizb-ul Mujaheddin. He had, however, been under surveillance from the government and both militant groups believed his death was caused by the security forces, although this was denied by the government. Once again there was anger that no enquiry took place. During his funeral procession, a large crowd assembled. 'There were 5 to 6,000 people but the BSF had cordoned off the area to the Martyrs graveyard and said that only a hundred people will go,' said a relative.[82] In the encounter which followed, the police opened fire and Dr Guru's brother-in-law, Ashiq Hussain, one of the pallbearers, was shot in the head and died instantly. 'Although the evidence does not indicate that the police targeted Hussain, it is evident from the testimony and photographs that they fired directly into the crowd,' stated Asia Watch.[83]

In February 1993 over thirty political parties had grouped together to form an umbrella organisation known as the All Parties Hurriyat (Freedom) Conference (APHC). Maulvi Farooq's teenage son, Omar, as the 'least objectionable leader to each of the factions of the Hurriyat',[84] became its chairman. The seasoned political element behind the APHC was provided by Syed Ali Shah Gilani of the Jamaat-i Islami, Abdul Gani Lone of the People's

Conference, Maulvi Abbas Ansari of the Liberation Council, and Professor Abdul Ghani of the Muslim Conference, all of whom were under arrest throughout most of this period. Proud of his achievement in bringing together so many disparate groups, Omar Farooq had also taken on his father's position as Mirwaiz of the Jama Masjid. Although the various components differed over whether they wanted independence or unification of the state with Pakistan, they had one common objective: that the people should be given the right to choose. It was the long-standing plea for self-determination and a plebiscite. But this time, the Kashmiris insisted that the third option of independence should not be excluded. Since the UN resolutions provide for a plebiscite to choose only between India and Pakistan, Omar Farooq suggested that 'a more equitable solution might be found in tripartite talks.'[85] The Hurriyat Conference gave the militants a united political platform through which they could voice their grievances, but their demands did not permit them to consider a solution which lay within the existing framework of the Indian Union.

Mindful of the harmful effects of censorship, practised during Jagmohan's days, Saxena lifted restrictions on the press: 'Right through my time in Kashmir, everyone was allowed in, all the press correspondents, journalists, TV teams, BBC, *Time*, *Newsweek*, German TV – you name it and they were there. I must have personally met over a hundred foreign journalists. Access to the valley was not denied. Even diplomats were able to meet top militants.' Only Amnesty International was persistently forbidden access. Saxena put this down to Pakistan's role. 'Any organisation like Amnesty, which has a tremendous international flavour will be exploited by Pakistan as a weapon for internationalising the issue.' He also maintained that the militants would use the presence of Amnesty to bring about a confrontation. 'I did not want the old phenomenon of hundreds of thousands of people marching in the streets.'[86]

During his three years as governor, Saxena was confident that the security situation 'qualitatively improved tremendously. 1990 and 1991 witnessed our efforts to contain militancy on the ground and that phase was over by early 1992, when the JKLF march also fizzled out on 11 February. Fear of the gun is still there, the militants still have significant striking capability. They can attack security forces at times, they can hit at soft targets'. Saxena also stressed that during his governorship, the lines of communication for a political dialogue with the militant outfits and the 'misguided youth' were kept open. Efforts were made through these channels to make them give up violence and join mainstream politics. The policy was never to settle the whole thing by force or political issues by guns.[87]

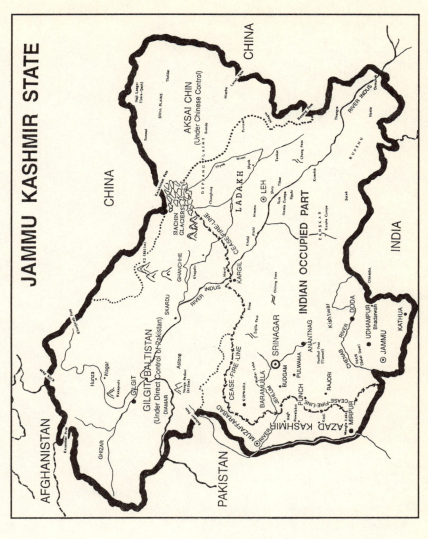

9. An Independent State of Jammu and Kashmir? (Source: Jammu and Kashmir Liberation Front)

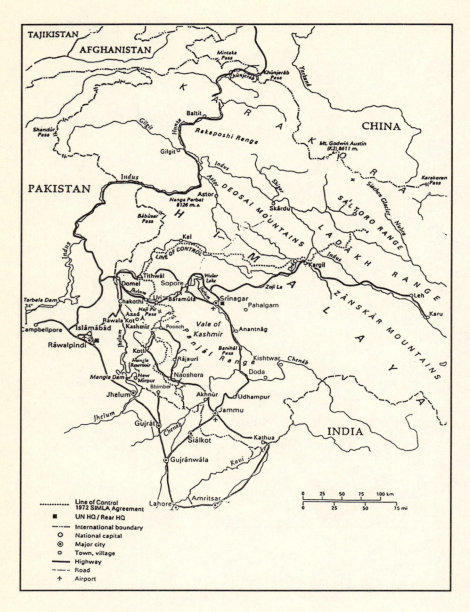

10. Jammu and Kashmir Today
(Source: United Nations Cartographic Section, 1994)

CHAPTER 15

Hearts and Minds

You can't just form a government and ignore that somehow you have to win their hearts again. Farooq Abdullah[1]

We should think about the hearts of the people, not the heads of government. Mirwaiz Omar Farooq[2]

By 1993 the Government of India was confident that the mass movement in the valley against India was weakening. There were no more large-scale demonstrations in the streets. People appeared to want their lives to return to normal. The problem remained how this was to be achieved. No political leader prepared to voice the demands of the Kashmiri activists and militants would be acceptable to Delhi; any leader of whom Delhi approved would be rejected by the militants. And, although the militancy had decreased in and around Srinagar, militants continued to operate throughout the countryside and were still capable of mounting serious attacks on the security forces. Pending a political settlement, the valley remained under siege. In addition, human rights groups, British MPs, US Congressmen and other international observers were beginning to look more critically than ever at events in the valley of Kashmir since the insurgency began.

Normalisation?

In March 1993 Girish Saxena was recalled and replaced by retired General Krishna Rao for a second term of office. 'That sent a mixed message to the people of the Kashmir valley,' stated the Srinagar correspondent of the *Economist*. 'As governor of the state in 1989, he bears some responsibility for the drift towards Kashmiri militancy during that time. On the other hand, General Rao's background as a professional soldier should help instil more discipline among the security forces.'[3] In July 1993, Rajesh Pilot, minister of state for internal security, reiterated that the government would respect human rights in its efforts to curb the 'separatist' movement in Jammu and Kashmir. The Indian government also permitted a team of international jurists to visit Kashmir during the summer.[4] In October the government set up the National Human Rights Commission under the Protection of Human Rights Act, 1993. But, according to Amnesty International, whose observers were still not allowed into the valley, its efficacy was reduced by the fact that it was not empowered to enquire into complaints of human rights violations by the army and paramilitary forces. 'All it can do when faced with complaints of this nature is to call for official reports from the government, effectively functioning as a 'post box' of official views.'[5]

In October 1993 the mosque at Hazratbal once more attracted international attention. Since the spring, the militants had been parading openly in the streets nearby. They were happy to talk to journalists and show off their weapons. 'I saw militant leaders, both JKLF and Hizb-ul Mujaheddin being escorted by armed bodyguards in public,' recalls one western journalist. 'I had several interviews with leaders in the open air. The area was completely controlled by the militants. There were no security forces around.'[6] By the autumn, the Indian government decided to take action. Azam Inquilabi, whose Operation Balakote militants were also at Hazratbal, said that the intention of the Indian army was to destroy the mosque:

> They wanted to humiliate the religious sentiments of the Kashmiris, to the extent that, once the shrine would have been demolished through shelling, they would then tell the Kashmiris "you see even after having this shrine demolished, Pakistani forces could not intervene. So they do not express solidarity with you struggling people. They are leaving you in the lurch; so this is hypocrisy of the Muslim world, therefore why should you fight for the Muslim world and you should reconcile yourselves to the situation as it was in 1989."[7]

Pakistan condemned the Indian action in surrounding the mosque as sacrilege and onlookers, both domestic and foreign, feared the outcome would be similar to the storming of the Golden Temple in Amritsar when the Indian army moved against Sikh militants in 1984.

M. N. Sabharwal, the director-general of the Jammu and Kashmir Police, had a different story to tell:

> A religious place which had been very dear to the Kashmiris was used by the militants, not only as a hideout but as an interrogation centre. We also had reason to believe that the locks where the holy relic is kept, were being tampered with by the militants. This was done to malign the security forces. So the security forces moved in to save the relic.[8]

The area was cordoned off leaving about a hundred militants and some civilians inside the mosque. Negotiations took place and after thirty-two days, the militants surrendered. Both sides prided themselves on the outcome. 'The militants did not let the Indians fire a bullet on the shrine,' says Inquilabi. The Indian authorities took credit for the care and restraint used by the security forces at Hazratbal. 'Food was sent in, so that neither the militants nor civilians starved,' says Sabharwal.

The image of Indian restraint was, however, undermined by the actions of the border security forces in Bijbihara when they shot at least thirty-seven unarmed demonstrators who were protesting against the siege of Hazratbal. Fourteen BSF members were held responsible. According to the Indian government, a Magisterial Inquiry and a Staff Court Inquiry were undertaken. The SCOI blamed four security force personnel for excessive use of force, while the Magisterial Inquiry indicted twelve people.[9] The magistrate also concluded that the shootings were unprovoked.[10]

In order to prevent the militants occupying the mosque again, the Indian government posted security forces in bunkers around Hazratbal. The Kashmiris objected to the mosque being 'fortified' by Indian troops. A year later Yasin Malik said that he put forward 'a daring initiative to lift the siege – I proposed to go for a fast until death and so there would be only two options for the government of India – either they should concede our death or they should remove their bunkers.' His suggestion, however, led to a temporary rift with the Hurriyat Conference. 'Their response was negative. They gave a statement that the fast was unislamic.'[11]

International concern over Kashmir reached a high point in February 1994 when the Pakistani prime minister, Benazir Bhutto, who had returned to office in October 1993, raised the issue in the United Nations Commission for Human Rights in Geneva. The situation in Kashmir was intolerable, she said, as was the world's silence. Despite its repression, India had failed to impose its will on the indomitable people of Jammu and Kashmir. Defending the Indian government's position, the finance minister, Dr Manmohan Singh, said that the prime minister of Pakistan had given a wholly erroneous view of the situation. Farooq Abdullah also defended India by once again condemning Pakistan for training and arming the militants.[12] Although Pakistan's resolution against India did not gain enough support and had to be withdrawn due to pressure from China and Iran, the fact that other countries were alerted to the human rights situation in Kashmir boosted the morale of the Kashmiri activists. It also surprised the government of India. 'Indian policy makers were jolted by the new Pakistani aggressiveness that could only be attributed to a growing belief in Islamabad that this Indian government was weak, focused exclusively on the economy and distracted from national security concerns,' reported Shekhar Gupta in *India Today*.[13]

Soon afterwards, Narasimha Rao, who called the Geneva resolution 'a tendentious ruse to secure other ends in Jammu and Kashmir,'[14] set up a cabinet committee to oversee Kashmiri policy with a view to starting a political dialogue. There was, writes Shekhar Gupta, 'a realisation that "Kashmir had been totally messed up by us" and any solution would have to be found in the Valley.'[15] Political process and normalisation became the key phrases of the Indian government's discussions on Jammu and Kashmir in order to hold elections to Jammu and Kashmir's state legislative assembly dissolved by Jagmohan in February 1990. Invitations were extended to Delhi-based ambassadors to visit Kashmir as well as those from the Organisation of Islamic Countries. Still out of the question, however, was any dialogue with Pakistan on an area which the Indian government continued to maintain was an integral part of India.

The militants' response to such initiatives was negative. The murder in March 1994 of Wali Mohammed Yattoo, a National Conference leader and former speaker of the Jammu & Kashmir Legislative Assembly, was taken to be a warning against attempts to introduce an unwanted political process in the valley. The government, however, pressed on with its initiative. Rajesh Pilot talked about 'rehabilitation'[16] of the Kashmiri youth; Karan Singh returned to the limelight by calling for a Kashmir Affairs ministry to be set up in order to begin 'a process of reconciliation'.[17] At India's independence day celebrations on 15 August 1994, Prime Minister Narasimha Rao formally announced that a political process would be initiated for the normalisation of affairs in the valley. In order to commence its dialogue, the government released some of the top political activists, including Shabir Shah, who had been in jail intermittently for nearly twenty years, as well as Syed Ali Shah Gilani and Abdul Gani Lone; 276 detainees were also released. Yasin Malik, under arrest since August 1990, had been released on bail in May 1994. At the end of October, however, the militants further attempted to derail the election process by stealing the electoral rolls for Srinagar from a government building and setting them on fire 'sending up in smoke the Indian government's latest attempts to bring peace to troubled Kashmir' wrote Tim McGirk in *The Independent*.[18]

Given the hostility of the militants to the proposal to hold elections, it was never clear how elections could be a practical option when there appeared to be no obvious contestants. 'Firstly, they don't have the right kind of infrastructure; there is no support for manning polling booths or acting as returning officers,' said Haroon Joshi, an Indian journalist based in Srinagar in 1995. 'Normally it is the task of the government employees but they don't want to do it; secondly, who will vote? and thirdly, whoever contests, what will happen to their family and friends?' Even if the polls were phased, holding them for one week in Jammu, a second week in Kashmir, and then in Ladakh, approximately 10,000 people (3,000 polling stations with three to a polling booth) would be needed to man the polls in the valley. 'But even if they were to find these officials by bringing them in from Jammu,' says Joshi 'there is still no strategy for getting people to stand.'[19]

When election speculation was at its height during the spring of 1995, one by one the members of the All Parties Hurriyat Conference said they would not participate. 'The Indian government has thrust this election process on us because they want to convey to the external world that they believe in the democratic system,' said Yasin Malik. He felt so strongly about the proposed elections that he threatened to immolate himself:

I am not doing this act against India. If the world conscience will come forward, they can stop the Indian government in this so-called election process. If they do not come forward then I will do this act against the world conscience; then I will be convinced that there is no one who can listen to the voice of the oppressed people.[20]

Shabir Shah, believed to be one of the few leaders who could be a unifying force throughout the state, said that he would not take part in the elections. 'We have no trust in Delhi. They have eroded our rights since 1953 and therefore we don't believe they will return them.'[21] Abdul Gani Lone was prepared to consider elections only as part of a process which would determine the future of the state:

> This is neither part of India nor part of Pakistan nor is it independent yet. The future disposition is to be settled through free and fair elections ... When we talk about our right of self-determination, no restrictions can be put on our choice. There are not two choices, the third option of independence is also there.'[22]

Professor Abdul Ghani of the Muslim Conference described the Indian government's attempt to hold elections as 'political prattle as opposed to political initiative.' As a supporter of accession to Pakistan, Ghani continues to reject the idea of independence. 'A small landlocked nation, surrounded by powerful neighbours could not survive.'[23]

'The Hurriyat conference has only one goal: that India should vacate Kashmir,' says Mian Abdul Qayum, president of the Srinagar Bar Association and member of the Hurriyat.[24] The Indian government, however, continues to woo the political leaders, pointing out that until they participate in elections, they cannot speak on behalf of the people. 'Let those who claim to represent the people, demonstrate their support in the elections, without the use of the gun,' said Governor Krishna Rao in April 1995.[25]

Despite assertions that elections could be held any time in 1995, the political impasse remained. Even Farooq Abdullah, who is committed to finding a solution within secular India, placed stringent conditions on his participation. 'We demand a return to autonomy as it existed before 1953 and a substantial economic package which must be announced formally in the Indian Parliament.'[26] Yet his association with the Government of India has lost him support in the valley. Although he appeared confident that his cadres were ready to contest an election, provided their terms were accepted, a National Conference electoral victory would most likely be seen as a step back to 1987 when the recent troubles began.

In November 1995 the Government of India once more demonstrated its commitment to the political process by sending election agents to Srinagar with the object of holding elections in December. This time a return to the status of Kashmir at the time of the 1975 accord between Sheikh Abdullah and Indira Gandhi was promised. Yet again the political parties, represented by the Hurriyat, indicated that they would not be willing to participate in an election process within the framework of the Indian constitution. 'Their idea of elections is just to create a government, a chief minister, an administration and then stop,' says Omar Farooq. 'While our stand is that elections cannot be a substitute for self-determination. If elections were a solution to the problem, we have already had eight or nine elections. But still the basic issue is unresolved.' He also believes that India's pledge to hold elections is for the benefit of the international community. 'India realises that they cannot make a dramatic change with elections, but they want to impress upon the international community that they are doing something and divert attention from the main issue of self-determination.'[27] Once more the December election date was postponed.

Mind of the military

Until a political process, acceptable to all protagonists, can be initiated, the Indian government has remained dependent upon the armed forces to control the insurgency in the valley of Kashmir. Their adjustment to a guerrilla war has not been easy. 'The man in uniform has been trained to fight an identifiable enemy,' said Brigadier Arjun Ray in 1995:

> The aim of a soldier is to kill, or capture; win or lose he must apply maximum force because of military considerations. But in Kashmir overnight he has to do a flip-flop. There is no enemy with whom he can identify. It is his own people who have taken up arms against him. Therefore, although you can win militarily, you can lose the war.[28]

The soldiers have also paid for their presence. According to military sources, the Indian army has suffered a proportionately high casualty rate. Coming from distant parts of India, they have no historical knowledge and little sympathy for the militants. Young soldiers have also suffered the trauma of war and hypertension is common. 'Troops have to stand in bunkers, constantly on vigil. One minute of negligence and it can be all over.'[29] On 29 March 1994 one of the more serious attacks against the military took place. An explosion at Badami Bagh cantonment outside Srinagar killed Major General E. W. Fernandes, who was to take over as director-general, Military Intelligence, and thirteen army men. Ten others were wounded. 'This incident is horrendous. Nobody will buy the line that it was an accident,' an army officer stated after the explosion.[30] The Jamiat-ul Mujaheddin, one of the smaller militant groups, claimed responsibility for the blast as well as a series of smaller bomb blasts on government vehicles following the expiry of a deadline for the removal of Indian troops still stationed around the Hazratbal mosque.

Opponents of India's military occupation of the valley of Kashmir continue to maintain that 600,000 troops are stationed throughout the state in what is the highest troops to civilian population density ratio in any region in the world.[31] This figure is taken to include over half of the 33 divisions of the regular army, border security forces (100,000) and Jammu and Kashmir Police (30,000). Indian authorities say this is a gross exaggeration. 'It is known that our army is just over 1 million. How we would possibly have half our army in Kashmir and leave our borders exposed elsewhere?' asked one army officer. But he was predictably evasive about how many troops were there.

Other sources suggest 'around 100,000 personnel of the paramilitary border security forces and 30,000 men of Kashmir's state police force,' with five divisions of the army.[32] A 'crack' corps of Rashtriya (National) Rifles (RR) was also brought into the valley to deal specifically with counter-insurgency.

Throughout the insurgency, the government has remained extremely sensitive about the behaviour of the security forces in Kashmir. Initially there was tremendous reluctance to acknowledge or publicise any of the alleged excesses, indiscriminate killing or arbitrary disappearances noted by the human rights groups for fear of humiliating and hence possibly demoralising the soldiers. But, as the insurgency continued, the Indian government came to realise that any abuses by the security forces created further alienation amongst the people and it was therefore important, for both international and domestic opinion, to pay greater attention to the behaviour of the soldiers. 'Nodal cells have been set up in the Army and in each of the paramilitary forces to monitor cases of delinquencies. Fortnightly reviews are being held at a senior level in the Ministry of Home Affairs with the representatives of the Army and the para-military forces.'[33] As noted by the report of the International Commission of Jurists after their visit in August 1993, 'the Army has become increasingly conscious of the need to improve its image, and has placed greater emphasis on human rights education with various "do's and don'ts". The jurists, however, also noted that the authorities had been 'tardy in instituting proceedings against governmental personnel who commit abuses against the people and have created an aura of impunity surrounding officials who violate human rights.' In conclusion, they stated:

> The Indian Government is genuinely anxious to improve its human rights record in Kashmir. Breaches of human rights are not in its interest ... There is, however, a long way still to go to overcome indiscipline and misconduct of the security forces, particularly the BSF, the persistent and regular use of torture in interrogation and the practice of extra-judicial execution.[34]

Since the insurgency began, torture of militants and suspected militants has been a feature of Indian counter-insurgency tactics as a means of extracting information, coercing confessions and punishment. According to Amnesty International, 'the brutality of torture in Jammu and Kashmir defies belief. It has left people mutilated and disabled for life. The severity of torture meted out by the Indian security forces in Jammu and Kashmir is the main reason for the appalling number of deaths in custody.'[35]

The torture generally includes electric shocks, beatings, and the use of a heavy roller on leg muscles, which can result in extensive muscle damage, leading to acute renal failure. Other forms of inhuman treatment on various parts of the body, including sexual molestation have also been reported. According to one victim, quoted by Amnesty, 'You always know in advance about the "current" because they send in the barber to shave you from head to foot. This is supposed to facilitate the flow of electricity. After he finishes shaving you, he hands you a cup of water to drink and then they attach the electrodes.'[36] Other common methods, described by the US Human Rights Agency, Asia Watch, include suspension by the hands or feet, stretching the legs apart and burning the skin with a clothes iron or other heated object. Victims have also been kicked and stamped on by security forces wearing spiked boots.[37]

Sixty-three interrogation centres where torture is routinely carried out are believed to exist in Jammu and Kashmir, mostly run by the BSF and the CRPF. Army camps, hotels and other buildings have been taken over by the security forces as detention centres. One BSF centre is located in one of the Maharaja's old guest houses overlooking Dal lake and the mountains. With faded wallpaper, worn carpets and stags' antlers on the walls, the luxuries of the past intrude inappropriately on the brutality of the present. Whereas an officer on duty will admit to the necessity of giving 'a few slaps' to captured militants to make them reveal where they have hidden their weapons, gruesome photographs of mutilated bodies are part of any press kit given to concerned journalists by human rights activists and militant sympathisers.

In its December 1993 report, Amnesty produced information about disappearances in Kashmir. In its response, the Indian government answered many of the allegations contained in Amnesty's report and supplied details on some of those listed as missing. 'The Government of India has never claimed that anything goes in the name of terrorism by way of complete freedom or immunity to the police and security forces.' Despite a dialogue initiated between the Indian government and Amnesty in 1992, the government continues to mistrust Amnesty's motivation. 'We do not look for kudos from Amnesty but equally we ask – is this an inquiry or an inquisition?'[38] Another report by Amnesty in January 1995 regarding 705 people who, since 1990, had died in custody as a result of torture, shooting, or medical neglect, produced yet another rebuttal from the Indian government. Amnesty, however, described their response as 'evasive and misleading. Complacently, the government refuses to recognise that there is an urgent need to take decisive action to put an end to the appalling human rights violations in Jammu and Kashmir.'[39]

In its reports Amnesty has also condemned the 'deliberate and arbitrary killings, torture and hostage-taking,' carried out by the militants, but the organisation maintains that 'however provocative' their abuses were, they could not justify excesses by the security forces. 'Such practices clearly contravene international human rights standards which the Indian government is bound to uphold.'[40]

Legal redress?

The nature of the legislation in force in the state of Jammu and Kashmir, which is described by the International Commission of Jurists as 'draconian', has given the military extensive powers without redress. According to

Amnesty, court orders to protect detainees are routinely flouted. Despite promises of enquiries into custodial deaths, official investigations are rare. When they have taken place, the evidence is not made public, which diminishes the credibility of government findings. 'It also makes a mockery of its expressed intention to eradicate human rights violations.'[41]

The Jammu and Kashmir Public Safety Act (1978) permits people to be detained for up to two years on vaguely defined grounds to prevent them acting 'in any manner prejudicial ... to the security of the state and the maintenance of public order.'[42] Detention without charge is possible for up to one year in the case of a threat to public order and for up to two years when there is a threat to the security of the state. The order must be communicated to the arrested person not later than five days after the arrest. In 1990 the act was amended in order to exempt the authorities from informing the detainee the reason for his arrest. In its report, the ICJ concluded that the law has led to 'hardships among those arrested under its scope. Its highly discretionary tone undermines efforts to discover the whereabouts of arrested persons and the quest for habeas corpus.'[43]

The Terrorist and Disruptive Activities (Prevention) Act 1987 (TADA) prohibits not only terrorist acts but also broadly defined 'disruptive' activities. The act established special courts to try those arrested. The term 'disruptive activities' is defined as including:

> any action, whether by act or by speech or through any other media or in any other manner, which questions, disrupts ... the sovereignty or territorial integrity of India, or which is intended to bring about or supports any claim for the cession of any part of India or the secession of any part of India from the Union.[44]

As the international jurists pointed out, the definition of 'disruptive activities' is 'a blatant contravention of the right to freedom of speech.' The two 'designated courts' are in Srinagar and Jammu, but the operations of the Srinagar court were temporarily suspended. Speedy hearing of bail applications was therefore impeded because of the necessity to go to the court at Jammu.

The discretionary nature of the Armed Forces (Jammu & Kashmir) Special Powers Act, introduced by Saxena in 1990, which gives the governor or the government in New Delhi the authority to declare all or part of the state a 'disturbed area' and to use the armed forces to assist the civil power, means that the military can be used 'to suppress legitimate political activity' and, according to the ICJ, cannot possibly be justified. Since the military have the power to shoot and kill, 'this involves a potential infringement of the right to life.'[45] Additional laws have been either introduced or revived 'with negative impact on human rights'. In February 1992 Presidential rule was extended, which dispensed with any obligation on the government to revert to an elected government. When this time period elapsed, a further amendment to the Constitution was passed.

The cumulative effect of such legislation is that the government has been able to act with relative impunity in the state of Jammu and Kashmir. Since the judicial system is 'almost dysfunctional'[46] there are long delays in court proceedings. 'The judiciary here in the state of Jammu and Kashmir has almost become irrelevant,' said Mian Abdul Qayum, president of the Srinagar Bar Association, in 1994. 'If they pass any kind of an order, those orders are not obeyed by anybody. Right now there are some 5,000 habeas corpus petitions pertaining to the people who are detained under preventive laws, pending in the High Court Srinagar and nobody is going to hear them.'[47] According to the Indian authorities, the state government has responded to '99 per cent' of all such petitions 'despite the tremendous strain under which the whole legal and administrative system has been put by the continuing violence and terrorism.'[48]

Mind of the militant

In the opinion of the Indian government the real culprits have always been the militants, whom they hold responsible for terrorising the people of Kashmir into open hostility against India and committing numerous extra-judicial executions, amongst whom they list Mirwaiz Maulvi Farooq, Professor Mushir-ul Haq, the vice chancellor of Kashmir University, Dr A. A. Guru, Maulana Masoodi, aged eighty-seven, a contemporary and colleague of Sheikh Abdullah who was shot in December 1990 allegedly for the part he played in the state of Jammu and Kashmir's accession to India. Through the efforts of the military, however, the insurgency has now been 'capped and brought down to acceptable levels,' said Brigadier Arjun Ray in 1995.[49] 'More and more people are coming to realise the futility of the gun,' says M. N. Sabharwal.[50] In 1995, the Indian government noted that the level of violence had declined still further except during the months of May, October and November, when announcements were made about elections.[51]

The Indian government also believes that militancy does not enjoy the popular support it had in the early 1990s. 'The militants lost some of their original élan,' says Balraj Puri, ' due to a number of reasons: a continuous proliferation of groups, confusion and division in their ranks, regarding their ultimate objective, and Pakistan's changing policy towards different groups of militants.'[52] Government analysts estimate that now no more than 6,000 militants are operating throughout the valley, which makes the ratio of their own troops to militants extremely high. Indian authorities also allege that young men have been abducted against their will to become militants. In August 1993 *The Times of India* reported how Indian forces had intercepted a large group of 'Kashmiri youth' who were being taken to Azad Kashmir at gun point by members of the Al Jehad militant group and that they had been promised sums ranging from Rs 2000 to Rs 10,000.[53]

In contrast to Jagmohan's assessment of the militants, General Krishna

Rao has adopted a conciliatory approach: 'We do not consider militants as enemies, but as our own kith and kin, although they have allowed themselves to be misled. The Government takes responsibility to rehabilitate them in an appropriate manner, provided they return to the path of sanity.'[54] The Indian government assesses the life expectancy of a militant at two years, after which time they either get killed or lose their enthusiasm for the fight. Militants who surrender are provided with a rudimentary rehabilitation programme and sometimes a change of identity.

Like the security forces, the militants are subject to allegations of excesses, mainly intimidation and extortion as well as their indiscriminate attacks on those suspected of sympathising with the Indian government. 'The lady next door was approached one night by militants and asked for money,' recalled a student in 1995; 'in the old days, she would have asked them in and given them food. This time she refused and shut the door in their face. So they pushed the door in and shot her.'[55] 'The militants would come to your door and ask for money or a son to fight. If you didn't have the money, then you would have to give up a son,' says a local Kashmiri. 'In 1993 the militants asked for 5 lakhs,' said one businessman in 1995, 'last year it was 3 lakhs; this year I am expecting them to ask for 1 lakh.'[56] Rich houseboat owners and carpet dealers have been targeted for money. They have also been afraid to speak out about loss of business because of the insurgency: 'They say to us: "You complain you are losing money, and we are losing our lives."'[57] Journalists are still threatened by the militants for writing reports interpreted as favourable to the government of India's position. In September 1995, a parcel bomb was sent to Yusuf Jameel, the BBC and Reuters correspondent in Srinagar. A photographer in his office opened the parcel and died in the explosion.

In June 1994 the JKLF admitted that atrocities committed by the militants had alienated the people and stated that strict action would be taken against 'erring elements' in the movement.[58] The most serious incident of a communal nature was the murder of sixteen male Hindus who were taken off a bus in Kishtwar on their way to Jammu on 14 August 1993 and shot. Both the JKLF and Hizb condemned the action. The murder of the vice-chancellor of Kashmir University in 1990 was described by activists as the work of 'renegades' amongst the numerous fringe groups which are operative.

Reports of rape by militants have also tarnished their image. 'While it is not clear that militant leaders have explicitly sanctioned such abuses,' states Asia Watch, 'there is little indication that the militants have done anything to stop their forces from committing rape. Some incidents of rape by militants appear to have been motivated by the fact that the victims or their families are accused of being informers.'[59] In 1994 former Governor Saxena rather surprisingly claimed that: 'For every allegation of rape by security persons, there will be a hundred by militants.'[60] In the early days of the insurgency, attacks were made on women for not adhering to the prescribed dress code, the wearing of the *burqah*. The Daughters of the Nation, an orthodox women's group, was particularly active in issuing threats and some women had to be hospitalised because acid was sprayed on their exposed faces. Due to adverse publicity, this has stopped and, especially in Srinagar, women do not feel obliged to wear the veil.

Allegations of corruption and drug dealing have also been levelled against some militants, in what the authorities call the 'criminalisation' of the movement, as well as military and government officials. 'There is a nexus,' says Farooq Abdullah ' between the militants, the paramilitary forces and some sections of the government, who have enjoyed absolute power and corruption that no government has ever enjoyed.'[61] There are allegations that militants and government officials split development funds; also that security forces not only sell back captured weapons but will allow border crossings at a price.[62] 'Many of the orchards in Kashmir, owned by the Hindus, who fled, have now divided between the top militants. They are changing the deeds and so it will be impossible to trace their original owners.'[63] The government maintains that the main incentive of many militants is money rather than political conviction. Yet despite such allegations, the militants still seek and obtain refuge amongst the people. 'How else do you think they are surviving?' asks Mirwaiz Omar Farooq, who insists that the militancy is still widely supported by the people.[64]

By 1993 the JKLF appeared to have lost its military ascendancy to the Hizb-ul Mujaheddin, although politically, the organisation claimed to have retained 85 per cent of the people's support. When Yasin Malik was released from jail in May 1994, he renounced the armed struggle and made an offer of political negotiations. 'We offered a unilateral ceasefire and offered to negotiate with all concerned powers – Pakistan, India and the Kashmiris – we believe all should be given equal status.' According to Malik, a message came through from the Government of India that negotiation would be possible, but only between the Government of India and the Kashmiri people, because they did not recognise Pakistan as a party to the talks. Malik disagreed on the grounds that Pakistan was a party to the dispute because nearly one-third of the state lies under its control. He also remains adamant that the third option of independence must be offered to the people of Jammu and Kashmir in order for a permanent solution to be reached. 'Until they put the third option of independence into the UN resolution, it will be unacceptable to the people of Jammu and Kashmir.'[65]

From his earlier days as one of the core 'Haji' group, reportedly involved in the kidnapping of Rubaiya Sayeed in December 1989, Malik now describes Mahatma Gandhi and his principles of non-violence as one of his motivating forces. This has led him to reaffirm the JKLF's secular nature, based on traditional Kashmiriyat, which includes Hindus. But his non-violent approach has caused a rift with Amanullah Khan, who has continued to operate as chairman of the JKLF *in absentia* from Rawalpindi and Muzaffarabad.

'Unfortunately our organisation is practically divided into two groups. Our basic difference was Yasin Malik's offer of a unilateral ceasefire, without informing us,' says Amanullah Khan.[66] At the end of 1995, Amanullah Khan removed Yasin Malik as president of the JKLF; in return Yasin Malik expelled Amanullah Khan as chairman. Shabir Ahmed Siddiqi, who was released from jail in the summer of 1995,[67] temporarily took over leadership of Amanullah's faction. Relations, however, are further complicated by Pakistan's recognition of Yasin Malik as the leader of the JKLF rather than Amanullah Khan, although Amanullah remains based in Pakistan.

Other militant groups have also been reassessing their position. In 1995, Azam Inquilabi of Operation Balakote left his base in Azad Kashmir and returned to Srinagar, where he has now declared himself in favour of working towards a 'political solution.' The Hizb-ul Mujaheddin, whose active strength is assessed by the Indian authorities at around 2,500, was able to gain its ascendancy militarily in the middle 1990s because of support from Jamaat sympathisers based in Pakistan. It dominates smaller pro-Pakistani groups and through the Jamaat-i Islami it also has a strong hold on the Hurriyat Conference. In the early days, Ahsan Dar, leader of Hizb, maintained that their strategy of making the country impassable for Indian security forces would eventually confine the army to their camps, where the militants would be able to attack them. But Ahsan Dar is now under arrest and the strategy failed. Their objectives are also split between ideological commitment to Pakistan and an undefined belief in freedom. A young militant stated that he wanted *azadi* and the decision on whether to join Pakistan would be taken by the elders; rather surprisingly, his mentor, in his mid-40s, affirmed that *azadi* meant freedom from both India and Pakistan.[68] The Harkat-ul Ansar operates alongside the Hizb. Al Barq and Al Jehad remain active in the Doda, Poonch and Rajauri areas.

Personal disagreements and rivalries have clearly reduced the efficacy of the militants. But, says Omar Farooq, 'in a movement like this there are ups and downs. There was a time when there were many inter-group clashes but if you study the situation now the graph has really come down. The differences have been resolved.' Omar Farooq believes that India's repressive tactics and counter-insurgency measures still remain a factor in uniting the people against India. The government, however, has detected a split in the leadership of the APHC which it believes is broadly divided between two factions – one includes Yasin Malik, Abdul Gani Lone and Syed Ali Shah Gilani, and the other Omar Farooq, Abdul Ghani, Maulvi Abbas Ansari, with tacit support from Shabir Shah.[69]

In 1996 the Indian government opened a dialogue with four former militants including two from the Hizb-ul Mujaheddin as well as Baba Badr, a former chief of the Muslim Janbaz, and Bilal Lodhi, former leader of Al Barq, in an attempt to create an alternative political base to the Hurriyat. The militants are also being challenged by a former folk singer, Kukka Parrey, who, with the support of the Indian government, assembled a group of over 1,000 fighters whose objective is the 'liberation' of part of the valley from control by the militants. Activists deny that Parrey has any standing amongst the Kashmiris. Even the four dissident militants insist that the Government of India should recognise that Kashmir is a historical and political problem.

On account of the war in Afghanistan and the plentiful weapons supplied to the Afghans, there has been an apparently inexhaustible supply of weapons for the Kashmiri militants. 'The US supplied the weapons to fight the war in Afghanistan against the Soviets,' said one Kashmiri, saddened by the gun culture prevalent in the valley, 'but they never returned to take the weapons away and now they are in the valley.' M. N. Sabharwal said that before the insurgency there were no Kalashnikov rifles in the valley. Now, however, there are quantities of weapons ranging from AK rifles, universal machine guns, Chinese pistols, snipers, rocket launchers and grenades. Just how many is indicated by government figures for those weapons captured between 1989 and 1995. These include 13,427 AK 47s, 750 rocket launchers, 1682 rockets, 54 light machine guns, 735 general purpose machine guns.[70] On average the government claims to recover 4,000 weapons a year of varying sophistication. In 1995 it retrieved 587 bombs compared with 300 in 1994.[71] The Kashmiris are, however, less well armed than the Afghans. To the obvious relief of the Indian security forces, to date, there have been no reports of the militants being able to bring in stingers. Nor have they, as yet, brought their struggle to the streets of Delhi, Calcutta or Bombay, where urban terrorism would have a greater impact on the lives of the Indian people and consequently the Indian government. Strangely, amongst the unsympathetic pro-government analysts, the belief persists that the Kashmiris, despite all their guns, are not good fighters: 'In Kashmir, you talk of paper-thin almonds, paper-thin walnuts – well, we also talk of paper-thin militants.'[72]

The proxy war

The Indian authorities continue to point to the 'foreign hand' in Kashmir, without which they believe the insurgency would never have gained momentum nor have been able to sustain itself. 'Pakistan took a firm and bold decision to meddle,' states former governor Saxena.

> This time they pulled out all the stops and went about creating trouble in a big way, training thousands of youths, giving huge quantities of arms to them, and not bothering so much as they earlier did about the threshold of India's tolerance, with the result that this environment acquired the proportions of a widespread terrorist movement and armed insurgency, which was conducted at the initiative of Pakistan by youth trained in Pakistan.[73]

The tactics the militants used to disrupt the government were considered to be similar to those used by Pakistanis sent into the valley in 1965: bomb blasts, cutting lines of communication, attacks on patrols and police.

Despite the Government of Pakistan's denials that their support is anything other than moral and diplomatic (and genuine uncertainty about Pakistan's actions before 1990), it is the common perception in India that Pakistan, through the ISI, is supplying material and financial support without which the movement would have been easier for the Indian army to suppress. 'Pakistan is unlikely to drop its covert support,' writes *Time* correspondent, Edward Desmond. 'the Kashmir issue is central to the nationalistic and Islamic identity of Pakistan.. the burden of assisting the rebels is light.'[74] 'On a scale of one to ten, if we were committed in Bangladesh up to ten, then the same is true for Pakistan's commitment in Kashmir,' says a Delhi based Indian journalist.[75] In support of this assertion, the Indian government quotes a February 1993 report by the US House of Representatives 'Task Force on Terrorism and Unconventional Warfare' which claimed that Pakistan 'began expanding its operation to sponsor and promote separatism and terrorism primarily in Kashmir, as a strategic long-term programme,' an allegation which the Government of Pakistan denies.[76]

Despite Indian attempts to seal the border, which it is impossible for a Western journalist to reach from the Indian side, the 450 mile line of control has remained open. The prime minister of Azad Kashmir, Sardar Abdul Qayum Khan, also admits that, from their side, the border is not sealed. 'We don't mind the boys coming in and going back.'[77] Militants and refugees take what they call the 'natural' route to cross from one side to the other. When the ICJ visited the area in 1993 they concluded that, despite Pakistani denials and the sensitivity of the issue, the presence of many representatives of militant groups in Azad Kashmir 'pointed to an affinity with operations in neighbouring Jammu and Kashmir.' The international jurists also considered that the provision of any military assistance would be in breach of obligations accepted by Pakistan under the Simla agreement and that therefore Pakistan should 'discontinue any support of a military nature (including the provision of finance for military purposes).'[78] It is, however, evident that the Jamaat-i Islami, and hence the Hizb, still has a considerable presence both in Azad Kashmir and in Pakistan. In November 1995 a BBC documentary programme showed evidence of camps supported by the Jamaat, where fighters were trained and openly professed their intention of going to fight a holy war in Kashmir.[79] And some sympathisers believe rightly so: 'After 1945 the world has shrunk. No one can give me one instance in the world in any liberation movement – in any country – which has started without a foreign base,' stated Muhammad Saraf. He also pointed to the genuine grievances of the local Kashmiris: 'You don't give people money and weapons and they just start dying. The question you have to ask is what made them prepared to start dying?'[80] Amongst some activists there is also a view that the Pakistani army should intervene overtly, not in order to claim the land for itself but in the same way the Indian army intervened in East Pakistan in 1971 to help the Bengalis.

Omar Farooq takes a pragmatic view. 'The issue of Pakistan giving support or not does not present a problem for us. The United States gave support to Afghanistan; they were not asked to explain why they were supporting the Afghans. So if Pakistan supports the Kashmiris on whatever grounds, it doesn't matter. You see ours is a totally indigenous movement and it is the Kashmiris who are getting killed.' Farooq includes in his analysis the support from Azad Kashmir. 'If they are helping us, no one should be concerned because, historically, they belong to the state of Jammu and Kashmir and they have a duty towards their people, who are occupied.'[81] Yasin Malik, however, is opposed to 'any kind of foreign presence in Kashmir, whether it is Pakistani or Indian foreign mercenaries.'[82]

Amongst the fighters who have crossed the line of control from Azad Kashmir and Pakistan are those who fought in Afghanistan. Their presence in the insurgency is facilitated by what is also a porous border in the tribal territory which divides Pakistan and Afghanistan and their numbers are believed to have increased after the fall of the Najibullah regime in Afghanistan in 1992.[83] The Kashmiris maintain that the Afghans, belonging mostly to the Harkat-ul Ansar, have come to support their struggle as Muslims after the help the Kashmiris gave during the Afghans own jihad against the Soviet Union. Between 1990 and 1995, the Indian government identified 297 'foreign mercenaries' arrested or killed, of which 213 were from Pakistan or Azad Kashmir, and 84 from Afghanistan.[84] In addition, the Indian government maintains that there are smaller numbers of Sudanese, Egyptians, Lebanese who have become attached to rival groups. Invariably, the reality of the insurgency in Kashmir has not matched their expectations: 'When I first came I thought it was for holy war, but then I heard about the struggle for power within the militant groups,' said Sheikh Jamaluddin, a nineteen year old from Gardez in Afghanistan who was captured by the security forces on the outskirts of Srinagar in 1993.[85]

The foreign presence in Kashmir became publicised when, in March 1995, Master Gul, a former shopkeeper from Pakistan's North-West Frontier, occupied the mosque at Charar Sharif about twenty-five miles from Srinagar which is revered for its association with Nund Rishi, the patron saint of the valley. Gul had trained during the war in Afghanistan and amongst his followers were what the Indian government referred to as about seventy 'mercenaries'. The militants claimed to have liberated the area from the Indian security forces, but the Indians responded by cordoning off the area as they had done at Hazratbal. This time, however, the mosque was destroyed by fire, which the militants blamed on the security forces, who in turn blamed the militants for starting it. Krishna Rao expressed 'grief and anguish' over the destruction of the shrine.[86] Security was increased to deter protests within the valley. Although over forty people were killed, Master Gul escaped to Pakistan, from where he continues to preach a holy war.[87] The presence of foreigners has, however, also had its repercussions amongst the local Kashmiris. 'They have been rather overbearing, they feel they've come to do a job and should be obeyed. They don't have any official position but they tend to bully,' said one Kashmiri militant.

Pakistan's official stand has been to highlight the abuse of human rights on the international stage and point to the alienation of the Kashmiris of the valley from Indian rule while putting the issue in its historical context and referring back to the UN resolutions. Obviously aware that self-determination is invariably interpreted by the valley Kashmiris as independence from India and Pakistan, Pakistani Foreign Secretary Nazimuddin Sheikh maintains that it is putting the cart before the horse to talk about independence at this stage. 'It requires a measure of sagacity to avoid entering a debate on this issue before India has granted the right of self-determination to the Kashmiri people.'[88]

'Free' Kashmir and the Northern Areas

The current insurgency has also affected the lives of the Azad Kashmiris, who are still waiting for their own constitutional position to be finalised. Wholehearted support for accession to Pakistan has now been tempered, for some, with their own dreams of independence. But whereas those in the valley have believed that it is within their reach, there is far less conviction amongst the Azad Kashmiris that life will ever be much different. If there were to be a change, Prime Minister Sardar Qayum has expressed his solidarity with the valley. 'We accept in final terms the leadership from the valley. They are the people, who are suffering, and there should be no dispute over power sharing.'[89] In November 1995, Mirwaiz Omar Farooq met Sardar Qayum in New York. 'He agreed,' says Omar Farooq 'that the All Parties Hurriyat Conference should represent them as well at the international level.'[90]

Traditionally, Azad Kashmiris have been sympathetic to the Kashmiris of the valley where many still have relatives. A 'liberation cell' has been operating in Muzaffarabad since 1987, which retains close links both with the AJK government in Muzaffarabad and Islamabad. Its representatives guide foreigners through the political issues at stake as well as the refugee camps which have been set up to accommodate those who fled from the border towns of Kupwara, Handwara, and Baramula in the early years of the insurgency. 'We eat and are clothed,' said one refugee from Ambore camp outside Muzaffarabad, 'but everything gets distasteful when we remember our brothers and sisters in occupied Kashmir.'[91] 'We notice the need for women to have psychiatric help,' says Nayyar Malik, who works as a voluntary social worker in the camps. 'They have seen such terrible things and they need to talk.'[92] A radio station has also been operating since 1960. It was initially set up to publicise the development activities of the Azad Jammu and Kashmir government. But, says Masood Kashfi, the station director, 'it was not possible to keep our eye shut on the situation in Occupied Kashmir, therefore, a fair proportion of its broadcast was reserved for broadcasting programmes on the subjects of freedom movement, freedom history and other relevant topics.' After the insurgency began in 1988, Azad Kashmir Radio changed its programme schedules to eliminate the 'entertaining aspects' and concentrate on 'inspiring' programmes related to the freedom struggle, which also includes relaying some programmes from Radio Pakistan. 'The stand of the government of Pakistan on the Kashmir issue is projected and the reaction of the people on both sides of the control line is depicted in a fair and balanced way,' says Kashfi. He believes that the Azad Kashmir radio is so popular in 'occupied Kashmir' that the Indian government has imposed a ban on listening to the station and 'is making her best efforts to jam the transmission.'[93]

The influx of Kashmiris from the valley in recent years has also created some friction between Kashmiri speakers from the valley, and those from Poonch and Rawalakot district. 'I am often told I am not a Kashmiri, because I don't speak Kashmiri,' says a Suddhan from Poonch whose father and grandfather were politically active in the 1940s. 'But politically I am Kashmiri because I belong to the state of Jammu and Kashmir.'[94] The Poonchis today still stress their historical legacy of independence. Many Azad Kashmiris are also far less concerned about independence than the absence of a proper status within Pakistan, enabling them to have access to the same funds, political rights and development aid granted to the other provinces. At the same time, the government is beholden to Islamabad. 'You see I have to keep in step; and to keep in step you cannot do things what you really wish to do at times, and so you have to cater to the situation,' says Prime Minister Sardar Qayum.[95]

Resentment has also been expressed by the Azad Kashmiris against their 'brethren' in Pakistan and the Muslim world for not doing enough over the years to help the cause of the Kashmiris of the valley. Those who would prefer to see the whole of the state of Jammu and Kashmir independent are as much opposed to Pakistan's 'occupation' of Azad Kashmir as they are with the Indian position in the valley. 'We are not satisfied with the de facto situation of Pakistan in Azad Kashmir,' said Azam Inquilabi in 1994. 'They have their forces there, they have a control there, we are tolerating this situation only to some extent.'[96] 'The reason we have not started a military movement there [in PoK]' says Yasin Malik, 'is because, so far as Pakistan is concerned it is their official stand to accept the right of self-determination for the people of Jammu and Kashmir.'[97]

Although geographically distant, the fate of the Northern Areas, with a population of a little over a million, remains directly affected by the current situation in Jammu and Kashmir. Despite the rebellion which took place in October/ November 1947, the Northern Areas have never been integrated into Pakistan. 'I was seven when I fought for Pakistan,' says Raja Nisar Wali, member of the Northern Areas Motahida Mahaz (joint platform) formed to press for political representation 'now I am fifty-seven and going grey and still I am struggling to be part of Pakistan.'[98] In 1975 Zulfikar Ali Bhutto abolished the old landholdings and kingdoms of Hunza and Nagar and re-organised the whole area into five administrative districts. 'He introduced far-reaching reforms,' says Wazir Firman Ali, who grew up in Skardu under 'the Dogra slavery' and later worked for fifteen years as a government servant in the Northern Areas. 'If Bhutto had lived, I think the Northern Areas would have become the fifth province, but under General Zia's military dictatorship, the Northern Areas became the 'fifth zone' – Zone E – and he did nothing for them.'

The JKLF in particular has made attempts to establish their representatives in Gilgit and Baltistan in order to foster the independence movement, but the people have little political affiliation with the valley, and are generally believed to favour full integration with Pakistan. 'The first choice would be integration with Pakistan and a provincial arrangement,' says Wazir Firman Ali, 'secondly, a set up similar to Azad Kashmir and thirdly, integration with Azad Jammu and Kashmir.'[99] In March 1993 the High Court of Azad Jammu and Kashmir declared that the Northern Areas were part of Azad Kashmir and ordered their administration to be returned to the government of Azad Kashmir. But the Shia population, who predominate in the Northern Areas, were reluctant to amalgamate with Sunni-dominated Azad Kashmir. The decision of the High Court was quashed on appeal in the Supreme Court.[100]

The Pakistani government has attempted to satisfy the lack of constitutional representation by a package of reforms. The government, however, has held back from formally integrating the Northern Areas within Pakistan lest such an action would jeopardise the Pakistani demand for the whole issue to be resolved under the terms of the UN resolutions. No attempt appears to have been made to make use of the British assessment in 1941 that the Gilgit Agency and related territories were considered only to be under the suzerainty of the state of Jammu and Kashmir and not part of it. Therefore, despite Pakistan's support of the Kashmiris' right to self-determination, it is not in the government's interest to support the demand for the 'third option' of independence of the entire state as it existed in 1947, which would include the Northern Areas. Gilgit and Hunza, which provide access to China through the Khunjerab pass along the Karakoram highway, opened in 1978, are as important to Pakistan strategically as they were to the British in the days of empire. Pending final resolution of the Jammu and Kashmir dispute, the Northern Areas remain administered by Pakistan, although not part of it. 'We have many suspension bridges in the Northern Areas, and our constitutional position is also in suspension,' states one local government official.

Civilians under siege

The losers in the insurgency against the Indian government, to date, are the Kashmiris. The city of Srinagar is dusty and dirty, with uncollected rubbish dumped on the roadside for dogs and cows to forage through. The streets are full of potholes. The charred remains of once revered buildings, such as the library next to the mosque at Hazratbal, are a visual reminder of past battles. Dal lake is thick and stagnant with weeds. The lives of the Kashmiris have been convulsed by bomb attacks, reprisals, crossfiring and curfew. Their homes have been raided and sometimes destroyed because of frequent security operations. Sopore is still half-gutted by fire. 'I used to be frightened when the army came, but now I am used to it,' said a young girl from Sopore. 'The searching totally destroys our houses. They scatter our belongings and break things.'[101]

For over seven years, the Kashmiris have lived in fear of the gun, whether it is that of the militants or the Indian security forces. Their sons, as militants, suspected militants or sympathisers, have been arrested, tortured, killed or just disappeared. 'In practice any young Muslim man living within a village, rural area or part of town noted for activities of any of the pro-independence or pro-Pakistan groups can become a suspect and a target for the large-scale and frequently brutal search operations,' stated Amnesty in 1993.[102] Extra-judicial executions of militants have often been publicised as death in 'an encounter.'

Nearly every Kashmiri has a sad tale to tell of a family member who had been picked up by the security forces on suspicion of being a militant. Dr Rashid is one of thousands who suffered personal loss:

> My brother was twenty-five years old. He was running a cosmetics shop. The BSF came and took him. In front of my father and family, he was killed. Someone had pointed him out as being a militant. He was not armed and in the news that evening they gave that there was an encounter, when there was no encounter at all.

Not long afterwards Dr Rashid's younger brother was also shot for being a suspected militant. Then he heard the news about his cousin's son:

> He was eighteen years old – he was a student. He was captured; I went to the police station and asked to see him because I had heard he had got some bullet injuries. They told me to wait and they would see where he was. For two hours I waited there. Then they brought his dead body. The report said he was running away and then they shot him. If he was running away he would have had bullet wounds on the back. But he had two bullet injuries at 2cm distance just on his heart in front.[103]

For the majority of the people the ill-effects of living under siege are tremendous. Although there have been no floods and the harvests have been good, no one has yet been able to evaluate the trauma of events on their lives since 1989. Children have frequently been unable to go to school and the standard of education has declined. Since 1950, the number of schools had increased ten times, but many schools have been burnt by 'renegade' militants who the Kashmiri activists believe are working against their cause.

Schools in rural areas have been occupied by the security forces, who have also installed themselves in university campuses. Official figures maintain that the schools functioned for ninety-three days in 1993–94 and 140 days in 1994–95 and primary education in general has regressed.[104] In higher education, Kashmiris had made great advances, but today the general disruption of the insurgency has once more reduced the level of education and general lawlessness prevails. Militancy for a number of Kashmiri youth has become a way of life. Young fighters show off their weapons and use their guns to resolve personal disputes. Older Kashmiri Muslims, who have known the valley at peace, regret the insurgency because they believe it has ruined the lives of so many without bringing about any political gains.

Medical facilities are insufficient and the hospitals are unhygienic. The doctors are overworked and many have fled. Some have been taken at gun point to treat injured militants and then returned. In 1995 the Bone and Joint Hospital had only three senior medical staff, besides nine registrars and six consultants. Immunisation programmes for children have fallen behind. On account of the insurgency, there are twenty times the number of psychiatric cases than in 1989.[105] Unofficial statistics estimate that 40,000 people have died since 1988, although the government puts the figure at about 13,500.[106] Of this number, less than half are militants. Amnesty bases its figures on police and hospital sources and assesses the number as in excess of 17,000. 'But we also believe there are several thousand more for whom we have no statistics,' says a representative of Amnesty.[107] The martyrs' graveyard in Srinagar is full of fresh graves with weeping mothers and onlookers standing by. The mausoleum to Maqbool Butt, who remains buried within the confines of Tihar jail in Delhi, is a painful reminder that the man who inspired so many in their fight for *azadi* has already been dead for over ten years.

Injury or death in crossfiring between militants and security forces has also taken a heavy toll. In 1994 M. N. Sabharwal, the director-general of Police in Srinagar admitted that at least 1,500 civilians had been killed in the crossfire, with many more injured. Just one of those casualties lay in a ward of the Bone and Joint Hospital in April 1994. He had been out shopping with his wife on his motorcycle. When firing began in a crowded street, soldiers shouted at them to get off the motorcycle and lie face down on the ground. Both he and his wife received bullet wounds. At first he thought they had been fired at on purpose, but then he realised that they were mere civilians caught in the crossfire. He was crying as he related his story: 'My Mrs is in the ladies hospital. I am here. What have we done to deserve this?' His own injury, close to his heart, was so serious that the doctor had only permitted him to be interviewed on the understanding that I did not tell him that his wife had already died. 'The shock,' warned the doctor 'might kill him.'[108]

By the beginning of 1996 the tremendous euphoria which lifted people's spirits in the early days of the movement had gone. The civilians of the valley are war weary. But the people's desire for their lives to return to normal, is tempered by a persistent rejection of a return to the status quo. 'Yes, they want peace,' says Omar Farooq, 'but at what cost?' Too much suffering has taken place for the clock to be put back. Despite all the disruption of the past seven years, taxi drivers, houseboat owners, shopkeepers still talk of independence, without being any closer to realising how it can be achieved. 'They demand *azadi* but it is a concept which has not been choreographed,' says Brigadier Arjun Ray.[109] *Azadi* means different things to different people. For some it is independence of the entire state; for those inhabitants of the valley it is preservation of their unique culture — Kashmiriyat — which includes both the Hindus and Muslims. For others, influenced by the Islamic resurgence, it means the creation of a theocratic state. 'It is not a geographical concept but an emotional one,' says Ashok Jaitley, 'the freedom to be themselves, with dignity and self-respect, wherever they can get it.'[110]

Farooq Abdullah, who prefers to talk about autonomy within the Indian union, describes 'azadi' as a bitter pill which has been covered with a sweetness:

> People would like to see *azadi* but they don't see the consequences of that 'azadi'. If we become independent, how are we going to sustain ourselves, where does the money come from? Where is it possible for us to develop? We are landlocked with powerful neighbours of China and Pakistan. If we get independence and India quits, I am sure Pakistan will march in overnight and take over. The people say we want *azadi*, without telling us what *azadi* will hold for us.[111]

Neither the Buddhists of Ladakh nor the Hindus of Jammu share the objectives of the Muslim Kashmiris of the valley. Their main concern is to press for autonomy against dominance from the more populous valley. 'Both feel the fruits of development have not reached them; most of the money has been spent on the valley,' says Ram Mahan Rao, adviser to the government of Jammu and Kashmir. 'A problem in our country is that we have a blanket which is too short. If it covers the head, then it is not able to cover the feet.'[112] Indian officials point out that there are eight linguistic and cultural districts in the Indian-administered state of Jammu and Kashmir, and Kashmiri is only one of them. The implication is that although in the valley Kashmiris may be numerically superior, their objectives cannot determine the future of the entire state.

In Ladakh, the troubles between Muslims of the Kargil district and Buddhists which erupted in 1989 have now subsided. 'There is little chance of the Hurriyat Conference gaining a standing in Ladakh,' says Ladakhi politician Pinto Narboo.[113] The objective of the Ladakh Autonomous Hill Development Council is to further the objectives of the approximately 150,000 Buddhist Ladakhis of the Leh area. But the valley Kashmiris have interpreted this as a move, backed by the Indian government, to divide the state on communal lines. However, even the Muslims of Jammu, who are not Kashmiri speaking, do not necessarily support the demands of the valley Kashmiri Muslims. 'The Jammu Muslims stand for the status quo and we support accession and integration,' said a Muslim Congress leader from Jammu in 1995. 'One-fifth of the total population of J & K state are Gujars, who do not speak Kashmiri; the Kashmiris have nothing in common with these people, other than a shared religion.'[114] Omar Farooq, however, maintains that in Jammu, the districts of Rajauri, Doda, Kishtwar, Poonch are not so wholeheartedly behind the Indian government as the politicians in New Delhi like to maintain and in 1996 the APHC plans to open an office in Jammu. 'We have been very democratic in our approach. We have said that all these regions, Gilgit, Baltistan too, should have a proper representation.' Mistrust, however, remains between Muslims and the displaced Kashmiri Pandits, some of whom are now demanding a separate homeland in the valley for the 700,000 Pandits living in different parts of India.

All communities have suffered during the insurgency. For those Kashmiri Muslims of the valley who so enthusiastically supported the demand for *azadi*, on the understanding that they had been promised a plebiscite in order to determine their future, the sense of betrayal is perhaps greatest. The repression of the 1990s, the indiscriminate and unnecessary killings have merely added fuel to their anger. Time and again I heard people say: 'How could we ever accept the Indian government again, after what the military did to our people?'

Kidnapping tourists

Since the conflict began in earnest in 1989, kidnapping civilians has been part of militant strategy. As with the kidnapping of Rubaiya Sayeed, the objective has generally been to keep them as hostages, pending the release of detained colleagues or to pressurise rival militant organisations. Several hundred Kashmiri civilians have also been kidnapped during the insurgency in order to extort money from their families. According to the Indian government, in 1995 430 people were kidnapped of which nearly half were killed, compared with the previous year, when 315 people were kidnapped, of which less than a quarter were killed.[115] But only on rare occasions were foreigners taken hostage.

As a result, with the exception of 1990, the government of India, with its own sense of bravado and its international image in mind, liked to maintain that the valley was not closed to tourism and that tourists are welcome. Those who visited the valley in the 1990s have often been surprised to find that provided they remained on their houseboats, they were not troubled by the insurgency and were able to enjoy their holiday. 'I was a bit alarmed when I arrived at the airport with all the military, but once I got on the houseboat I felt all right,' said Stephen Humphrey, an accountant from

Birmingham, who visited Kashmir in April 1994.[116] Robert Shadworth of Top Deck bus tours has taken tourists to Kashmir, as part of a tour from Nepal to London, twice a year, with the exception of 1990. Sylvain Soudain takes select parties of Europeans heli-skiing. Their main problem is not the insurgency but the government-run Centaur hotel on the outskirts of Srinagar which lacks basic facilities and hygiene.

The record numbers of nearly 80,000 foreign tourists who visited the valley in 1989 are reduced to about 9,000. Isolated incidents of kidnapping foreigners who were either working in Kashmir or had come as tourists, as well as the rape of a Canadian girl in October 1990 by two army officers, acted as an obvious deterrent. So too the militarisation of the valley and the paradox of enjoying a holiday, while the local people were subjected to crackdowns and crossfiring. The lack of tourists has, of course, meant that the business of the local Kashmiris has suffered accordingly: houseboat owners, the Hanjis, who, for generations have managed the houseboats, the shikara wallahs, taxi drivers, tonga drivers, hotel owners, and those who depended on selling their handicrafts to visiting tourists, have all lost what was the only avenue of income open to them. 'This houseboat which used to be so popular is now nearly gone,' said Iqbal Chapra, founder president of the Houseboat Owners Association.[117] 'We pray for peace in our valley and then the tourists will come,' says Muhammed Kotru, president of the Houseboat Owners Association in 1994.[118] Only the privileged few have been able to continue to export and sell carpets, handicrafts, and embroidery throughout India and abroad. A Kashmiri Pandit who has fled from the valley maintains that some Muslim Kashmiris are now better off because they no longer have to go through the Hindus as middlemen.

In 1994 the attention of the Western media was focused on the valley because two men, one of whom was the son of former *Financial Times* journalist David Housego, were kidnapped. The Housego family were on holiday in Kashmir to celebrate Jenny Housego's fiftieth birthday. On 6 June, when they reached the village of Aru, after three days in the mountains near Pahalgam, they were held up and robbed of money, watches and clothing. They were taken to a hotel where they met another couple David and Cathy Mackie who were also being held at gun point. They too had been trekking in the mountains. The militants took the Housegos' son, Kim, 16, and David Mackie, 36, leaving the Housego parents and Cathy Mackie to negotiate through a series of intermediaries for their release. After their release seventeen days later, Mackie made some revealing comments about the militants: 'They had heard on the BBC that I had a bad knee and next morning provided me with a stick and detailed one of the party to stay close to me. I was allowed to walk at my own pace.'[119] 'They made sure we had the best places by the camp fire,' said Kim Housego. 'They listened to the BBC Urdu service and translated for us.'[120] Harkat-ul Ansar were held responsible for the kidnapping, which was believed to have been a mistake.

By the following year the incident had almost been forgotten. As the winter snows melted, small numbers of tourists, who had either not heard about the troubles or were not sufficiently disturbed by them arrived in the valley. Martha Fichtinger, an Austrian woman, who visited Kashmir in April 1995, said that she did not find travelling on her own in Kashmir any more daunting than previous trips to South America and had heard very little about the insurgency.[121] Sam Valani, a Ugandan Asian and his family, now living in Canada, had always wanted to come to Kashmir but thought it was too dangerous.' But when an Indian airline official in Delhi told us that it was possible, we cancelled our trip to Udaipur and Jaipur and came to Kashmir instead.'[122] Gary Lazzarini, a shoe shop owner, and Philip Peters, a construction engineer from London, spent sixteen days in Kashmir with the intention of going skiing in once fashionable Gulmarg. Finding that the slopes were virtually closed, they stayed on a houseboat whose owner's only request was for them to send him some flies and lines for trout fishing when they returned to England. 'Everyone had something to say about the troubles going on. They didn't seem very optimistic and were more interested in getting their lives back to normal. But they were worried about human rights.'[123] A South African couple preferred to stay at Ahdoo's hotel in central Srinagar, because they felt trapped on the houseboats. Ahdoo's is still the only hotel which remains open, the lights sometimes fail, the telephones generally work, and the food is just bearable. The manager of Ahdoo's was delighted with the presence of the South African couple: 'These are the first tourists we have had. Otherwise it has been just journalists who come to report on the insurgency.'[124]

In July 1995 the hopes of those who were trying to say the valley was safe for tourism were once more dashed. Six foreigners were kidnapped and held by what was referred to as a 'little known' militant group, Al Faran, believed to be a radical wing of Harkat-ul Ansar. The tourists had also been trekking in Pahalgam and were apprehended in three separate incidents. One tourist, John Childs, escaped within days of being kidnapped. The others were Donald Hutchings, an American, Paul Wells and Keith Mangan, both British, Dirk Hasert, a German and a Norwegian, Hans Christian Ostro. The kidnappers demanded the release of twenty-one militants held by the Indian authorities, mostly belonging to Harkat-ul Ansar. Unless the militants were released, the kidnappers threatened to kill the hostages. On 17 July a hand-written statement was received by the news agencies in Srinagar: 'The Indian government is not showing any interest in securing the release of the hostages. The international community, particularly those who have appealed to us [to release the foreigners] should pressurise India to stop human rights violations in Kashmir and accept our demands immediately.'[125] The group's objective in taking the tourists was regarded as another variation on the persistent theme of the insurgency: the involvement of the international community in the 'just cause' of the Kashmiris.

Despite the release of the militants in 1989 after Dr Rubaiya Sayeed's kidnapping and the numerous other incidents where bargains had been made the Indian government publicly refused to consider an exchange.' There is no question of releasing any militant [in exchange for the five abducted tourists]', stated the home secretary, K. Padmanabhaiah, in the first of many refusals.[126] While the Indian authorities tried to contact Al Faran, deadlines for the killing of the hostages came and went. The JKLF condemned the kidnapping, as did Omar Farooq, who claimed the APHC had tried but failed to get in touch with the Al Faran militants. Pakistan also condemned the kidnapping and some commentators even believed that the incident was an elaborate ploy by Indian intelligence to discredit the Kashmiri movement and, indirectly, Pakistan. 'Although Pakistan has undoubtedly not got anything to do with this kidnapping, their overall support of the insurgency would make them responsible,' commented a Western analyst who believes Pakistan has supplied weapons to the insurgents. 'In the same way, if you give a child a gun and leave him a in a room with his siblings and he shoots them, you are responsible for their murder.'

On 13 August, the decapitated body of Hans Christian Ostro was found by the roadside. By murdering a foreigner, the kidnappers succeeded in attracting world-wide publicity, but for the wrong reasons. The action was condemned by both the political and other militant groups. A one-day strike throughout the valley was intended to show that the Kashmiris dissociated themselves from the murder, which Omar Farooq called an act of terrorism. Because of the potential publicity damage to their movement, he and many others were sceptical about the group's origins and their motivation. 'Who are these people who come into existence at a time when we are trying to gain support for our movement day and night? I do not believe that they are in anyway committed to the Kashmiris' struggle.'[127] In December 1995 three members of the Al Faran group were captured by Indian security forces. They confirmed that the hostages were still alive, but no information was given regarding their release. By 1996 it was feared they were dead.

The diametrically opposed viewpoints of Pakistan and India on the kidnapping demonstrate how far apart they still are over what takes place in Kashmir. On the one hand, the Indian government is convinced the group are foreign mercenaries, aided and abetted by Pakistan. On the other, Pakistanis believe that they are agents of the Indian government, paid to discredit the Kashmiris' struggle for self-determination and, by association, Pakistan. In the midst of these conflicting views, the Kashmiri people are, as ever, caught in their verbal crossfire. The valley, surrounded by the magnificent Himalayan mountains, whose beauty has, for centuries, attracted visitors from far and wide, is still the home of tragedy.

Behold! The valley, lush and green;
Splendid and serene in all its majesty.
Paradise of peasants, kings and queens
Throughout the ages.
Trees stand tall in verdurous grandeur
Bowing not to time nor wind
But man is blind and cannot see that
Every noble head's in sorrow bent,
Each leaf is shedding tears,
Each bough is breaking
With its heavy burden of grief
For man is deaf, he cannot hear
The wailing in the wind.

Sahira Jamila[128]

Conclusion

Fifty years of failed bilateralism has proved that India and Pakistan are not in a position to solve the issue without the consent of the Kashmiri people. Omar Farooq[1]

They have no love for the Kashmiris, only for the land. Kashmiri Militant[2]

The Kashmiri conflict, which has lasted half a century, has been inherited by the next and the next generation. Many of those in the forefront of the struggle today were not born when it all began, nor were those who have died fighting in the cause of Kashmir. As in 1947, the fear of a full-scale war on the sub-continent is a determining factor in arousing international interest in the problem. The state of Jammu and Kashmir remains, as ever, poised strategically between powerful and competing neighbours: China to the east, the new Central Asian republics to the north and west and the land mass of the sub-continent to the south. The world, however, has become much more dangerous since 1947. Yet the basic demand of those Kashmiris challenging the Indian government is the same: the right to determine their future. Should the valley of Kashmir remain part of India? Should it accede to Pakistan? Should it become independent, in which case, does this mean prising the Northern Areas and Azad Kashmir away from allegiance to Pakistan, and Ladakh and Jammu away from India? Could the valley survive as an autonomous unit in its own right? What is the threshold of tolerance of both India and Pakistan in terms of what, if anything, they are prepared to concede? Most importantly, how can a lasting solution be achieved?

World opinion

Throughout their struggle the Kashmiri political activists and militants have felt helpless about the inability or unwillingness of the rest of the world to assist them in what they perceive to be a 'just' cause. They are mindful of the support given to the Afghans during their struggle against the Soviet Union, aware of the military might of the United States and conscious of the sub-continent's past history in which Britain played its own, at times controversial, role. Their optimistic belief, however, that they had only to create enough trouble in the valley to attract international support did not materialise. 'No country was willing to risk its entire agenda with New Delhi over the Kashmir cause,' writes *Time* correspondent Edward Desmond 'especially when it was clear that New Delhi had no intention of backing down.'[3]

British MPs, Euro MPs, US congressmen as well as Muslim countries all played a role in listening to the grievances of the Kashmiris; but once they had lodged their complaints and written their reports, there was very little action they could take. International opinion was as much concerned about Pakistan's own alleged role in 'exporting terrorism' and its potential nuclear capability as it was about events in what India terms an integral part of its territory. Kashmir also appears remote, an issue which does not have the same immediacy as Bosnia, Northern Ireland or the Middle East.

The toughest international criticism which India faced was in the early months of the insurgency over violations of human rights. When foreign observers took up the refrain of plebiscite and self-determination, as recommended by the United Nations resolutions, the commentators found themselves on less secure ground. Not only do the UN resolutions make no specific reference to the 'third option' of independence for the Kashmiri people, but to call for their implementation would also unearth all the old reasons why the plebiscite was never held. In the Indian armoury of excuses is the fact that Pakistan has never vacated that part of the state of Jammu and Kashmir which it is occupying in the Northern Areas and Azad Kashmir and which was a prerequisite for the holding of a plebiscite. 'We have always said that the whole of Jammu and Kashmir acceded to India and if we are going to talk in legal terms, then the whole state should be united and become part of the Indian republic, ' states Indian former foreign secretary, J. N. Dixit.[4] Moreover, one of the strongest arguments put forward by the Indian government is that if the state of Jammu and Kashmir left the Indian Union, other disaffected parts of the country might also wish to secede, and no member of the international community wishes to see the sub-continent destabilised.

The Kashmiris who are challenging Indian rule, however, believe that it is the moral duty of the international community to support their cause precisely because successive resolutions, unanimously adopted by the Security Council, called for the settlement of the dispute by means of a free and impartial plebiscite under the auspices of the United Nations. They refer in particular to the UNCIP resolution of 13 August 1948 which makes no mention of accession to India or Pakistan but calls for the status of Jammu and Kashmir to be determined according to the will of the people, and does not therefore preclude independence. 'The people should be given free choice to accede to India or Pakistan or to become independent,' says Yasin Malik. 'And whatever the people decide, we will accept this democratic decision wholeheartedly, because we believe in the democratic process.'[5] The Kashmiris refute India's suggestion that if Kashmir secedes it will lead to the break-up of India. 'We have a legal case, supported by United Nations resolutions. There are commitments made by India,' says Omar Farooq, chairman of the All Parties Hurriyat Conference:

We are not like Punjab or Assam in India, where the situation was quite different. We are not telling the governments of Britain and the United States that they should impose economic sanctions. What we need is that there should be a little bit of push. Mere submission of reports does not mean that India stops the crimes in Kashmir. There should also be pressure so that India talks to the people of Kashmir and Kashmiris in Pakistan.

Omar Farooq also believes that India does not have to retain Kashmir for the sake of its 'secular' image. 'There are over 100 million Muslims in India, which make it secular, without India having to hold onto Kashmir.'[6]

After its early diplomatic initiatives in the 1950s and 1960s the United States kept aloof from the Kashmiri issue. In the 1990s, without the weight of the Soviet Union to balance power in the region, the United States has now taken more interest in what James Woolsey, head of the CIA in 1994, assessed as posing 'perhaps the most probable prospect for future use of weapons of mass destruction, including nuclear weapons.'[7] The prospect of a war between India and Pakistan over rival claims to the Siachen glacier, where their troops have clashed intermittently over the past decade, is chilling indeed. The fear of such a local dispute spreading into a greater conflict was fundamental to the shift in emphasis of US foreign policy. 'We felt it was time to get out our Kashmir file, dust it off and see what could be done,' said a State Department official in 1995.[8]

Furthermore, as the US administration involved itself in the issue, so its officials began to appreciate the sensitivities felt by both the Indian and Pakistani governments. When, in October 1993, Robin Raphael, assistant secretary of state on South Asian affairs, commented that the US still regarded the status of Jammu and Kashmir as a 'disputed territory and that means we do not recognise the Instrument of Accession as meaning that Kashmir is for evermore an integral part of India', her remarks caused an outcry in New Delhi.[9] In April 1994, when US deputy secretary of state, Strobe Talbott, visited New Delhi and Islamabad, both countries reacted nervously at any perceived favouritism towards the other. 'The US has good relations with India and with Pakistan,' Talbott declared at his press conference in New Delhi.[10] British foreign secretary, Douglas Hurd's remarks that the UN resolutions no longer had the same relevance upset the Pakistanis during his visit to Islamabad at the end of 1994. So too did the statement in 1995 by Robin Cook, British opposition spokesman on foreign affairs, who indicated that Kashmir was a part of India. He was obliged to clarify his remarks by emphasising that his statement was meant to reflect the situation on the ground rather than the legal situation.[11]

While US support is courted by the Kashmiris for its international clout, that of the UK is seen as a natural extension of the 'unfinished' business of partition. There is a widespread belief, on both sides of the line of control, that the United Kingdom has a moral responsibility to solve the Kashmir issue, not just because of suspicions of Mountbatten's favouritism towards

India in 1947, but also because the British masterminded the sale of Kashmir in 1846. Yet although there may be some amongst the older generation of British who remember partition, and who feel some concern that Britain's role was not as even-handed as it should have been, the Kashmiris are also dealing with a new post-colonial generation who need to understand the complexities of the subject before they can take any action. The official Foreign Office attitude towards Kashmir, influenced by Britain's historical, trading and economic ties, has been to maintain good relations with both India and Pakistan as two important members of the Commonwealth.

The Kashmiris are also apprehensive that adverse publicity regarding the militancy means that their struggle is misunderstood by the world community. The kidnapping of the western hostages and murder of one of them in 1995 did not help their movement. 'It is portrayed as a terrorist and Islamic fundamentalist movement, while that is not the case.' says Omar Farooq. 'It is important for both the UK and the US to understand the Kashmiris' point of view. We are not fanatics.' They also regret the departure of the Hindus, which has detracted from Kashmiriyat, their unique cultural heritage, established over centuries of co-existence between Hindus and Muslims. 'It is not normally realised that there are still many Sikhs and Hindus living in the valley. We want the Kashmiri Pandits to return.'[12]

Western inability to pressurise the Indian government in any world forum to modify its stand has not only been interpreted as a sign of their lack of basic resolve, but has also generated considerable anti-western feeling against an alleged 'pro India tilt'. Kashmiri sympathisers point to examples where Western powers have intervened forcefully, such as in the Gulf, when their interests were obviously at stake. 'The West has absolute double standards,' says Abdul Suhrawardy, one of the early generation of 'freedom fighters'. 'They have no morality; they talk of democracy, they talk of human rights but these are just hypocritical slogans.'[13]

However, given the unwillingness of the Indian government to consider the demands of the Kashmiris and their own realisation that the militants are unlikely to defeat the Indian army, the Kashmiris still see that the best solution lies in pressure from the international community. The Kashmiris who are opposing India do not see themselves as remote and rate their struggle on the same basis as other troublespots. 'We see issues like Bosnia, Ireland, Middle East getting solved,' says Omar Farooq, 'therefore we have high hopes of getting the international community involved to solve the issue in Kashmir.' Yasin Malik applauds US official policy which states that the Kashmiri aspirations should be taken into consideration. 'This is a positive change.'[14] At the same time, Prime Minister Sardar Abdul Qayyum Khan of Azad Jammu and Kashmir warns against US attempts to encourage Pakistan unilaterally to sign the Nuclear Non-proliferation treaty before the Kashmir issue is resolved. 'Signing the NPT without resolving the Kashmir issue will completely destroy our position and we will have no bargaining power.'[15]

Failed bilateralism?

The insurgency waged within the valley of Kashmir against the Government
of India is only one war. The other is the undeclared psychological war
which has existed between India and Pakistan over Kashmir ever since
partition. Although conventional wars were fought in 1947, 1965, and 1971,
there has never been a mutually acceptable outcome to the Kashmir issue,
which means that the future of other parts of the state is also unresolved.
'It is one of those tragic cases in which neither Pakistan nor India can resile
from their positions.' says L. P. Singh, Indian home secretary in the 1960s,
who is one of a dying generation who remembers partition, Tashkent and
Simla.[16] India may have unilaterally decided that the Kashmir issue was
resolved, but Pakistan never has. Although at the time it was hoped that the
1972 Simla agreement would resolve the problem, it merely shelved discussion
and lulled the rest of the world into thinking that they need not concern
themselves with what was now a bilateral issue.

Since Simla, however, not only has the Government of India shown
extreme sensitivity over criticism of its Kashmiri policy by the international
community, but it has refused to discuss the Kashmir issue with Pakistan
either bilaterally or through a third party. Inconclusive talks between their
respective foreign ministers have led to a stalemate of rhetoric over the
whole subject. The government of New Delhi's stance remains that the State
of Jammu and Kashmir belongs to India and is non-negotiable. India's complaints against Pakistan for waging a 'proxy war' have still further embittered
relations between the two countries. Thus, even the element of bilateralism
has disappeared.

By excluding Pakistan from any discussions relating to the valley, however,
the Indian political leaders leave themselves open to the continuation of a
struggle which began in 1947 partly because of Pakistan's own thwarted
territorial ambitions and has been intensified because of the valley Kashmiris
alienation against the Indian government. The Pakistani government never
made any secret of its disappointment that the state did not accede to Pakistan
at independence and Mr Jinnah considered the Instrument of Accession to
have been an act of 'fraud and violence'. Is it perhaps so surprising that, in
the absence of political discussion, the spirit of the jihad of 1947 fuelled by
world-wide Islamic resurgence, was revitalised in 1987, forty years later?

Nonetheless, given the commitment enshrined at Simla to deal with Jammu
and Kashmir bilaterally, the Government of India has strongly objected to
Pakistan's re-introduction of the Kashmir issue on the international platform,
be it at the United Nations, the Organisation of Islamic Countries, the
Commonwealth or in meetings with other foreign leaders. The 'international-
isation' of the issue was most vocally demonstrated when the prime minister
of Pakistan, Benazir Bhutto, raised it at the United Nations Commission for
Human Rights at Geneva in February 1994. The disappointment felt by the

Kashmiris at the withdrawal of the resolution was tempered by the evidence of how much support there was amongst UN members for their cause.

Bilateralism, however, clearly failed long before Pakistan re-introduced the issue at the international level. Simla was rejected by the Kashmiris on both sides of the line of control in 1972 because their views were not included. 'Tashkent and Simla failed,' says Shabbir Shah 'because they did not include the view of the sons of the soil.'[17] Paradoxically, given Sheikh Abdullah's own intermittent leanings towards independence, only his son, Farooq Abdullah, amongst Kashmiri leaders today, is willing to let the Indian government speak on his behalf.

Bygones

Much of the current discussion about Kashmir relates to past events which still cause bitterness. Those Kashmiris challenging the Government of India continually refer back to the sale of Kashmir in 1846, the award of Gurdaspur, Mountbatten's role, the Instrument of Accession, almost as though in an attempt to unscramble history they can rewrite it. In 1946 Sheikh Abdullah seemed seriously to believe that the Kashmiris could reverse the Treaty of Amritsar by offering to collect enough money to buy back the state purchased by Hari Singh's great-grandfather in 1846. In 1994 I met a young girl in Sopore who had heard how Professor Alastair Lamb, had questioned the validity of the Instrument of Accession. She also seemed to believe that it might be possible to redefine the status of Jammu and Kashmir in the light of his revelations.

Although history cannot be re-written, an analysis of all the relevant aspects of the struggle makes it easier to understand the depth of disappointment and, at times, hatred which these issues have created on all sides. Balraj Puri, one of the few surviving commentators who has followed the freedom struggle since it began against the maharaja in the 1930s, explains how the discontented Kashmiris related the spirit of *azadi* back to Kashmir's last phase of independence in the sixteenth century. 'When the organised movement against autocracy started in 1931, its leaders linked it with the four centuries old urge for freedom of the people of Kashmir. It culminated in the Quit Kashmir movement in 1946 which, though addressed to the last ruler, a Dogra Hindu, Maharaja Hari Singh, promised to undo Akbar's act of enslaving the Kashmiris in 1586.'[18]

The Indian government has shown little inclination to look back: whether the British should have annexed Kashmir instead of selling it to Gulab Singh in 1846, when, precisely, Hari Singh signed the Instrument of Accession in 1947, whether a plebiscite should have been held, are all regarded as largely irrelevant issues. 'All these legalities are not going to make an iota of difference,' says J. N. Dixit:

> Everybody who has a sense of history knows that legality only has a relevance up to the threshold of transcending political realities. And especially in inter-state relations ... so to quibble about points of law and hope, that by proving a legal point, you can reverse the process of history is living in a somewhat contrived utopia. It won't work.[19]

The history of Kashmir may be relevant to understand the depth of feeling, but once understood, the challenge is to move on. World parameters have changed. They have also hardened. Nationalist feeling, the breaking down of old frontiers, especially the creation of the five Central Asian republics within the former Soviet Union, and alienation towards the Indian government in New Delhi have made the valley Kashmiris' demand for self-determination even stronger. The reunification of East and West Germany was particularly symbolic 'We felt if the Berlin Wall could be dismantled so too could the line of control,' said Dr Hamida Bano, professor of English at the University of Kashmir in Srinagar.[20] Vision is also required on the Pakistani side, since they must now realise that many of the Kashmiris are no longer fighting for accession to Pakistan. When I asked the young girl from Sopore whether, as a Muslim, she would like to accede to Pakistan, she replied incredulously: 'Do you think I would want to exchange one set of masters for another?'

What has not changed, however, is the belief that a plebiscite is the time-honoured way to finalise the issue. 'Even if the plebiscite goes against us, we will accept that decision,' says Shabir Shah.[21] Regardless of prior elections, accords and economic packages, the Kashmiri people have never been allowed to exercise their right of self-determination. After examining the issue in its report, the mission of the International Commission of Jurists concluded 'that the right of self-determination to which the peoples of Jammu and Kashmir became entitled as part of the process of partition has neither been exercised nor abandoned, and thus remains exercisable today.'[22] Unless the Kashmiris themselves can be made to feel that they have been given the freedom to choose their destiny, the issue may never be laid to rest. If this generation is silenced, the next will learn the history, read about the plebiscite and seek, perhaps again through armed struggle, to achieve their aims. Sir Frederic Bennett is just one of many Western observers who has spent a lifetime speaking out on behalf of the Kashmiris.

> In the cause of essential justice, which is intrinsically worth pursuing, it must be the fervently held faith of all of us that in the end the people of that unhappy and luckless, but beautiful land of Kashmir will at last be given the opportunity of settling their own future, which they were promised so many weary years go.'

It is rather disheartening to realise that he made this statement as a young member of parliament in 1958.[23] After the 1965 war, Josef Korbel warned that 'as profound as is the crevasse between India and Pakistan' it was necessary for them to reach a solution over Kashmir otherwise they and the rest of the world 'may reap the harvest of short-sightedness and indecision of unpredictable dimensions.'[24] Thirty years later no lasting solution has been reached. Today there are Indians, Pakistanis, Kashmiris, who dismiss all the high-sounding principles as political posturing for the benefit of their respective domestic public opinion. They cynically maintain that no one wants a resolution of the issue because their own positions are better served by retaining the status quo.

If, however, one can look forward into the twenty-first century and reason that India and Pakistan do both want a lasting peace, given the domestic problems they both face, they may find that it better suits their mutual interests to let bygones be bygones in an attempt to resolve their differences. Is it really in the interest of India – respected as the largest democracy in the world – to face the prospect of condemnation by the international community because of its continuing military presence and human rights record in the valley of Kashmir? Is it really in the interest of Pakistan – a country which fought so hard for its existence – to face the threat of censure because of the allegation that it is 'exporting terrorism'? Do they both want to continue spending so much of their limited resources on military equipment which their people can ill afford? Is it really in the international interest to see two countries, who have so much in common, live side by side in hatred? Non-governmental conferences and meetings between Indians and Pakistanis testify that they want to live in harmony. Why not then their governments? The answer is always Kashmir.

Genuine accord means both countries may have to give away the moral high ground and admit some incontrovertible truths. There were compelling reasons, emotional and strategic, why both Dominions wanted and worked towards obtaining the accession of the state of Jammu and Kashmir; the tribal invasion did precipitate Hari Singh's accession to India, but there was already an indigenous rebellion which opposed the maharaja and whose adherents would have preferred accession to Pakistan; the accounts of the signing of the Instrument of Accession are inconsistent; Sheikh Abdullah's dominating personality and belief in secularism did push the state towards India, yet this affiliation never satisfied those whose allegiance lay with Muslim Pakistan; the Government of India did erode the special status promised to Kashmir; independence has become a 'third option' in the minds of many Kashmiris.

Discontent in the valley did not begin with the insurgency of the 1990s. The Government of India had nearly fifty years to win over the hearts of the Kashmiris and, if the Indian government finds its actions have come under greater scrutiny than those of Pakistan, it is because it is its authority in the valley which is being challenged. Even during periods of stability and apparent calm the acquiescence of the people was never whole-hearted or unanimous. The popularity of Kashmir's leaders was only ever measured in relation to their stance towards New Delhi. Farooq Abdullah was a hero in the valley in 1984 because he stood up to New Delhi; when he made an accord with Rajiv Gandhi in 1986 he became 'India's man'. 'If he had really understood the wishes of the people and worked for his people, he would have been the most respected man in Kashmir,' says Omar Farooq. The 'rigged' elections of 1987, combined with economic grievances, corruption and unfulfilled expectations, completed the process of alienation. 'Believe me, we are not against the Indian people. We are opposed to the wrong policies the Indian government has committed in Kashmir.'[25] India's persistent belief that Pakistan instigated the Kashmiri problem has also prevented a thorough analysis of the Indian government's handling of the situation. 'I do not believe that any foreign hand engineered the Kashmir problem,' stated George Fernandes in 1990. 'The problem was created by us, and if others decided to take advantage of it, I do not believe that one should make that an issue; given the nature of the politics of our subcontinent, such a development was inevitable.'[26]

Is there a solution?

'Our first goal should be that we should be in a position to decide our future,' says Omar Farooq.

> In consultation with the political leadership of Azad Kashmir, we could take a decision. The first phase is reunification; secondly, all Kashmiris should sit and discuss what will be the future of the state. Until we can discuss with our brothers across the border it is very difficult for us to take a single-handed decision. We should also discuss what Ladakhis want, and the people from Gilgit, Baltistan and Jammu.

Spoken so convincingly, it all sounds easy. 'We have given proposals to the Indian government,' Farooq continues. 'If you stop human rights abuses, allow in Amnesty and other organisations, release political prisoners, if you accept that Kashmir is part of a dispute, maybe then the Hurriyat can get the militants to stop their activities for a certain time, and we can have a ceasefire and pursue the political ground.'

The Kashmiri political leaders appreciate that the militancy cannot go on indefinitely and now, more than ever, they seem eager to talk. 'We feel that the battle has to be fought on political grounds,' says Omar Farooq. 'We have seen what has happened in Afghanistan. We know that the gun cannot really be the answer to the problem. It introduced the Kashmiri issue at the international level, by bringing it out of cold storage into the limelight, but now it is the job of the political leaders to work for the movement.'[27] The Kashmiris also realise that the amount of money, which is spent on the insurgency and counter-insurgency detracts from other programmes which could benefit all the people of the sub-continent. In November 1995, the Hurriyat opened a 'Kashmir Awareness' bureau in New Delhi to establish contact with people throughout India in order to explain how much the Kashmiri conflict is affecting their lives.

In order for the long-awaited plebiscite to be held, the Kashmiri activists have optimistically suggested that both India and Pakistan should vacate the areas which each country is administering and for UN troops to safeguard the frontiers so that the state of Jammu and Kashmir can be left alone from outside interference for a period of five, even ten years. Then without external pressure, from either India or Pakistan, the will of the people could be ascertained. But, although the UN could well have a role to play in future deliberations, this proposal presupposes that both India and Pakistan would be prepared to surrender all the territory they hold, including the strategically important areas of Ladakh and the Northern Areas. When such suggestions have been raised in international fora, the Government of India has listened, at times more patiently than others, but has shown no desire to accede to any of them. The Government of Pakistan, whilst supporting the Kashmiris right of self-determination, is most unlikely to agree to surrender its control over the Northern Areas, whose political leaders have not shown any obvious support of the independence movement.

In addition, although the All Parties Hurriyat Conference has attempted to broaden its following, it still has no significant standing in Ladakh, whose preference is for greater autonomy within the Indian Union. It is also most unlikely that the Hindu areas of Jammu would want a departure from the status quo. 'Why is it that everybody is only talking of the valley?' asks former Indian foreign secretary, J. N. Dixit. He also points to the dangers of political fragmentation, which is an inherent fear amongst all Indian politicians: 'Once you have the argument of ethno-religiosity as the basis for statehood or new territorial arrangements, it has a cascading effect of generating further claims of further sub-identities.' The APHC's position is weakened by its own divisions – whether its ultimate objective is independence or accession to Pakistan. Despite the rift within the JKLF, its objective remains independence of the entire state, regardless of its lack of homogeneity. 'I don't think there is any country in the world today which is a single cultural, religious, ethnic unit. If you break up Kashmir you might as well break up Pakistan,' says Amanullah Khan.[28] J. N. Dixit, however, believes that: 'An independent Kashmir would be landlocked. They would have to depend either on India or Pakistan, and that would create problems for them, because if they decide to join one or the other, purely in speculative terms, the other country which has been rejected will create pressure.'[29]

As of writing, there is little scope for an agreement between the Indian government and the discontented Kashmiris. The deadlock is compounded by increased tension between India and Pakistan. In the absence of any accord between the protagonists, the Indian authorities will most probably continue to suppress the insurgency in the valley, for which they have the militarily capability, at the same time as promising economic aid and some degree of autonomy in the attempt to hold elections to the state of Jammu and Kashmir Legislative Assembly. Pending a settlement with the Government of Pakistan, this option will leave a running sore along the 450-mile line of control, which Pakistan and the Azad Kashmiris refuse to recognise as an international border. Nor will it answer the Kashmiris' demand for self-determination. After the defeat of Narasimha Rao in India's general election held in May 1996, it remains to be seen what fresh policy the successor government will adopt on Kashmir. Although the election was contested under heavy security by candidates in the valley of Kashmir for their six representatives to the Indian parliament, the APHC and the National Conference refused to take part. Only Congress, BJP and independents agreed to stand.[30]

Kashmiri political activists continue to maintain that elections are no substitute for a plebiscite. Ever since Sir Owen Dixon suggested a regional plebiscite and Sheikh Abdullah talked of confederation, variations on the theme of a plebiscite according to the UN resolutions have been suggested and rejected. Sadly, after so many years, impartial observers are beginning to conclude that there will never be a generally acceptable solution. But, if India and Pakistan were ever to see a way to relax their established positions, the one scenario which seems viable is to consider holding a plebiscite or referendum on a regional basis so that each component can determine its own preference. Depending on the outcome it might be possible to restore the natural geographical link of the valley with Azad Kashmir with a 'soft' border along the line of control, so that those who have suffered by having their families separated could once more visit them freely. This smaller area, comparable in size to Switzerland, could form an 'autonomous' region, equivalent to an 'independent' Kashmir, which would have its historical foundation in the independent kingdom, as it existed before its absorption into the Mughal, Afghan and Sikh kingdoms and before the Dogras of Jammu extended their somewhat unnatural dominance over Ladakh, Baltistan and Gilgit in the nineteenth century. In any such arrangement, the future of the Kashmiri Pandits must also be determined. Where in the polarised atmosphere which exists between Hindus and Muslims, do they now belong? Could Kashmir ever revive its Sufist reputation for religious tolerance and show the way forward to greater religious harmony between Muslims and Hindus throughout the sub-continent, or will the Kashmiri Pandits have to resign themselves to being exiles from their own land? No one, said Sheikh Abdullah in 1964, must be left with a sense of defeat.

Any initiative would require immense courage from all protagonists because inevitably it would involve a voluntary compromise either in terms of objective or territory. Security arrangements between India, Pakistan and Kashmir, perhaps initially safeguarded by the United Nations, would be needed to reduce mutual concern over each other's territorial ambitions. Pakistan's fears of domination by India, expressed when Sheikh Abdullah first suggested confederation in 1964, would have to be assuaged. India would likewise have to be assured that the spectre of 'jihad' will be laid to rest. The

Kashmiris would need safeguards from both sides that the *azadi* which they cherish would be honoured. As the Indian journalist, Pan Chopra, has said, it would be much better if India and Pakistan could take the initiative to resolve the conflict themselves, 'instead of being summoned to appear at alien tables by third countries.'[31]

A change to the status quo will only stand a chance of succeeding if, in the process, it can dispel the long-standing hostility and suspicion which has existed between India and Pakistan ever since 1947, and which perhaps explains why no lasting solution has ever been reached. The Kashmiris have been the unwitting victims of that enmity. Too often I heard both Indians and Pakistanis lament how much money and effort was being spent on the Kashmiri conflict and yet 'the Kashmiris don't want to be with either of us.' At present neither India nor Pakistan appears to be in a position to alter its established rhetoric. The Government of India maintains that the state of Jammu and Kashmir is an integral part of India. The Government of Pakistan remains committed to calling for the self-determination of the Kashmiri people; yet it also insists on the implementation of the UN resolutions without the 'third option'. Equally, those committed to fighting for complete independence of the former princely state or accession to Pakistan do not wish to deviate from their respective objectives.

However, if a solution could be reached which involves a genuine dialogue on all sides appropriate to the world as it is in the 1990s and not how it was in 1947, India could take pride in having fulfilled its pledge to ascertain the will of the Kashmiri people in determining their future; Pakistan would be free, at last, from a national preoccupation and able to focus attention on developing valuable relations not only with India but with the new Muslim republics in Central Asia. A stable sub-continent would also act as a suitable counterpoise to China which, in recent years, has adopted a more neutral stance over Kashmir and has shown a desire to maintain good relations with both its sub-continental neighbours.[32]

Without a generally acceptable settlement, the Kashmir issue is likely to remain indefinitely on the international agenda of unresolved conflicts, which may yet become more explosive. It is a testimony to the Kashmiris' own endurance that, despite all they have suffered, they are still looking forward to the day when their land will become 'not a cot of hatred between India and Pakistan but a bridge of friendship.'[33]

Glossary

anna	one-sixteenth of a rupee
azad	free
azadi	freedom
bandh	strike
bazaar	market
begar	forced labour
burqah	garment which covers women completely
crore(s)	10 million or 100 lakhs
darbar	the court of a ruler
hartal	strike
gaddi	throne
goonda	hooligan
izzat	honour
jagir	an assignment of the land revenue of a territory to a chief or noble for a specific service
jagirdar	big landlord; one who hold a jagir
jamiat	association of Muslim clerics
jawan	private soldier in the Indian army
jihad	holy war; war waged for a religious cause
jirga	tribal assembly
kashmir	also Cashmere, Kasmir, Kasmira
khalsa	Sikh army
khan	Muslim ruler of a small Indian state; tribal leader
khel	clan
khutba	sermon
lakh	100,000
laskhar	tribal army
maharaja	Hindu ruler of an Indian state
masjid	mosque
maulana	'our master' – a term of reverence
mir	a chief or leader
mirwaiz	chief preacher
misl	confederacy
mujaheddin	soldiers of the holy war; holy warriors; freedom fighters
mullah	Muslim preacher
nanga parbat	naked lady

nawab	Muslim ruler of an Indian state; also used by big Muslim landlords
nishat	abode of gladness
panch	executive body of Sikh army
panchayat	village council of five members
pandit	Prefix to a name. Generally denotes members of the Brahmin caste; learned or wise man
puphi	aunt
purdah	veil
qaum	nation
quaid-i azam	the great leader
rakaposhi	one who guards
raj	kingdom; used to denote British rule in India (1858–1947)
rajah	Hindu ruler of a small Indian state
rani	wife of a rajah
rupee	currency of India, Pakistan. In British India one rupee was worth about 1s 6d (7.5 new pence)
sabha	assembly or conference
sardar	chief, nobleman
sepoy	Indian soldier
shalimar	abode of love
shikar	big game hunting
swaraj	self-rule
tehsil	sub-division of an administrative district
tonga	two-wheeled horse-drawn carriage
UNCIP	United Nations Commission in India and Pakistan
UNMOGIP	United Nations Military Observer Group in India and Pakistan
vakil	lawyer or advocate
yuvaraj	Hindu heir-apparent
zar	gold

For purposes of consistency I have used the names by which the respective governments prefer to call that part of Kashmir which lies under their control – thus 'Azad Jammu and Kashmir' for that part held by Pakistan and 'Jammu and Kashmir.' for that part held by India.

When I refer to Kashmiris, I generally mean the inhabitants of the valley, although I fully understand that all inhabitants of the state of Jammu and Kashmir are, politically speaking, Kashmiris.

Notes

Chapter 1

1. Emperor Jehangir, Tuzuk-i Jahanguri, as quoted in Ajit Bhattacharjea, *Kashmir: The Wounded Valley*, New Delhi, 1994, p. 21.
2. William Wakefield, *The Happy Valley*, London, 1879, p. 3.
3. Sir Francis Younghusband, *Kashmir*, London, 1924, p. 17.
4. Sanskrit is taken from samskrta, meaning 'adorned, cultivated, perfected'.
5. Dr Radha Krishan Parmu, *Muslim Rule in Kashmir, 1320–1819*, New Delhi, 1969, p. 34.
6. Kalhana, *Chronicle of Kings*, Preface, p. xxiv.

Chapter 2

1. Kalhana's Rajatarangini, *Saga of the Kings of Kashmir*, tr. R. S. Pandit (New Delhi, 1991), Vol. I, p. 24.
2. Kalhana, *Chronicle of Kings*, Vol. I, p. 16.
3. Ibid., p. 45.
4. Ibid., p. 108.
5. Ibid., p. 171.
6. Ibid., p. 293.
7. Prem Nath Bazaz, *History of Struggle for Freedom*, New Delhi, 1954, p. 10.
8. As quoted in Younghusband, *Kashmir*, p. 120.
9. Bazaz, *Struggle for Freedom*, p. 12.
10. Ibid., p. 32.
11. Kalhana, *Chronicle of Kings*, Vol. IV, p. 131.
12. Ibid., p. 347–8.
13. Ibid., p. 181.
14. Captain C-M. Enriquez, *Realm of the Gods*, London, 1915, p 126.
15. Younghusband, *Kashmir*, p. 125.
16. M. L. Kapur, *Eminent Rulers of Kashmir*, Delhi, 1975, p. 37.
17. Kalhana, *Chronicle of Kings*, Vol. V, p. 1.
18. Ibid., p. 88–90.
19. Ibid., p. 102.
20. Walter Lawrence, *The Valley of Kashmir*, London, 1895, p. 187.
21. Kapur, *Eminent Rulers*, p. 49.
22. Kalhana, *Chronicle of Kings*, Vol. V, p. 174.
23. Ibid., p. 184.
24. Ibid., p. 136.
25. Ibid., p. 218.

26. Nehru, as quoted in his Foreword to Kalhana's *Saga of Kings*, p. x.
27. See Bazaz, *Struggle for Freedom*, p. 22.
28. Kapur, *Eminent Rulers*, p. 68.
29. Kalhana, *Chronicle of Kings*, Vol. VI, p. 151.
30. Ibid., p. 189.
31. Kalhana, *Chronicle of Kings*, VI, 313.
32. Ibid., p. 315.
33. Ibid., p. 326.
34. Ibid., p. 360.
35. Kalhana, *Chronicle of Kings*, Vol. VII, p. 423–4.
36. Ibid., p. 444.
37. Ibid., p. 478.
38. Ibid., p. 507.
39. Ibid., p. 1072.
40. Ibid., p. 1092.
41. Ibid., p. 1146.
42. Ibid., p. 1243.
43. Kalhana, *Chronicle of Kings*, Vol.VIII, p. 3405.
44. As quoted in M. J. Akbar, *Kashmir: Behind the Vale*, New Delhi, 1991, p. 17.
45. Prithivi Nath Kaul Bamzai, *A History of Kashmir from Earliest Times to the Present Day*, 1973, p. 163–4.
46. Bazaz, *Struggle for Freedom*, p. 48–9.
47. Bamzai, *History of Kashmir*, p. 424.
48. Jonaraja, *Kings of Kashmira*, Vol III, p. 32, as quoted in Bazaz, *Struggle for Freedom*, p. 45.
49. Jonaraja *Kings of Kashmira*, Vol III, p. 32, as quoted in ibid., p. 48.
50. Kalhana, *Chronicle of Kings*, p. 130.
51. Jonaraja, *Kings of Kashmira*, Vol III, p. 59–60, as quoted in Bazaz, *Struggle for Freedom*, p. 53.
52. Bazaz, *Struggle for Freedom*, p. 53.
53. Ibid., p. 56.
54. N. K. Zutshi, *Sultan Zain-ul Abidin of Kashmir*, Jammu & Lucknow, 1976, p. 212.
55. Jonaraja, as quoted in Zutshi, *Sultan Zain-ul Abidin*, p. 222.
56. George Forster, as quoted in Bamzai, *History of Kashmir*, p. 452.
57. Zutshi, *Sultan Zain-ul Abidin*, p. 215.
58. Bazaz, *Struggle for Freedom*, p. 63.
59. Wakefield, *Happy Valley*, p. 193.
60. Parmu, *Muslim Rule in Kashmir*, p. 37.

Chapter 3

1. From G. L. Tikku, *Persian Poetry in Kashmir 1339–1846*, California, 1971, p. 159.
2. Kalhana, *Chronicle of Kings*, Vol. I, p. 131.
3. As quoted in Bhattacharjea, *Wounded Valley*, p. 41.
4. Henry Sender, *The Kashmiri Pandits*, Delhi, 1988, p. 29.
5. Dr Nizam-ud Din Wani, *Muslim Rule in Kashmir 1554–86*, Jammu, 1987, p. 125.
6. Abul Fazl, as quoted in *The History of the Sikhs*, Calcutta, 1846, p. 39–40.
7. Moore, *Lalla Rookh*, p. 260.

8. Younghusband, *Kashmir*, p. 139.

9. François Bernier, *Travels in the Mogul Empire, ad 1656–1668*, Delhi, 1969, p. 352.

10. Ibid., p. 400.

11. Ibid., p. 397.

12. Sender, *Kashmiri Pandits*, p. 2.

13. Ippolito Desideri, *An Account of Tibet*, London, 1932, p. 71–2.

14. Sender, *Kashmiri Pandits*, p. 34.

15. Bazaz, *Struggle for Freedom*, p. 111.

16. Ibid.

17. Ibid., p. 112.

18. Sender, *Kashmiri Pandits*, p. 44.

19. As quoted in Bhattacharjea, *Wounded Valley*, p. 46.

20. See Bhattacharjea, *Wounded Valley*, p. 46.

21. Baron Charles von Huegel, *Travels in Kashmir and the Panjab*, ed. T. B. Jervis, London, 1845, p. 106.

22. Lawrence, *Valley of Kashmir*, p. 197.

23. Sender, *Kashmiri Pandits*, p. 45.

24. Von Huegel, *Travels*, p. 7.

25. J. D. Cunningham, *History of the Sikhs*, London, 1849, p. 162.

26. Ibid., p. 164.

27. Godfrey Vigne, *Travels in Kashmir, Ladak, Iskardo*, 1842, Vol. 1, p. 254.

28. Lawrence, *Valley of Kashmir*, p. 198.

29. Saraf, *Kashmiris Fight*, Vol. I, p. 73.

30. Lawrence, *Valley of Kashmir*, p. 198.

31. Cunningham, *History of the Sikhs*, p. 169.

32. *The History of the Sikhs 1846*, p. 48.

33. Lawrence, *Valley of Kashmir*, p. 197–9.

34. Bamzai, *History of Kashmir*, p. 426.

35. Sender, *Kashmiri Pandits*, p. 45.

36. Kusum Pant, *The Kashmiri Pandit*, New Delhi, 1987, p. 15.

Chapter 4

1. Saraf, *Kashmiris Fight*, Vol. I, p. 141.

2. Von Huegel, *Travels in Kashmir and the Panjab*, p. xvi.

3. *The History of the Sikhs 1846*, p. 146.

4. Ibid., p. 150.

5. Bazaz, *Struggle for Freedom*, p. 117.

6. See Ibid., p. 118.

7. Saraf, *Kashmiris Fight*, Vol. 1, p. 119.

8. William Moorcroft, *Travels in the Himalayan Provinces of Hindustan and the Punjab*, London, 1841, p. 123.

9. Ibid., p. 124.

10. Ibid., p. 248.

11. Ibid., p. 294.

12. Ibid., p. 293.

13. Saraf, *Kashmiris Fight*, Vol. I, p. 121.

14. Ibid., p. 129.

15. Ibid., p. 121.
16. Vigne, *Travels*, Vol. 1, p. 281.
17. Victor Jacquemont, *Correspondance inédite, 1824–32*, Paris, 1867, p. 97.
18. Joseph Wolff, *Travels and Adventures*, London, 1861, p. 404.
19. Dewan Sharma, *Kashmir under the Sikhs*, Delhi, 1983, p. 4.
20. Vigne, *Travels*, Vol. I, p. 318-9.
21. Ibid., p. 317.
22. Ibid., p. 204.
23. Quoted in Vigne, *Travels*, Vol. I, p. 203.
24. Vigne, *Travels*, Vol. I, p. 257.
25. Von Huegel, *Travels*, p. 115.
26. Bazaz, *Struggle for Freedom*, p. 121.
27. Saraf, *Kashmiris Fight*, Vol. I, p. 65.
28. Ellenborough to Queen Victoria, 16 February 1844, *Punjab Papers*, ed. Bikrama Jit Hasrat, Punjab, 1970, p. 71.
29. K. M. Panikkar, *The Founding of the Kashmir State*, London, 1953, p. 16.
30. Ibid, p. 32.
31. *History of Sikhs, 1846*, p. 158.
32. Panikkar, *Kashmir State*, p. 38.
33. Victor Jacquemont, Correspondence, as quoted in Singh, *Jammu Fox*, p. 15.
34. Vigne, *Travels*, Vol. I, p. 184.
35. Ibid., p. 241.
36. As quoted in Singh, *Jammu Fox*, p. 189.
37. Vigne, *Travels*, Vol. I, p. 184.
38. Ibid., p. 218.
39. Singh, *Jammu Fox*, p. 39.
40. Vigne, *Travels*, Vol. I, p. 318.
41. Singh, *Jammu Fox*, p. 51.
42. Lepel Griffin, as quoted in Robert Thorp, *Cashmere Misgovernment*, London, 1870, p. 63.
43. Sir James Douie, *The Panjab, North-West Frontier Province & Kashmir*, Cambridge, 1916, p. 314.
44. Singh, *Jammu Fox*, p. 34.
45. H. B. Bayley to John Hobhouse, 11 January 1841, as quoted in Singh, *Jammu Fox*, p. 88.
46. George Clerk to Herbert Maddock, political secretary to Governor-General Auckland, as quoted in Singh, *Jammu Fox*, p. 89.
47. Herbert Edwardes & Herman Merivale, *Sir Henry Lawrence*, London, 1872, Vol. I, p. 324.
48. Henry Lawrence, as quoted in Panikkar, *Kashmir State*, p. 55.
49. Singh, *Jammu Fox*, p. 61.

Chapter 5

1. Sir Muhammad Iqbal, as quoted in Saraf, *Kashmiris Fight*, Vol. I, p. 201.
2. *History of the Sikhs 1846*, p. 185.
3. Major G. Carmichael Smyth, 1847, as quoted in Saraf, *Kashmiris Fight*, Vol. I, p. 171.

4. Hardinge, as quoted in Singh, *Jammu Fox*, p. 100.

5. Cunningham, *History of the Sikhs*, p. 304.

6. The acknowledged boundary between British and Sikh territory since 1809.

7. *The Times*, (no date given) as quoted in Singh, *Jammu Fox*, p. 109.

8. Lieutenant Edward Lake to Captain Mills, 'Enclosures to Secret Letters in India', Vol. 103, Enclosure 2, letter 59, L/P & S/5/184. Muhammad Saraf, M. J. Akbar and Ajit Bhattercharjea quote Khushwant Singh and attribute the message given by Lake to Gulab Singh, as Gulab Singh's message to the British. This is not correct.

9. Singh, *Jammu Fox*, p. 110.

10. 'Items of Lahore Intelligence', 30 January, dated 3 February 1846, ESLI, Vol. 103.

11. Hardinge, 31 January 1846, *Punjab Papers*, edited by Bikrama Jit Hasrat, Punjab, 1970, p. 101.

12. Colonel Gardner, as quoted in Saraf, *Kashmiris Fight*, p. 180.

13. *History of the Sikhs 1846*, p. 186.

14. Lionel Trotter, *History of the British Empire, 1844–1862*, London, 1866, Vol. I, p. 65.

15. Sir Hugh Gough, as quoted in Donald Featherstone, *Victorian Colonial Warfare: India*, London, 1992.

16. *History of the Campaign on the Sutlej & the War in the Punjaub, From Authentic Sources*, 2nd edition, London, 1846, p. 40–1.

17. *Campaign on the Sutlej*, p. 46.

18. Lord Hardinge to Queen Victoria, 19 Feb. 1846, in Younghusband, *Kashmir*, p. 153.

19. Lord Hardinge to the Secret Committee, 19 February 1846 as quoted in Bhattacharjea, *Wounded Valley*, p. 54.

20. W. Napier, *Life of Charles Napier*, as quoted in Singh, *Jammu Fox*, p. 119.

21. Herbert Edwardes, *Edwardes Memorials*, 24 September 1846, as quoted in Singh, *Jammu Fox*, p. 184.

22. Saraf, *Kashmiris Fight*, Vol. 1, p. 191.

23. Hardinge, 2 March 1846, *The Punjab Papers*, p. 104.

24. Lord Hardinge to Secret Committee, 14 March 1846, as quoted in Saraf, *Kashmiris Fight*, p. 192.

25. Viscount Hardinge, *Rulers of India: Hardinge*, Oxford, 1891, p. 132–3.

26. Trotter, *British Empire*, p. 72.

27. Treaty of Lahore, as quoted in *Enclosures to Secret Letters in India*, Vol. 103, enc. 2, letter 3.

28. Treaty of Amritsar, in Aitchinson, *A Collection of Treaties*, Vol. XII, Part 1, No. I, pp. 21–2 and Singh, *Jammu Fox*, Appendix B, p. 190–1.

29. *History of the Sikhs 1846*, p. 179.

30. See B. S. Singh, *Jammu Fox*, p. 119.

31. Hardinge as quoted in *Viscount Hardinge, Rulers of India*, Oxford 1891, p. 138.

32. Akbar, *Behind the Vale*, p. 59.

33. Hardinge to Ellenborough, 7 June 1846, *Punjab Papers*, p. 94.

34. Panikkar, *Kashmir State*, p. 100.

35. Mian Abdul Qayum, interview, Srinagar, 14 April 1994.

36. Henry Lawrence Collection, MSS Eur F. 85/6, Jan 1846–Feb 1847.

37. See Singh, *Jammu Fox*, Appendix C, p. 192.

38. Hardinge, *Rulers of India*.

39. Edwardes & Merivale, *Sir Henry Lawrence* p. 78.

40. Charles Napier, 2 November 1846, as quoted in Singh, *Jammu Fox*, p. 133.

41. Arthur Neve, *Thirty Years in Kashmir*, London, 1913, p. 252.

42. Henry Lawrence, *Collection*, p. 84.

43. Ibid., p. 95.

44. Lieutenant-Colonel Henry Torrens, *Travels in Ladak, Tartary & Kashmir*, London, 1862, p. 300.

45. Younghusband, *Kashmir*, p. 152.

46. Cunningham, *History of the Sikhs*, p. 330.

47. Thorp, *Cashmere Misgovernment*, p. 66.

48. Ibid., p. 60.

49. Younghusband, *Kashmir*, p. 165.

50. K. M. Teng, Bhatt, R. K. Kaul & S. Kaul, *Kashmir: Documents on Constitutional History*, India 1977, p. 16.

51. Ellenborough to the Duke of Wellington, 20 October 1843, *Punjab Papers*, p. 67–8.

52. Bazaz, *Struggle for Freedom*, p. 123.

53. Sheikh Abdullah, *Flames of the Chinar*, New Delhi, 1993, p. 79.

54. *Muslim Outlook*, 29 Sept 1925, in 'Documents Relating to the Death of the Maharaja of Kashmir', R1/1/1477 (2) OIOC.

Chapter 6

1. Edwardes, *Edwardes Memorials*, 1:73, 24 Sept 1846, as quoted in Singh, *Jammu Fox*, p. 166.

2. Bazaz, *Struggle for Freedom*, p. 127.

3. Torrens, *Travels*, London, 1862, p. 301.

4. Edwardes & Merivale, *Henry Lawrence*, p. 80.

5. The tradition of providing orphanages has been continued and a trust to supervise them is now run by the last maharaja's ADC, Captain Dewan Singh.

6. Henry Lawrence to George Lawrence, Henry Lawrence Collection, MSS EUR F 85 Jan 1846–Feb 1847, p. 239.

7. Ibid., 20 April 1847, p. 127.

8. Lieutenant Reynell Taylor, *Punjab Political Diaries*, p. 42, as quoted in Saraf, *Kashmiris Fight* Vol. I, p. 236.

9. See Singh, *Jammu Fox*, Appendix D, p. 193–4.

10. Sri Nandan Prasad, *Paramountcy under Dalhousie*, Delhi, 1964, p. 168.

11. Frederic Drew, *The Northern Barrier of India*, London, 1877, p. 44.

12. Lawrence, *Valley of Kashmir*, p. 201.

13. Lord Hardinge, as quoted in Saraf, *Kashmiris Fight*, p. 210.

14. Singh, *Jammu Fox*, p. 151.

15. Lord Dalhousie, *Punjab Papers*, ed. Bikrama Jit Hasrat, Punjab, 1970, p. 265.

16. George Clerk, as quoted in Edwardes & Merivale, *Henry Lawrence*, p. 60.

17. Marquess of Dalhousie to George Couper, 10 July 1849, *Private Letters*, ed. J. G. A. Baird, Blackwood, Edinburgh & London, 1910, p. 84.

18. Ibid., p. 100.

19. Lt Gen. Sir Charles James Napier, GCB, *Defects, Civil & Military of the Indian Government*, London, 1853, 27 November 1849, p. 371.

20. Napier, *Defects*, p. 401.

21. Ibid., p. 51.

22. Dalhousie, 6 January 1851, *Private Letters*, p. 150.

23. Lord Dalhousie, 'Dalhousie's Minute' p. 112, as quoted in Singh, *Jammu Fox*, p. 158.

24. Ibid., p. 179.

25. Ibid., p. 162.

26. Edwardes, *Edwardes Memorials*, as quoted in Singh, *Jammu Fox*, p. 162.

27. Adoption Sunnad to Maharajah Runbeer Singh, Cashmere, 5 March 1862, in C. V. Aitchinson, ed., *A Collection of Treaties, Engagements and Sanads*: Vol. XII, part 1, No. IV, Calcutta 1931, p. 26.

28. Torrens, *Travels*, p. 306.

29. Frederic Drew, *The Northern Barrier*, London, 1877, p. 47.

30. Colonel Ralph Young, *Journal of a Trip to Cashmere, 1867*, MSS Eur, B 133, p. 16.

31. Wakefield, *Happy Valley*, London, p. 88.

32. Lawrence, *Valley of Kashmir*, p. 202–3.

33. Torrens, *Travels*, p. 310.

34. Robert Thorp, *Cashmere Misgovernment*, Longmans, Green & Co. 1870, p. 8–9.

35. Saraf, *Kashmiris Fight*, p. 262.

36. See Alastair Lamb, *Kashmir: A Disputed Legacy*, 1846–1990, Roxford, Herts, 1991, p. 13.

37. Neve, *Thirty Years in Kashmir*, p. 30

38. Ibid., p. 37–8.

39. Lord Kimberley to the Government of India, as quoted in Lamb, *Disputed Legacy*, p. 13.

40. Major W. Sedgwick, *India for Sale: Kashmir Sold*, Calcutta, 1886, p. 29.

Chapter 7

1. Colonel Algernon Durand, *The Making of a Frontier*, London, 1900, p. 68.

2. Sedgwick, *India for Sale*, p. 23.

3. Lord Lytton as quoted in Garry Alder, 'British Policy on the Roof of the World, 1865–1895', PhD, University of Bristol, Sept. 1959, p. 227.

4. John Lawrence, as quoted in Madhavi Yasin, *British Paramountcy in Kashmir*, New Delhi, 1985, p. xvii.

5. Hemen Ray, *How Moscow Sees Kashmir*, Bombay, 1985, p. 3.

6. Lord Mayo, as quoted in Alder, 'Roof of the World', p. 193.

7. Lord Lytton, as quoted in Alder, 'Roof of the World', p. 209.

8. As recorded by Lieutenant Col. C. D. Ogilvie, 'Memorandum on the Future of the Gilgit Agency', 18 December 1930, L/P & S/12/3287, OIOC.

9. Lord Lytton, as quoted in Alder, 'Roof of the World', p. 235.

10. F. Henvey, 15 May 1880, as quoted in Alder, 'Roof of the World', p. 235.

11. Oglivie in *Memorandum on the Future of the Gilgit Agency*, 18 December 1930.

12. Teng, Kaul & Bhatt, *Documents*, p. 23.

13. Lamb, *Disputed Legacy*, p. 21.

14. Margaret Fisher, Leo E. Rose & Robert A. Huttenback, *Himalayan Battleground*, London, 1963, p. 63.

15. Lamb, *Disputed Legacy*, p. 24.

16. Fisher, Rose & Huttenback, *Himalayan Battleground*, p. 69.

17. Yasin, *British Paramountcy*, p. 131.

18. Akbar, *Behind the Vale*, p. 64.

19. Patrick French, *Sir Francis Younghusband*, London, 1994, p. 264.

20. Teng, Kaul & Bhatt, *Documents*, p. 27.

21. Lawrence, *Valley of Kashmir*, p. 2.

22. Ibid., p. 400.

23. Ibid., p. 3.

24. E. F. Knight, *Where Three Empires Meet*, London, 1893, p. 42.

25. Ibid., p. 44.

26. Lawrence, *Valley of Kashmir*, p. 4.

27. Parry Nisbet to Durand, 27 Feb. 1889, 'Maharaja's Edict', Teng, Kaul & Bhatt, *Documents*, p. 32–3.

28. William Digby, *Condemned Unheard*, in Teng, Kaul & Bhatt, *Documents*, p. 37.

29. See Dilip Ghose, *Kashmir in Transition*, Calcutta, 1975, p. 222.

30. Yasin, *British Paramountcy*, p. 79.

31. Durand, *Making of a Frontier*, p. 300.

32. Ibid., p. 66.

33. Ibid., p. 300.

34. Neve, *Thirty Years*, p. 139.

35. Durand, *Making of a Frontier*, p. 308.

36. As quoted in Knight, *Three Empires*, p. 361.

37. Ibid., p. 377.

38. Ibid., p. 381–2.

39. Ibid., p. 390.

40. Durand, *Making of a Frontier*, p. 344.

41. Dr Hugh Bixby Luard, 'Personal Memoirs, 1890–99', MSS. Eur. C 262, p. 105.

42. Durand, *Making of a Frontier*, p. 348.

43. See Dr Shanka Sanya, *The Boats and Boatmen of Kashmir*, New Delhi, 1979.

44. Iqbal Chapra, interview, Srinagar, April 1994.

45. Torrens, *Travels*, p. 266.

46. David Lockhart Lorimer, Lorimer Papers, MSS Eur.D 922, p. 29.

47. Ibid., p. 40.

48. French, *Younghusband*, p. 266.

49. Enriquez, *The Realm of the Gods*, p. 99.

50. Ernest F. Neve, *A Crusader in Kashmir*, London, 1928, p. 15.

51. Canon Tyndale-Biscoe, *Autobiography*, London, 1951, p. 52.

52. Neve, *Thirty Years*, p. 43.

53. Arthur Neve, *The Tourist's Guide to Kashmir, Ladakh, Skardo etc.*, Lahore 1938, p. vii.

54. C. E. Tyndale-Biscoe, *Elizabeth Mary Newman*, London 1933.

55. Knight, *Where Three Empires Meet*, p. 175.

56. Pratap Singh to Lord Lansdowne, in Teng, Kaul & Bhatt, *Documents*, p. 39.

57. Pratap Singh to Lord Minto, 27 May 1907, 'Adoption by the Maharaja of the Second Son of the Raja of Poonch', OIOC.

58. Pratap Singh to the Resident, in Teng, Kaul & Bhatt, *Documents*, p. 47.

59. Younghusband to Pratap Singh, ibid., p. 48.

60. Bazaz, *Struggle for Freedom*, p. 135.

61. Council Intelligence Dept, 10 June 1907, 'Sedition in Kashmir', Foreign Dept, OIOC.

62. Younghusband to E. Barnes, Asst Secr, 22 June 1907, ibid.

63. Ibid., 15 June 1907.

64. Col Ramsey, C.I.E., 'General Reports', 8 April 1910, R/1/1/879, OIOC.

65. Tyndale-Biscoe, *Autobiography*, p. 52.

66. Abdullah, *Flames*, p. 5.

67. Bazaz, *Struggle for Freedom*, p. 137.

68. Private note entitled 'Kashmir Affairs', to Hon J. B. Wood 15 Oct. 1917 in 'Documents Relating to a Suitable Occupation for Raja Hari Singh', For & Pol Dept, 1918, OIOC.

69. Rose to Hon J. B. Wood, Pol. Sec to the Gov of India, 19 Nov 1917, in ibid.

70. Montagu & Chelmsford, 'Report on Indian Constitutional Reform', 22 April 1918, MSS Eur C 264/42, OIOC, p. 141.

71. 'Kashmir Affairs', Rose to Hon J. B. Wood, Pol Sec to the Gov. of India, For & Pol Dept, 19 Nov 1917.

72. Quoted in Montagu & Chelmsford, 'Report', p. 5.

73. Ibid., p. 76.

74. Col Bannerman, Resident, to Foreign & Pol Dept, 16 August 1920 in 'Documents Relating to Raj Kumar Jagat Dev Singh', OIOC.

75. G. R. Lowndes, 16 Dec 1920, in ibid.

76. Maharaja Pratap Singh, 'Speech', in 'Kashmir Reforms Scheme, 1922', OIOC.

77. Colonel Windham to Political Secretary, 17 January 1922, ibid.

78. Sir John Wood, Resident, to For & Pol Dept, 25 July 1923, ibid.

79. Bazaz, *Struggle for Freedom*, p. 144.

80. Allama Iqbal as quoted in Abdullah, *Flames*, p. 3.

81. *Muslim Outlook*, 5 May 1923, quoted in *Punjab Press Abstract*, 12 May 1923, Crown Representatives' Records, OIOC.

82. Representation to the Viceroy, Lord Reading by Khadmans of Khanqah Muallah, Shah Hadman, Srinagar, 29 Sept 1924 quoted in 'Muslims of Kashmir', OIOC.

83. G. K. S. Fitze, to Syed Mohsin Shah, 1 July 1925, ibid.

84. Major Searle, 'Diary, 1924–5', MSS Eur A 165, OIOC, p. 27.

85. Britain and Afghanistan had fought a third war in 1919.

86. J. P. Thompson, pol sec, to Sir Denys Bray, for sec, 26 Sept. 1925, 'Documents Relating to the Death of His Highness the Maharaja of Kashmir', 1925, OIOC.

87. Telegram to Resident, 27 Sept 1925, ibid.

88. Letter from Gov. of India to Resident, 7 Oct. 1925, ibid.

Chapter 8

1. Abdullah, *Flames*, p. 13.

2. Ibid.

3. Saraf, *Kashmiris Fight*, p. 342–3.

4. A. H. Suhrawardy, interview, Rawalpindi, 24 March 1994.

5. As quoted in Saraf, *Kashmiris Fight*, Vol. I, p. 349.

6. Maharaja of Bikaner, *Round Table Conference*, Madras, 1931, p. 32.

7. Karan Singh, *Heir Apparent*, Oxford, 1982, p. 4.

8. Hari Singh in Teng, Bhatt & Kaul, *Documents*, p. 342.

9. Prem Nath Bazaz says that he made 'a violent speech advocating massacre of Hindus', *Struggle for Freedom*, p. 152.

10. Tyndale Biscoe, *Autobiography*, p. 237.

11. Abdullah, *Flames*, p. 24.

12. Ibid., p. 3.

13. Ibid., p. 9.

14. Ibid., p. 21.

15. Ibid., p. 10.

16. Ibid., p. 18.

17. Bilqees Taseer, *The Kashmir of Sheikh Abdullah*, Lahore, 1986, p. 18.

18. Abdullah, *Flames*, p. 25.

19. Bazaz, *Struggle for Freedom*, p. 162.

20. Abdullah, *Flames*, p. 38.

21. Bazaz, *Struggle for Freedom*, p. 164.

22. Saraf, *Kashmiris Fight*, p. 482.

23. Muhammad Iqbal, 'A Sincere Appeal to the Mussulmans of Kashmir', 1933, in 'Copies of Selected Documents relating to Sir Muhammad Iqbal', Photo Eur 209, 1909–34, OIOC.

24. Letter from Garbett, Punjab Civil Secretariat, to R. Wingate, 5 August 1933, in ibid.

25. As quoted in Akbar, *Behind the Vale*, p. 175.

26. Abdullah, *Flames*, p. 45.

27. Lieutenant Col C. D. Oglivie, 'Memorandum on the Future of the Gilgit Agency, 18 Dec 1930' L/P & S/12/3287, OIOC.

28. E. W. R. Lumby, *British Policy Towards the Indian States, 1940–7*, as quoted in *The Partition of India, Policies and Perspectives, 1935–1947*, ed. C. H. Philips & Mary Doreen Wainwright, London, 1970, p. 95; Lumby was assistant editor, India Office Records project on the transfer of power.

29. H. V. Hodson, *The Great Divide*, London, 1969, p. 57; Hodson was constitutional adviser to the Viceroy from 1941–42.

30. Abdullah, *Flames*, p. 47.

31. Sir Francis Wylie, *Federal Negotiations in India 1935–39 and After*, as quoted in *The Partition of India*, Philips & Wainwright, p. 521.

32. See Taseer, *Sheikh Abdullah*, p. 138.

33. Abdullah, as quoted in Bazaz, *Struggle for Freedom*, p. 168.

34. Bazaz, *Struggle for Freedom*, p. 169–70.

35. Ibid.

36. As quoted in Bazaz, *Struggle for Freedom*, p. 171.

37. As quoted in Akbar, *Behind the Vale*, p. 77.

38. Hodson, *The Great Divide*, p. 78.

39. As quoted in Hodson, *The Great Divide*, p. 79.

40. See Ayesha Jalal, *The Sole Spokesman*, Cambridge, 1985, p. 12 fn. 14.

41. Ibid., p. 208.

42. Gandhi, as quoted in Michael Edwardes, *The Last Years of British Empire*, London, 1969, p. 79.

43. Linlithgow to Amery, Secretary of State for India & Burma, *Transfer of Power*, ed. E. W. R. Lumby, Vol. II, Doc 633, p. 827.

44. Hodson, *Great Divide*, p. 111.

45. As quoted in Akbar, *Behind the Vale*, p. 84.

46. Inder Gujral, interview, New Delhi, 9 April 1994.

47. Pranay Gupte, *Mother India*, New York, 1992, p. 270. A footnote mentions the unsubstantiated rumour that Sheikh Abdullah was the illegitimate son of Motilal Nehru.

48. Congress Working Committee, 29 July–1 August 1935, as quoted in Akbar, *Behind the Vale*, p. 81.

49. Mohammad Ali Jinnah, 17 June 1947, *Speeches and Statements*, Government of Pakistan, 1989, p. 17.

50. Professor Zaidi, interview, Islamabad, April 1994.

51. Jinnah to Linlithgow, 30 September 1943, *Transfer of Power*, Vol. III, Doc 153, p. 338.

52. Abdullah, *Flames*, p. 59.

53. Ibid., p. 47.

54. Saraf, *Kashmiris Fight*, Vol. I, p. 623.

55. As quoted in Saraf, *Kashmiris Fight*, Vol. I, p. 624.

56. Jinnah quoted in ibid., p. 637.

57. Abdullah, as quoted in Akbar, *Behind the Vale*, p. 86.

58. K. H. Khurshid, *Memories of Jinnah*, ed. Khalid Hassan, Karachi, 1990, p. 13.

59. Saraf, *Kashmiris Fight*, Vol. I, p. 638.

60. Abdullah, *Flames*, p. 61.

61. Singh, *Heir Apparent*, p. 39.

62. Abdullah, *Flames*, p. 83.

63. See Sher Ali Pataudi, *The Elite Minority, The Princes of India*, Lahore, 1989, p. 1; 565 is normally given as the number of princely states, but it is also put at 584 or 562.

64. Abdullah, *Flames*, p. 78.

65. Abdullah, 'Quit Kashmir' speech, 26 May 1946, in Teng, Kaul & Bhatt, *Documents*, p. 528.

66. Bazaz, *Struggle for Freedom*, p. 186.

67. Mir Abdul Aziz, 14 March 1947, *Jinnah Papers*, Doc 128, p. 249.

68. Lamb, *Disputed Legacy*, p. 95.

69. Josef Korbel, *Danger in Kashmir*, Princeton, 1954 & 1966, p. 23.

70. Singh, *Heir Apparent*, p. 40.

71. Lamb, *Disputed Legacy*, p. 96.

72. Mohi-ud Din, 11 March 1947, *Jinnah Papers*, Doc 220, p. 114.

73. Shaukat Ali, 24 March 1947, *Jinnah Papers*, Doc 207, p. 383.

74. Singh, *Heir Apparent*, p. 41.

75. Ibid., p. 42.

76. Ibid., p. 53.

77. Ibid., p. 38.

Chapter 9

1. Mountbatten, as quoted in Michael Edwardes, *The Last Years of British India*, p. 89.

2. Hodson, *The Great Divide*, p. 83.

3. Wavell, *The Viceroy's Journal*, London, 1973, p. 199–200.

4. Attlee, quoted in Philip Ziegler, *Mountbatten*, London, 1985, p. 359.

5. Mountbatten, quoted in Hodson, *The Great Divide*, p. 289.

6. Mountbatten, quoted in ibid., p. 293.

7. Alan Campbell-Johnson, 'Address to Pakistan Society', 12 October 1995.

8. W. H. Morris-Jones, 'Thirty-six Years Later: the Mixed Legacies of Mountbatten's Transfer of Power', *International Affairs*, Autumn 1983, p. 624.

9. Ibid., p. 625; he was constitutional adviser to Mountbatten from June–August 1947.

10. Sir Conrad Corfield, *Some Thoughts on British Policy and the Indian States, 1935–47*, as quoted in Philips & Wainwright, *The Partition of India*, p. 531.

11. Nehru to Mountbatten, 17 June 1947, in *Transfer*, Vol. XI, Doc. 229, p. 443–4.

12. Mountbatten to Saraf, 3 November 1978, as quoted in *Kashmiris Fight*, Vol. II, p. 1395.

13. V. P. Menon, *The Story of the Integration of the Indian States*, Calcutta, 1956, p. 394.

14. Singh, *Heir Apparent*, p. 48.

15. Captain Dewan Singh, interview, Jammu, 11 April 1994.

16. Alan Campbell-Johnson, *Mission with Mountbatten*, London, 1977, p. 120.

17. Nehru to Mountbatten, 27 July 1947, in *Transfer*, Vol. XII, Doc. 249, p. 368.

18. Ismay, *The Memoirs of General the Lord Ismay*, London, 1960, p. 433.

19. Menon, *Integration*, p. 395.

20. Campbell-Johnson, *Mission*, p. 120.

21. Patel to Hari Singh, 3 July 1947, in *Patel Correspondence*, Vol. I, Doc. 34, p. 33.

22. Lord Mountbatten, *Time Only to Look Forward*, London, 1949, p. 52.

23. Mountbatten in *Transfer*, Vol. XI, Doc. 319, p. 593.

24. Mountbatten to Webb, 28 June 1947, *Transfer*, Vol. XI, Doc. 387, p. 720.

25. Viceroy's Report, 1 August 1947, No. 15, *Transfer*, Vol. XII, Doc. 302, p. 449.

26. Saraf, interview, Rawalpindi, March 1994.

27. Shahid Hamid, *Disastrous Twilight*, Great Britain 1986, p. 273.

28. Mir Abdul Aziz, interview, Rawalpindi, March 1994.

29. Mohammad Ali Jinnah, *India News*, 13 July 1947, in *Transfer of Power*, Vol. XII, Doc. 87, p. 128.

30. Mohammad Ali Jinnah, 17 June 1947, *Speeches and Statements*, p. 17.

31. Sir Walter Monckton to Lord Ismay, 9 June 1947, *Transfer*, Vol. XI, Doc. 112, p. 216.

32. Ismay to Mountbatten, 7 April 1948, Dr Kirpal Singh (ed.), *The Partition of the Punjab*, New Delhi, 1991, Doc. 238, p. 706.

33. Mountbatten, *Time Only*, p. 30.

34. Chaudhri Muhammad Ali, *The Emergence of Pakistan*, New York, 1967, p. 218–9.

35. Quoted in Hugh Tinker, 'Pressure, Persuasion, Decision: Factors in the Partition of the Punjab, August 1947', *The Journal of Asian Studies*, August 1977, p. 702.

36. Lord Wavell to Lord Pethick-Lawrence, 7 February 1946, *Transfer*, Vol. VI, Doc. 406, p. 912.

37. 'Draft Statement to be made by Parliamentary Spokesman', as quoted in Hugh Tinker, 'Pressure, Persuasion, Decision', p. 704.

38. Abell to Abbott, 8 August 1947, *The Partition of the Punjab, 1947*, Lahore, 1983, Vol. 1, Doc. 198, p. 245.

39. Ismay to Mountbatten, 7 April 1948, *Partition of the Punjab, 1947*, ed. Kirpal Singh, Delhi 1991, Doc. 238, p. 706.

40. Ali, *Emergence*, p. 213.

41. 'Report of the interview between Mountbatten and Nawab of Bhopal and Nawab of Mysore', 4 August 1947, *Transfer*, Vol. XII, Doc. 335 , p. 509.

42. Wavell, *Viceroy's Journal*, p. 384.

43. Letter to Peter Scott, 17 July 1947, *Transfer*, Vol. XII, Doc. 151, p. 214.

44. Lord Birdwood, *Two Nations and Kashmir*, London, 1956, p. 74.

45. Ali, *Emergence*, p. 215.

46. Akbar, *Behind the Vale*, p. 98.

47. Christopher Beaumont, correspondence with the author, 10/17 October 1995.

48. Campbell-Johnson, 'Address'.

49. Professor Zaidi, interview, Islamabad, April 1994.

50. Ibid.

51. Morris-Jones, 'Thirty-six Years Later', p. 628.

52. Suhrawardy, A. H., *Kashmir: The Incredible Freedom Fight*, Lahore, 1991, p. 36.

53. As quoted in ibid., p. 37.

54. Mountbatten to Listowel, 8 August 1947, *Transfer*, Vol. XII, Doc. 383, p. 586–7.

55. Singh, *Heir Apparent*, p. 55.

56. Lamb, *Birth of a Tragedy*, p. 52.

57. Viceroy's Personal Report, No. 17, *Transfer*, Vol. XII, Doc. 489, para 51, p. 757.

58. Menon, *Integration*, p. 395.

59. Suhrawardy, *Incredible Freedom Fight*, p. 25.

60. Muhummad Saraf, interview, April 1994.

61. See Korbel, *Danger in Kashmir*, p. 54.

62. Horace Alexander, *Kashmir*, Friends Peace Committee, London, 1953, p. 7.

63. Richard Symonds, as quoted in Korbel, *Danger in Kashmir*, p. 68.

64. Sardar Muhammad Ibrahim Khan, interview, Islamabad, 24 March 1994.

65. Sardar Abdul Qayum Khan, interview, Islamabad, March 1994.

66. Singh, *Heir Apparent*, p. 54.

67. George Cunningham, 23 September 1947, 'Diary', MSS Eur D 670/6, OIOC.

68. Alexander, *Kashmir*, p. 7.

69. Ian Stephens, *Pakistan*, London, 1963, p. 200.

70. Lamb, *Disputed Legacy*, p. 123.

71. Lamb, *Birth of a Tragedy*, p. 70.

72. Bhattacharjea, *Wounded Valley*, p. 177.

73. Korbel, *Danger in Kashmir*, p. 66.

74. Nehru to Patel, *Patel Correspondence*, 27 September 1947, Vol. I, Doc. 49, p. 45.

75. Abdullah, 'Speech at Huzoori Bagh', 2 October 1947, in *Flames*, p. 86.

76. Kachru to Nehru, 4 October 1947, *Patel Correspondence*, Vol. I, Doc. 57, enclosure, p. 54–5.

77. Patel to Nehru, 8 October 1948, ibid., Vol. 1, Doc. 58, p. 56.

78. Lamb, *Birth of a Tragedy*, p. 67.

79. Taseer, *Sheikh Abdullah*, pp. 50 & 271.

80. Abdullah, *Flames*, p. 88.

81. Recorded by Cunningham, 'Diary', 18 October 1947.

82. Mehr Chand Mahajan, *Looking Back*, London, 1963, p. 133.

83. Quaid-i Azam, Mohammad Ali Jinnah, *Speeches and Statements, 1947–48*, Government of Pakistan, 1989, p. 91–2; see also Korbel, *Danger in Kashmir*, p. 69–70.

84. Patel to Mahajan, 21 October 1947, *Patel Correspondence*, Vol. I, Doc. 65, p. 62.
85. Mahajan to Patel, 23 October 1947, ibid., Doc. 66, p. 63.
86. Press note, 23 October 1947, ibid., Vol. I, Doc. 67, p. 65.
87. As quoted in Taseer, *Sheikh Abdullah*, p. 145.
88. Faiz as quoted in ibid., p. 145.

Chapter 10

1. Singh, *Heir Apparent*, p. 57.
2. Maj-Gen Akbar Khan, *Raiders in Kashmir*, Karachi, 1970, p. 11.
3. Sardar Muhammad Ibrahim, interview, Islamabad, 24 March 1994.
4. Akbar Khan, *Raiders*, p. 17.
5. Sir George Cunningham, 15 October 1947, Diary, MSS Eur D 670/6, OIOC; Cunningham is probably referring to the Pakistan National Guard set up on 7 October under Major-General Shahid Hamid as a voluntary force to supplement the Pakistani armed forces. 'Many' units took part in the Kashmir operations; see Shahid Hamid, *Early Years of Pakistan*, Lahore, 1993, p. 62.
6. Cunningham, 'Diary', 20 October 1947.
7. Ibid., 22 October 1947.
8. Stephens, *Pakistan*, p. 202.
9. Alexander, *Kashmir*, p. 8.
10. Ayesha Jalal, *The State of Martial Rule*, Cambridge, 1990, p. 58.
11. Professor H. Zaidi, interview, Islamabad, 18 April 1994.
12. Muhammad Saraf, interview, Rawalpindi, March 1994; *Kashmiris Fight*, Vol. 2, p. 988.
13. K. H. Khurshid as quoted in Rajendra Sareen, *Pakistan: The India Factor*, New Delhi, 1984, p. 221.
14. Cunningham, 'Diary', 26 October 1947
15. See Bhattacharjea, *Wounded Valley*, p. 136.
16. Menon, *Integration of the Indian States*, p. 410.
17. *Dawn*, 7 December 1947.
18. Lamb, *Disputed Legacy*, p. 131.
19. Menon, *Integration of the Indian States*, p. 397.
20. There are conflicting reports on whether or not this was because of an attack by the tribesmen.
21. Korbel, *Danger in Kashmir*, p. 77.
22. Singh, *Heir Apparent*, p. 57.
23. Campbell-Johnson, *Mission with Mountbatten*, p. 224.
24. Gopal, *Nehru*, p. 19.
25. Menon, *Integration of the Indian States*, p. 397–8.
26. Captain Dewan Singh, interview, Jammu, 11 April 1994.
27. Singh, *Heir Apparent*, p. 59.
28. Mehr Chand Mahajan, *Looking Back*, London, 1963, p. 151.
29. Indian White Paper, 3 March 1948, in 'Kashmir, Internal Situation', L/P & S/13, OIOC.
30. Menon, *Integration of the Indian States*, p. 400; Captain Dewan Singh, interview, Jammu, April 1994.
31. Dewan Singh, interview, Jammu, April 1994.

32. Menon, *Integration of the Indian States*, p. 400.

33. *Documents on Kashmir Problem*, Vol. XIV, New Delhi, 1991, as quoted in Bhattacharjea, *Wounded Valley*, p. 150.

34. Korbel, *Danger in Kashmir*, p. 84.

35. Mahajan, *Looking Back*, p. 152.

36. Ibid. p. 154.

37. Lamb, *Birth of a Tragedy*, p. 96.

38. Collins and Lapierre say the journey took seventeen hours; see *Freedom at Midnight*, p. 355.

39. Singh, *Heir Apparent*, p. 58–9.

40. Mahajan, *Looking Back*, p. 152.

41. Ibid., p. 150.

42. Ibid., p. 276; see also Campbell-Johnson, *Mission with Mountbatten*, p. 224.

43. Collins & Lapierre, *Freedom at Midnight*, p. 356.

44. Alexander Symon to Sir Archibald Carter, 27 October 1947 in 'Kashmir Internal Situation', L/P&S/13, OIOC.

45. *Selected Works of Jawaharlal Nehru*, Vol. 4, 2nd edition, ed S. Gopal, New Delhi, 1986, p. 278.

46. B. G. Verghese, 'Lamb's Tales from Kashmir', *Sunday Mail*, 14–20 June 1992, as quoted in *The Kashmir Issue*, High Commission of India, London, 1993, p. 155.

47. See Lamb, *Birth of a Tragedy*, p. 99–100.

48. Ibid., p. 102–3.

49. Korbel, *Danger in Kashmir*, p. 79.

50. Ziegler, *Mountbatten*, p. 446.

51. Quoted in Korbel, *Danger in Kashmir*, p. 76.

52. Major Khurshid Anwar's account, as reported in *Dawn*, 7 December 1947.

53. Cunningham, 'Diary', 10 November 1947.

54. Brigadier L. P. Sen, as quoted in Rajesh Kadian, *The Kashmir Tangle*, New Delhi, 1992, p. 93.

55. Stephens, *Pakistan*, p. 202.

56. Muhammad Saraf, interview, Rawalpindi, March 1994.

57. Prem Nath Bazaz, *Azad Kashmir*, Lahore, p. 33.

58. Commonwealth Relations Office Note, 1 December 1947, in 'Kashmir Internal Situation', L/P. &S/13, OIOC.

59. Mahajan to Mountbatten, 27 October 1947. *Patel Correspondence*, Vol. I, Doc. 70, p. 69.

60. Hamid, *Disastrous Twilight*, p. 278.

61. Cunningham, 'Diary', 28 October 1947.

62. Ibid., 7 November 1947.

63. Ali, *Emergence*, p. 293.

64. Mountbatten to Nehru, 2 November 1947, *Patel Correspondence*, Vol. I, Doc 72, p. 71–81.

65. Liaquat Ali Khan to Nehru, *White Paper on Jammu and Kashmir*, as quoted in Korbel, *Danger in Kashmir*, p. 96.

66. As quoted in Menon, *Integration of the Indian States*, p. 406.

67. Ibid., p. 400.

68. 'Status of Hunza, Nagar and Political Districts', OIOC.

69. Menon, *Integration of the Indian States*, p. 393.

70. Chenevix-Trench, *Frontier Scouts*, p. 273.

71. Major William Brown, as quoted in *The Scotsman*, 22 March 1994.

72. Chenevix-Trench, *Frontier Scouts*, p. 276.

73. Major William Brown, as quoted in *The Scotsman*, 22 March 1994.

74. Chenevix-Trench, *Frontier Scouts*, p. 269.

75. Muhammad Saraf, interview, Rawalpindi, 24 March 1994.

76. Arif Aslam Khan, interview, en route to Baltistan, 17 April 1995.

77. Menon, *Integration of the Indian States*, p. 410.

78. Mountbatten, quoted in Hodson, *The Great Divide*, p. 462–3.

79. Mountbatten, quoted in ibid., p. 465.

80. Commonwealth Relations Office, note, 1 December 1947, in Kashmir Internal Situation', L/P&S/13, OIOC.

81. British High Commissioner's opdom No. 3, 8 January 1948, as quoted in Jalal, *State of Martial Law*, p. 58.

82. *Times*, 13 Jan 1948, quoted in Korbel, *Danger in Kashmir*, p. 84.

83. Akbar Khan, *Raiders*, p. 13. The INA fought against the British in World War II.

84. *Dawn*, 7 December 1947.

85. Akbar Khan, *Raiders*, p. 100.

86. Eas Bokhari, *Kashmir Operations 1947–48*, ISPR forum, Lahore, August 1990.

87. En route to Leh, April 1995.

88. Nehru to Patel, 30 May 1948, *Patel Correspondence*, Vol. I, Doc 152, p. 190–1.

89. Patel to Nehru, 4 June 1948, ibid., Vol. I, Doc 153, p. 192–3.

90. Patel to Ayyangar, 4 June 1948, ibid., Vol. 1, Doc 156, p. 199.

91. Sher Ali Pataudi, *The Story of Soldiering and Politics*, Lahore, 1988, p. 119.

92. General Sher Ali Pataudi, interview, Islamabad, 14 April 1995.

93. Mountbatten, as quoted in Hodson, *The Great Divide*, p. 465.

94. Hodson, *The Great Divide*, p. 466

95. Jawaharlal Nehru, as quoted in Korbel, *Danger in Kashmir*, p. 98.

96. Sir Zafrullah Khan, 'Speech to Security Council', 16 January 1948, as quoted in Khan, *Troubled Frontiers*, p. 281.

97. See Gopal, *Nehru*, Vol. II, p. 23.

98. V. Shankar, unpublished memoirs, p. 607.

99. *Patel Correspondence*, 3 July 1948, Vol. VI, Doc. 327, p. 387.

100. Resolution 39, 20 January 1948, Doc No S/654, quoted in *Kashmir in the Security Council*, Government of Pakistan, Islamabad, p. 2.

101. Resolution 47, 21 April 1948, Doc S/726, quoted in *Kashmir in the Security Council*, p. 7.

102. Resolution, 13 August 1947, Doc No S/1100, dated 9 November 1948, quoted in *Kashmir in the Security Council*.

103. Nehru to Patel, 27 October 1948, *Patel Correspondence*, Vol. VII, Doc. 576, p. 665.

104. Resolution, 5 January 1949, Doc No S/1196, dated 10 January 1949, as quoted in *Kashmir in the Security Council*, p. 16.

105. Akbar Khan, *Raiders*, p. 155.

106. Colonel Abdul Haq Mirza, *The Withering Chinar*, Islamabad, 1991, p. 173.

107. Pataudi, *Soldiering*, p. 119–120.

108. Menon, *Integration of the Indian States*, p. 412.

109. Kashmir Papers, Reports of the United Nations Commission for India and

Pakistan, June 1948–December 1949, Government of India, New Delhi, 1952.
110. As quoted in UN Commission's Report, Government of India, 1952.

Chapter 11

1. Singh, *Tragedy of Errors*, p. xi.
2. Captain Dewan Singh, interview, Jammu, 11 April 1994.
3. Quoted in Akbar, *Behind the Vale*, p. 135.
4. Singh, *Heir Apparent*, p. 83.
5. Nehru, IV, p. 325, as quoted in Bhattacharjea, *Wounded Valley*, p. 166 and Singh, *Heir Apparent*, p. 83.
6. Nehru to Mahajan, 1 Dec 1947, *Patel's Correspondence*, Vol. I, Doc. 88, p. 101.
7. Singh, *Heir Apparent*, p. 85.
8. Mahajan to Patel, 24 Dec 1947, *Patel's Correspondence*, Vol. I, Doc. 103, p. 128.
9. Mahajan to Patel, 11 Dec 1947, ibid., Vol. I, Doc. 92, p. 113.
10. Hari Singh to Patel, 31 Jan 1948, ibid., Vol. I, Doc. 124, p. 162–3.
11. Patel to Hari Singh, 9 Feb 1948, ibid., Vol. I, Doc. 127, p. 166.
12. Nehru to V Shankar, private secretary to Sardar Patel, 3 April 1948, ibid., Vol. I, Doc. 138, p. 175.
13. Nehru to Patel, 12 May 1948, ibid., Vol. 1, Doc 149, p. 189.
14. Nehru to Patel, 5 June 1948, ibid., Vol. I, Doc. 157, p. 200.
15. Hari Singh to Patel, 9 September 1948, ibid., Vol. I, Doc. 180, p. 225.
16. Singh, *Heir Apparent*, p. 92.
17. Quoted in Singh, *Heir Apparent*, p. 96.
18. Captain Dewan Singh, interview, Jammu, 11 April 1994.
19. Singh, *Heir Apparent*, p. 101.
20. Ibid., p. 104.
21. Abdullah, *Flames*, p. 108.
22. As quoted in Akbar, *Behind the Vale*, p. 137.
23. Akbar, *Behind the Vale*, p. 139.
24. See Bhattacharjea, *Wounded Valley*, p. 181, note 26.
25. Taseer, *Sheikh Abdullah*, p. 51.
26. Ayyangar, as quoted in Abdullah, *Flames*, p. 113.
27. Krishan Mohan Teng & Santosh Kaul, *Kashmir's Special Status*, Delhi, 1975, p. 45.
28. Patel to Nehru, 27 June 1950, *Patel Correspondence*, Vol. X, Doc. 247, p. 353.
29. Patel to Nehru, 3 July 1948, ibid., Vol. X, Doc. 250, p. 357.
30. Abdullah, as quoted in Teng & Kaul, *Kashmir's Special Status*, Appendix IV, p. 198.
31. Sheikh Abdullah, 10 April 1952, Ranbir Singhpura, Jammu, as quoted in Balraj Puri, *Triumph and Tragedy*, New Delhi, 1981, p. 99.
32. Abdullah, *Flames*, p. 118.
33. Balraj Puri, *Kashmir: Towards Insurgency*, London, 1993, p. 27.
34. Balraj Puri, *Jammu: A Clue to the Kashmir Tangle*, Delhi, 1966, p. 7–8.
35. Puri, *Triumph and Tragedy*, p. 94.
36. Puri, *Jammu*, p. 11.
37. Lamb, *Disputed Legacy*, p. 197.
38. Puri, *Kashmir Tangle*, p. 93.
39. Ibid., p. 98.
40. Janet Rizvi, *Ladakh*, Oxford, 1983, p. 70.

41. Abdullah, *Flames*, p. 121.

42. As quoted in P. S. Verma, *Jammu and Kashmir at the Political Crossroads*, New Delhi, 1994, p. 42.

43. Puri, *Triumph & Tragedy*, p. 93.

44. Singh, *Heir Apparent*, p. 92.

45. Patel to Nehru, 27 June 1950, *Patel Correspondence*, Vol. X, Doc. 247, p. 353.

46. Gopal, *Nehru*, Vol. II, p. 90.

47. Letter dated 15 September 1950 from Sir Owen Dixon to the Security Council quoted in Korbel, *Danger in Kashmir*, p. 172–3.

48. Resolution 91 (1951) Doc No S/2017/REV.I, quoted in *Kashmir in the Security Council*.

49. Korbel, *Danger in Kashmir*, p. 179.

50. Jalal, *The State of Martial Law*, p. 120.

51. Ibid., p. 117.

52. Ibid., p. 132.

53. Nehru to Bakshi Ghulam Muhammed, 18 August 1953, quoted in Gopal, *Nehru*, Vol. II, p. 182.

54. Gowher Rizvi, 'Nehru and the Indo–Pakistan Rivalry over Kashmir', *Contemporary South Asia*, March 1995, Vol. IV, No. 1, p. 27.

55. Nehru to Muhammed Ali Bogra, 10 November 1953, as quoted in Gopal, *Nehru*, Vol. II, p. 185.

56. Nirad C. Chaudhri, as quoted in Sam Burke, *Mainsprings of Indian and Pakistani Foreign Policies*, Minneapolis, 1974, p. 143.

57. Jain, ed. *Soviet–South Asian Relations*, Vol. I, p. 4.

58. Khrushchev, as quoted in Abdullah, *Flames*, p. 134.

59. Burke, *Indian and Pakistani Foreign Policies*, p. 148.

60. B. L. Kak, *The Fall of Gilgit*, New Delhi, 1977, p. 31.

61. Stanley Wolpert, *Zulfi Bhutto of Pakistan*, Oxford, 1993, p. 64.

62. Louis D. Hayes, *The Impact of U.S. Policy on the Kashmir Conflict*, Texas, 1971. p. 28.

63. The Karakoram highway was opened in 1978.

64. Resolution 126, 2 December 1957, quoted in *Kashmir in the Security Council*, p. 38.

65. Morozov, 21 June 1962, as quoted in Jain, *Soviet–South Asian Relations*, Vol. 1, p. 45.

66. Leo Rose, 'The Politics of Azad Kashmir', in *Perspectives on Kashmir*, ed. Raju G. C. Thomas, Colorado, 1992, p. 237.

67. Saraf, *Kashmiris Fight*, Vol. II, p. 1289–90.

68. Mir Abdul Aziz, interview, 24 March 1994.

69. Rose, 'The Politics of Azad Kashmir', p. 238.

70. Korbel, *Danger in Kashmir*, p. 200.

71. See Ian Stephens, *Horned Moon*, London, 1953, p. 138.

72. Saraf, *Kashmiris Fight*, Vol. II, p. 1294.

73. Lamb, *Disputed Legacy*, p. 189.

74. Abdullah, 10 April 1952, as quoted in Saraf, *Kashmiris Fight*, Vol. II, p. 1200.

75. Abdullah, *Flames*, p. 122.

76. See Puri, *Towards Insurgency*, p. 20.

77. Verma, *Crossroads*, p. 46.

78. Abdullah, *Flames*, p. 127.

79. Singh, *Heir Apparent*, p. 160.
80. Gopal, *Nehru*, p. 133.
81. Nehru to G. S. Bajpai, 30 July 1953, as quoted in Gopal, *Nehru*, p. 132.
82. See Lamb, *Disputed Legacy*, p. 199.
83. *The Times*, 8 May 1952, as quoted in Taseer, *Abdullah*, p. 148.
84. Stephens, *Horned Moon*, p. 210–11.
85. Taseer, *Abdullah*, p. 23.
86. Kak, *Fall of Gilgit*, p. 27.
87. *New York Times*, 28/30 July 1955, as quoted in Korbel, *Danger in Kashmir*, p. 319.
88. Abdullah, *Flames*, p. 128.
89. Abdullah, February 1958, as quoted in Lamb, *Disputed Legacy*, p. 203.
90. As quoted in Korbel, *Danger in Kashmir*, 1966, p. 322.
91. Saraf, *Kashmiris Fight*, Vol. II, p. 1322.
92. Excerpts from Sheikh Abdullah's latest statements, *Kashmir & the Peoples Voice*, 1964.
93. Abdullah, *Flames*, p. 143.
94. *Daily Express*, 5 February 1957, as quoted in Saraf, *Kashmiris Fight*, Vol. II, p. 1226.
95. Mir Qasim, p. 82, as quoted in Verma, *Crossroads*, p. 52.
96. Nehru as quoted in Gopal, *Nehru*, Vol. 3 1956–1964, p. 262.
97. Prem Nath Bazaz, *The Shape of Things in Kashmir*, New Delhi, 1965.

Chapter 12

1. John Kenneth Galbraith, US Ambassador in New Delhi, 19 January 1963, as quoted in Altaf Gauhar, *Ayub Khan*, Lahore, 1993, p. 227 fn. 41.
2. Burke, *Indian and Pakistani Foreign Policies*, p. 187.
3. Nehru, quoted in Gopal, *Nehru*, Vol. III, p. 223.
4. Burke, *Indian and Pakistani Foreign Policies*, p. 166, p. 169.
5. President Kennedy, as quoted in Gauhar, *Ayub Khan*, p. 215 fn. 28.
6. Kak, *Fall of Gilgit*, p. 43.
7. Gopal, *Nehru*, Vol. III, p. 256.
8. Ziegler, *Mountbatten*, p. 601.
9. Kak, *Fall of Gilgit*, p. 47.
10. Gopal, *Nehru*, p. 258.
11. James, *Pakistan Chronicle*, p. 97.
12. State Department telegram, dated 9 March 1963, as quoted in James, *Pakistan Chronicle*, p. 96.
13. Rostow was chairman of the Policy Planning Council at the US State Department; see James, *Pakistan Chronicle*, p. 98.
14. See Sisir, Gupta, *Kashmir: A Study of India–Pakistan Relations*, London, 1966, p. 355.
15. James, *Pakistan Chronicle*, p. 102.
16. See James, *Pakistan Chronicle*, p. 101.
17. Kak, *Fall of Gilgit*, p. 48–9.
18. Zulfikar Ali Bhutto, as quoted in Wolpert, *Bhutto*, p. 74.
19. Amanullah Khan, interview, Rawalpindi, April 1995.
20. Zulfikar Ali Bhutto, as quoted in Wolpert, *Bhutto*, p. 77.
21. Document dated 18 May 1964, S/PV 1117, *Kashmir in the Security Council*, p. 42.

22. Bazaz, *The Shape of Things in Kashmir*.
23. *Observer*, 16 December 1960, as quoted in Abdullah, *Flames*, p. 144.
24. Abdullah, *Flames*, p. 144.
25. Sheikh Abdullah, reported by *The Times of India*, 10 April 1964, as quoted in *Kashmir and the Peoples Voice*.
26. Krishna Menon, 13 April 1964, as quoted in ibid.
27. *Indian Express*, editorial, 13 April 1964, as quoted in ibid.
28. *The Times of India*, editorial, 16 April 1964, as quoted in ibid.
29. Gopal, *Nehru*, p. 264.
30. Abdullah, *Flames*, p. 152.
31. Ibid., p. 154.
32. Gauhar, *Ayub Khan*, p. 257.
33. Ibid., p. 260.
34. Ibid., p. 265.
35. Abdullah, *Flames*, p. 155.
36. James, *Pakistan Chronicle*, p. 114.
37. See Wolpert, *Bhutto*, p. 78.
38. Abdullah, *Flames*, p. 157.
39. Ibid., p. 158.
40. Abdullah, as quoted in Burke, *Indian and Pakistani Foreign Policy*, p. 186.
41. Abdullah, *Flames*, p. 160.
42. Burke, *Indian and Pakistani Foreign Policy*, p. 186–7.
43. Gauhar, *Ayub Khan*, p. 290.
44. Johnson was annoyed that Pakistan's US Patton tanks were moving towards the Indo–Pakistani border. They had been sold to Pakistan on the understanding that they would not be used against India.
45. Gauhar, *Ayub Khan*, p. 301.
46. James, *Pakistan Chronicle*, p. 126.
47. Ibid., p. 129.
48. Gauhar, *Ayub Khan*, p. 312.
49. Shahid Hamid, *Early Years of Pakistan*, Lahore, 1993, p. 177.
50. Gauhar, *Ayub Khan*, p. 493.
51. Karim, *Troubled Frontiers*, p. 80.
52. Lamb, *Disputed Legacy*, p. 261.
53. Gauhar, *Ayub Khan*, p. 326.
54. Hamid, *Early Years of Pakistan*, p. 177.
55. Ayub Khan, 29 August 1965, as quoted in Wolpert, *Bhutto*, p. 90.
56. Akbar, *Behind the Vale*, p. 171.
57. Gauhar, *Ayub Khan*, p. 330.
58. Ibid., p. 334.
59. James, *Pakistan Chronicle*, p. 136.
60. Burke, *Indian and Pakistani Foreign Policy*, p. 190.
61. James, *Pakistan Chronicle*, p. 141.
62. Gauhar, *Ayub Khan*, p. 342.
63. As quoted in Gauhar, *Ayub Khan*, p. 347.
64. See James, *Pakistan Chronicle*, p. 144.
65. *The Times*, London, 18 Sept 1965 as quoted in Gauhar, *Ayub Khan*, p. 348.
66. Gauhar, Ayub Khan, p. 352–3.

67. Hamid, *Early Years of Pakistan*, p. 184.
68. Zulfikar Ali Bhutto, 22/23 Sept 1965, as quoted in Wolpert, *Bhutto*, p. 94.
69. James, *Pakistan Chronicle*, p. 150.
70. Korbel, *Danger in Kashmir*, p. 347.
71. James, *Pakistan Chronicle*, p. 166.
72. Feldman, *From Crisis to Crisis*, p. 159.
73. James, *Pakistan Chronicle*, p. 157.
74. *Dawn*, 16 March 1966, as quoted in Gauhar, *Ayub Khan*, p. 404.
75. See Maleeha Lodhi, 'Bhutto, the Pakistan Peoples Party and Political Development in Pakistan, 1967–77', PhD Econ, 1981, London School of Economics.
76. Justice Abdul Majeed Mallick, interview, Mirpur, 30 March 1995.
77. *Washington Post*, 14 August 1965, as quoted in Korbel, *Danger in Kashmir*, 1966, p. 341.
78. Inder Gujral, interview, New Delhi, 9 April 1994.
79. Dharma Vira, interview, New Delhi, April 1994.
80. Saraf, *Kashmiris Fight*, Vol. II, p. 1378.
81. Amanullah Khan, interview, Rawalpindi, March 1994.
82. Maqbool Butt, as quoted in B. L. Kak, *The Untold Story of Men and Matters*, Jammu, 1987, p. 76.
83. Kak, *Untold Story*, p. 77.
84. Saraf, *Kashmiris Fight*, Vol. II, p. 1379.
85. Jai Prakash Narayan, confidential letter to Mrs Gandhi, 26 June 1966, as quoted in Akbar, *Behind the Vale*, p. 183.
86. As quoted in Verma, *Crossroads*, p. 53.
87. See Lamb, *Disputed Legacy*, p. 290–4.
88. Amanullah Khan, interview, Rawalpindi, March 1994.
89. Akbar, *Behind the Vale*, p. 173.
90. Inder Malhotra, *Indira Gandhi*, London, 1989, p. 133.
91. J. N. Dixit, interview, New Delhi, April 1994.
92. Gandhi to Nixon, 15 Dec 1971, in Indira Gandhi, *India*, London 1975, p. 173.
93. Simla is now written Shimla; I have retained the original spelling as it was at the time of the agreement.
94. White Paper, 1977, as quoted in Lamb, *Disputed Legacy*, p. 27.
95. Simla agreement, sub-clause 4 (ii), as quoted in Lamb, *A Disputed Legacy*, p. 297 and other publications.
96. T. N. Kaul, *Sunday Times of India*, 17 October 1993.
97. Zulfikar Ali Bhutto, *If I am Assassinated*, New Delhi, 1979, p. 130.
98. Ibid., p. 131.
99. P. N. Dhar, *The Times of India*, 4 April 1995.
100. J. N. Dixit, *The Times of India*, 7 April 1995.
101. Saraf, interview, March 1994.
102. P. N. Haksar, telephone interview, New Delhi, April 1995.
103. Bhattacharjea, *Wounded Valley*, p. 232–3.
104. Girish Saxena, interview, New Delhi, 16 April 1994.
105. Z. A. Bhutto, speech in the National Assembly, as quoted in the *Pakistan Times*, 19 July 1972.
106. Farooq visited Pakistan during negotiations for the Kashmir accord.
107. Farooq Abdullah, as quoted in Akbar, *Behind the Vale*, p. 186.

108. Farooq Abdullah, interview, Srinagar, 5 April 1995.
109. Wolpert, *Bhutto*, p. 192.
110. Interview, Muzaffarabad, March 1994.
111. Figures from *Azad Kashmir at a Glance, 1993*, Planning & Development Dept, Azad Govt of the State of Jammu and Kashmir.
112. Farooq Abdullah, interview, Srinagar, 5 April 1995.
113. Rose, 'The Politics of Azad Kashmir', p. 241.
114. Sheikh Abdullah, *Hindustan Times*, 5 March 1972 in Verma, *Crossroads*, p. 122.
115. Mir Qasim, *Hindustan Times*, 18 March 1972, ibid., p. 122.
116. Mir Qasim, *My Life and Times*, New Delhi, 1992, p. 132.
117. Sheikh Abdullah, interview with *The Times*, London, 8 March 1972, as quoted in Bhattacharjea, *Wounded Valley*, p. 234.
118. Sheikh Abdullah, *Flames*, p. 164.
119. Ibid., p. 165.
120. Akbar, *Behind the Vale*, p. 188.
121. Kashmir accord, as quoted in Verma, *Crossroads*, p. 58 Saraf, *Kashmiris Fight*, Vol. II, p. 1276.
122. Verma, *Crossroads*, p. 57.
123. Lamb, *Disputed Legacy*, p. 309.
124. See Akbar, *Behind the Vale*, p. 189.
125. Mir Qasim, *My Life and Times*, p. 145.
126. Prem Nath Bazaz, as quoted in Lamb, *Disputed Legacy*, p. 312.
127. Sheikh Abdullah, *Flames*, p. 168.
128. Verma, *Crossroads*, p. 129; interviews with APHC in Islamabad, March 1995.
129. Interview, Muzaffarabad, March 1994.
130. Ali, interview, Srinagar, March 1981.
131. Verma, *Crossroads*, p. 62.
132. Azam Inquilabi, interview, Islamabad, April 1994.

Chapter 13

1. Sheikh Abdullah, Iqbal Park, 21 August 1981, as quoted in Akbar, *Behind the Vale*, p. 197.
2. Farooq Abdullah, 24 September 1989, as quoted in Puri, *Towards Insurgency*, p. 57.
3. Bhutto was executed on 4 April 1979 on a charge of conspiracy to murder a political opponent.
4. Sheikh Abdullah, as quoted in Singh, *Tragedy of Errors*, p. 16.
5. Singh, *Tragedy of Errors*, p. 18.
6. Bhattacharjea, *Wounded Valley*, p. 241.
7. Singh, *Tragedy of Errors*, p. 19.
8. Ibid., pp. 20–2.
9. As quoted in Taseer, *Sheikh Muhammad Abdullah*, Lahore, p. 67.
10. Prime Minister Sardar Abdul Qayum, interview, Islamabad, 25 March 1994.
11. Amanullah Khan, interview, Rawalpindi, 24 March 1944.
12. Singh, *Tragedy of Errors*, p. 24.
13. Mir Abdul Aziz, interview. Rawalpindi, 24 March 1994.
14. M. J. Akbar, *Behind the Vale*, p. 199.

15. When Indira Gandhi broke with the old guard of the Congress Party in 1969 it split into several factions. In 1978 she formed her own party, known as Congress(I) i.e. Indira.

16. Farooq Abdullah, interview, New Delhi, April 1994.

17. Singh, *Tragedy of Errors*, p. 34.

18. Ibid., p. 30.

19. Inder Malhotra, *Indira Gandhi*, London, 1989, p. 278.

20. Supporters of the Mirwaiz were called 'goats' because of the tradition of wearing a beard.

21. Akbar, *Behind the Vale*, p. 202.

22. Ibid., p. 205.

23. Verma, *Crossroads*, p. 129 & 143.

24. Tavleen Singh, interview, New Delhi, April 1994.

25. Singh, *Tragedy of Errors*, p. 38.

26. Ibid., p. 40.

27. Malhotra, *Indira Gandhi*, p. 279.

28. Bhattacharjea, *Wounded Valley*, p. 245.

29. Akbar, *Behind the Vale*, p. 207.

30. Ibid., p. 206.

31. Singh, *Tragedy of Errors*, p. 53.

32. Bhattacharjea, *Wounded Valley*, p. 246.

33. Singh, *Tragedy of Errors*, p. 54.

34. Malhotra, *Indira Gandhi*, p. 295.

35. Bhattacharjea, *Wounded Valley*, p. 248.

36. Singh, *Tragedy of Errors*, p. 68.

37. Jagmohan, *Frozen Turbulence*, p. 286.

38. Singh, *Tragedy of Errors*, p. 68.

39. Abdullah, *My Dismissal*, p. 11.

40. Ibid., p. 32.

41. Mir Qasim, *My Life and Times*, p. 163.

42. Singh, *Telegraph*, India, 11 July 1984, as quoted in *Tragedy of Errors*, p. 74.

43. Malhotra, *Indira Gandhi*, p. 297.

44. Singh, *Tragedy of Errors*, p. 79.

45. Jagmohan, *Frozen Turbulence*, p. 346.

46. Singh, *Tragedy of Errors*, p. 98.

47. Akbar, *Behind the Vale*, p. 213.

48. See Verma, *Crossroads*, p. 74.

49. As quoted in Verma, *Crossroads*, p. 159.

50. Verma, *Crossroads*, p. 137.

51. *Times of India*, 26 March 1987, as quoted in Verma, *Crossroads*, p. 141.

52. As quoted in Verma, *Crossroads*, p. 141.

53. Farooq Abdullah, interview, New Delhi, 15 April 1994.

54. Singh, *Tragedy of Errors*, p. 102.

55. Mir Abdul Aziz, interview, March 1994.

56. As quoted in Verma, *Crossroads*, p. 79.

57. Farooq Abdullah, interview, New Delhi, 1994; Bhattacharjea, *Wounded Valley*, p. 253.

58. Amanullah Khan, interview, Rawalpindi, March 1995.

59. Rodney Cowton, *The Times*, 27 December 1985.
60. Edward Desmond, 'The Insurgency in Kashmir (1989–91), *Contemporary South Asia*, March 1995, Vol. IV, No. 1, pp. 6–7.
61. Yasin Malik, *Our Real Crime*, Srinagar 1994, p. 1.
62. Singh, *Tragedy of Errors*, p. 108.
63. Ibid., p. 107.
64. Jagmohan, *Frozen Turbulence*. p.111–13.
65. Verma, *Crossroads*, p. 229.
66. Bhattacharjea, *Wounded Valley*, p. 255.
67. Verma, *Crossroads*, p. 208.
68. Rajendra Sareen, *Pakistan: the India Factor*, New Delhi, 1984, p. 40.
69. Desmond, 'The Insurgency in Kashmir', p. 8.
70. Singh, *Tragedy of Errors*, p. 204.

Chapter 14

1. *Sunday Observer*, 10 August 1990 quoted in Kadian, *The Kashmir Tangle*, p. 147.
2. Reeta Chowdhari Tremblay, 'Kashmir: The Valley's Political Dynamics', *Contemporary South Asia*, March 1995. Vol. IV, No. 1, p. 81.
3. Verma, *Crossroads*, p. 230.
4. Ibid., p 236.
5. Jagmohan, *Frozen Turbulence*, p. 125.
6. Bhattacharjea, *Wounded Valley*, p. 257.
7. Puri, *Towards Insurgency*, p. 58.
8. Singh, *Tragedy of Errors*, p.110.
9. Puri, *Towards Insurgency*, p. 56.
10. Farooq Abdullah, interview, New Delhi, 15 April 1994.
11. *Peace Initiatives*, ed. Sundeep Waslekar, Vol. I, No. 2, Sept–Oct 95, p 16–18.
12. Jagmohan listed 44 'terrorist organisations' at the beginning of 1990; see *Frozen Turbulence*, Appendix XV, p. 751–2.
13. Azam Inquilabi, interview, Islamabad, 25 March 1994.
14. Ibid.
15. Mufti Muhammed Sayeed, as quoted in Singh, *Tragedy of Errors*, p. 120.
16. Dr Major (retd) Muzafar Shah, interview, Lahore, 7 April 1994.
17. Jagmohan, *Frozen Turbulence*, p. 373.
18. Farooq Abdullah, interview, New Delhi, 15 April 1994.
19. See Akbar, *Behind the Vale*, p. 281.
20. Jagmohan, *Frozen Turbulence*, p. 342.
21. Singh, *Tragedy of Errors*, p. 131.
22. See Puri, *Towards Insurgency*, p. 60.
23. Haseeb, interview, Srinagar, 7 April 1995.
24. See Singh, *Tragedy of Errors*, p. 132.
25. Tony Allen-Mills, *The Independent on Sunday*, 28 January 1990.
26. *Daily Telegraph*, 22 January 1990.
27. Puri, *Towards Insurgency*, p. 60.
28. Akbar, *Behind the Vale*, p. 219.
29. Haseeb, interview, Srinagar, April 1995.
30. Desmond, 'The Insurgency in Kashmir', p. 8.

31. Inder Gujral as quoted in *Newsline*, May 1990, p. 17.

32. Puri, *Towards Insurgency*, p. 63.

33. Singh, *Tragedy of Errors*, p. 205.

34. Jagmohan, *Frozen Turbulence*, p. 34.

35. Ibid., p. 364.

36. Ved Bhasin, interview, Jammu, 10 April 1994.

37. See *Asia Watch*, May 1991, p. 57.

38. Jagmohan, *Frozen Turbulence*, p. 419.

39. Shiraz Sidhva, 'Present Insurgency is a Peoples Movement', as quoted in *Kashmir Bleeds*, p. 34.

40. *The Guardian*, 24 February 1990.

41. Singh, *Tragedy of Errors*, p.144.

42. Jagmohan, *Frozen Turbulence*, p. 21.

43. Ibid., p. 465.

44. George Fernandes, 'India's Policies in Kashmir, quoted in Perspectives on Kashmir', ed. Raju G. C. Thomas, p. 288.

45. The figure of 250,000 has also been given out of a total of 300,000 Kashmiri Pandits in the valley ('Report of a Mission', International Commission of Jurists, 1994).

46. Jawaharlal, interview, Mishriwalla camp, Jammu, 10 April 1994.

47. Dr Pamposh Ganju, interview, London, February 1996.

48. Jagmohan. *Frozen Turbulence*. p. 492.

49. Fernandes, 'India's Policies in Kashmir', p. 291.

50. Puri, *Towards Insurgency*, p. 65.

51. Report of Tarkunde, Sachar, Singh, Puri, as quoted in Bhattacharjea, *Wounded Valley*, p. 267.

52. Omar Farooq, interview, London, 9 November 1995.

53. Singh, *Tragedy of Errors*, p. 152.

54. Punjab Human Rights Organisation, Report, 1990.

55. Satish Jacob, 'Interview with Punjab Human Rights Organisation', 1995.

56. Punjab Human Rights Organisation Report, 1990.

57. Jagmohan, *Current. 26 May–1 June. 1990*, as quoted in PHRO Report, 1990.

58. Ashok Jaitley, as quoted in Desmond, 'The Insurgency in Kashmir', p. 6.

59. Singh, *Tragedy of Errors*, p. 157.

60. Girish Saxena, interview, New Delhi, 16 April 1994.

61. Derek Brown, *The Guardian*, 14 February 1990.

62. David Housego, *The Financial Times*, 6 June 1990.

63. Azam Inquilabi, interview, Islamabad, 25 March 1994.

64. V. M. Tarkunde, *Radical Humanist*, New Delhi, March 1990.

65. As quoted in Kadian, *The Kashmir Tangle*, p. 141.

66. Kadian, *The Kashmir Tangle*, p. 142.

67. Mian Zahid Sarfraz, interview, *Friday Times*, 6–21 June 1991.

68. Asia Watch, *Human Rights in India, Kashmir Under Siege*, May 1991, p. 5.

69. Desmond, 'The Insurgency in Kashmir', p. 15.

70. Christopher Thomas, *The Times*, 4 April 1991.

71. *Response of the Indian Government*, p. 17.

72. *Human Rights in Kashmir, Report of a Mission*, ICJ, 1994.

73. David Housego, *The Financial Times*, 22 April 1991.

74. Tony Allen Mills, *The Independent*, 2 June 1991.

75. Tim McGirk, *The Independent*, 17 September 1991.
76. Anwar Iqbal, *The News*, 8 February, 1992.
77. Puri, *Towards Insurgency*, p. 67.
78. Asia Watch, *The Human Rights Crisis in Kashmir*, June 1993, p. 45.
79. Dr Farida Ashai, as quoted in Asia Watch, *Human Rights Crisis*, p. 44.
80. *Asia Watch*, June 1993, p. 45.
81. Girish Saxena, interview, New Delhi, 16 April 1994.
82. Interview, Karachi, 1 April 1994.
83. *Asia Watch*, June 1993. p. 55.
84. Aditya Sinya, *The Pioneer*, 11 April 1994.
85. Mirwaiz Umar Farooq, telephone interview, Srinagar. April 1995.
86. Saxena, interview, New Delhi, 16 April 1994.
87. Ibid.

Chapter 15

1. Farooq Abdullah, interview, New Delhi, 15 April 1994.
2. Mirwaiz Omar Farooq, interview, London, 9 November 1995.
3. *The Economist*, 'Kashmir: Another Try', 27 March 1993, p. 81.
4. The members of the mission were: Sir William Goodhart, UK, Dr Dalmo Dallari, Brazil, Ms Florence Butegwa, Uganda, Professor Vitit Muntarbhorn, Thailand. Their report was issued in November 1994.
5. Amnesty International, *Torture and Deaths in Custody in Jammu and Kashmir*, 31 January 1995, p. 8.
6. Journalist, interview, London, September 1995.
7. Azam Inquilabi, interview, Islamabad, 25 March 1994.
8. M. N. Sabharwal, director-general of J&K police, interview, Srinagar, April 1994.
9. *Response of the Government of India to Report of Amnesty International on Torture and Deaths in Custody in Jammu and Kashmir*, p 22.
10. Amnesty, *Torture and Deaths in Custody*, p. 7.
11. Yasin Malik, interview, Srinagar, 6 April 1995.
12. UN Commission for Human Rights, Geneva, February 1994, E/CN.4/1994.
13. Shekhar Gupta, 'On a Short Fuse', *India Today*, 15 March 1994, p. 26.
14. Narasimha Rao, 'Don't Underestimate Us', *India Today*, 15 March 1994, p. 34.
15. Shekhar Gupta, *India Today*, 15 March 1994, p. 29.
16. Ahmad, Sajjad, *Greater Kashmir*, 12 April 1994.
17. Dr Karan Singh, in *The Times of India*, Bangalore, 11 April 1994.
18. Tim McGirk, *The Independent*, 31 October 1994.
19. Haroon Joshi, interview, Srinagar, April 1995.
20. Yasin Malik, interview, Srinagar, 6 April 1995.
21. Shabir Shah, interview, Srinagar, 5 April 1995.
22. Abdul Gani Lone, interview, Srinagar, 5 April 1995.
23. Professor Abdul Ghani, as quoted in *Asian Age*, 12 April 1994.
24. Mian Abdul Qayum, advocate, interview, Srinagar, 14 April 1994.
25. Governor General (retd.) Krishna Rao, 'Statement on Doordashan', Jammu, 3 April 1995.
26. Farooq Abdullah, interview, Srinagar, 5 April 1995.
27. Mirwaiz Omar Farooq, interview, London, 9 November 1995.

28. Brigadier Arjun Ray, General Staff, Corps HQ, interview, Srinagar, April 1995.

29. *Peace Initiatives*, ed. Sundeep Waslekar, Vol. I, No. 2, Sept–Oct 1995, p. 13.

30. As quoted in 'Faltering Steps' by Shiraz Sidhva, *Frontline*, New Delhi, 9–22 April 1994, p. 4.

31. Kaleem Omar, 'Special Report on Kashmir', *The News on Friday*, 28 July 1995.

32. Rahul Bedi, 'On the Kashmir Beat', *Jane's Defence Weekly*, 21 May 1994, p. 19.

33. *Response of the Indian Government*, p. 21.

34. *Human Rights in Kashmir, Report of a Mission*, International Commission of Jurists, Geneva, November 1994.

35. Amnesty, *Torture and Deaths in Custody*, January 1995, p. 2.

36. *The Observer*, London, 13 November 1994, as quoted in Amnesty, *Torture and Deaths in Custody*, January 1995, p. 19.

37. Asia Watch, 'The Human Rights Crisis in Kashmir, A Pattern of Impunity', Rawalpindi, June 1993, p. 58.

38. *Response of the Government of India*, p. 22–3.

39. Amnesty International, *India: Analysis of the Government of India's response to Amnesty International's Report on Torture and Deaths in Custody in Jammu and Kashmir*, March 1995, p. 1.

40. Amnesty, *Torture and Deaths in Custody* January 1995, p. 60–1.

41. Ibid., p. 10.

42. Section 8(1) as quoted in *Human Rights in Kashmir*, ICJ report.

43. *Human Rights in Kashmir*, ICJ report.

44. Section 4, as quoted in *Human Rights in Kashmir*, ICJ report.

45. *Human Rights in Kashmir*, ICJ report.

46. Ibid.

47. Mian Abdul Qayum, interview, Srinagar, April 1994.

48. *Response of the Indian government*, p. 10.

49. Brigadier Arjun Ray, interview, Srinagar, April 1995.

50. M. N. Sabharwal, director-general J & K Police, interview, Srinagar, April 1994.

51. Indian High Commission, London, February 1996.

52. Puri, *Towards Insurgency*, p. 78.

53. Dinesh Kumar, *The Times of India*, August 1993.

54. Governor Gen (retd) K. V. Kirshna Rao, 'Statement on Doordashan', Jammu, 3 April 1995.

55. Student, interview, Srinagar, April 1995.

56. Businessman, interview, Srinagar, April 1995.

57. Houseboat Owner, interview, Srinagar, April 1995.

58. Amnesty, *Torture and Deaths in Custody*, January 1994, p. 59.

59. Asia Watch, *The Human Rights Crisis in Kashmir*, June 1993, p. 98.

60. Girish Saxena, interview, New Delhi, 16 April 1994.

61. Farooq Abdullah, interview, Srinagar, 5 April 1995.

62. See *Human Rights in Kashmir*, ICJ report.

63. Interview, Srinagar, April 1995.

64. Mirwaiz Omar Farooq, interview, London, 9 November 1995.

65. Yasin Malik, interview, Srinagar, 6 April 1995.

66. Amanullah Khan, telephone interview, February 1996.

67. Siddiqi was amongst 32 killed in police firing in March 1996 when the mosque at Hazratbal was once more placed under siege.

68. Interviews, Srinagar, April 1995.

69. Indian High Commission, London, February 1996.

70. Statistics to end March 1995, supplied by Ram Mahan Rao, Adviser to Government of J&K, New Delhi, April 1995.

71. Indian High Commission, London, February 1996.

72. Interview, Srinagar, April 1994.

73. Girish Saxena, interview, New Delhi, April 1994.

74. Desmond, 'The Insurgency in Kashmir', p. 15.

75. Interview, New Delhi, 1995.

76. *Response of the Government of India*, p. 5.

77. Prime Minister Sardar Abdul Qayyum Khan, interview, Islamabad, March 1995.

78. *Human Rights in Kashmir*, ICJ report .

79. 'The Islamic Blowback', BBC 2, 11 November 1995.

80. Muhammad Saraf, interview, Rawalpindi, March 1994; he died in November 1994.

81. Mirwaiz Omar Farooq, interview, London, 9 November 1995.

82. Yasin Malik, interview, Srinagar, April 1995.

83. Anthony Davis, *Jane's Intelligence Review*, Vol. VII No 1.

84. Indian High Commission, London, February 1996.

85. Sheikh Jamaluddin, interview, Srinagar, April 1994.

86. Izhar Wani, *The Daily Telegraph*, 12 May 1995.

87. Master Gul's role was publicised in the documentary, 'The Islamic Blowback', broadcast on BBC 2 on 11 November 1995.

88. Nazimuddin Sheikh, interview, Islamabad, 29 March 1995.

89. Prime Minister Sardar Abdul Qayum, interview, Islamabad, 25 March 1994.

90. Mirwaiz Omar Farooq, interview, London, 9 November 1995.

91. Ambore camp, interview, Muzaffarabad, 29 March 1994.

92. Nayyar Malik, interview, Muzaffarabad, 29 March 1994.

93. Masood Kashfi, Station Director, interview, Muzaffarabad, 29 March 1994.

94. Interview, Rawalpindi, April 1995.

95. Prime Minister Sardar Qayum Khan, interview, Islamabad, March 1994.

96. Azam Inquilabi, interview, Islamabad, March 1994.

97. Yasin Malik, interview, Srinagar, April 1995.

98. Raja Nisar Wali, interview, Gilgit, 16 April 1994.

99. Wazir Firman Ali, interview, Islamabad, 14 April 1995.

100. See Verdict on Gilgit & Baltistan (Northern Area) Mirpur, 1993.

101. Student, interview, Sopore, April 1994.

102. Amnesty, *An Unnatural Fate*, December 1993, p. 7.

103. Dr Rashid, interview, Srinagar, April 1994.

104. *Peace Initiatives*, ed. Sundeep Waslekar, New Delhi, September–October 1995, Vol. I, No. 2, p. 15.

105. *Peace Initiatives*, p. 11.

106. Indian government figures for 1995 are 2,796 persons killed; for 1994, 2,899 killed. This compares with 31 killed in 1988, 92 killed in 1989, 1,177 killed in 1990. Indian High Commission, London, February 1996. Unofficial statistics are much higher.

107. Amnesty, interview, London, October 1995.

108. Bone and Joint hospital, interview, Srinagar, April 1994.

109. Brigadier Arjun Ray, interview, Srinagar, April 1995.

110. Ashok Jaitley, telephone interview, New Delhi, 11 April 1995.

111. Farooq Abdullah, interview, Srinagar, 5 April 1995.

112. Ram Mahan Rao, interview, New Delhi, 10 April 1995.

113. Pinto Narboo, interview, New Delhi, 10 April 1995; also P. K. Triparthi, District Commissioner, interview, Leh, 12 April, 1995.

114. Congress politician, interview, Jammu, April 1995.

115. Indian High Commission, London, February 1996: in 1995 45 per cent were killed, compared with 20 per cent in 1994.

116. Stephen Humphrey, interview, Srinagar, April 1994.

117. Iqbal Chapra, interview, Srinagar, April 1994.

118. Muhammed Kotru, interview, Srinagar, April 1994.

119. David Mackie, *The Daily Telegraph*, 24 June 1994.

120. Kim Housego in ibid.

121. Martha Fichtinger, interview, Srinagar, April 1995.

122. Sam Valani, interview, Srinagar, April 1995.

123. Gary Lazzarini, interview, Srinagar, April 1995.

124. Manager, Ahdoo's Hotel, interview, Srinagar, April 1995.

125. Kaleem Omar, Special Report on Kashmir, *The News on Friday*, 28 July 1995.

126. K. Padmanabhaiah in *The News on Friday*, 28 July 1995.

127. Omar Farooq, interview, London, 9 November 1995.

128. As quoted in 'Kashmir Calling', Lahore, 16–31 March 1994, p. 5.

Conclusion

1. Mirwaiz Omar Farooq, interview, London, 9 November 1995.

2. Kashmiri Militant, April 1995.

3. Desmond, 'The Insurgency in Kashmir', p. 8.

4. J. N. Dixit, interview, New Delhi, April 1994.

5. Yasin Malik, interview, Srinagar, 6 April 1995.

6. Mirwaiz Omar Farooq, interview, London, 9 November 1995.

7. James Woolsey, as quoted in *The Economist*, 7 January 1994.

8. Interview, March 1995.

9. Robin Raphael, as quoted in the *Financial Times*, 1 November 1994.

10. Strobe Talbott, press conference, New Delhi, 8 April 1994.

11. *Guardian*, 7 August 1995.

12. Mirwaiz Omar Farooq, interview, London, 9 November 1995.

13. A. H. Suhrawardy, interview , Rawalpindi, March 1994.

14. Yasin Malik, interview, Srinagar, 6 April 1995.

15. Sardar Abdul Qayyum Khan, interview, Islamabad, March 1995.

16. L. P. Singh, interview, New Delhi, 16 April 1994.

17. Shabir Shah, interview, Srinagar, 5 April 1995.

18. Balraj Puri, 'Kashmiriyat: the Vitality of Kashmiri Identity', *Contemporary South Asia*, March 1995, Vol. IV, No. 1, p. 62.

19. J. N. Dixit, interview, New Delhi, April 1994.

20. Interview, London, April 1996.

21. Shabir Shah, interview, Srinagar, 5 April 1995.

22. International Commission of Jurists, *Human Rights in Kashmir, Report of a Mission*, Geneva, November 1994.

23. Sir Frederic Bennett, *Speaking Frankly*, London, 10 July 1958.

24. Korbel, *Danger in Kashmir*, p. 353.

25. Mirwaiz Omar Farooq, interview, London, 9 November 1995.

26. George Fernandes, 12 October 1990, 'India's Policies in Kashmir: An Assessment and Discourse', in Thomas, ed., *Perspectives of Kashmir*.

27. Mirwaiz Omar Farooq, interview, London, 9 November 1995.

28. Amanullah Khan, interview, Rawalpindi, March 1995.

29. J. N. Dixit, interview, New Delhi, April 1994.

30. In the 1989 and 1991 general elections no candidates from Jammu and Kashmir took part and the seats remained vacant.

31. Pran Chopra, *India, Pakistan and the Kashmir Tangle*, New Delhi, 1995, p. 3.

32. See Samina Yasmeen, 'The China Factor in the Kashmir Issue,' in Thomas, ed., *Perspectives on Kashmir*.

33. Mirwaiz Omar Farooq, interview, London, November 1995.

Bibliography

Unpublished sources

THE BRITISH LIBRARY, ORIENTAL AND INDIA OFFICE COLLECTION

'Adoption by the Maharaja of the Second Son of the Raja of Poonch, 1906–7'.
Chelmsford Collection, 'Report on Indian Constitutional Reforms', 22 April 1918.
'Copies of Selected Documents Relating to Sir Muhammad Iqbal'.
Crown Representatives' Records, 1923.
Cunningham, Sir George, 'Diary, 1947'.
'Death of His Highness the Maharaja of Kashmir', 1925.
'Documents Relating to Raj Kumar Jagat Dev Singh', For & Pol Dept, 1924.
'Documents Relating to a Suitable Occupation for Raja Hari Singh', For & Pol Dept, 1918.
'Enclosures to Secret Letters in India', Vol. 103.
'Fortnightly Reports of the Resident in Kashmir 1924, 1925–26, 1927'.
General Reports by Colonel Ramsey, C. I. E., Resident in Kashmir, 1910.
'Kashmir Internal Situation' 1947–48'.
'Kashmir Reforms Scheme', For & Pol Dept, 1922.
Lawrence, Henry, 'Henry Lawrence Collection, Jan 1846–Feb 1847'.
Lorimer, David Lockhart, 'Lorimer Papers'.
Luard, Dr Hugh Bixby, Personal Memoirs, 1890–99.
'Memorandum on the Future of the Gilgit Agency, 1930'.
'Muslims of Kashmir', For & Pol Dept, 1924.
Poonch State Affairs, 1892.
Searle, Major, 'Diary, 1924'.
'Sedition in Kashmir', Foreign Dept, 1907.
'Status of Hunza and Nagar and Political Districts', For & Pol Dept, 1941.
Young, Colonel Ralph, 'Journal of a Trip to Cashmere, 1867'.

OTHER UNPUBLISHED DOCUMENTS AND MANUSCRIPTS

Alder, Garry, 'British Policy on the Roof of the World, 1865–95', PhD thesis, Sept 1959, University of Bristol.
Lodhi, Maleeha, Bhutto, 'The Pakistan Peoples Party and Political Development in Pakistan, 1967–77', PhD thesis, London School of Economics, 1981.
Shankar, V., 'Memoirs' (by kind permission of Miss Rashmi Shankar).
United Nations Commission for Human Rights, Geneva, February 1994, E/CN.4/ 1994, (UN Library, London).

Interviews and briefings

Abbasi, Fayyaz Ali, Assistant Commissioner: Mirpur, March 1995.

Abdullah, Dr Farooq, former Chief Minister of Jammu and Kashmir: Srinagar & New Delhi, 1994 & 1995.

Ahdoo's Hotel, Manager: Srinagar, April 1995.

Ahmad, Sardar Riaz, Secretary Agriculture, Chattar, AJK: March 1994.

Ahmed, Nasir, Deputy Commissioner: Gilgit, April 1994.

Advani, Muhstaq Ahmed, Muslim Conference: Rawalpindi, March 1995.

Akbar, Chaudhri Latif, advocate and former minister, PPP: Muzaffarabad, March 1994.

Akhtar, Prof. Sharifa, J & K Action Committee: Karachi, April 1994.

Akhtar, Miss Rumina, J & K Action Committee: Karachi, April 1994.

Akhtar, Miss Shahbina, J & K Action Committee: Karachi, April 1994.

Ali, Mr, Carpet dealer: Srinagar, March 1981.

Ali, Wazir Firman, former Joint Secretary, Ministry of Kashmir Affairs: Islamabad, April 1995.

Ambore refugee camp, Muzaffarabad: March 1994.

Ansari, Abdul Khaliq, advocate: Mirpur, March 1995.

Ashraf, Malik Muhd, Inspector-General Police: Gilgit, April 1994.

Atta, Mrs Saleema, Associate Professor Economics, University College, Muzaffarabad: March 1994.

Azim, Muhammed, advocate: Mirpur, March 1995.

Aziz, Mir Abdul, journalist: Rawalpindi, March 1994.

Aziz, Tahir, research officer, Azad government of Jammu and Kashmir: Islamabad, March 1995.

Balti, Iqbal, journalist: Islamabad, April 1995.

Bandey, Abdul Majid, advocate, Srinagar: London, April 1996.

Bano, Dr Hamida, University of Kashmir, Srinagar: London, April 1996.

Beaumont, Christopher, former Secretary to the Boundary Commission, correspondence with the author: October 1995.

Bedi, Rahul, journalist: New Delhi April 1994/ 1995.

Bhasin, Ved, journalist: Jammu, April 1994.

Bercha, Sher Baz Ali Khan, assistant librarian and writer: Gilgit, April 1994.

Bhattacharya, Subhabrata, journalist: New Delhi, April 1994.

Bone & Joint Hospital: Srinagar, doctors & patients, April 1994.

Brown, Mrs Margaret: Islamabad, April 1994.

Butt, Gulam, houseboat owner, Srinagar: March 1981, April 1994, April 1995.

Campbell-Johnson, Alan, Address to Pakistan Society: London, October 1995.

Chapra, Iqbal, Houseboat Owners Association: Srinagar, April 1994.

Chaudhri, Dr Muhd Khairyat, Dean of Arts Faculty, University of Azad Jammu and Kashmir, March 1994.

Dhar, Vijay: New Delhi, April 1994/1995.

Dixit, J. N., former Foreign Secretary for the Government of India: New Delhi, April 1994.

Dongola, Abdul Hamid, taxi driver: Srinagar, April 1994 & 1995.

Doucet, Lyse, journalist: Febuary 1996.

Farooq, Mirwaiz Omar, Srinagar/London: April/November 1995.

Farooqi, Siddique, Secretary, AJK government: Muzaffarabad, March 1994.

Fichtinger, Martha, tourist: Srinagar, April 1995.

Ganju, Dr Pamposh, Indo–European Kashmir forum: London, February 1996.

Gujral, Inder, former Foreign Minister of India, New Delhi, April 1994.

Guru, M. R., Srinagar: April 1994.

Haksar, P. N., civil servant: telephone interview, New Delhi, April 1995.

Hamilton, Mollie Kaye, author: Surrey, June 1995.

Haseeb, medical student: Srinagar, April 1995.

Hijazi, Dr Haider, JKLF: Rawalpindi, March 1995.

Humphrey, Stephen, tourist: Srinagar, April 1994.

Hussain, Shahmat, medical student: Srinagar, April 1995.

Inquilabi, Azam, Jammu and Kashmir Plebiscite Front/ Operation Balakote: Islamabad, March 1994.

Jaitley, Ashok, civil servant: telephone interview, New Delhi, April 1995.

Jamaluddin, Sheikh, Afghan prisoner, former militant: Srinagar, April 1994.

Jameel, Yusuf, journalist: Srinagar, April 1994.

James, Wing-Cdr A. G.: London, 1994.

Jawaharlal, teacher and refugee: Jammu, April 1994.

Joshi, Haroon, journalist: Srinagar, April 1995.

Kashfi, Masood, radio station director: Muzaffarabad, March 1994.

Kaul, H. K. Librarian, India International Centre: New Delhi, March 1994.

Khalid, Dr Nazir A., J & K Action Committee: Karachi, April 1994.

Khan, Sardar Abdul Qayum Khan, Prime Minister of the Azad government of Jammu and Kashmir: Islamabad, March 1994, March 1995.

Khan, Abdul Wahid, ex-Joint Secretary: Gilgit, April 1994.

Khan, Aftab Ahmed, Secretary, Northern Areas: Islamabad, March 1994.

Khan, Amanullah, JKLF, Rawalpindi, March 1994, March 1995, February 1996.

Khan, Arif Aslam: en route to Baltistan, April 1995.

Khan, Farooq Ahmed, Secretary for Tourism, AJK: Muzaffarabad, March 1994.

Khan, Habib, Inspector General Police, Muzaffarabad: March 1994.

Khan, Khalid Ibrahim, son of Sardar Mohammad Ibrahim Khan: Islamabad, March 1994.

Khan, Muhammad Afzal, Minister, Northern Areas: Islamabad, March 1995.

Khan, Mahmood, Chief Commissioner: Gilgit, April 1994.

Khan, Nisar Hussain, Joint Secretary, Ministry of Industries and Production: Islamabad, April 1995.

Khan, Riaz Ahmed, Secretary, Dept of Agriculture & Livestock: Muzaffarabad, March 1994.

Khan, Sardar Mohammad Ibrahim, Founder/President of Azad Government of Jammu & Kashmir: Islamabad, March 1994.

Khan, Sardar Muhd Latif Khan, Secretary for Education, AJK: Muzaffarabad, March 1994.

Khan, Shaharyar Muhammad, former Foreign Secretary to the Government of Pakistan: Islamabad, March 1994.

Khan, Tanveer Ahmed, Foreign Secretary to the Government of Pakistan, Islamabad, March 1994.

Khashif, Zahid Amin, Chairman of Development Authority: Muzaffarabad, March 1994.

Khel, Shafqat Kaka, Ministry of Foreign Affairs: Islamabad, March 1994.

Khurshid Library: Muzaffarabad, March 1994.

Koker, A. S., advocate: Mirpur, March 1995.

Kotru, Muhammad, Houseboat Owners Association: Srinagar, April 1994.

Khwaja, Mrs Faiza: Islamabad, March 1994.

Lamb, Prof. Alastair, Address to Pakistan Society, London: March 1996.

Latif, Mr Ch. Muhammad and Mrs Tanveer: Muzaffarabad, March 1994.

Lazzarini, Gary, tourist: Srinagar, April 1995.

Lone, Abdul Gani, Peoples Conference: Srinagar, April 1995.

Malik, Mrs Nayyar, social worker: Muzaffarabad, March 1994.

Malik, Yasin, JKLF: Srinagar, 1995.

Mallick, Justice Abdul Majeed: Mirpur, March 1995.

Masood, Khalid, Agricultural Training Institute, Ghari Dopatta, AJK: March 1994.

Masood, Tahir, Ittehad-ul Muslimeen: Rawalpindi, March 1995.

Masud, Tariq, Kashmir House: Islamabad, March 1994/1995.

Mehmood, Khwaja Ahsan, J & K Action Committee: Karachi, April 1994.

Mishriwalla refugee camp: Jammu, April 1994.

Militants from JKLF, Hizb-ul Mujaheddin, Harkat-ul Ansar: Srinagar, April 1995.

Muhammad, Noor, Regional Programme Officer, Agha Khan Project: Hunza, April 1994.

Mushtaq, Dr Muhammed, Jamaat-i Islami: Muzaffarabad, March 1994.

Mustafa, Gulam, Assistant Commissioner: Muzaffarabad, March 1994.

Naik, Niaz, former Foreign Secretary to the Government of Pakistan: Islamabad, March 1994.

Narboo, Pinto, former minister, Ladakh: New Delhi, April 1995.

Naseem, Syed Yousuf, Peoples Conference: Rawalpindi, March 1995.

Naqshbandi, Fez, research officer, Azad Government of Jammu and Kashmir: Islamabad, March 1994.

Pataudi, General Sher Ali: Islamabad, April 1995.

Peters, Philip, tourist: Srinagar, April 1995.

Puri, Balraj, author: telephone interview, Jammu, April 1995.

Qayum, Mian Abdul, advocate: Srinagar, April 1994.

Quereshi, Khalil Ahmad, Board of Revenue and Secretary to AJK government: Muzaffarabad, March 1994.

Rao, Ram Mahan, adviser to Government of J & K: New Delhi, April 1995.

Rashid, Doctor: Srinagar, April 1994.

Rashid, Malik Abdul, Secretary Kashmir Cell: Muzaffarabad, March 1994.

Rathore, Mr and Mrs Mohd Amin, J & K Action Committee: Karachi, April 1994.

Ray, Brigadier Arjun, General Staff, Corps Headquarters: Srinagar, April 1995.

Sabharwal, M. N., Director-General of J & K Police: Srinagar, April 1994.

Safi, Ghulam Muhammad, APHC: Rawalpindi, March 1995, London, April 1996.

Saghar, Mehmood Ahmed, Peoples League: Rawalpindi, March 1995.

Saraf, Chief Justice (retd) Muhammad Yusuf: Rawalpindi, March/April 1994.

Saxena, Girish, former governor of the state of Jammu & Kashmir: New Delhi, April 1994.

Shah, Major Hussain, Northern Areas Joint Platform: Gilgit, April 1994.

Shah, Dr Major (retd) Muzaffar, Kashmir Action Committee: Lahore, April 1994.

Shah, Shabir, Peoples League: Srinagar, April 1995.

Shah, Syed Fazil, Director, Pakistan Information Dept: Gilgit, April 1994.

Shankar, V., former private secretary to Sardar Patel: New Delhi, March 1981.

Sheikh, Nazimuddin: Foreign Secretary to the Government of Pakistan: Islamabad, March 1995.

Sidhvar, Shiraz, journalist, New Delhi, April 1994.

Singh, Mrs Arjun, New Delhi, April 1995.

Singh, Captain Dewan, former ADC to Maharaja Hari Singh: Jammu, April 1994.

Singh, Dr Karan Singh, son of Maharaja Hari Singh, former Sadar-i-Riyasat: New Delhi, April 1994.

Singh, L. P., former Indian Home Secretary: New Delhi, April 1994.

Singh Tavleen, journalist: New Delhi, April 1994.

Suhrawardy, Abdul H., author: Rawalpindi, March 1994.

Talbott, Strobe, US Deputy Secretary of State, press conference: New Delhi, April 1994.

Talib, Rasheed, journalist: New Dehli, April 1994.

Thapar, Karan, journalist: New Dehli, April 1994.

Thukar, Dr Ayyub, World Kashmir Freedom Movement, London 1994, 1996.

Triparthi, P. K., District Commissioner: Leh, April 1995.

Valani, Sam, tourist: Srinagar, April 1995.

Vira, Dharma, civil servant: New Delhi, April 1994.

Wali, Raja Nisar, Northern Areas Joint Platform: Gilgit, April 1994.

Wani, Dr Ghulam Qadir, J & K Islamic Students League: Islamabad, March 1994.

Wani, Muhstaq Ahmad, Muslim Conference: Rawalpindi, March 1995.

Wani, Mumtaz Ahmed, advocate, Srinagar: London, April 1996.

Waverley, Viscount: London, October 1995.

Zafar, Colonel, Line of Control: Chakoti, March 1994.

Zaidi, Professor Z. H.: Islamabad, March/April 1994.

Note: Positions and professions relate to the dates of interviews. Many others guided me to these interviews. I also spoke with a number of people whom I have not quoted directly, but whose views have contributed to my analyses. Several people spoke to me in confidence and requested that their names should not be included.

Newspapers and periodicals

INDIA

The Times of India, The Sunday Times of India, Indian Express, The Hindustan Times, Frontline, The Pioneer, India Today, Rashtriya Sahara, Greater Kashmir, Kashmir Times, Asian Age.

PAKISTAN

The Pakistan Times, The Muslim, The Frontier, Dawn, The News, The Nation, The Friday Times, The News on Friday, The Herald, Newsline, Kashmir Calling.

UNITED KINGDOM

The Times, The Independent, The Daily Telegraph, The Financial Times, The Guardian, The Scotsman, Time, Newsweek.

Books, articles and published papers

Abdullah, Farooq, *My Dismissal*, New Delhi, 1985.

Abdullah, Sheikh Mohammad, *Flames of the Chinar*, New Delhi, 1993. tr. from the Urdu by Khushwant Singh.

Aitchinson, C. V., ed. *A Collection of Treaties, Engagements and Sanads*, Vol. XII Part I, Calcutta, 1931.

Alexander, Horace, *Kashmir*, Friends Peace Committee, London, 1953.

Ali, Chaudhri Muhammad, *The Emergence of Pakistan*, New York, 1967.

Akbar, M. J., *Kashmir: Behind the Vale*, New Delhi, 1991.

Amnesty International, *'An Unnatural Fate', Disappearances and Impunity in the Indian States of Jammu and Kashmir and Punjab*, December 1993.

—— *Torture and Deaths in Custody in Jammu and Kashmir*, January 1995.

—— *India*, March 1995.

Asia Watch, *Human Rights in India: Kashmir under Siege*, May 1991.

—— *The Human Rights Crisis in Kashmir: A Pattern of Impunity*, June 1993.

Azad Government of the State of Jammu and Kashmir, *Azad Kashmir at a Glance*, 1993.

Baird, J. G. A., ed. *Private Letters of the Marquess of Dalhousie*, Edinburgh & London, 1910.

Bamzai, Prithivi Nath Kaul, *A History of Kashmir, Political, Social, Cultural from the Earliest Times to the Present Day*, New Dehli, 1973.

Bazaz, Prem Nath, *Azad Kashmir*, Lahore, 1951.

—— *History of Struggle for Freedom*, New Delhi, 1954.

—— *The Shape of Things in Kashmir*, New Delhi, 1965.

Bedi, Rahul, 'On the Kashmir Beat, *Jane's Defence Weekly*, 21 May 1994.

—— 'Casualties Rise in Kashmir', *Jane's Defence Weekly*, 28 January 1995.

Beg, Mirza Afzal, *Sheikh Abdullah Defended*, Srinagar, 1962.

Bennett, Frederic, *Speaking Frankly*, London, 1958.

Bernier, François, *Travels in the Mogul Empire, AD 1656–1668*, ed. Archibald Constable, Delhi, 1969.

Bhattacharjea, Ajit, *Kashmir: The Wounded Valley*, New Delhi, 1994.

Bhutto, Zulfikar Ali, *If I am Assassinated*, New Delhi, 1979.

Bikrama Jit Hasrat, (ed.) *The Punjab Papers*, Punjab, 1970.

Birdwood, Lord, *Two Nations & Kashmir*, London, 1956.

Burke, Samuel M., *Mainsprings of Indian and Pakistani Foreign Policies*, Minneapolis, 1974.

Campbell-Johnson, Alan, *Mission with Mountbatten*, London, 1972.

Chenevix-Trench, Charles, *The Frontier Scouts*, London, 1985.

Chopra, Pran, *India, Pakistan and the Kashmir Tangle*, New Delhi, 1994.

Collins, Larry & Lapierre, Dominique, *Freedom at Midnight*, London, 1975.

Corfield, Sir Conrad, 'Some Thoughts on British Policy and the Indian States, 1935–47, in C. H. Philips & Mary Doreen Wainright (eds) *The Partition of India*, London, 1970.

Cunningham, J. D., *The History of the Sikhs*, London, 1849.

Davis, Anthony, 'The Conflict in Kashmir', *Jane's Intelligence Review*, Vol. 7, No. 1, January 1995.

Desmond, Edward W., 'The Insurgency in Kashmir 1989–1991', in *Contemporary South Asia*, Vol. 4, No. 1, March 1995.

Douglas, William O., *Beyond the High Himalayas*, London, 1953.

Douie, Sir James, *The Panjab, North-West Frontier Province & Kashmir*, Cambridge, 1916.

Drew, Frederic, *The Northern Barrier of India*, London, 1877.

Durand, Colonel Algernon, *The Making of a Frontier*, London, 1900.

Dutt, Dr Nalinaksha, *Buddhism in Kashmir*, Delhi, 1985.

Edwardes, Herbert & Merivale, Herman, *The Life of Sir Henry Lawrence*, London, 1872.

Edwardes, Michael, *The Last Years of British India*, London, 1963.

Enriquez, Captain C-M, *The Realm of the Gods*, London, 1915.

Featherstone, Donald, *Victorian Colonial Warfare: India*, London, 1992.

Feldman, Herbert, *From Crisis to Crisis, Pakistan 1962–1969*, Oxford, 1972.

Ferguson, James P. *Kashmir: an Historical Introduction*, London, 1961.

Fernandes, George, 'India's Policies in Kashmir: An Assessment and Discourse' in Ragu G. C. Thomas (ed.) *Perspectives on Kashmir*, Colorado, 1992.

Fisher, Margaret, Rose, Leo E., Huttenback, Robert A., *Himalayan Battleground*, London, 1963.

French, Patrick, *Sir Francis Younghusband*, London, 1994.

Gandhi, Indira, *India*, London, 1975

Ghose, Dilip Kumar, *Kashmir in Transition*, Calcutta, 1975.

Gauhar, Altaf, *Ayub Khan, Pakistan's First Military Ruler*, Lahore, 1993.

Gopal, Sarvepalli, *Jawaharlal Nehru*, Vols, 1,2,3, London, 1975, 1979, 1984.

Government of India, Foreign Dept, *Visitor's Rules for Jammu and Kashmir*, 1916.

—— White Paper (India), 3 March 1948.

Government of India, 'Response of the Government of India to Report of Amnesty International titled *An Unnatural Fate*', December 1993.

Government of Pakistan, *Kashmir in the Security Council*, Islamabad, March 1990.

Gupta, Sisir, *Kashmir A Study in India–Pakistan Relations*, London, 1966.

Gupte, Pranay, *Mother India*, New York, 1992.

Hamid, Shahid, *Karakuram Hunza*, Karachi, 1979.

—— *Disastrous Twilight*, Great Britain, 1986.

—— *Early Years of Pakistan*, Lahore, 1993.

Hardinge, Viscount, *Rulers of India: Hardinge*, Oxford, 1891.

Hayes, Louis D., *The Impact of US. Policy on the Kashmir Conflict*, Arizona, 1971.

History of the Campaign on the Sutlej & the War in the Punjaub, from authentic sources, 2nd edition, London, 1846.

History of the Sikhs: A Concise Account of the Punjaub & Cashmere, compiled from authentic sources, Calcutta, 1846.

High Court of Judicature, Azad Jammu and Kashmir, 'Verdict on Gilgit and Baltistan (Northern Area)', Mirpur, 1993.

Hodson, H. V., *The Great Divide*, London, 1969.

International Commission of Jurists, *Report of a Mission: Human Rights in Kashmir*, Geneva, 1994.

Ippolito, Desideri, *An Account of Tibet*, London, 1932.

Ismay, *The Memoirs of General the Lord Ismay*, London, 1960.

Jacquemont, Victor, *Correspondance inédite*, 1824–32, Paris, 1867.

Jaffar, S. M., *Kashmir Sold and Resold*, Lahore, 1992.

Jagmohan, *My Frozen Turbulence*, New Delhi, 1994.

Jain, R. K., *Soviet–South Asian Relations, 1947–78*, Vols 1 & 2, New Dehli, 1978.

Jalal, Ayesha, *The Sole Spokesman*, Cambridge, 1985.

—— *The State of Martial Rule*, Cambridge, 1990.

James, Sir Morrice, *Pakistan Chronicle*, London, 1993.

Kadian, Rajesh, *The Kashmir Tangle, Issues & Options*, New Delhi, 1992.

Kak, B. L., *The Fall of Gilgit: the Untold Story of Indo–Pak Affairs from Jinnah to Bhutto*, New Delhi, 1977.

—— *The Untold Story of Men and Matters*, Jammu, 1987.

Kalhana, *Rajatarangini, The Chronicle of the Kings of Kasmir*, tr. M. A. Stein, London, 1900.

—— *Rajatarangini, The Saga of the Kings of Kasmir*, tr. Ranjit Sitaram Pandit, New Delhi, 1991.

Kalla, Aloke, *Kashmiri Pandits and Their Diversity*, Delhi, 1985.

Kapur, M. L., *Eminent Rulers of Kashmir*, New Delhi, 1975.

Karim, Maj. Gen. Afsir, *Kashmir: The Troubled Frontiers*, New Delhi, 1994.

Khan, Akbar, *Raiders in Kashmir*, Karachi, 1970.

Khan, Amanullah, 'Oppressor v/s Oppressed', Court of Appeal, Brussels, 16 December 1993, Rawalpindi, 1993.

Khanna, Professor D. D., *Defence Studies Papers*, No. 1, University of Allahabad, 1981.

Khurshid, K. H., *Memories of Jinnah*, ed. Khalid Hasan, Karachi, 1990.

Klaproth, M., *Histoire du Kachmir*, Paris, 1825.

Knight, E. F., *Where Three Empires Meet*, London, 1893.

Korbel, Joseph, *Danger in Kashmir*, Princeton, 1955 & 1966.

Lamb, Alastair, *Crisis in Kashmir*, London, 1966.

—— *Kashmir: A Disputed Legacy 1846–1990*, Herts, 1991.

—— *Birth of a Tragedy*, Herts, 1994.

Lawrence, Walter, *The Valley of Kashmir*, London, 1895.

Lumby, E. W. R., 'British Policy Towards the Indian States, 1940–7' in C. H. Philips & Mary Doreen Wainright (eds) *The Partition of India*, London, 1970.

Mahajan, Mehr Chand, *Looking Back*, London, 1963.

Malhotra, Inder, *Indira Gandhi*, London, 1989.

Malik, Yasin, *Our Real Crime*, Srinagar, 1994.

Malleson, George Bruce, *The Indian Mutiny*, London 1891/1983.

Mansbergh, Nicholas, (editor-in-chief), *The Transfer of Power*, 1942–47, Vols I–XII. London, 1970–83.

Masani, Zareer, *Indira Gandhi*, London, 1975.

Menon, V. P., *The Story of the Integration of the Indian States*, Calcutta, 1956.

——*The Transfer of Power in India*, New Delhi, 1957, 1981.

Mirza, Colonel Abdul Haq, *The Withering Chinar*, Islamabad, 1991.

Moorcroft, William, *Travels in the Himalayan Provinces of Hindustan and the Punjab*, London, 1841.

Moore, Thomas, *Lalla Rookh*, London, 1986.

Morris-Jones, W. H., 'Thirty-six Years Later, The Mixed Legacies of Mountbatten's Transfer of Power', *International Affairs*, Autumn 1983.

Mountbatten, Lord, *Time Only to Look Forward*, London, 1949.

Napier, Lt Gen. Sir Charles, *Defects, Civil & Military of the Indian Government*, London, 1853.

National Documentation Centre, Lahore, *The Partition of the Punjab*, 1947, Lahore, 1983.

Nehru, Jawaharlal, *Selected Works*, ed. Sarvepalli Gopal, Vol. 4, 2nd edition, New Delhi, 1986.

Neve, Arthur, *Thirty Years in Kashmir*, London, 1913.
—— *The Tourist's Guide to Kashmir, Ladakh, Skardo, etc.*, Lahore, 1938.
Neve, Ernest, *A Crusader in Kashmir*, London, 1928.
Nugent, Nicholas, *Rajiv Gandhi*, London, 1990.
Panikkar, K. M., *The Founding of the Kashmir State*, London, 1953.
Pant, Kusum, *The Kashmiri Pandit*, New Delhi, 1987.
Parmu, Dr Radha Krishnan, *Muslim Rule in Kashmir, 1320–1819*, New Delhi, 1969.
Pataudi, Sher Ali, *The Story of Soldiering and Politics*, Lahore, 1988.
—— *The Elite Minority, The Princes of India*, Lahore, 1989.
Patel, Sardar, *Correspondence*, ed. Durga Das, Ahmedabad, 1971.
Philips, C. H., & Wainwright, Mary Doreen, (eds) *The Partition of India, Policies and Perspectives 1935-1947*, London, 1970.
Prasad, Sri Nandan, *Paramountcy under Dalhousie*, Delhi, 1964.
Punjab Human Rights Organisation, *The Kashmir Massacre, A Report on the Assassination of Mirwaiz Mauvi Farooq and its Aftermath*, Punjab, 1990.
Punjabi, Riaz, 'Kashmir Imbroglio: the Socio-political Roots', *Contemporary South Asia*, Vol. 4, No. 1, March 1995.
Puri, Balraj, *Jammu: A Clue to the Kashmir Tangle*, New Delhi, 1966.
—— *Triumph and Tragedy*, New Dehli, 1981.
—— *Kashmir: Towards Insurgency*, London, 1993.
—— 'Kashmiriyat: the Vitality of Kashmiri Identity', *Contemporary South Asia*, Vol. 4, No. 1, March 1995.
Qasim, Mir, *My Life and Times*, New Delhi, 1992.
Rabbani, G. M., *Ancient Kashmir*, Srinagar, 1981.
Ray, Hermen, *How Moscow sees Kashmir*, Bombay, 1985.
Rizvi, Gowher, 'Nehru and the Indo-Pakistan Rivalry Over Kashmir, 1947–1963', *Contemporary South Asia*, Vol. 4, No. 1, March 1995.
Rizvi, Janet, *Ladakh*, Oxford, 1983.
Rose, Leo E., 'The Politics of Azad Kashmir', in Ragu G. C. Thomas, (ed.) *Perspectives on Kashmir*, Colorado, 1992.
Round Table Conference, *India's Demand for Dominion Status: Speeches by the King, the Premier, the British Party Leaders and the Representatives of the Princes and People of India*, Madras, 1931.
Sanya, Dr Shanka, *The Boats and Boatmen of Kashmir*, New Delhi, 1979.
Saraf Muhammad, *Kashmiris Fight for Freedom*, Lahore, 1977.
Sareen, Rajendra, *Pakistan: The India Factor*, New Delhi, 1984.
Sedgwick, W., *India for Sale: Kashmir Sold*, Calcutta, 1886.
Sender, Henry, *The Kashmiri Pandits*, Delhi, 1988.
Sharma, Dewan, *Kashmir under the Sikhs*, Delhi, 1983.
Singh, B. S., *The Jammu Fox*, Southern Illinois, 1974.
Singh, Karan, *Heir Apparent*, Oxford, 1982.
Singh, Dr Kirpal, (ed.) *Partition of the Punjab – 1947, Select Documents*, New Delhi, 1991.
Singh, Raghubir, *Kashmir: Garden of the Himalayas*, London, 1983.
Singh, Tavleen, *Kashmir: A Tragedy of Errors*, New Delhi, 1995.
Stephens, Ian, *Horned Moon*, London, 1953.
—— *Pakistan*, London 1963.
Suhrawardy, A. H., *Kashmir: The Incredible Freedom Fight*, Lahore, 1991.
Tarkunde, V. M., 'Kashmir for Kashmiris', *Radical Humanist*, New Delhi, March 1990.

Taseer, C. Bilqees, *The Kashmir of Sheikh Muhammad Abdullah*, Lahore, 1986.

Teng, K. M. and Kaul, S., *Kashmir's Special Status*, Delhi, 1975.

Teng, K. M., Bhatt, Kaul,R. K. and Kaul, S., *Kashmir: Documents on Constitutional History*, India, 1977.

Thomas, Raju G. C. (ed.) *Perspectives on Kashmir*, Colorado, 1992.

Thorp, Robert, *Cashmere Misgovernment*, London, 1870.

Tinker, Hugh, *India and Pakistan*, London, 1962.

—— 'Pressure, Persuasion, Decision: Factors in the Partition of the Punjab, August 1947, *Journal of Asian Studies*, Vol. XXXVI, No. 4, August 1977.

Torrens, Lieut.-Col. Henry, *Travels in Ladak, Tartary & Kashmir*, London, 1862.

Tremblay, Reeta Chowdhari, 'Kashmir: the Valley's Political Dynamics' in *Contemporary South Asia*, Vol. 4, No. 1, March 1995.

Trotter, Lionel, *History of the British Empire, 1844–1862*, London, 1866.

Tyndale-Biscoe, Canon C. E, *Elizabeth Mary Newman*, London, 1933.

—— *An Autobiography*, London, 1951.

United Nations Commission for India and Pakistan, Kashmir Papers: *Reports of UNCIP, June 1948-December 1949*, Government of India, New Delhi, 1952.

Verghese, B. G., 'Lamb's Tales from Kashmir', in *The Kashmir Issue*, High Commission of India, London, 1993.

Verma, P. S., *Jammu and Kashmir at the Political Crossroads*, New Delhi, 1994.

Vigne, Godfrey, *Travels in Kashmir, Ladak, Iskardo*, London, 1842.

Von Huegel, Baron Charles, *Travels in Kashmir and the Panjab*, ed. T. B. Jervis, London, 1845.

Wakefield, William, *The Happy Valley*, London, 1879.

Walker, Annabel, *Aurel Stein*, London, 1995.

Wani, Dr Nizam-ud din, *Muslim Rule in Kashmir (1554–86)*, Jammu, 1987.

Waslekar, Sundeep, (ed.) *Peace Initiatives*, Vol. 1, No. 2, Sept–Oct 1995, New Dehli, 1995.

Wavell, *The Viceroy's Journal*, ed. Penderel Moon, London, 1973.

Wessels, C. S. J., *Early Jesuit Travellers in Central Asia 1603–1721*, The Hague, 1924.

Wolff, Joseph, *Travels and Adventures*, London, 1861.

Wolpert, Stanley, *Jinnah of Pakistan*, Oxford, 1984.

—— *Zulfi Bhutto of Pakistan*, Oxford, 1993.

Wylie, Sir Francis, 'Federal Negotiations in India 1935–39 and After' in C. H. Philips & Mary Doreen Wainright (eds) *The Partition of India*, London, 1970.

Yasin, Madhavi, *British Paramountcy in Kashmir*, New Delhi, 1985.

Yasmeen, Samina, 'The China Factor in the Kashmir Issue' in Ragu G. C. Thomas (ed.) *Perspectives on Kashmir*, Colorado, 1992.

Younghusband, Francis, *Kashmir*, London, 1924.

Zaidi, Professor Z. H., (ed.) *Jinnah Papers, Prelude to Partition*, National Archives of Pakistan, 1993.

Ziegler, Philip, *Mountbatten, The Official Biography*, London, 1985.

Zutshi, N. K., *Sultan Zain-ul Abidin of Kashmir*, Jammu & Lucknow, 1976.

Index